ToolKit: Docker

Swarm

Building, testing, deploying, and monitoring services inside
Docker Swarm clusters

Viktor Farcic

BIRMINGHAM - MUMBAI

The DevOps 2.1 Toolkit: Docker Swarm

First published: May 2017

Production reference: 1020517

Published by Packt Publishing Ltd.

Livery Place
35 Livery Street
Birmingham
B3 2PB, UK.
ISBN 978-1-78728-970-3

www.packtpub.com

Credits

Author
Viktor Farcic

Acquisition Editor
Frank Pohlmann

Technical Editors
Joel Wilfred D'souza
Devesh Chugh

Production Coordinator
Shraddha Falebhai

Indexer
Francy Puthiry

About the Author

Viktor Farcic is a senior consultant at *CloudBees* (`https://www.cloudbees.com/`), a member of the *Docker Captains* (`https://www.docker.com/community/docker-captains`) group, and an author.

He codes using a plethora of languages starting with Pascal (yes, he is old), Basic (before it got the Visual prefix), ASP (before it got the .NET suffix), C, C++, Perl, Python, ASP.NET, Visual Basic, C#, JavaScript, Java, Scala, and so on. He never worked with Fortran. His current favorite is Go.

Viktor's big passions are Microservices, Continuous Deployment, and Test-Driven Development (TDD).

He often speaks at community gatherings and conferences. Viktor wrote *Test-Driven Java Development* by *Packt Publishing*, and *The DevOps 2.0 Toolkit*. His random thoughts and tutorials can be found in his blog *TechnologyConversations.com* (`https://technologyconversations.com/`).

www.PacktPub.com

For support files and downloads related to your book, please visit www.PacktPub.com.

Did you know that Packt offers eBook versions of every book published, with PDF and ePub files available? You can upgrade to the eBook version at www.PacktPub.com and as a print book customer, you are entitled to a discount on the eBook copy. Get in touch with us at service@packtpub.com for more details.

At www.PacktPub.com, you can also read a collection of free technical articles, sign up for a range of free newsletters and receive exclusive discounts and offers on Packt books and eBooks.

https://www.packtpub.com/mapt

Get the most in-demand software skills with Mapt. Mapt gives you full access to all Packt books and video courses, as well as industry-leading tools to help you plan your personal development and advance your career.

Why subscribe?

- Fully searchable across every book published by Packt
- Copy and paste, print, and bookmark content
- On demand and accessible via a web browser

Customer Feedback

Thanks for purchasing this Packt book. At Packt, quality is at the heart of our editorial process.

If you'd like to join our team of regular reviewers, you can e-mail us at customerreviews@packtpub.com. We award our regular reviewers with free eBooks and videos in exchange for their valuable feedback. Help us be relentless in improving our products!

Table of Contents

Preface

At the beginning of 2016, I published *The DevOps 2.0 Toolkit* (`https://www.amazon.com/dp/B01BJ4V66M`). It took me a long time to finish it. Much longer than I imagined.

I started by writing blog posts in *TechnologyConversations.com* (`https://technologyconversations.com/`). They become popular and I received a lot of feedback. Through them, I clarified the idea behind the book. The goal was to provide a guide for those who want to implement DevOps practices and tools. At the same time, I did not want to write a material usable to any situation. I wanted to concentrate only on people that truly want to implement the latest and greatest practices. I hoped to make it go beyond the "traditional" DevOps. I wished to show that the DevOps movement matured and evolved over the years and that we needed a new name. A reset from the way DevOps is implemented in some organizations. Hence the name, *The DevOps 2.0 Toolkit* (`https://www.amazon.com/dp/B01BJ4V66M`)

As any author will tell you, technical books based mostly on hands-on material do not have a long time span. Technology changes ever so quickly and we can expect tools and practices that are valid today to become obsolete a couple of years afterward. I expected *The DevOps 2.0 Toolkit* to be a reference for two to three years (not more). After all, how much can things change in one year? Well, Docker proved me wrong. A lot changed in only six months since I made the book public. The new Swarm was released. It is now part of *Docker Engine v1.12+*. Service discovery is bundled inside it. Networking was greatly improved with load balancing and routing mesh. The list can go on for a while. The release 1.12 is, in my opinion, the most significant release since the first version that went public.

I remember the days I spent together with Docker engineers in Seattle during *DockerCon 2016*. Instead of attending the public sessions, I spent four days with them going through the features that will be released in version 1.12 and the roadmap beyond it. I felt I understood all the technical concepts and features behind them. However, a week later, when I went back home and started "playing" with the new *Docker Swarm Mode*, I realized that my brain was still wired to the way the things were working before. Too many things changed. Too many new possibilities emerged. It took a couple of weeks until my brain reset. Only then I felt I truly understood the scope of changes they introduced in a single release. It was massive.

In parallel with my discovery of the Swarm Mode, I continued receiving emails from *The DevOps 2.0 Toolkit* (`https://www.amazon.com/dp/B01BJ4V66M`) readers. They wanted more. They wanted me to cover new topics as well as to go deeper into those already explored.

One particular request was repeated over and over. "I want you to go deeper into clustering." Readers wanted to know in more detail how to operate a cluster and how to combine it with continuous deployment. They requested that I explore alternative methods for zero-downtime deployments, how to monitor the system more efficiently, how to get closer to self-healing systems, and so on. The range of topics they wanted me to cover was massive, and they wanted it as soon as possible.

Hence, I decided to start a new book and combine my amazement with Docker 1.12 with some of the requests from the readers. *The DevOps 2.1 Toolkit* was born, and, more importantly, *The DevOps Toolkit Series* came into existence.

Overview

This book explores the practices and tools required to run a Swarm cluster. We'll go beyond a simple deployment. We'll explore how to create a **Continuous Deployment** process. We'll set up multiple clusters. One will be dedicated to testing and the other for production. We'll see how to accomplish zero-downtime deployments, what to do in case of a failover, how to run services at scale, how to monitor the systems, and how to make it heal itself. We'll explore the processes that will allow us to run the clusters on a laptop (for demo purposes) as well as on different providers. I'll try to cover as many different hosting solutions as possible. However, time and space are limited, and the one you use (be it public or on-premise) might not be one of them. Fear not! The processes, the tools, and the practices can be easily applied to almost any. As always, this book is very hands-on oriented, but the goal is not to master a particular set of tools but to learn the logic behind them so that you can apply it to your job no matter whether your choice ends up being different.

This book does not make *The DevOps 2.0 Toolkit* (https://www.amazon.com/dp/B01BJ4V66M)obsolete. I think that the logic behind it will continue being valid for a while longer. *The DevOps 2.1 Toolkit* builds on top of it. It goes deeper into some of the subjects explored before and explains others that could not fit in *2.0*. While I did my best to write this book in a way that prior knowledge is not required, I strongly recommend starting with *The DevOps 2.0 Toolkit* (https://www.amazon.com/dp/B01BJ4V66M). The first book in the series sets the stage for this one as well as those that will come afterward. Please consider this book as the second episode in *The DevOps Toolkit Series*.

The first few chapters might, on the first look, seem repetitive to the readers of *The DevOps 2.0 Toolkit*. Never the less, they are important because they unravel some of the problems we'll face when working inside a cluster. They set the stage for the chapters that follow. While you might be tempted to skip them, my recommendation is to read everything. As in any good story, the start sets the stage, the middle develops the story, and the end reveals an unexpected outcome. Some of the theory will be the same as described in *The DevOps 2.0 Toolkit*. In such cases, I will clearly indicate it and let you choose whether to skip it or read it as a way to refresh your memory.

While there will be a lot of theory, this is a hands-on book. You won't be able to complete it by reading it in a metro on the way to work. You'll have to read this book while in front of a computer getting your hands dirty. Eventually, you might get stuck and in need of help. Or you might want to write a review or comment on the book's content. Please post your thoughts on *The DevOps 2.1 Toolkit channel in Disqus* (https://disqus.com/home/channel/thedevops21toolkit/). If you prefer a more direct communication, please join the *DevOps2.0* (http://slack.devops20toolkit.com/) Slack channel. All the books I wrote are very dear to me, and I want you to have a good experience reading them. Part of that experience is the option to reach out to me. Don't be shy.

Please note that this, just as the previous book, is self-published. I believe that having no intermediaries between the writer and the reader is the best way to go. It allows me to write faster, update the book more frequently, and have a more direct communication with you. Your feedback is part of the process. No matter whether you purchased the book while only a few or all chapters were written, the idea is that it will never be truly finished. As time passes, it will require updates so that it is aligned with the change in technology or processes. When possible, I will try to keep it up to date and release updates whenever that makes sense. Eventually, things might change so much that updates are not a good option anymore, and that will be a sign that a whole new book is required. *As long as I continue getting your support, I will keep writing.*

Audience

This book is for professionals interested in the full microservices life cycle combined with continuous deployment and containers. Due to the very broad scope, target audience could be *architects* who want to know how to design their systems around microservices. It could be *DevOps* wanting to know how to apply modern configuration management practices and continuously deploy applications packed in containers. It is for *developers* who would like to take the process back into their hands as well as for *managers* who would like to gain a better understanding of the process used to deliver software from the beginning to the end. We'll speak about scaling and monitoring systems. We'll even work on the design (and implementation) of self-healing systems capable of recuperation from failures (be it of hardware or software nature). We'll deploy our applications continuously directly to production without any downtime and with the ability to rollback at any time.

This book is for *everyone wanting to know more about the software development lifecycle* starting from requirements and design, through development and testing all the way until deployment and post-deployment phases. We'll create the processes taking into account best practices developed by and for some of the biggest companies.

1

Continuous Integration with Docker Containers

It is paradoxical, yet true, to say, that the more we know, the more ignorant we become in the absolute sense, for it is only through enlightenment that we become conscious of our limitations. Precisely one of the most gratifying results of intellectual evolution is the continuous opening up of new and greater prospects.

—*Nikola Tesla*

To fully understand the challenges and benefits that Docker Swarm brings, we need to start from the beginning. We need to go back to a code repository and decide how are we going to build, test, run, update, and monitor the services we're developing. Even though the objective is to implement continuous deployment to a Swarm cluster, we need to step back and explore **Continuous Integration (CI)** first. The steps we'll define for the CI process will dictate how we proceed towards **Continuous Delivery (CD)**, from there towards **Continuous Deployment (CDP)**, and, finally, how we ensure that our services are monitored and able to self-heal. This chapter explores Continuous Integration as a prerequisite for the more advanced processes.

A note to The DevOps 2.0 Toolkit readers
The text that follows is identical to the one published in *The DevOps 2.0 Toolkit*. If it is still fresh in your mind, feel free to jump to the sub-section *Defining a fully Dockerized manual Continuous Integration flow* . Since I wrote the 2.0, I discovered a few better ways to implement CI processes. I hope you'll benefit from this chapter even if you consider yourself a veteran CI practitioner.

To understand Continuous Deployment we should first define its predecessors, Continuous Integration and Continuous Delivery.

Integration phase of a project development tended to be one of the most painful stages of **Software Development Life Cycle (SDLC)**. We would spend weeks, months or even years working in separate teams dedicated to separate applications and services. Each of those teams would have their set of requirements and tried their best to meet them. While it wasn't hard to periodically verify each of those applications and services in isolation, we all dreaded the moment when team leads would decide that the time has come to integrate them into a unique delivery. Armed with the experience from previous projects, we knew that integration would be problematic. We knew that we would discover problems, unmet dependencies, interfaces that do not communicate with each other correctly and that managers will get disappointed, frustrated, and nervous. It was not uncommon to spend weeks or even months in this phase. The worse part of all that was that a bug found during the integration phase could mean going back and redoing days or weeks worth of work. If someone asked me how I felt about integration back then, I'd say that it was closest I could get to becoming permanently depressed. Those were different times. We thought that was the *right* way to develop applications.

A lot changed since then. **Extreme Programming (XP)** and other agile methodologies became familiar, automated testing became frequent, and Continuous Integration started to take ground. Today we know that the way we developed software back then was wrong. The industry moved a long way since those days.

Continuous Integration usually refers to integrating, building, and testing code within the development environment. It requires developers to integrate code into a shared repository often. How often is often can be interpreted in many ways and it depends on the size of the team, the size of the project and the number of hours we dedicate to coding. In most cases, it means that coders either push directly to the shared repository or merge their code with it. No matter whether we're pushing or merging, those actions should, in most cases, be done at least a couple of times a day. Getting code to the shared repository is not enough, and we need to have a pipeline that, as a minimum, checks out the code and runs all the tests related, directly or indirectly, to the code corresponding to the repository. The result of the execution of the pipeline can be either *red* or *green*. Something failed, or everything was run without any problems. In the former case, minimum action would be to notify the person who committed the code.

The Continuous Integration pipeline should run on every commit or push. Unlike Continuous Delivery, Continuous Integration does not have a clearly defined goal of that pipeline. Saying that one application integrates with others does not tell us a lot about its production readiness. We do not know how much more work is required to get to the stage when the code can be delivered to production. All we are striving for is the knowledge that a commit did not break any of the existing tests. Nevertheless, CI is a vast improvement when done right. In many cases, it is a very hard practice to implement, but once everyone is comfortable with it, the results are often very impressive.

Integration tests need to be committed together with the implementation code, if not before. To gain maximum benefits, we should write tests in **Test-Driven Development (TDD)** fashion. That way, not only that tests are ready for commit together with implementation, but we know that they are not faulty and would not pass no matter what we do. There are many other benefits TDD brings to the table and, if you haven't already, I strongly recommend to adopt it. You might want to consult the *Test-Driven Development* (http://tec hnologyconversations.com/category/test-driven-development/) section of the *Technology Conversations* (http://technologyconversations.com/) blog.

Tests are not the only CI prerequisite. One of the most important rules is that when the pipeline fails, fixing the problem has higher priority than any other task. If this action is postponed, next executions of the pipeline will fail as well. People will start ignoring the failure notifications and, slowly, CI process will begin losing its purpose. The sooner we fix the problem discovered during the execution of the CI pipeline, the better we are. If corrective action is taken immediately, knowledge about the potential cause of the problem is still fresh (after all, it's been only a few minutes between the commit and the failure notification) and fixing it should be trivial.

Defining a fully Dockerized manual Continuous Integration flow

Every Continuous Integration process starts with a code that is checked out from a repository. We'll use the GitHub repository vfarcic/go-demo (https://github.com/vfar cic/go-demo) throughout the book. It contains the code of the service we'll use throughout the book. The service is written in *Go* (https://golang.org/). Fear not! Even though I consider it one of the best currently available languages, you will not be required to learn Go. We'll use the go-demo service only as a demonstration of the processes explained throughout the book. Even though I strongly recommend learning Go, the book does not assume any knowledge of the language. All the examples will be programming language agnostic.

 All the commands from this chapter are available in the 01-continuous-integration.sh (https://gist.github.com/vfarcic/886ae97fe7a 98864239e9c61929a3c7c) Gist.

A note to Windows users
Please make sure that your Git client is configured to check out the code *AS-IS*. Otherwise, Windows might change carriage returns to the Windows format.

Let's get going and check out the `go-demo` code:

```
git clone https://github.com/vfarcic/go-demo.git

cd go-demo
```

Some of the files will be shared between the host file system and Docker Machines we'll start creating soon. Docker Machine makes the whole directory that belongs to the current user available inside the VM. Therefore, please make sure that the code is checked out inside one of the user's sub-folders.

Now that we have the code checked out from the repository, we need a server that we'll use to build and run tests. For now, we'll use Docker Machine, since it provides an easy way to create a "Docker ready" VMs on our laptops.

The *Docker Machine* (`https://docs.docker.com/machine/overview/`) is a tool that lets you install Docker Engine on virtual hosts, and manage the hosts with the `docker-machine` commands. You can use Machine to create Docker hosts on your local Mac or Windows box, on your company network, in your data center, or on cloud providers like AWS or DigitalOcean.

Using `docker-machine` commands, you can start, inspect, stop, and restart a managed host, upgrade the Docker client and daemon, and configure a Docker client to talk to your host.

Machine was the only way to run Docker on Mac or Windows previous to *Docker v1.12*. Starting with the beta program and *Docker v1.12*, Docker for Mac and Docker for Windows are available as native apps and the better choice for this use case on newer desktops and laptops. I encourage you to try out these new apps. The installers for Docker for Mac and Docker for Windows include Docker Machine, along with Docker Compose.

The examples that follow assume that you have *Docker Machine version v0.9* (`https://www.docker.com/products/docker-machine`) that includes *Docker Engine v1.13+* (`https://www.docker.com/products/docker-engine`). The installation instructions can be found in the *Install Docker Machine* (`https://docs.docker.com/machine/install-machine/`) **page.**

A note to Windows users

The recommendation is to run all the examples from *Git Bash* (installed through *Docker Toolbox* as well as Git). That way the commands you'll see throughout the book will be same as those that should be executed on *OS X* or any *Linux* distribution.

A note to Linux users

Docker Machine on Linux might not be able to mount a host volume inside VMs. The problem is related to the fact that both host and Docker Machine OSes use /home directory. Mounting /home from the host would overwrite some of the required files. If you experience problems with mounting of the host volume, please export the VIRTUALBOX_SHARE_FOLDER variable:
export VIRTUALBOX_SHARE_FOLDER="$PWD:$PWD"
If machines are already created, you'll have to destroy them and create them again.
Please note that this problem should be fixed in newer Docker Machine versions so use this workaround only if you notice that the volume is not mounted (files from the host are not available inside VMs).

Let's create our first server called go-demo use the following command:

```
docker-machine create -d virtualbox go-demo
```

A note to Windows users

If you're using *Docker for Windows* instead of *Docker Toolbox*, you will need to change the driver from virtualbox to Hyper-V. The problem is that Hyper-V does not allow mounting host volumes, so it is still highly recommended to use *Docker Toolbox* when working with *Docker Machine*. The reason behind the choice of running *Docker* inside *Docker Machines* instead natively on the host lies in the need to run a cluster (coming in the next chapter). *Docker Machine* is the easiest way to simulate a multi-node cluster.

The command should be self-explanatory. We specified virtualbox as the driver (or Hyper-V if you're running *Docker for Windows*) and named the machine go-demo:

A note to Windows users

In some cases, Git Bash might think that it is still running as BAT. If you experience a problem with the docker-machine env commands, please export the SHELL variable:
export SHELL=bash

Now that the machine is running, we should instruct our local Docker Engine to use it, use the following command:

```
docker-machine env go-demo
```

The `docker-machine env go-demo` command outputs environment variables required for the local engine to find the server we'd like to use. In this case, the remote engine is inside the VM we created with the `docker-machine create` command.

The output is as follows:

```
export DOCKER_TLS_VERIFY="1"
export DOCKER_HOST="tcp://192.168.99.100:2376"
export DOCKER_CERT_PATH="/Users/vfarcic/.docker/machine/machines/go-demo"
export DOCKER_MACHINE_NAME="go-demo"
```

We can envelop the `env` command into an `eval` that will evaluate the output and, in this case, create the environment variables using the following command:

```
eval $(docker-machine env go-demo)
```

From now on, all the Docker commands we execute locally will be channeled to the engine running inside the `go-demo` machine.

Now we are ready to run the first two steps in the CI flow. We'll execute unit tests and build the service binary.

Running unit tests and building service binary

We'll use Docker Compose for the CI flow. As you will see soon, Docker Compose has little, if any, value when operating the cluster. However, for operations that should be performed on a single machine, Docker Compose is still the easiest and the most reliable way to go.

Compose is a tool for defining and running multi-container Docker applications. With Compose, you use a Compose file to configure your application's services. Then, using a single command, you create and start all the services from your configuration. Compose is great for development, testing, and staging environments, as well as CI workflows.

The repository that we cloned earlier, already has all the services we'll need defined inside the `docker-compose-test-local.yml` (https://github.com/vfarcic/go-demo/blob/master/docker-compose-test-loc) file.

Let's take a look at the content of the `docker-compose-test-local.yml` (https://github
b.com/vfarcic/go-demo/blob/master/docker-compose-test-local.yml) file:

```
cat docker-compose-test-local.yml
```

The service we'll use for our unit tests is called `unit`. It is as follows:

```
unit:
    image: golang:1.6
    volumes:
      - .:/usr/src/myapp
      - /tmp/go:/go
    working_dir: /usr/src/myapp
    command: bash -c "go get -d -v -t && go test --cover -v \
./... && go build -v -o go-demo"
```

It is a relatively simple definition. Since the service is written in *Go*, we are using the
`golang:1.6` image.

Next, we are exposing a few volumes. Volumes are directories that are, in this case,
mounted on the host. They are defined with two arguments. The first argument is the path
to the host directory while the second represents a directory inside the container. Any file
already inside the host directory will be available inside the container and vice versa.

The first volume is used for the source files. We are sharing the current host directory .
with the container directory `/usr/src/myapp`. The second volume is used for *Go* libraries.
Since we want to avoid downloading all the dependencies every time we run unit tests,
they will be stored inside the host directory `/tmp/go`. That way, dependencies will be
downloaded only the first time we run the service.

Volumes are followed with the `working_dir` instruction. When the container is run, it will
use the specified value as the starting directory.

Finally, we are specifying the command we want to run inside the container. I won't go into
details since they are specific to *Go*. In short, we download all the dependencies `go get -d
-v -t`, run unit tests `go test --cover -v ./...`, and build the go-demo binary `go
build -v -o go-demo`. Since the directory with the source code is mounted as a volume,
the binary will be stored on the host and available for later use.

With this single Compose service, we defined two steps of the CI flow. It contains unit tests
and build of the binary.

Please note that even though we run the service called `unit`, the real purpose of this CI step
is to run any type of tests that do not require deployment. Those are the tests we can
execute before we build the binary and, later on, Docker images.

Let's run the following code:

```
docker-compose \
    -f docker-compose-test-local.yml \
    run --rm unit
```

A note to Windows users

You might experience a problem with volumes not being mapped correctly. If you see an `Invalid volume specification` error, please export the environment variable `COMPOSE_CONVERT_WINDOWS_PATHS` set to `0`:

`export COMPOSE_CONVERT_WINDOWS_PATHS=0`

If that fixed the problem with volumes, please make sure that the variable is exported every time you run `docker-compose`.

We specified that Compose should use `docker-compose-test-local.yml` file (default is `docker-compose.yml`) and run the service called `unit`. The `--rm` argument means that the container should be removed once it stops. The run command should be used for services that are not meant to run forever. It is perfect for batch jobs and, as in this case, for running tests.

As you can see from the output, we pulled the `golang` image, downloaded service dependencies, successfully ran the tests, and built the binary.

We can confirm that the binary is indeed built and available on the host by listing the files in the current directory using the following command. For brevity, we'll filter the result:

```
ls -l *go-demo*
```

Now that we passed the first round of tests and have the binary, we can proceed and build the Docker images.

Building service images

Docker images are built through a definition stored in a Dockerfile. With few exceptions, it takes a similar approach as if we would define a simple script. We will not explore all the options we can use when defining a Dockerfile, but only those used for the `go-demo` service. Please consult the *Dockerfile reference* (`https://docs.docker.com/engine/referen ce/builder/`) page for more info.

The `go-demo` Dockerfile is as follows:

```
FROM alpine:3.4
MAINTAINER Viktor Farcic <viktor@farcic.com>

RUN mkdir /lib64 && ln -s /lib/libc.musl-x86_64.so.1 /lib64/ld-linux-
x86-64.so.2

EXPOSE 8080
ENV DB db
CMD ["go-demo"]
HEALTHCHECK --interval=10s CMD wget -qO- localhost:8080/demo/hello

COPY go-demo /usr/local/bin/go-demo
RUN chmod +x /usr/local/bin/go-demo
```

Each of the statements will be built as a separate image. A container is a collection of images stacked one on top of the other.

Every Dockerfile starts with the `FROM` statement. It defines the base image that should be used. In most cases, my preference is to use `alpine` Linux. With its size being around 2MB it is probably the smallest distribution we can use. That is aligned with the idea that containers should have only things that are needed and avoid any extra overhead.

`MAINTAINER` is for informational purposes only.

The `RUN` statement executes any command set as its argument. I won't explain this one since it is very specific to the service we're building.

The `EXPOSE` statement defines the port the service will be listening to. It is followed by the definition of the environment variable `DB` that tells the service the address of the database. The default value is `db` and, as you'll see soon, it can be changed at runtime. The `CMD` statement represents the command that will be run when containers start.

The `HEALTHCHECK` instruction tells Docker how to test a container to check that it is still working. This can detect cases such as a web server that is stuck in an infinite loop and unable to handle new connections, even though the server process is still running. When a container has a healthcheck specified, it has a health status in addition to its normal status. This status is initially starting. Whenever a health check passes, it becomes healthy (from whatever state it was previously in). After a certain number of consecutive failures, it becomes unhealthy.

In our case, the healthcheck will be executed every ten seconds. The command sends a simple request to one of the API endpoints. If the service responds with status 200, the wget command will return 0 and Docker will consider the service healthy. Any other response will be considered as unhealthy and Docker Engine will perform certain actions to fix the situation.

Finally, we copy the go-demo binary from the host to the /usr/local/bin/ directory inside the image and give it executable permissions with the chmod command.

To some, the order of the statements might not look logical. However, there is a good reason behind such declarations and their order. Those that are less likely to change are defined before those that are prone to changes. Since go-demo will be a new binary every time we build the images, it is defined last.

The reasons behind such order lie in the way Docker Engine creates images. It starts from the top-most definition and checks whether it changed since the last time the build was run. If it didn't, it moves to the next statement. As soon as it finds a statement that would produce a new image, it, and all the statements following it are built into Docker images. By placing those that are less likely to change closer to the top, we can reduce the build time, disk usage, and bandwidth.

Now that we understand the Dockerfile behind the go-demo service, we can build the images.

The command is very straightforward and is as follows:

```
docker build -t go-demo .
```

As an alternative, we can define build arguments inside a Docker Compose file. The service defined in docker-compose-test-local.yml (https://github.com/vfarcic/go-demo /blob/master/docker-compose-test-local.yml) file is as follows:

```
app:
  build: .
  image: go-demo
```

In both cases, we specified that the current directory should be used for the build process . and that the name of the image is go-demo.

We can run the build through Docker compose with the command that is as follows:

```
docker-compose \
    -f docker-compose-test-local.yml \
    build app
```

We'll use the latter method throughout the rest of the book.

We can confirm that the image was indeed built, by executing the `docker images` command as follows:

```
docker images
```

The output is as follows:

```
REPOSITORY TAG      IMAGE ID      CREATED        SIZE
go-demo    latest  5e90126bebf1  49 seconds ago 23.61 MB
golang     1.6     08a89f0a4ee5  11 hours ago   744.2 MB
alpine     latest  4e38e38c8ce0  9 weeks ago    4.799 MB
```

As you can see, `go-demo` is one of the images we have inside the server.

Now that the images are built, we can run staging tests that depend on the service and its dependencies to be deployed on a server.

Running staging tests

Please note that the real purpose of this step in the CI flow is to run the tests that require the service and its dependencies to be running. Those are still not integration tests that require production or production-like environment. The idea behind those tests is to run the service together with its direct dependencies, run the tests, and, once they're finished, remove everything and free the resources for some other task. Since these are still not integration tests, some, if not all, dependencies can be mocks.

Due to the nature of these tests, we need to split the task into three actions:

1. Run the service and all the dependencies.
2. Run the tests.
3. Destroy the service and all the dependencies.

The dependencies are defined as the `staging-dep` service inside the `docker-compose-test-local.yml` (https://github.com/vfarcic/go-demo/blob/master/docker-compose-test-local.yml) file. The definition is as follows:

```
staging-dep:
  image: go-demo
  ports:
    - 8080:8080
  depends_on:
    - db

db:
  image: mongo:3.2.10
```

The image is `go-demo`, and it exposes the port `8080` (both on the host and inside the container). It depends on the service `db` which is a `mongo` image. Services defined as `depends_on` will be run before the service that defines the dependency. In other words, if we run the `staging-dep` target, Compose will run the `db` first.

Let's run the dependencies as shown in the following code:

```
docker-compose \
    -f docker-compose-test-local.yml \
    up -d staging-dep
```

Once the command is finished, we will have two containers running (`go-demo` and `db`). We can confirm that by listing all the processes:

```
docker-compose \
    -f docker-compose-test-local.yml \
    ps
```

The output is as follows:

```
Name                      Command                 State   Ports
-------------------------------------------------------------------------
godemo_db_1               /entrypoint.sh mongod   Up      27017/tcp
godemo_staging-dep_1      go-demo                 Up      0.0.0.0:8080->8080/tcp
```

Now that the service and the database it depends on are running, we can execute the tests. They are defined as the service staging. The definition is as follows:

```
staging:
  extends:
    service: unit
  environment:
    - HOST_IP=localhost:8080
```

```
network_mode: host
command: bash -c "go get -d -v -t && go test --tags integration -v"
```

Since the definition of the staging tests is very similar to those we run as unit tests, the staging service extends unit. By extending a service, we inherit its full definition. Further on, we defined an environment variable HOST_IP. The tests code uses that variable to determine the location of the service under test. In this case, since the go-demo service is running on the same server as tests, the IP is server's localhost. Since, by default, localhost inside a container is not the same as the one on the host, we had to define network_mode as host. Finally, we defined the command that should be executed. It will download tests dependencies go get -d -v -t and run the tests go test --tags integration -v.

Let's run the following commands:

```
docker-compose \
    -f docker-compose-test-local.yml \
    run --rm staging
```

All the tests passed, and we are one step closer to the goal of having full confidence that the service is indeed safe to be deployed to production.

We don't have any use for keeping the service and the database running so let's remove them and free the resources for some other task:

```
docker-compose \
    -f docker-compose-test-local.yml \
    down
```

The down command stops and removes all services defined in that Compose file. We can verify that by running the following ps command:

```
docker-compose \
    -f docker-compose-test-local.yml \
    ps
```

The output is as follows:

```
Name    Command    State    Ports
-------------------------------
```

There is only one thing missing for the CI flow to be complete. At this moment we have the go-demo image that is usable only inside the go-demo server. We should store it in a registry so that it can be accessed from other servers as well.

Pushing images to the registry

Before we push our `go-demo` image, we need a place to push to. Docker offers multiple solutions that act as a registry. We can use *Docker Hub* (`https://hub.docker.com/`), *Docker Registry* (`https://docs.docker.com/registry/`), and *Docker Trusted Registry* (`https://docs.docker.com/docker-trusted-registry/`). On top of those, there are many other solutions from third party vendors.

Which registry should we use? Docker Hub requires a username and password, and I do not trust you enough to provide my own. One of the goals I defined before I started working on the book is to use only open source tools so Docker Trusted Registry, while being an excellent choice under different circumstances, is also not suitable. The only option left (excluding third party solutions), is *Docker Registry* (`https://docs.docker.com/registry/`).

The registry is defined as one of the services inside the `docker-compose-local.yml` (`https://github.com/vfarcic/go-demo/blob/master/docker-compose-local.yml`) Compose file. The definition is as follows:

```
registry:
  container_name: registry
  image: registry:2.5.0
  ports:
    - 5000:5000
  volumes:
    - .:/var/lib/registry
  restart: always
```

We set registry as an explicit container name, specified the image, and opened the port `5000` (both on the host and inside the container).

Registry stores the images inside the `/var/lib/registry` directory, so we mounted it as a volume on the host. That way, data will not be lost if the container fails. Since this is a production service that could be used by many, we defined that it should always be restarted on failure.

Let's run the following commands:

```
docker-compose \
    -f docker-compose-local.yml \
    up -d registry
```

Now that we have the registry, we can do a dry-run. Let's confirm that we can pull and push images to it:

```
docker pull alpine

docker tag alpine localhost:5000/alpine

docker push localhost:5000/alpine
```

Docker uses a naming convention to decide where to pull and push images from. If the name is prefixed with an address, the engine will use it to determine the location of the registry. Otherwise, it assumes that we want to use Docker Hub. Therefore, the first command pulled the alpine image from Docker Hub.

The second command created a tag of the alpine image. The tag is a combination of the address of our registry localhost:5000 and the name of the image. Finally, we pushed the alpine image to the registry running on the same server.

Before we start using the registry in a more serious fashion, let's confirm that the images are indeed persisted on the host:

```
ls -1 docker/registry/v2/repositories/alpine/
```

The output is as follows:

```
_layers
_manifests
_uploads
```

I won't go into details what each of those sub-directories contains. The important thing to note is that registry persists the images on the host so no data will be lost if it fails or, in this case, even if we destroy the VM since that Machine directory is mapped to the same directory on our laptop.

We were a bit hasty when we declared that this registry should be used in production. Even though data is persisted, if the whole VM crashes, there would be a downtime until someone brings it up again or creates a new one. Since one of the goals is to avoid downtime whenever possible, later on, we should look for a more reliable solution. The current setup should do for now.

Now we are ready to push the go-demo image to the registry:

```
docker tag go-demo localhost:5000/go-demo:1.0

docker push localhost:5000/go-demo:1.0
```

As with the Alpine example, we tagged the image with the registry prefix and pushed it to the registry. We also added a version number 1.0.

The push was the last step in the CI flow. We run unit tests, built the binary, built the Docker image, ran staging tests, and pushed the image to the registry. Even though we did all those things, we are not yet confident that the service is ready for production. We never tested how it would behave when deployed to a production (or production-like) cluster. We did a lot, but not enough.

If CI were our final objective, this would be the moment when manual validations should occur. While there is a lot of value in manual labor that requires creativity and critical thinking, we cannot say the same for repetitive tasks. Tasks required for converting this Continuous Integration flow into Continuous Delivery and, later on, deployment are, indeed repetitive.

We have the CI process done, and it is time to do the extra mile and convert it into Continuous Delivery.

Before we move into the steps required for the Continuous Integration process to become Continuous Delivery, we need to take a step back and explore cluster management. After all, in most cases, there is no production environment without a cluster.

We'll destroy the VMs at the end of each chapter. That way, you can come back to any of part of the book and do the exercises without the fear that you might need to do some steps from one of the earlier chapters. Also, such a procedure will force us to repeat a few things. Practice makes perfect. To reduce your waiting times, I did my best to keep things as small as possible and keep download times to a minimum. Execute the following command:

```
docker-machine rm -f go-demo
```

The next chapter is dedicated to the setup and operation of a Swarm cluster.

2

Setting Up and Operating a Swarm Cluster

Organizations which design systems ... are constrained to produce designs which are copies of the communication structures of these organizations

—M.Conway

Many will tell you that they have a *scalable system*. After all, scaling is easy. Buy a server, install WebLogic (or whichever other monster application server you're using) and deploy your applications. Then wait for a few weeks until you discover that everything is so *fast* that you can click a button, have some coffee, and, by the time you get back to your desk, the result will be waiting for you. What do you do? You scale. You buy a few more servers, install your monster application servers and deploy your monster applications on top of them. Which part of the system was the bottleneck? Nobody knows. Why did you duplicate everything? Because you must. And then some more time passes, and you continue scaling until you run out of money and, simultaneously, people working for you go crazy. Today we do not approach scaling like that. Today we understand that scaling is about many other things. It's about elasticity. It's about being able to quickly and easily scale and de-scale depending on variations in your traffic and growth of your business, and that you should not go bankrupt during the process. It's about the need of almost every company to scale their business without thinking that IT department is a liability. It's about getting rid of those monsters.

A note to The DevOps 2.0 Toolkit readers
The text that follows is identical to the one published in *The DevOps 2.0 Toolkit*. If it is still fresh in your mind, feel free to jump to the section *Docker Swarm Mode* of this chapter. You'll see that a lot has changed. One of those changes is that the old Swarm running as a separate container is deprecated for *Swarm Mode*. There are many other new things we'll discover along the way.

Scalability

Let us, for a moment take a step back and discuss why we want to scale applications. The main reason is *high availability*. Why do we want high availability? We want it because we want our business to be available under any load. The bigger the load, the better (unless you are under DDoS). It means that our business is booming. With high availability our users are happy, and many of us simply leave the site if it takes too long to load. We want to avoid having outages because every minute our business is not operational can be translated into a money loss. What would you do if an online store is not available? Probably go to another. Maybe not the first time, maybe not the second, but, sooner or later, you would get fed up and switch it for another. We are used to everything being fast and responsive, and there are so many alternatives that we do not think twice before trying something else. And if that something else turns up to be better. One man's loss is another man's gain. Do we solve all our problems with scalability? Not even close. Many other factors decide the availability of our applications. However, scalability is an important part of it, and it happens to be the subject of this chapter.

What is scalability? It is a property of a system that indicates its ability to handle increased load in a graceful manner or its potential to be enlarged as demand increases. It is the capacity to accept increased volume or traffic.

The truth is that the way we design our applications dictates the scaling options available. Applications will not scale well if they are not designed to scale. That is not to say that an application not designed for scaling cannot scale. Everything can scale, but not everything can scale well.

Commonly observed scenario is as follows.

We start with a simple architecture, sometimes with load balancer sometimes without, setup a few application servers and one database. Everything is great, complexity is low, and we can develop new features very fast. The cost of operations is low, income is high (considering that we just started), and everyone is happy and motivated.

Business is growing, and the traffic is increasing. Things are beginning to fail, and performance is dropping. Firewalls are added, additional load balancers are set up, the database is scaled, more application servers are added and so on. Things are still relatively straightforward. We are faced with new challenges, but we can overcome obstacles in time. Even though the complexity is increasing, we can still handle it with relative ease. In other words, what we're doing is still, more or less, the same but bigger. Business is doing well, but it is still relatively small.

And then it happens. The big thing you've been waiting for. Maybe one of the marketing campaigns hit the spot. Maybe there was an adverse change in your competition. Maybe that last feature was indeed a killer one. No matter the reasons, business got a big boost. After a short period of happiness due to this change, your pain increases tenfold. Adding more databases does not seem to be enough. Multiplying application servers does not appear to fulfill the needs. You start adding caching and what not. You start getting the feeling that every time you multiply something, benefits are not equally big. Costs increase, and you are still not able to meet the demand. Database replications are too slow. New application servers do not make such a big difference anymore. Operational costs are increasing faster than you expected. The situation hurts the business and the team. You are starting to realize that the architecture you were so proud of cannot fulfill this increase in load. You cannot split it. You cannot scale things that hurt the most. You cannot start over. All you can do is continue multiplying with ever decreasing benefits of such actions.

The situation described above is quite common. What was good at the beginning, is not necessarily right when the demand increases. We need to balance the need for **You ain't gonna need it** (YAGNI) principle and the longer term vision. We cannot start with the system optimized for large companies because it is too expensive and does not provide enough benefits when business is small. On the other hand, we cannot lose the focus from one of the primary objectives of any business. We cannot not think about scaling from the very first day. Designing scalable architecture does not mean that we need to start with a cluster of a hundred servers. It does not mean that we have to develop something big and complex from the start. It means that we should start small, but in the way that, when it becomes big, it is easy to scale. While microservices are not the only way to accomplish that goal, they are indeed a good way to approach this problem. The cost is not in development but operations. If operations are automated, that cost can be absorbed quickly and does not need to represent a massive investment. As you already saw (and will continue seeing throughout the rest of the book), there are excellent open source tools at our disposal. The best part of automation is that the investment tends to have lower maintenance cost than when things are done manually.

We already discussed microservices and automation of their deployments on a tiny scale. Now it's time to convert this small scale to something bigger. Before we jump into practical parts, let us explore what are some of the different ways one might approach scaling.

We are often limited by our design and choosing the way applications are constructed limits our choices severely. Although there are many different ways to scale, the most common one is called *Axis Scaling*.

Axis scaling

Axis scaling can be best represented through three dimensions of a cube; *X-Axis*, *Y-Axis*, and *Z-Axis*. Each of those dimensions describes a type of scaling:

- X-Axis: Horizontal duplication
- Y-Axis: Functional decomposition
- Z-Axis: Data partitioning

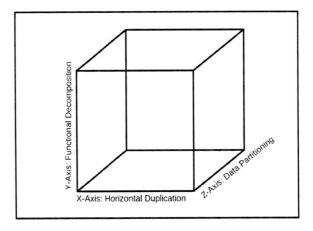

Figure 2-1: Scale cube

Let's go through the Axes, one at a time.

X-axis scaling

In a nutshell, *x-axis* scaling is accomplished by running multiple instances of an application or a service. In most cases, there is a load balancer on top that makes sure that the traffic is shared among all those instances. The biggest advantage of *x-axis* scaling is simplicity. All we have to do is deploy the same application on multiple servers. For that reason, this is the most commonly used type of scaling. However, it comes with its set of disadvantages when applied to monolithic applications.

Having a large application usually requires a big cache that demands heavy usage of memory. When such an application is multiplied, everything is multiplied with it, including the cache. Another, often more important, problem is an inappropriate usage of resources. Performance issues are almost never related to the whole application. Not all modules are equally affected, and, yet, we multiply everything. That means that even though we could be better off by scaling only part of the application that requires such an action, we scale everything. Nevertheless, *x- axis* scaling is important no matter the architecture. The major difference is the effect that such a scaling has.

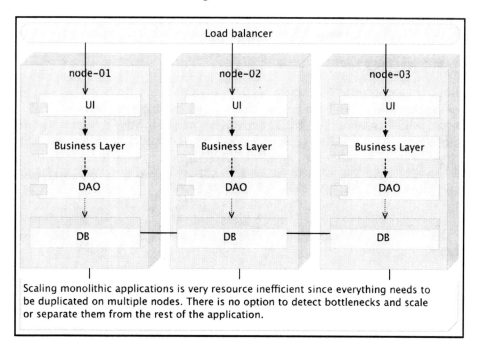

Figure 2-2: Monolithic application scaled inside a cluster

By using microservices, we are not removing the need for *x-axis* scaling but making sure that due to their architecture such scaling has more effect than with alternative and more traditional approaches to architecture. With microservices, we have the option to fine-tune scaling. We can have many instances of services that suffer a lot under heavy load and only a few instances of those that are used less often or require fewer resources. On top of that, since they are small, we might never reach a limit of a service. A small service in a big server would need to receive a truly massive amount of traffic before the need for scaling arises. Scaling microservices is more often related to fault tolerance than performance problems. We want to have multiple copies running so that, if one of them dies, the others can take over until recovery is performed.

Y-axis scaling

Y-axis scaling is all about decomposition of an application into smaller services. Even though there are different ways to accomplish this decomposition, microservices are probably the best approach we can take. When they are combined with immutability and self-sufficiency, there is indeed no better alternative (at least from the prism of y-axis scaling). Unlike x-axis scaling, the y-axis is not accomplished by running multiple instances of the same application but by having multiple different services distributed across the cluster.

Z-axis scaling

Z-axis scaling is rarely applied to applications or services. Its primary and most common usage is among databases. The idea behind this type of scaling is to distribute data among multiple servers thus reducing the amount of work that each of them needs to perform. Data is partitioned and distributed so that each server needs to deal only with a subset of the data. This type of separation is often called **sharding**, and there are many databases specially designed for this purpose. Benefits of z-axis scaling are most noticeable in I/O and cache and memory utilization.

Clustering

A server cluster consists of a set of connected servers that work together and can be seen as a single system. They are usually connected to a fast **Local Area Network (LAN)**. The significant difference between a cluster and a group of servers is that the cluster acts as a single system trying to provide high availability, load balancing, and parallel processing.

If we deploy applications, or services, to individually managed servers and treat them as separate units, the utilization of resources is sub-optimum. We cannot know in advance which group of services should be deployed to a server and utilize resources to their maximum. Moreover, resource usage tends to fluctuate. While, in the morning, some service might require a lot of memory, during the afternoon that usage might be lower. Having predefined servers prevents us from having elasticity that would balance that usage in the best possible way. Even if such a high level of dynamism is not required, predefined servers tend to create problems when something goes wrong, resulting in manual actions to redeploy the affected services to a healthy node:

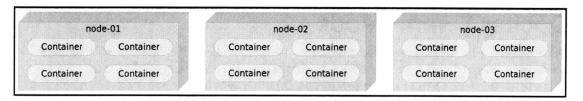

Figure 2-3: Cluster with containers deployed to predefined servers

Real clustering is accomplished when we stop thinking in terms of individual servers and start thinking of a cluster; of all servers as one big entity. That can be better explained if we drop to a bit lower level. When we deploy an application, we tend to specify how much memory or CPU it might need. However, we do not decide which memory slots our application will use nor which CPUs it should utilize. For example, we don't specify that some application should use CPUs 4, 5 and 7. That would be inefficient and potentially dangerous. We only decide that three CPUs are required. The same approach should be taken on a higher level. We should not care where an application or a service will be deployed but what it needs. We should be able to define that the service has certain requirements and tell some tool to deploy it to whichever server in our cluster, as long as it fulfills the needs we have. The best (if not the only) way to accomplish that is to consider the whole cluster as one entity.

We can increase or decrease the capacity of a cluster by adding or removing servers but, no matter what we do, it should still be a single entity. We define a strategy and let our services be deployed somewhere inside the cluster. Those using cloud providers like **Amazon Web Services (AWS)**, Microsoft Azure and **Google Compute Engine (GCE)** are already accustomed to this approach, even though they might not be aware of it.

Throughout the rest of this chapter, we'll explore ways to create our cluster and explore tools that can help us with that objective. The fact that we'll be simulating the cluster locally does not mean that the same strategies cannot be applied to public or private clouds and data centers. Quite the opposite:

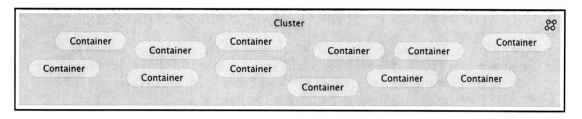

Figure 2-4: Cluster with containers deployed to servers based on a predefined strategy

Docker Swarm Mode

Docker Engine v1.12 was released in July 2016. It is the most significant version since *v1.9*. Back then, we got Docker networking that, finally, made containers ready for use in clusters. With *v1.12*, Docker is reinventing itself with a whole new approach to cluster orchestration. Say goodbye to Swarm as a separate container that depends on an external data registry and welcome the *new Docker Swarm* or *Swarm Mode*. Everything you'll need to manage your cluster is now incorporated into Docker Engine. Swarm is there. Service discovery is there. Improved networking is there. That does not mean that we do not need additional tools. We do. The major difference is that Docker Engine now incorporates all the "essential" (not to say minimal) tools we need.

The old Swarm (before *Docker v1.12*) used *fire-and-forget principle*. We would send a command to Swarm master, and it would execute that command. For example, if we would send it something like `docker-compose scale go-demo=5`, the old Swarm would evaluate the current state of the cluster, discover that, for example, only one instance is currently running, and decide that it should run four more. Once such a decision is made, the old Swarm would send commands to Docker Engines. As a result, we would have five containers running inside the cluster. For all that to work, we were required to set up Swarm agents (as separate containers) on all the nodes that form the cluster and hook them into one of the supported data registries (Consul, etcd, and Zookeeper).

The problem was that Swarm was executing commands we send it. It was not maintaining the desired state. We were, effectively, telling it what we want to happen (example: scale up), not the state we wanted (make sure that five instances are running). Later on, the old Swarm got the feature that would reschedule containers from failed nodes. However, that feature had a few problems that prevented it from being a reliable solution (example: failed containers were not removed from the overlay network).

Now we got a brand new Swarm. It is part of Docker Engine (no need to run it as separate containers), it has incorporated service discovery (no need to set up Consul or whatever is your data registry of choice), it is designed from the ground up to accept and maintain the desired state, and so on. It is a truly major change in how we deal with cluster orchestration.

In the past, I was inclined towards the old Swarm more than Kubernetes. However, that inclination was only slight. There were pros and cons for using either solution. Kubernetes had a few features Swarm was missing (example: the concept of the desired state), the old Swarm shined with its simplicity and low usage of resources.

With the new Swarm (the one that comes with *v1.12*), I have no more doubts which one to use. *The new Swarm is often a better choice than Kubernetes.* It is part of Docker Engine, so the whole setup is a single command that tells an engine to join the cluster. The new networking works like a charm. The bundle that can be used to define services can be created from Docker Compose files, so there is no need to maintain two sets of configurations (Docker Compose for development and a different one for orchestration). Most importantly, the new Docker Swarm continues being simple to use. From the very beginning, Docker community pledged that they are committed to simplicity and, with this release, they, once again, proved that to be true.

And that's not all. The new release comes with a lot of other features that are not directly related with Swarm. However, this book is dedicated to cluster management. Therefore, I'll focus on Swarm and leave the rest for one of the next books or a blog article.

Since I believe that code explains things better than words, we'll start with a demo of some of the new features introduced in *version 1.12*.

Setting up a Swarm cluster

We'll continue using Docker Machine since it provides a very convenient way to simulate a cluster on a laptop. Three servers should be enough to demonstrate some of the key features of a Swarm cluster:

 All the commands from this chapter are available in the `02-docker-swarm.sh` (`https://gist.github.com/vfarcic/750fc4117bad9d8619004081af171896`) Gist

```
for i in 1 2 3; do
    docker-machine create -d virtualbox node-$i
done
```

At this moment, we have three nodes. Please note that those servers are not running anything but Docker Engine.

We can see the status of the nodes by executing the following `ls` command:

```
docker-machine ls
```

The output is as follows (ERROR column removed for brievity):

```
NAME     ACTIVE  DRIVER      STATE   URL                     SWARM DOCKER
node-1   -       virtualbox  Running tcp://192.168.99.100:2376 v1.12.1
node-2   -       virtualbox  Running tcp://192.168.99.101:2376 v1.12.1
node-3   -       virtualbox  Running tcp://192.168.99.102:2376 v1.12.1
```

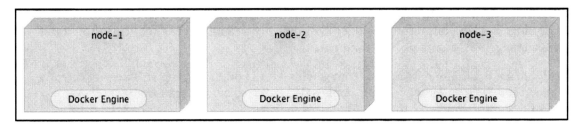

Figure 2-5: Machines running Docker Engines

With the machines up and running we can proceed and set up the Swarm cluster.

The cluster setup consists of two types of commands. We need to start by initializing the first node which will be our manager. Refer to the following illustration:

```
eval $(docker-machine env node-1)

docker swarm init \
    --advertise-addr $(docker-machine ip node-1)
```

The first command set environment variables so that the local Docker Engine is pointing to the node-1. The second initialized Swarm on that machine.

We specified only one argument with the swarm init command. The --advertise-addr is the address that this node will expose to other nodes for internal communication.

The output of the swarm init command is as follows:

```
Swarm initialized: current node (1o5k7hvcply6g2excjiqqf4ed) is now a
manager.

To add a worker to this swarm, run the following command:
    docker swarm join \
--token SWMTKN-1-3czblm3rypyvrz6wyijsuwtmk1ozd7giqip0m \
6k0b3hllycgmv-3851i2gays638e7unmp2ng3az \
192.168.99.100:2377

To add a manager to this swarm, run the following command:
    docker swarm join \
--token SWMTKN-1-3czblm3rypyvrz6wyijsuwtmk1ozd7giqi \
```

```
p0m6k0b3h11ycgmv-6oukeshmw7a295vudzmo9mv6i \
192.168.99.100:2377
```

We can see that the node is now a manager and we've got the commands we can use to join other nodes to the cluster. As a way to increase security, a new node can be added to the cluster only if it contains the token generated when Swarm was initialized. The token was printed as a result of the `docker swarm init` command. You can copy and paste the code from the output or use the `join-token` command. We'll use the latter.

Right now, our Swarm cluster consists of only one VM. We'll add the other two nodes to the cluster. But, before we do that, let us discuss the difference between a *manager* and a *worker*.

A Swarm manager continuously monitors the cluster state and reconciles any differences between the actual state and your expressed desired state. For example, if you set up a service to run ten replicas of a container, and a worker machine hosting two of those replicas crashes, the manager will create two new replicas to replace the ones that failed. Swarm manager assigns new replicas to workers that are running and available. A manager has all the capabilities of a worker.

We can get a token required for adding additional nodes to the cluster by executing the `swarm join-token` command.

The command to obtain a token for adding a manager is as follows:

```
docker swarm join-token -q manager
```

Similarly, to get a token for adding a worker, we would run the command that follows:

```
docker swarm join-token -q worker
```

In both cases, we'd get a long hashed string.

The output of the worker token is as follows:

```
SWMTKN-1-3czblm3rypyvrz6wyijsuwtmk1ozd7giqip0m6k0b3hll \
ycgmv-3851i2gays638\
e7unmp2ng3az
```

Please note that this token was generated on my machine and, in your case, it will be different.

Let's put the token into an environment variable and add the other two nodes as workers:

```
TOKEN=$(docker swarm join-token -q worker)
```

Now that have the token inside a variable, we can issue the command that follows:

```
for i in 2 3; do
eval $(docker-machine env node-$i)

  docker swarm join \
    --token $TOKEN \
    --advertise-addr $(docker-machine ip node-$i) \
    $(docker-machine ip node-1):2377
done
```

The command we just ran iterates over nodes two and three and executes the swarm join command. We set the token, the advertise address, and the address of our manager. As a result, the two machines joined the cluster as workers. We can confirm that by sending the node ls command to the manager node node-1:

```
eval $(docker-machine env node-1)

docker node ls
```

The output of the node ls command is as follows:

```
ID                            HOSTNAME   STATUS  AVAILABILITY  MANAGER STATUS
3vlq7dsa8g2sqkp6vl911nha8     node-3     Ready   Active
6cbtgzk19rne5mzwkwugiolox     node-2     Ready   Active
b644vkvs6007rpjre2bfb8cro *   node-1     Ready   Active        Leader
```

The asterisk tells us which node we are currently using. The MANAGER STATUS indicates that the node-1 is the *leader:*

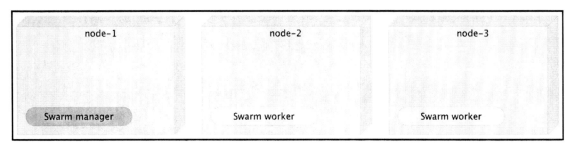

Figure 2-6: Docker Swarm cluster with three nodes

In a production environment, we would probably set more than one node to be a manager and, thus, avoid deployment downtime if one of them fails. For the purpose of this demo, having one manager should suffice.

Deploying services to the Swarm cluster

Before we deploy a demo service, we should create a new network so that all containers that constitute the service can communicate with each other no matter on which nodes they are deployed:

```
docker network create --driver overlay go-demo
```

The next chapter will explore networking in more details. Right now, we'll discuss and do only the absolute minimum required for an efficient deployment of services inside a Swarm cluster.

We can check the status of all networks with the command that follows:

```
docker network ls
```

The output of the `network ls` command is as follows:

```
NETWORK ID     NAME             DRIVER   SCOPE
e263fb34287a bridge            bridge   local
c5b60cff0f83 docker_gwbridge bridge   local
8d3gs95h5c5q go-demo          overlay  swarm
4d0719f20d24 host              host     local
eafx9zd0czuu ingress          overlay  swarm
81d392ce8717 none             null     local
```

As you can see, we have two networks that have the `swarm` scope. The one named `ingress` was created by default when we set up the cluster. The second `go-demo` was created with the `network create` command. We'll assign all containers that constitute the `go-demo` service to that network.

The next chapter will go deep into the Swarm networking. For now, it is important to understand that all services that belong to the same network can speak with each other freely.

The *go-demo* application requires two containers. Data will be stored in MongoDB. The back-end that uses that `DB` is defined as `vfarcic/go-demo` container.

Let's start by deploying the `mongo` container somewhere within the cluster.

Usually, we'd use constraints to specify the requirements for the container (example: HD type, the amount of memory and CPU, and so on). We'll skip that, for now, and tell Swarm to deploy it anywhere within the cluster:

```
docker service create --name go-demo-db \
    --network go-demo \
    mongo:3.2.10
```

Please note that we haven't specified the port Mongo listens to 27017. That means that the database will not be accesible to anyone but other services that belong to the same go-demo network .

As you can see, the way we use service create is similar to the Docker run command you are, probably, already used to.

We can list all the running services:

```
docker service ls
```

Depending on how much time passed between service create and service ls commands, you'll see the value of the REPLICAS column being zero or one. Immediately after creating the service, the value should be *0/1*, meaning that zero replicas are running, and the objective is to have one. Once the mongo image is pulled, and the container is running, the value should change to *1/1*.

The final output of the service ls command should be as follows (IDs are removed for brevity):

```
NAME         MODE        REPLICAS   IMAGE
go-demo-db   replicated  1/1        mongo:3.2.10
```

If we need more information about the go-demo-db service, we can run the service inspect command:

```
docker service inspect go-demo-db
```

Now that the database is running, we can deploy the go-demo container:

```
docker service create --name go-demo \
    -e DB=go-demo-db \
    --network go-demo \
    vfarcic/go-demo:1.0
```

There's nothing new about that command. The service will be attached to the go-demo network. The environment variable DB is an internal requirement of the go-demo service that tells the code the address of the database.

At this point, we have two containers (`mongo` and `go-demo`) running inside the cluster and communicating with each other through the `go-demo` network. Please note that none of them is *yet* accessible from outside the network. At this point, your users do not have access to the service API. We'll discuss this in more details soon. Until then, I'll give you only a hint: *you need a reverse proxy* capable of utilizing the new Swarm networking.

Let's run the `service ls` command one more time:

```
docker service ls
```

The result, after the `go-demo` service is pulled to the destination node, should be as follows (IDs are removed for brevity):

```
NAME         MODE        REPLICAS  IMAGE
go-demo      replicated  1/1       vfarcic/go-demo:1.0
go-demo-db   replicated  1/1       mongo:3.2.10
```

As you can see, both services are running as a single replica:

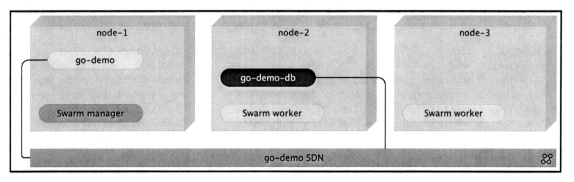

Figure 2-8: Docker Swarm cluster containers communicating through the go-demo SDN

What happens if we want to scale one of the containers? How do we scale our services?

Scaling services

We should always run at least two instances of any given service. That way they can share the load and, if one of them fails, there will be no downtime. We'll explore Swarm's failover capability soon and leave load balancing for the next chapter.

We can, for example, tell Swarm that we want to run five replicas of then `go-demo` service:

```
docker service scale go-demo=5
```

With the `service scale` command, we scheduled five replicas. Swarm will make sure that five instances of `go-demo` are running somewhere inside the cluster.

We can confirm that, indeed, five replicas are running through the, already familiar, `service ls` command:

```
docker service ls
```

The output is as follows (IDs are removed for brevity):

```
NAME         MODE        REPLICAS  IMAGE
go-demo      replicated  5/5       vfarcic/go-demo:1.0
go-demo-db   replicated  1/1       mongo:3.2.10
```

As we can see, five out of five `REPLICAS` of the `go-demo` service are running.

The `service ps` command provides more detailed information about a single service:

```
docker service ps go-demo
```

The output is as follows (IDs and ERROR PORTs columns are removed for brevity):

```
NAME        IMAGE                NODE    DESIRED STATE CURRENT STATE
go-demo.1   vfarcic/go-demo:1.0  node-3  Running       Running 1 minute ago
go-demo.2   vfarcic/go-demo:1.0  node-2  Running       Running 51 seconds ago
go-demo.3   vfarcic/go-demo:1.0  node-2  Running       Running 51 seconds ago
go-demo.4   vfarcic/go-demo:1.0  node-1  Running       Running 53 seconds ago
go-demo.5   vfarcic/go-demo:1.0  node-3  Running       Running 1 minute ago
```

We can see that the `go-demo` service is running five instances distributed across the three nodes. Since they all belong to the same **go-demo SDN**, they can communicate with each other no matter where they run inside the cluster. At the same time, none of them is accessible from outside:

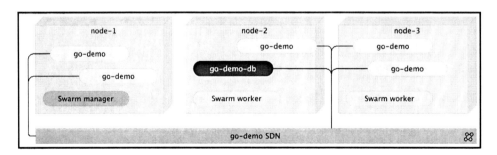

Figure 2-9: Docker Swarm cluster with go-demo service scaled to five replicas

What happens if one of the containers is stopped or if the entire node fails? After all, processes and nodes do fail sooner or later. Nothing is perfect, and we need to be prepared for such situations.

Failover

Fortunately, failover strategies are part of Docker Swarm. Remember, when we execute a `service` command, we are not telling Swarm what to do but the state we desire. In turn, Swarm will do its best to maintain the specified state no matter what happens.

To test a failure scenario, we'll destroy one of the nodes:

```
docker-machine rm -f node-3
```

Swarm needs a bit of time until it detects that the node is down. Once it does, it will reschedule containers. We can monitor the situation through `service ps command`:

```
docker service ps go-demo
```

The output (after rescheduling) is as follows (`ID` is removed for brevity):

```
NAME          IMAGE                  NODE    DESIRED STATE CURRENT STATE              \ERROR PORTS
go-demo.1     vfarcic/go-demo:1.0 node-2 Running       Running 13 seconds ago
 _ go-demo.1 vfarcic/go-demo:1.0 node-3 Shutdown      Running about a minute ago
go-demo.2     vfarcic/go-demo:1.0 node-2 Running       Running about a minute ago
go-demo.3     vfarcic/go-demo:1.0 node-2 Running       Running about a minute ago
go-demo.4     vfarcic/go-demo:1.0 node-1 Running       Running about a minute ago
go-demo.5     vfarcic/go-demo:1.0 node-1 Running       Running 13 seconds ago
 _ go-demo.5 vfarcic/go-demo:1.0 node-3 Shutdown      Running about a minute ago
```

As you can see, after a short period, Swarm rescheduled containers among healthy nodes (node-1 and node-2) and changed the state of those that were running on the failed node to Shutdown. If your output still shows that some instances are running on the node-3, please wait for a few moments and repeat the `service ps command`.

What now?

That concludes the exploration of basic concepts of the new Swarm features we got with *Docker v1.12+*.

Is this everything there is to know to run a Swarm cluster successfully? Not even close! What we explored by now is only the beginning. There are quite a few questions waiting to be answered. How do we expose our services to the public? How do we deploy new releases without downtime? I'll try to give answers to those and quite a few other questions in the chapters that follow. The next one will be dedicated to the exploration of the ways we can expose our services to the public. We'll try to integrate a proxy with a Swarm cluster. To do that, we need to dive deeper into Swarm networking.

Now is the time to take a break before diving into the next chapter. As before, we'll destroy the machines we created and start fresh:

```
docker-machine rm -f node-1 node-2
```

3
Docker Swarm Networking and Reverse Proxy

The most compelling reason for most people to buy a computer for the home will be to link it to a nationwide communications network. We're just in the beginning stages of what will be a truly remarkable breakthrough for most people - as remarkable as the telephone.
—Steve Jobs

Software-Defined Network (SDN) is a cornerstone of efficient cluster management. Without it, services distributed across the cluster would not be able to find each other.

Having proxies based on static configuration does not fit the world of highly dynamic scheduling. Services are created, updated, moved around the cluster, scaled and de-scaled, and so on. In such a setting, information changes all the time.

One approach we can take is to use a proxy as a central communication point and make all the services speak with each other through it. Such a setting would require us to monitor changes in the cluster continuously and update the proxy accordingly. To make our lives easier, a monitoring process would probably use one of the service registries to store the information and a templating solution that would update proxy configuration whenever a change in the registry is detected. As you can imagine, building such a system is anything but trivial.

Fortunately, Swarm comes with a brand new networking capability. In a nutshell, we can create networks and attach them to services. All services that belong to the same network can speak with each other using only the name of the service. It goes even further. If we scale a service, Swarm networking will perform round-robin load balancing and distribute the requests across all the instances. When even that is not enough, we have a new network called ingress with routing mesh that has all those and a few additional features.

Efficient usage of Swarm networking is not sufficient by itself. We still need a reverse proxy that will be a bridge between the external world and our services. Unless there are special requirements, the proxy does not need to perform load balancing (Swarm networking does that for us). However, it does need to evaluate request paths and forward requests to a destination service. Even in that case, Swarm networking helps a lot. Configuring reverse proxy becomes a relatively easy thing to do as long as we understand how networking works and can harness its full potential.

Let's see the networking in practice.

Setting up a cluster

We'll create a similar environment as we did in the previous chapter. We'll have three nodes which will form a Swarm cluster.

All the commands from this chapter are available in the 03-networking.sh (https://gist.github.com/vfarcic/fd7d7e04e1133fc3c90084c4c1a919fe) Gist.

By this time, you already know how to set up a cluster so we'll skip the explanation and just do it:

```
for i in 1 2 3; do
  docker-machine create -d virtualbox node-$i
done

eval $(docker-machine env node-1)

docker swarm init \
  --advertise-addr $(docker-machine ip node-1)

TOKEN=$(docker swarm join-token -q worker)

for i in 2 3; do
eval $(docker-machine env node-$i)

  docker swarm join \
    --token $TOKEN \
    --advertise-addr $(docker-machine ip node-$i) \
    $(docker-machine ip node-1):2377
done

eval $(docker-machine env node-1)

docker node ls
```

The output of the last command `node ls` is as follows (IDs were removed for brevity):

```
HOSTNAME    STATUS    AVAILABILITY    MANAGER STATUS
node-2      Ready     Active
node-1      Ready     Active          Leader
node-3      Ready     Active
```

As you can see, we have a cluster of three nodes with `node-1` being the only manager (and hence the leader).

Now that we have a fully operating cluster, we can explore the benefits Docker networking provides in conjunction with Swarm. We already worked with Swarm networking in the previous chapter. Now its time to go deeper, gain a better understanding of what we already saw, and unlock some new features and use cases.

Requirements of secured and fault tolerant services running with high availability

Let us quickly go over the internals of the *go-demo* application. It consists of two services. Data is stored in a MongoDB. The database is consumed by a backend service called `go-demo`. No other service should access the database directly. If another service needs the data, it should send a request to the `go-demo` service. That way we have clear boundaries. Data is owned and managed by the `go-demo` service. It exposes an API that is the only access point to the data.

The system should be able to host multiple applications. Each will have a unique base URL. For example, the `go-demo` path starts with `/demo`. The other applications will have different paths (example: `/users`, `/products`, and so on). The system will be accessible only through ports `80` for HTTP and `443` HTTPS. Please note that there can be no two processes that can listen to the same port. In other words, only a single service can be configured to listen to port `80`.

To meet load fluctuations and use the resources effectively, we must be able to scale (or de-scale) each service individually and independently from the others. Any request to any of the services should pass through a load balancer that will distribute the load across all instances. As a minimum, at least two instances of any service should be running at any given moment. That way, we can accomplish high availability even in case one of the instances stops working. We should aim even higher than that and make sure that even a failure of a whole node does not interrupt the system as a whole.

To meet performance and fail-over needs services should be distributed across the cluster.

We'll make a temporary exception to the rule that each service should run multiple instances. Mongo volumes do not work with Docker Machine on OS X and Windows. Later on, when we reach the chapters that provide guidance towards production setup inside major hosting providers (example: AWS), we'll remove this exception and make sure that the database is also configured to run with multiple instances.

Taking all this into account, we can make the following requirements:

1. A **load balancer** will distribute requests evenly (*round-robin*) across all instances of any given service (**proxy** included). It should be fault tolerant and not depend on any single node.
2. A reverse proxy will be in charge of routing requests based on their base URLs.
3. The **go-demo** service will be able to communicate freely with the **go-demo-db** service and will be accessible only through the reverse proxy.
4. The database will be isolated from any but the service it belongs to **go-demo**.

A logical architecture of what we're trying to accomplish can be presented with the diagram that follows:

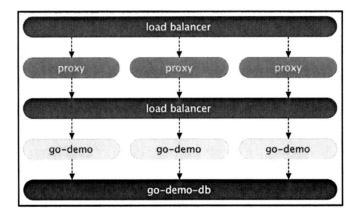

Figure 3-1: A logical architecture of the go-demo service

How can we accomplish those requirements?

Let us solve each of the four requirements one by one. We'll start from the bottom and move towards the top.

The first problem to tackle is how to run a database isolated from any but the service it belongs to.

Running a database in isolation

We can isolate a database service by not exposing its ports. That can be accomplished easily with the `service create` command:

```
docker service create --name go-demo-db \
    mongo:3.2.10
```

We can confirm that the ports are indeed not exposed by inspecting the service:

```
docker service inspect --pretty go-demo-db
```

The output is as follows:

```
ID:             rcedo70r2f1njpm0eyb3nwf8w
Name:           go-demo-db
Service Mode:   Replicated
 Replicas:      1
Placement:
UpdateConfig:
 Parallelism:   1
 On failure:    pause
 Max failure ratio: 0
ContainerSpec:
 Image:         mongo:3.2.10@sha256:532a19da83ee0e4e2a2ec6bc4212fc4af\
26357c040675d5c2629a4e4c4563cef
 Resources:
Endpoint Mode: vip
```

As you can see, there is no mention of any port. Our `go-demo-db` service is fully isolated and inaccessible to anyone. However, that is too much isolation. We want the service to be isolated from anything but the service it belongs to `go-demo`. We can accomplish that through the usage of Docker Swarm networking.

Let us remove the service we created and start over:

```
docker service rm go-demo-db
```

This time, we should create a network and make sure that the `go-demo-db` service is attached to it:

```
docker network create --driver overlay go-demo

docker service create --name go-demo-db \
    --network go-demo \
    mongo:3.2.10
```

We created an overlay network called `go-demo` followed with the `go-demo-db service`. This time, we used the `--network` argument to attach the service to the network. From this moment on, all services attached to the `go-demo` network will be accessible to each other.

Let's inspect the service and confirm that it is indeed attached to the network:

```
docker service inspect --pretty go-demo-db
```

The output of the `service inspect` command is as follows:

```
ID:              ktrxcgp3gtszsjvi7xg0hmd73
Name:            go-demo-db
Service Mode:    Replicated
 Replicas:       1
Placement:
UpdateConfig:
 Parallelism:    1
 On failure:     pause
 Max failure ratio: 0
ContainerSpec:
 Image:
mongo:3.2.10@sha256:532a19da83ee0e4e2a2ec6bc4212fc4af26357c040675d
5c2629a4e4c4563cef
Resources:
Networks:        go-demo
Endpoint Mode: vip
```

As you can see, this time, there is a `Networks` entry with the value set to the ID of the `go-demo` network we created earlier.

Let us confirm that networking truly works. To prove it, we'll create a global service called `util`:

```
docker service create --name util \
    --network go-demo --mode global \
    alpine sleep 1000000000
```

Just as `go-demo-db`, the `util` service also has the `go-demo` network attached.

A new argument is `--mode`. When set to global, the service will run on every node of the cluster. That is a very useful feature when we want to set up infrastructure services that should span the whole cluster.

We can confirm that it is running everywhere by executing the `service ps` command:

```
docker service ps util
```

The output is as follows (IDs and ERROR PORTS columns are removed for brevity):

```
NAME      IMAGE           NODE     DESIRED STATE CURRENT STATE
util...   alpine:latest   node-1   Running        Running 6 minutes ago
util...   alpine:latest   node-3   Running        Running 6 minutes ago
util...   alpine:latest   node-2   Running        Running 6 minutes ago
```

As you can see, the `util` service is running on all three nodes.

We are running the `alpine` image (a minuscule Linux distribution). We put it to sleep for a very long time. Otherwise, since no processes are running, the service would stop, Swarm would restart it, it would stop again, and so on.

The purpose of the `util` service will be to demonstrate some of the concepts we're exploring. We'll exec into it and confirm that the networking truly works.

To enter the `util` container, we need to find out the ID of the instance running on the `node-1` (the node our local Docker is pointing to):

```
ID=$(docker ps -q --filter label=com.docker.swarm.service.name=util)
```

We listed all the processes `ps` in quiet mode so that only IDs are returned `-q`, and limited the result to the service name util:

```
--filter label=com.docker.swarm.service.name=util
```

The result is stored as the environment variable ID.

We'll install a tool called *drill*. It is a tool designed to get all sorts of information out of a DNS and it will come in handy very soon:

```
docker exec -it $ID apk add --update drill
```

Alpine Linux uses the package management called `apk`, so we told it to add drill.

Now we can see whether networking truly works. Since both `go-demo-db` and util services belong to the same network, they should be able to communicate with each other using DNS names. Whenever we attach a service to the network, a new virtual IP is created together with a DNS that matches the name of the services.

Let's try it out as follows:

```
docker exec -it $ID drill go-demo-db
```

We entered into one of the instances of the `util` service and "drilled" the DNS `go-demo-db`. The output is as follows:

```
;; ->>HEADER<<- opcode: QUERY, rcode: NOERROR, id: 5751
;; flags: qr rd ra ; QUERY: 1, ANSWER: 1, AUTHORITY: 0, ADDITIONAL: 0
;; QUESTION SECTION:
;; go-demo-db.    IN      A

;; ANSWER SECTION:
go-demo-db.        600      IN       A       10.0.0.2

;; AUTHORITY SECTION:

;; ADDITIONAL SECTION:

;; Query time: 0 msec
;; SERVER: 127.0.0.11
;; WHEN: Thu Sep  1 12:53:42 2016
;; MSG SIZE  rcvd: 54
```

The response code is `NOERROR` and the `ANSWER` is 1 meaning that the DNS `go-demo-db` responded correctly. It is reachable.

We can also observe that the `go-demo-db` DNS is associated with the IP `10.0.0.2`. Every service attached to a network gets its IP. Please note that I said service, not an instance. That's a huge difference that we'll explore later. For now, it is important to understand that all services that belong to the same network are accessible through service names:

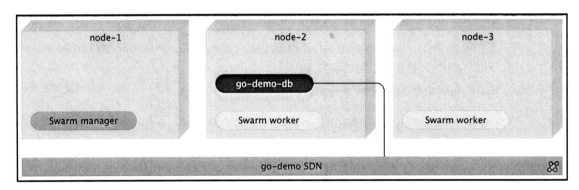

Figure 3-2: go-demo-db service attached to the go-demo network

Let's move up through the requirements.

Running a service through a reverse proxy

We want the go-demo service to be able to communicate freely with the go-demo-db service and to be accessible only through the reverse proxy. We already know how to accomplish the first part. All we have to do is make sure that both services belong to the same network go-demo.

How can we accomplish the integration with a reverse proxy?

We can start by creating a new network and attach it to all services that should be accessible through a reverse proxy:

```
docker network create --driver overlay proxy
```

Let's list the currently running overlay networks:

```
docker network ls -f "driver=overlay"
```

The output is as follows:

```
NETWORK ID    NAME     DRIVER   SCOPE
b17kzasd3gzu go-demo overlay swarm
0d7ssryojcyg ingress overlay swarm
9e4o7abyts0v proxy    overlay swarm
```

We have the go-demo and proxy networks we created earlier. The third one is called ingress. It is set up by default and has a special purpose that we'll explore later.

Now we are ready to run the go-demo service. We want it to be able to communicate with the go-demo-db service so it must be attached to the go-demo network. We also want it to be accessible to a proxy (we'll create it soon) so we'll attach it to the proxy network as well.

The command that creates the go-demo service is as follows:

```
docker service create --name go-demo \
  -e DB=go-demo-db \
  --network go-demo \
  --network proxy \
  vfarcic/go-demo:1.0
```

It is very similar to the command we executed in the previous chapter with the addition of the `--network proxy` argument:

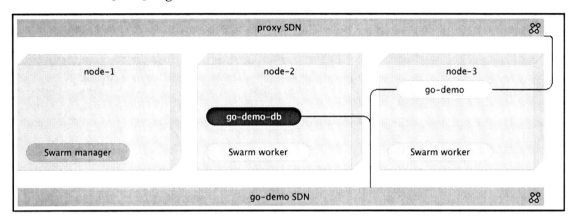

Figure 3-3: Docker Swarm cluster with three nodes, two networks and a few containers

Now both services are running somewhere inside the cluster and can communicate with each other through the `go-demo` network. Let's bring the proxy into the mix. We'll use the *Docker Flow Proxy* (`https://github.com/vfarcic/docker-flow-proxy`) project that is a combination of HAProxy (`http://www.haproxy.org/`) and a few additional features that make it more dynamic. The principles we'll explore are the same no matter which one will be your choice.

Please note that, at this moment, none of the services are accessible to anyone except those attached to the same network.

Creating a reverse proxy service in charge of routing requests depending on their base URLs

We can implement a reverse proxy in a couple of ways. One would be to create a new image based on HAProxy (`https://hub.docker.com/_/haproxy/`) and include configuration files inside it. That approach would be a good one if the number of different services is relatively static. Otherwise, we'd need to create a new image with a new configuration every time there is a new service (not a new release).

The second approach would be to expose a volume. That way, when needed, we could modify the configuration file instead building a whole new image. However, that has downsides as well. When Deploying to a cluster, we should avoid using volumes whenever they're not necessary. As you'll see soon, a proxy is one of those that do not require a volume. As a side note, `--volume` has been replaced with the `docker service` argument `--mount`.

The third option is to use one of the proxies designed to work with Docker Swarm. In this case, we'll use the container `vfarcic/docker-flow-proxy` (https://hub.docker.com/r /vfarcic/docker-flow-proxy/) It is based on HAProxy with additional features that allow us to reconfigure it by sending HTTP requests.

Let's give it a spin.

The command that creates the `proxy` service is as follows:

```
docker service create --name proxy \
    -p 80:80 \
    -p 443:443 \
    -p 8080:8080 \
    --network proxy \
    -e MODE=swarm \
    vfarcic/docker-flow-proxy
```

We opened ports `80` and `443` that will serve Internet traffic (HTTP and HTTPS). The third port is 8080. We'll use it to send configuration requests to the proxy. Further on, we specified that it should belong to the proxy network. That way, since go-demo is also attached to the same network, the proxy can access it through the proxy-SDN.

Through the **proxy** we just ran, we can observe one of the cool features of the network routing mesh. It does not matter which server the **proxy** is running in. We can send a request to any of the nodes and Docker networking will make sure that it is redirected to one of the proxies. We'll see that in action very soon.

The last argument is the environment variable MODE that tells the proxy that containers will be deployed to a Swarm cluster. Please consult the project README (`https://github.com/vfarcic/docker-flow-proxy`) for other combinations.

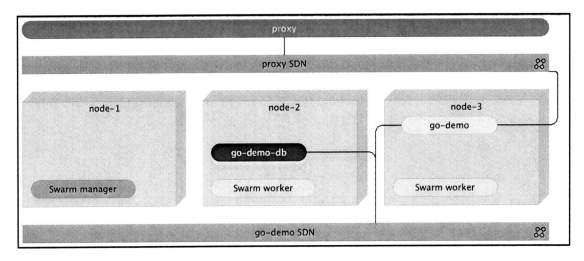

Figure 3-4: Docker Swarm cluster with the proxy service

Please note that the **proxy**, even though it is running inside one of the nodes, is placed outside to illustrate the logical separation better.

Before we move on, let's confirm that the proxy is running.

```
docker service ps proxy
```

We can proceed if the CURRENT STATE is Running. Otherwise, please wait until the service is up and running.

Now that the proxy is Deployed, we should let it know about the existence of the go-demo service:

```
curl "$(docker-machine ip node-1):8080/v1/docker-flow-\
proxy/reconfigure?serviceName=go-demo&servicePath=/demo&port=8080"
```

The request was sent to reconfigure the proxy specifying the service name go-demo, base URL path of the API /demo, and the internal port of the service 8080. From now on, all the requests to the proxy with the path that starts with /demo will be redirected to the go-demo service. This request is one of the additional features Docker Flow Proxy provides on top of HAProxy.

Please note that we sent the request to node-1. The proxy could be running inside any of the nodes and, yet, the request was successful. That is where Docker's Routing Mesh plays a critical role. We'll explore it in more detail later. For now, the important thing to note is that we can send a request to any of the nodes, and it will be redirected to the service that listens to the same port (in this case 8080).

The output of the request is as follows (formatted for readability):

```
{
    "Mode": "swarm",
    "Status": "OK",
    "Message": "",
    "ServiceName": "go-demo",
    "AclName": "",
    "ConsulTemplateFePath": "",
    "ConsulTemplateBePath": "",
    "Distribute": false,
    "HttpsOnly": false,
    "HttpsPort": 0,
    "OutboundHostname": "",
    "PathType": "",
    "ReqMode": "http",
    "ReqRepReplace": "",
    "ReqRepSearch": "",
    "ReqPathReplace": "",
    "ReqPathSearch": "",
    "ServiceCert": "",
    "ServiceDomain": null,
    "SkipCheck": false,
    "TemplateBePath": "",
    "TemplateFePath": "",
    "TimeoutServer": "",
    "TimeoutTunnel": "",
    "Users": null,
    "ServiceColor": "",
    "ServicePort": "",
    "AclCondition": "",
    "FullServiceName": "",
    "Host": "",
    "LookupRetry": 0,
    "LookupRetryInterval": 0,
    "ServiceDest": [
      {
        "Port": "8080",
        "ServicePath": [
            "/demo"
        ],
```

```
        "SrcPort": 0,
        "SrcPortAcl": "",
        "SrcPortAclName": ""
    }
  ]
}
```

I won't go into details but note that the `Status` is `OK` indicating that the `proxy` was reconfigured correctly.

We can test that the `proxy` indeed works as expected by sending an HTTP request:

```
curl -i "$(docker-machine ip node-1)/demo/hello"
```

The output of the `curl` command is as follows.

```
HTTP/1.1 200 OK
Date: Thu, 01 Sep 2016 14:23:33 GMT
Content-Length: 14
Content-Type: text/plain; charset=utf-8

hello, world!
```

The `proxy` works! It responded with the HTTP status `200` and returned the API response `hello, world!`. As before, the request was not, necessarily, sent to the node that hosts the service but to the routing mesh that forwarded it to the `proxy`.

As an example, let's send the same request but this time, to `node-3`:

```
curl -i "$(docker-machine ip node-3)/demo/hello"
```

The result is still the same.

Let's explore the configuration generated by the `proxy`. It will give us more insights into the Docker Swarm Networking inner workings. As another benefit, if you choose to roll your own `proxy` solution, it might be useful to understand how to configure the `proxy` and leverage new Docker networking features.

We'll start by examining the configuration *Docker Flow Proxy* (https://github.com/vfa rcic/docker-flow-proxy) created for us. We can do that by entering the running container to take a sneak peek at the file /cfg/haproxy.cfg. The problem is that finding a container run by Docker Swarm is a bit tricky. If we deployed it with Docker Compose, the container name would be predictable. It would use the format <PROJECT>_<SERVICE>_<INDEX>.

The `docker service` command runs containers with hashed names. The `docker-flow-proxy` created on my laptop has the name `proxy.1.e07jvhdb9e6s76mr9ol41u4sn`. Therefore, to get inside a running container deployed with Docker Swarm, we need to use a filter with, for example, an image name.

First, we need to find out on which node the `proxy` is running execute the following command:

```
NODE=$(docker service ps proxy | tail -n +2 | awk '{print $4}')
```

We listed the `proxy` service processes `docker service ps proxy`, removed the header `tail -n +2`, and output the node that resides inside the fourth column `awk '{print $4}'`. The output is stored as the environment variable `NODE`.

Now we can point our local Docker Engine to the node where the `proxy` resides:

```
eval $(docker-machine env $NODE)
```

Finally, the only thing left is to find the ID of the `proxy` container. We can do that with the following command:

```
ID=$(docker ps -q \
    --filter label=com.docker.swarm.service.name=proxy)
```

Now that we have the container ID stored inside the variable, we can execute the command that will retrieve the HAProxy configuration:

```
docker exec -it \
$ID cat /cfg/haproxy.cfg
```

The important part of the configuration is as follows:

```
frontend services
    bind *:80
    bind *:443
    mode http

    acl url_go-demo8080 path_beg /demo
    use_backend go-demo-be8080 if url_go-demo8080

backend go-demo-be8080
    mode http
    server go-demo go-demo:8080
```

The first part `frontend` should be familiar to those who have used HAProxy. It accepts requests on ports 80 HTTP and 443 HTTPS. If the path starts with `/demo`, it will be redirected to the `backend go-demo-be`. Inside it, requests are sent to the address `go-demo` on the port 8080. The address is the same as the name of the service we deployed. Since `go-demo` belongs to the same network as the `proxy`, Docker will make sure that the request is redirected to the destination container. Neat, isn't it? There is no need, anymore, to specify IPs and external ports.

The next question is how to do load balancing. How should we specify that the `proxy` should, for example, perform round-robin across all instances? Should we use a `proxy` for such a task?

Load balancing requests across all instances of a service

Before we explore load balancing, we need to have something to balance. We need multiple instances of a service. Since we already explored scaling in the previous chapter, the command should not come as a surprise:

```
eval $(docker-machine env node-1)

docker service scale go-demo=5
```

Within a few moments, five instances of the `go-demo` service will be running:

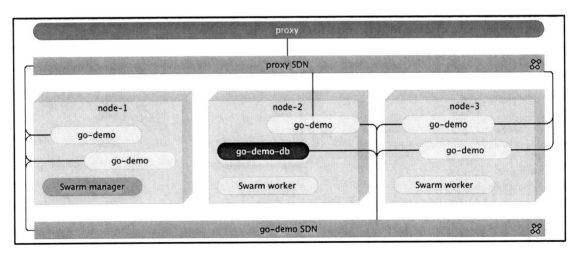

Figure 3-5: Docker Swarm cluster with the go-demo service scaled

What should we do to make the **proxy** load balance requests across all instances? The answer is nothing. No action is necessary on our part. Actually, the question is wrong. The **proxy** will not load balance requests at all. Docker Swarm networking will. So, let us reformulate the question. What should we do to make the *Docker Swarm network* load balance requests across all instances? Again, the answer is nothing. No action is necessary on our part.

To understand load balancing, we might want to go back in time and discuss load balancing before Docker networking came into being.

Normally, if we didn't leverage Docker Swarm features, we would have something similar to the following **proxy** configuration mock-up:

```
backend go-demo-be
    server instance_1 <INSTANCE_1_IP>:<INSTANCE_1_PORT>
    server instance_2 <INSTANCE_2_IP>:<INSTANCE_2_PORT>
    server instance_3 <INSTANCE_3_IP>:<INSTANCE_3_PORT>
    server instance_4 <INSTANCE_4_IP>:<INSTANCE_4_PORT>
    server instance_5 <INSTANCE_5_IP>:<INSTANCE_5_PORT>
```

Every time a new instance is added, we would need to add it to the configuration as well. If an instance is removed, we would need to remove it from the configuration. If an instance failed… Well, you get the point. We would need to monitor the state of the cluster and update the `proxy` configuration whenever a change occurs.

If you read *The DevOps 2.0 Toolkit*, you probably remember that I advised a combination of *Registrator* (`https://github.com/gliderlabs/registrator`), *Consul* (`https://www.consul.io/`), and *Consul Template* (`https://github.com/hashicorp/consul-template`). Registrator would monitor Docker events and update Consul whenever a container is created or destroyed. With the information stored in Consul, we would use Consul Template to update nginx or HAProxy configuration. There is no need for such a combination anymore. While those tools still provide value, for this particular purpose, there is no need for them.

We are not going to update the `proxy` every time there is a change inside the cluster, for example, a scaling event. Instead, we are going to update the proxy every time a new service is created. Please note that service updates (Deployment of new releases) do not count as service creation. We create a service once and update it with each new release (among other reasons). So, only a new service requires a change in the `proxy` configuration.

The reason behind that reasoning is in the fact that load balancing is now part of Docker Swarm networking. Let's do another round of drilling from the `util` service:

```
ID=$(docker ps -q --filter label=com.docker.swarm.service.name=util)

docker exec -it $ID apk add --update drill

docker exec -it $ID drill go-demo
```

The output of the previous command is as follows:

```
;; ->>HEADER<<- opcode: QUERY, rcode: NOERROR, id: 50359
;; flags: qr rd ra ; QUERY: 1, ANSWER: 1, AUTHORITY: 0, ADDITIONAL: 0
;; QUESTION SECTION:
;; go-demo.        IN      A

;; ANSWER SECTION:
go-demo.           600     IN      A       10.0.0.8

;; AUTHORITY SECTION:

;; ADDITIONAL SECTION:

;; Query time: 0 msec
;; SERVER: 127.0.0.11
;; WHEN: Thu Sep  1 17:46:09 2016
;; MSG SIZE  rcvd: 48
```

The IP `10.0.0.8` represents the `go-demo` service, not an individual instance. When we sent a drill request, Swarm networking performed **load balancing** (**LB**) across all of the instances of the service. To be more precise, it performed *round-robin* LB.

Besides creating a virtual IP for each service, each instance gets its own IP as well. In most cases, there is no need discovering those IPs (or any Docker network endpoint IP) since all we need is a service name, which gets translated to an IP and load balanced in the background.

What now?

That concludes the exploration of basic concepts of the Docker Swarm networking.

Is this everything there is to know to run a Swarm cluster successfully? In this chapter, we went deeper into Swarm features, but we are not yet done. There are quite a few questions waiting to be answered. In the next chapter, we'll explore *service discovery* and the role it has in the Swarm Mode.

Now is the time to take a break before diving into the next chapter. As before, we'll destroy the machines we created and start fresh:

```
docker-machine rm -f node-1 node-2 node-3
```

4

Service Discovery inside a Swarm Cluster

It does not take much strength to do things, but it requires a great deal of strength to decide what to do.

-Elbert Hubbard

If you used the old Swarm, the one shipped as a standalone product before *Docker 1.12*, you were forced to set up a service registry alongside it. You might have chosen Consul, etcd, or Zookeper. The standalone Swarm could not work without one of them. Why is that? What was the reason for such a strong dependency?

Before we discuss reasons behind using an external service registry with the old Swarm, let's discuss how would Swarm behave without it.

What would Docker Swarm look like without?

Let's say we have a cluster with three nodes. Two of them run **Swarm managers**, and one is a worker. Managers accept our requests, decide what should be done, and send tasks to **Swarm workers**. In turn, workers translate those tasks into commands that are sent to the local **Docker Engine**. Managers act as workers as well.

If we describe the flow we did earlier with the `go-demo` service, and imagine there is no service discovery associated with Swarm, it would be as follows.

A user sends a request to one of the managers. The request is not a declarative instruction but an expression of the desired state. For example, I want to have two instances of the go-demo service and one instance of the DB running inside the cluster:

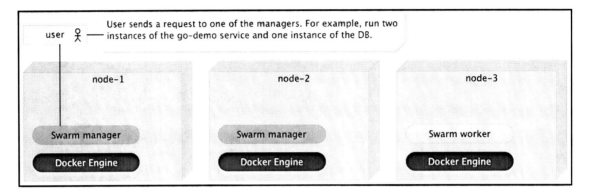

Figure 4-1: User sends a request to one of the managers

Once **Swarm manager** receives our request for the desired state, it compares it with the current state of the cluster, generates tasks, and sends them to **Swarm workers**. The tasks might be to run an instance of the go-demo service on **node-1** and **node-2**, and an instance of the go-demo-db service on **node-3**:

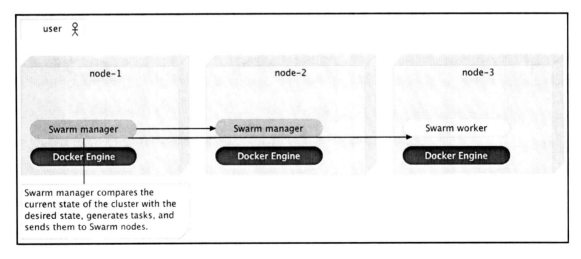

Figure 4-2: Swarm manager compares the current state of the cluster with the desired state, generates tasks, and sends them to Swarm workers.

Swarm workers receive tasks from the managers, translate them into Docker Engine commands, and send them to their local **Docker Engine** instances:

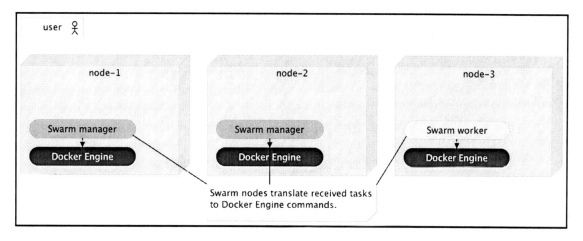

Figure 4-3: Swarm nodes translate received tasks to Docker Engine commands

Docker Engine receives a command from the Swarm worker and executes it:

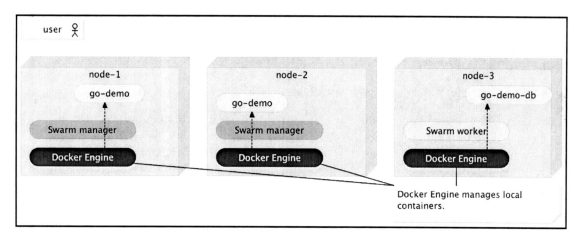

Figure 4-4: Docker Engine manages local containers.

Next, let's say that we send a new desired state to the manager. For example, we might want to scale the number of the **go-demo** instances to **node-3**. We would send a request to the **Swarm manager** on **node-1**, it would consult the cluster state it stored internally and make a decision to, for example, run a new instance on **node-2**. Once the decision is made, the manager would create a new task and send it to the **Swarm worker** on **node-2**. In turn, the worker would translate the task into a Docker command, and send it to the local engine. Once the command is executed, we would have the third instance of the **go-demo** service running on **node-2**:

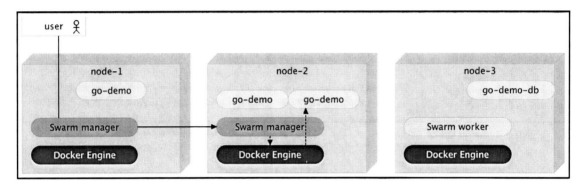

Figure 4-5: A scale request is sent to the Swarm manager

If the flow were as described, we would have quite a lot of problems that would make such a solution almost useless.

Let's try to list some of the issues we would face.

A Docker manager uses the information we sent to it. That would work as long as we always use the same manager and the state of the cluster does not change due to factors outside the control of the manager. The important thing to understand is that the information about the cluster is not stored in one place, nor it is complete. Each manager knows only about the things it did. Why is that such a problem?

Let's explore a few alternative (but not uncommon) paths.

What would happen if we sent the request to scale to three instances to the manager on **node-2**? That manager would be oblivious of the tasks created by the manager in **node-1**. As a result, it would try to run three new instances of the **go-demo** service resulting in five instances in total. We'd have two instances created by the manager in **node-1** and three by the manager in **node-2**.

It would be tempting always to use the same manager, but, in that case, we would have a single point of failure. What would happen if the whole **node-1** fails? We would have no managers available or would be forced to use the manager on **node-2**.

Many other factors might produce such discrepancies. Maybe one of the containers stopped unexpectedly. In such a case, when we decide to scale to three instances, the manager on **node-1** would think that two instances are running and would create a task to run one more. However, that would not result in three but two instances running inside the cluster.

The list of things that might go wrong is infinite, and we won't go into more examples.

The important thing to note is that it is unacceptable for any single manager to be stateful in isolation. Every manager needs to have the same information as any other. On the other hand, every node needs to monitor events generated by Docker Engine and make sure that any change to its server is propagated to all managers. Finally, we need to oversee the state of each server in case one of them fails. In other words, each manager needs to have an up-to-date picture of the entire cluster. Only then it can translate our requests for the desired state into tasks that will be dispatched to the Swarm nodes.

How can all the managers have a complete view of the whole cluster no matter who made a change to it?

The answer to that question depends on the requirements we set. We need a place where all the information is stored. Such a place need to be distributed so that the failure of one server does not affect the correct functioning of the tool. Being distributed provides fault tolerance, but that, by itself, does not mean data is synchronized across the cluster. The tool needs to maintain data replicated across all the instances. Replication is not anything new except that, in this case, it needs to be very fast so that the services that would consult it can receive data in (near) real-time. Moreover, we need a system that will monitor each server inside the cluster and update the data if anything changes.

To summarize, we need a distributed service registry and a monitoring system in place. The first requirement is best accomplished with one of the service registries or key-value stores. The old Swarm (standalone version before Docker 1.12) supports *Consul* (`https://www.consul.io/`), *etcd* (`https://github.com/coreos/etcd`), and *Zookeeper* (`https://zookeeper.apache.org/`). My preference is towards Consul, but any of the three should do.

For a more detailed discussion about service discovery and the comparison of the major service registries, please consult the service discovery: The Key to Distributed services chapter of *The DevOps 2.0 Toolkit*.

What does standalone Docker Swarm look like with service discovery?

Now that we have a better understanding of the requirements and the reasons behind the usage of service discovery, we can define the (real) flow of a request to a Docker Swarm manager.

Please note that we are still exploring how the old (standalone) Swarm is working:

1. A user sends a request with the desired state to one of the Swarm managers.
2. The Swarm manager gets the cluster information from the service registry, creates a set of tasks, and dispatches them to Swarm workers.
3. Swarm workers translate the tasks into commands and send them to the local Docker Engine which, in turn, runs or stops containers.
4. Swarm workers continuously monitor Docker events and update the **service registry**.

That way, information about the whole cluster is always up-to-date. The exception is when one of the managers or workers fails. Since managers are monitoring each other, the failure of a manager or a worker is considered a failure of the whole node. After all, without a worker, containers cannot be scheduled on that node:

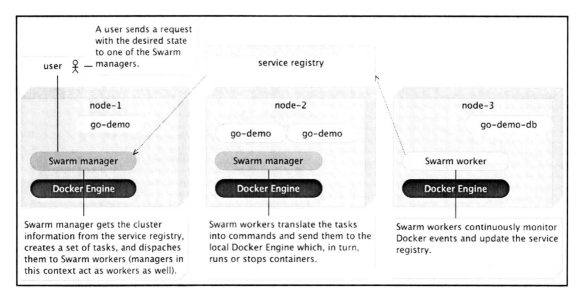

Figure 4-6: Docker Swarm (standalone) flow

Now that we established that service discovery is an essential tool for managing a cluster, the natural question is what happened to it in Swarm Mode (*Docker 1.12*)?

Service discovery in the Swarm cluster

The old (standalone) Swarm required a service registry so that all its managers can have the same view of the cluster state. When instantiating the old Swarm nodes, we had to specify the address of a service registry. However, if you take a look at setup instructions of the new Swarm (Swarm Mode introduced in *Docker 1.12*), you'll notice that we did not set up anything beyond Docker Engines. You will not find any mention of an external service registry or a key-value store.

Does that mean that Swarm does not need service discovery? Quite the contrary. The need for service discovery is as strong as ever, and Docker decided to incorporate it inside Docker Engine. It is bundled inside just as Swarm is. The internal process is, essentially, still very similar to the one used by the standalone Swarm, only with less moving parts. Docker Engine now acts as a Swarm manager, Swarm worker, and service registry.

The decision to bundle everything inside the engine provoked a mixed response. Some thought that such a decision creates too much coupling and increases Docker Engine's level of instability. Others think that such a bundle makes the engine more robust and opens the door to some new possibilities. While both sides have valid arguments, I am more inclined towards the opinion of the latter group. Docker Swarm Mode is a huge step forward, and it is questionable whether the same result could be accomplished without bundling service registry inside the engine.

Knowing how Docker Swarm works, especially networking, the question that might be on your mind is whether we need service discovery (beyond Swarms internal usage). In *The DevOps 2.0 Toolkit*, I argued that service discovery is a must and urged everyone to set up *Consul* (https://www.consul.io/) or *etcd* (https://github.com/coreos/etcd) as service registries, Registrator as a mechanism to register changes inside the cluster, and Consul Template or confd (https://github.com/kelseyhightower/confd) as a templating solution. Do we still need those tools?

Do we need service discovery?

It is hard to provide a general recommendation whether service discovery tools are needed when working inside a Swarm cluster. If we look at the need to find services as the main use case for those tools, the answer is usually no. We don't need external service discovery for that. As long as all services that should communicate with each other are inside the same network, all we need is the name of the destination service. For example, for the go-demo (`https://github.com/vfarcic/go-demo`) service to find the related database, it only needs to know its DNS `go-demo-db`. The `Chapter 3`, *Docker Swarm Networking and Reverse Proxy* proved that proper networking usage is enough for most use cases.

However, finding services and load balancing requests among them is not the only reason for service discovery. We might have other uses for service registries or key-value stores. We might need to store some information such that it is distributed and fault tolerant.

An example of the need for a key-value store can be seen inside the *Docker Flow Proxy* (`http s://github.com/vfarcic/docker-flow-proxy`) project. It is based on HAProxy which is a stateful service. It loads the information from a configuration file into memory. Having stateful services inside a dynamic cluster represents a challenge that needs to be solved. Otherwise, we might lose state when a service is scaled, rescheduled after a failure, and so on.

Before we go into more details and problems related with stateful services, let's see how we could set up Consul as our key-value store of choice and go through its basic features.

Setting up Consul as service registry inside a Swarm cluster

As before, we'll start by setting up a Swarm cluster. From there on, we'll proceed with the Consul setup and a quick overview of the basic operations we can do with it. That will give us the knowledge necessary for the rest of this chapter.

A note to The DevOps 2.0 Toolkit readers
You might be tempted to skip this sub-chapter since you already learned how to set up Consul. I recommend you read on. We'll use the official Consul image that was not available at the time I wrote the previous book. At the same time, I promise to keep this sub-chapter as brief as possible without confusing the new readers too much.

Practice makes perfect, but there is a limit after which there is no reason to repeat the same commands over and over. I'm sure that, by now, you got tired of writing the commands that create a Swarm cluster. So, I prepared the `scripts/dm-swarm.sh` (https://github.com/vfarcic/cloud-provisioning/blob/master/scripts/dm-swarm.sh) script that will create Docker Machine nodes and join them into a Swarm cluster.

All the commands from this chapter are available in the `04-service-discovery.sh` (https://gist.github.com/vfarcic/fa57e88faf09651c9a7e9e46c8950ef5) Gist.

Let's clone the code and run the script:

Some of the files will be shared between the host file system and Docker Machines we'll create soon. Docker Machine makes the whole directory that belongs to the current user available inside the VM. Therefore, please make sure that the code is cloned inside one of the user's sub-folders.

```
git clone https://github.com/vfarcic/cloud-provisioning.git

cd cloud-provisioning

scripts/dm-swarm.sh

eval $(docker-machine env swarm-1)

docker node ls
```

The output of the `node ls` command is as follows (IDs are removed for brevity):

```
HOSTNAME STATUS AVAILABILITY MANAGER STATUS
swarm-2 Ready Active Reachable
swarm-3 Ready Active Reachable
swarm-1 Ready Active Leader
```

Please note that this time there was a slight change in the commands. We used the `manager` token so that all three nodes are set up as managers.

As a general rule, we should have a least three Swarm managers. That way, if one of them fails, the others will reschedule the failed containers and can be used as our access points to the system. As is often the case with solutions that require a quorum, an odd number is usually the best. Hence, we have three.

You might be tempted to run all nodes as managers. I advise you against that. Managers synchronize data between themselves. The more manager instances are running, the more time the synchronization might last. While that is not even noticeable when there are only a few, if, for example, you'd run a hundred managers there would be some lag. After all, that's why we have workers. Managers are our entry points to the system and coordinators of the tasks, while workers do the actual work.

With that out of the way, we can proceed and set up Consul.

We'll start by downloading the `docker-compose.yml` (https://github.com/vfarcic/doc ker-flow-proxy/blob/master/docker-compose.yml) file from the *Docker Flow Proxy* (http s://github.com/vfarcic/docker-flow-proxy) project. It already contains Consul defined as Compose services.

```
curl -o docker-compose-proxy.yml \
    https://raw.githubusercontent.com/\
vfarcic/docker-flow-proxy/master/docker-compose.yml

cat docker-compose-proxy.yml
```

Just as Docker Swarm node can act as a manager or a worker, Consul can be run as a server or an agent. We'll start with the server.

The Compose definition of the Consul service that acts as a server is as follows:

```
consul-server:
  container_name: consul
  image: consul
  network_mode: host
  environment:
    - 'CONSUL_LOCAL_CONFIG={"skip_leave_on_interrupt": true}'
  command: agent -server -bind=$DOCKER_IP -bootstrap-expect=1 -
client=$DOCKER_IP
```

The important thing to note is that we set up the network mode as `host`. That means that the container will share the same network as the host it is running on. This is followed by an environment variable and the command.

The command will run the agent in server mode and, initially, it expects to be the only one in the cluster `-bootstrap-expect=1`.

You'll notice the usage of the `DOCKER_IP` environment variable. Consul expects the information about the binding and the client address. Since we don't know the IP of the servers in advance, it had to be a variable.

At this moment you might be wondering why are we talking about Docker Compose services inside a Swarm cluster. Shouldn't we run `docker service create` command? The truth is, at the time of this writing, the official consul image is still not adapted to the "Swarm way" of running things. Most images do not require any changes before launching them inside a Swarm cluster. Consul is one of the very few exceptions. I will do my best to update the instructions as soon as the situation changes. Until then, the good old Compose should do:

```
export DOCKER_IP=$(docker-machine ip swarm-1)

docker-compose -f docker-compose-proxy.yml \
    up -d consul-server
```

You'll notice `WARNING: The Docker Engine you're using is running in swarm mode` message in the output. It is only a friendly reminder that we are not running this as Docker service. Feel free to ignore it.

Now that we have a Consul instance running, we can go through the basic operations.

We can, for example, put some information into the key-value store:

```
curl -X PUT -d 'this is a test' \
    "http://$(docker-machine ip swarm-1):8500/v1/kv/msg1"
```

The `curl` command put this is a test value as the `msg1` key inside Consul.

We can confirm that the key-value combination is indeed stored by sending a `GET` request:

```
curl "http://$(docker-machine ip swarm-1):8500/v1/kv/msg1"
```

The output is as follows (formatted for readability):

```
[
  {
    "LockIndex": 0,
    "Key": "msg1",
    "Flags": 0,
    "Value": "dGhpcyBpcyBhIHRlc3Q=",
    "CreateIndex": 17,
    "ModifyIndex": 17
  }
]
```

You'll notice that the value is encoded. If we add the `raw` parameter to the request, Consul will return only the value in its raw format:

```
curl "http://$(docker-machine ip swarm-1):8500/v1/kv/msg1?raw"
```

The output is as follows:

```
this is a test
```

Right now, we have only one Consul instance. If the node it is running in fails `swarm-1`, all the data will be lost and service registry will be unavailable. That's not a good situation to be in.

We can create fault tolerance by running a few more Consul instances. This time, we'll run agents.

Just as the Consul server instance, the agent is also defined in the `docker-compose.yml` (h ttps://github.com/vfarcic/docker-flow-proxy/blob/master/docker-compose.yml) file in the *Docker Flow Proxy* (https://github.com/vfarcic/docker-flow-proxy) project. Remember, we downloaded it with the name `docker-compose-proxy.yml`. Let's take a look at the service definition:

```
cat docker-compose-proxy.yml
```

The part of the output that defines the `Consul-agent` service is as follows:

```
consul-agent:
  container_name: consul
  image: consul
  network_mode: host
  environment:
    - 'CONSUL_LOCAL_CONFIG={"leave_on_terminate": true}'
  command: agent -bind=$DOCKER_IP -retry-join=$CONSUL_SERVER_IP \
-client=$DOCKER_IP
```

It is almost the same as the definition we used to run the Consul server instance. The only important difference is that the `-server` is missing and that we have the `-retry-join` argument. We're using the latter to specify the address of another instance. Consul uses the gossip protocol. As long as every instance is aware of at least one other instance, the protocol will propagate the information across all of them.

Let's run agents on the other two nodes `swarm-2` and `swarm-3`:

```
export CONSUL_SERVER_IP=$(docker-machine ip swarm-1)

for i in 2 3; do
    eval $(docker-machine env swarm-$i)

    export DOCKER_IP=$(docker-machine ip swarm-$i)

    docker-compose -f docker-compose-proxy.yml \
        up -d consul-agent
done
```

Now that we have three Consul instances running inside the cluster (one on each node), we can confirm that gossip indeed works.

Let's request the value of the `msg1` key. This time, we'll request it from the Consul instance running on `swarm-2`:

```
curl "http://$(docker-machine ip swarm-2):8500/v1/kv/msg1"
```

As you can see from the output, even though we put the information to the instance running on `swarm-1`, it is available from the instance in `swarm-2`. The information is propagated through all the instances.

We can give the gossip protocol one more round of testing:

```
curl -X PUT -d 'this is another test' \
 "http://$(docker-machine ip swarm-2):8500/v1/kv/messages/msg2"

curl -X PUT -d 'this is a test with flags' \
 "http://$(docker-machine ip swarm-3):8500/v1/kv/messages/msg3?\
flags=1234"

curl "http://$(docker-machine ip swarm-1):8500/v1/kv/?recurse"
```

We sent one `PUT` request to the instance running in `swarm-2` and another to the instance in `swarm-3`. When we requested all the keys from the instance running in `swarm-1`, all three were returned. In other words, no matter what we do with data, it is always in sync in all of the instances.

Similarly, we can delete information:

```
curl -X DELETE "http://$(docker-machine ip swarm-2):\
8500/v1/kv/?recurse"

curl "http://$(docker-machine ip swarm-3):8500/v1/kv/?recurse"
```

We sent the request to the `swarm-2` to delete all keys. When we queried the instance running in `swarm-3`, we got an empty response meaning that everything is, indeed, gone.

With a setup similar to the one we explored, we can have a reliable, distributed, and fault-tolerant way for storing and retrieving any information our services might need.

We'll use this knowledge to explore a possible solution for some of the problems that might arise when running stateful services inside a Swarm cluster. But before we start discussing the solution, let's see what the problem is with stateful services.

Problems when scaling stateful instances

Scaling services inside a Swarm cluster is easy, isn't it? Just execute `docker service scale <SERVICE_NAME>=<NUMBER_OF_INSTANCES>` and, all of a sudden, the service is running multiple copies.

The previous statement is only partly true. The more precise wording would be that "scaling stateless services inside a Swarm cluster is easy".

The reason that scaling stateless services is easy lies in the fact that there is no state to think about. An instance is the same no matter how long it runs. There is no difference between a new instance and one that run for a week. Since the state does not change over time, we can create new copies at any given moment, and they will all be exactly the same.

However, the world is not stateless. State is an unavoidable part of our industry. As soon as the first piece of information is created, it needs to be stored somewhere. The place we store data must be stateful. It has a state that changes over time. If we want to scale such a stateful service, there are at least two things we need to consider:

1. How do we propagate a change of state of one instance to the rest of the instances?
2. How do we create a copy (a new instance) of a stateful service, and make sure that the state is copied as well?

We usually combine stateless and stateful services into one logical entity. A back-end service could be stateless and rely on a database service as an external data storage. That way, there is a clear separation of concerns and a different lifecycle of each of those services.

Before we proceed, I must state that there is no silver bullet that makes stateful services scalable and fault-tolerant. Throughout the book, I will go through a couple of examples that might, or might not, apply to your use case. An obvious, and very typical example of a stateful service is a database. While there are some common patterns, almost every database provides a different mechanism for data replication. That, in itself, is enough to prevent us from having a definitive answer that would apply to all. We'll explore scalability of a MongoDB later on in the book. We'll also see an example with Jenkins that uses a file system for its state.

The first case we'll tackle will be of a different type. We'll discuss scalability of a service that has its state stored in a configuration file. To make things more complicated, the configuration is dynamic. It changes over time, throughout the lifetime of the service. We'll explore ways to make HAProxy scalable.

If we use the official *HAProxy* (`https://hub.docker.com/_/haproxy/`) image, one of the challenges we would face is deciding how to update the state of all the instances. We'd have to change the configuration and reload each copy of the `proxy`.

We can, for example, mount an NFS volume on each node in the cluster and make sure that the same host volume is mounted inside all HAProxy containers. At first, it might seem that that would solve the problem with the state since all instances would share the same configuration file. Any change to the config on the host would be available inside all the instances we would have. However, that, in itself, would not change the state of the service.

HAProxy loads the configuration file during initialization, and it is oblivious to any changes we might make to the configuration afterward. For the change of the state of the file to be reflected in the state of the service, we'd need to reload it. The problem is that instances can run on any of the nodes inside the cluster. On top of that, if we adopt dynamic scaling (more on that later on), we might not even know how many instances are running. So we'd need to discover how many instances we have, find out on which nodes they are running, get IDs of each of the containers, and, only then, send a signal to reload the `proxy`. While all this can be scripted, it is far from an optimum solution. Moreover, mounting an NFS volume is a single point of failure. If the server that hosts the volume fails, data is lost. Sure, we can create backups, but they would only provide a way to restore lost data partially. That is, we can restore a backup, but the data generated between the moment the last backup was created, and the node failure would be lost.

An alternative would be to embed the configuration into HAProxy images. We could create a new Dockerfile that would be based on `haproxy` and add the `COPY` instruction that would add the configuration. That would mean that every time we want to reconfigure the proxy, we'd need to change the config, build a new set of images (a new release), and update the `proxy` service currently running inside the cluster. As you can imagine, this is also not practical. It's too big of a process for a simple proxy reconfiguration.

Docker Flow Proxy uses a different, less conventional, approach to the problem. It stores a replica of its state in Consul. It also uses an undocumented Swarm networking feature (at least at the time of this writing).

Using service registry to store the state

Now that we have Consul instances set up let us explore how to exploit them to our own benefit. We'll study the design of the *Docker Flow Proxy* as a way to demonstrate some of the challenges and solutions you might want to apply to your own services.

Let us create the `proxy` network and the service:

```
eval $(docker-machine env swarm-1)

docker network create --driver overlay proxy

docker service create --name proxy \
    -p 80:80 \
    -p 443:443 \
    -p 8080:8080 \
    --network proxy \
    -e MODE=swarm \
    --replicas 3 \
    -e CONSUL_ADDRESS="$(docker-machine ip swarm-1):8500 \
,$(docker-machine ip \
swarm-2):8500,$(docker-machine ip swarm-3):8500" \
    vfarcic/docker-flow-proxy
```

The command we used to create the **proxy** service is slightly different than before. Namely, now we have the `CONSUL_ADDRESS` variable with the comma separated addresses of all three **Consul** instances. The **proxy** is made in a way that it will try the first address. If it does not respond, it will try the next one, and so on. That way, as long as at least one **Consul** instance is running, the **proxy** will be able to fetch and put data. We would not need to do this loop if **Consul** would run as a Swarm service. In that case, all we'd need to do is put both inside the same network and use the service name as the address.

Unfortunately, **Consul** cannot, yet, run as a Swarm service, so we are forced to specify all addresses, refer to the following diagram:

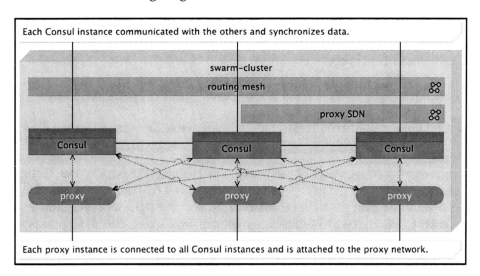

Figure 4-7: The proxy scaled to three instances

Before we proceed, we should make sure that all instances of the proxy are running:

```
docker service ps proxy
```

Please wait until the current state of all the instances is set to Running.

Let's create the go-demo service. It will act as a catalyst for a discussion around challenges we might face with a scaled reverse proxy:

```
docker network create --driver overlay go-demo

docker service create --name go-demo-db \
    --network go-demo \
    mongo:3.2.10

docker service create --name go-demo \
    -e DB=go-demo-db \
    --network go-demo \
    --network proxy \
    vfarcic/go-demo:1.0
```

There's no reason to explain the commands in detail. They are the same as those we've run in the previous chapters.

Please wait until the current state of the `go-demo` service is Running. Feel free to use `docker service ps go-demo` command to check the status.

If we would repeat the same process we used in the `Chapter 3`, *Docker Swarm Networking and Reverse Proxy* the request to reconfigure the proxy would be as follows (please do not run it).

```
curl "$(docker-machine ip swarm-1):8080/v1/\
proxy/reconfigure?serviceName=go-demo&servicePath=/demo&port=8080"
```

We would send a reconfigure request to the `proxy` service. Can you guess what would be the result?

A user sends a request to reconfigure the **proxy**. The request is picked by the routing mesh and load balanced across all the instances of the **proxy**. The request is forwarded to one of the instances. Since the **proxy** is using **Consul** to store its configuration, it sends the info to one of the **Consul** instances which, in turn, synchronizes the data across all others.
As a result, we have **proxy** instances with different states. The one that received the request is reconfigured to use the `go-demo` service. The other two are, still, oblivious to it. If we try to ping the `go-demo` service through the **proxy**, we will get mixed responses. One out of three times, the response would be status `200`. The rest of the time, we would get `404`, not found:

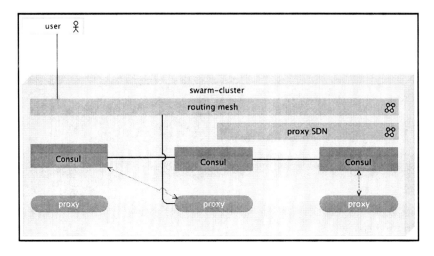

Figure 4-8: A request to reconfigure the proxy

We would experience a similar result if we scale MongoDB. The **routing mesh** would load balance across all instances, and their states would start to diverge. We could solve the problem with MongoDB by using replica sets. That's the mechanism that allows us to replicate data across all DB instances. However, HAProxy does not have such a feature. So, I had to add it myself.

The correct request to reconfigure the proxy running multiple instances is as follows:

```
curl "$(docker-machine ip swarm-1):8080/v1/\
docker-flow-proxy/reconfigure \
serviceName=go-demo&servicePath=/demo&port=8080&distribute=true"
```

Please note the new parameter `distribute=true`. When specified, the **proxy** will accept the request, reconfigure itself, and resend the request to all other instances:

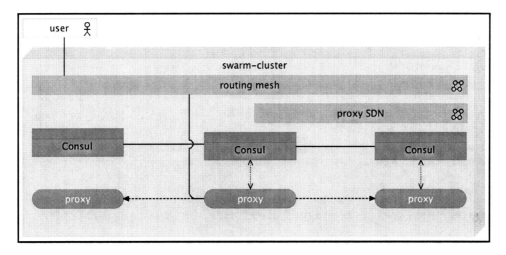

Figure 4-9: The proxy instance that received the request and resent it to all others

That way, the **proxy** implements a mechanism similar to replica sets in MongoDB. A change to one of the instances is propagated to all others.

Let us confirm that it indeed works as expected:

```
curl -i "$(docker-machine ip swarm-1)/demo/hello"
```

The output is as follows:

```
HTTP/1.1 200 OK
Date: Fri, 09 Sep 2016 16:04:05 GMT
Content-Length: 14
Content-Type: text/plain; charset=utf-8

hello, world!
```

The response is 200 meaning that the go-demo service received the request forwarded by the proxy service. Since the routing mesh is in play, the request entered the system, was load balanced and resent to one of the proxy instances. The proxy instance that received the request evaluated the path and decided that it should go to the go-demo service. As a result, the request is resent to the go-demo network, load balanced again and forwarded to one of the go-demo instances. In other words, any of the proxy and go-demo instances could have received the request. If the proxy state was not synchronized across all the instances, two out of three requests would fail.

Feel free to repeat the curl -i $(docker-machine ip swarm-1)/demo/hello command. The result should always be the same.

We can double check that the configuration is indeed synchronized by taking a peek into one of the containers.

Let's take a look at, let's say, proxy instance number three.

The first thing we should do is find out the node the instance is running in:

```
NODE=$(docker service ps proxy | grep "proxy.3" | awk '{print $4}')
```

We listed all proxy service processes docker service ps proxy, filtered the result with the third instance grep "proxy.3", and returned the name of the node stored in the fourth column of the output awk '{print $4}'. The result was stored in the environment variable NODE.

Now that we know the server this instance is running in, we can enter the container and display the contents of the configuration file:

```
eval $(docker-machine env $NODE)

ID=$(docker ps | grep "proxy.3" | awk '{print $1}')
```

We changed the Docker client to point to the node. That was followed with the command that lists all running processes `docker ps`, filters out the third instance `grep "proxy.3"`, and outputs the container ID stored in the first column `awk '{print $1}'`. The result was stored in the environment variable ID.

With the client pointing to the correct node and the ID stored as the environment variable ID, we can, finally, enter the container and display the configuration:

```
docker exec -it $ID cat /cfg/haproxy.cfg
```

The relevant part of the output is as follows:

```
frontend services
    bind *:80
    bind *:443
    mode http

    acl url_go-demo8080 path_beg /demo
    use_backend go-demo-be8080 if url_go-demo8080

backend go-demo-be8080
    mode http
    server go-demo go-demo:8080
```

As you can see, the third instance of the `proxy` is indeed configured correctly with the go-demo service. Feel free to repeat the process with the other two instances. The result should be exactly the same proving that synchronization works.

How was it done? How did the `proxy` instance that received the request discover the IPs of all the other instances? After all, there is no Registrator that would provide the IPs to Consul, and we cannot access Swarms internal service discovery API.

Discovering addresses of all instances that form a service

If you browse through the official Docker documentation, you will not find any reference to addresses of individual instances that form a service.

The previous sentence might not be true at the time you're reading this. Someone might have updated the documentation. However, at the time I'm writing this chapter, there is not a trace of such information.

The fact that something is not documented does not mean that it does not exist. Indeed, there is a special DNS that will return all IPs.

To see it in action, we'll create the global service called util and attach it to the `proxy` network:

```
docker service create --name util \
    --network proxy --mode global \
    alpine sleep 1000000000

docker service ps util
```

Before proceeding, please wait until the current state is set to running.

Next, we'll find the ID of one of the util instances and install drill that will show us the information related to DNS entries:

```
ID=$(docker ps -q --filter label=com.docker.swarm.service.name=util)

docker exec -it $ID apk add --update drill
```

Let's start by drilling the DNS proxy:

```
docker exec -it $ID drill proxy
```

The output is as follows:

```
;; ->>HEADER<<- opcode: QUERY, rcode: NOERROR, id: 31878
;; flags: qr rd ra ; QUERY: 1, ANSWER: 1, AUTHORITY: 0, ADDITIONAL: 0
;; QUESTION SECTION:
;; proxy.                IN              A

;; ANSWER SECTION:
proxy.          600             IN              A          10.0.0.2

;; AUTHORITY SECTION:

;; ADDITIONAL SECTION:

;; Query time: 0 msec
;; SERVER: 127.0.0.11
;; WHEN: Fri Sep 9 16:43:23 2016
;; MSG SIZE rcvd: 44
```

As you can see, even though we are running three instances of the service, only one IP is returned 10.0.0.2. That is the IP of the service, not an individual instance. To be more concrete, it is the IP of the `proxy` service network end-point. When a request reaches that end-point, Docker network performs load balancing across all the instances.

In most cases, we do not need anything else. All we have to know is the name of the service and Docker will do the rest of the work for us. However, in a few cases, we might need more. We might need to know the IPs of every single instance of a service. That is the problem *Docker Flow Proxy* faced.

To find the IPs of all the instances of a service we can use the "undocumented" feature. We need to add the tasks prefix to the service name.

Let's drill again:

```
docker exec -it $ID drill tasks.proxy
```

This time, the output is different:

```
;; ->>HEADER<<- opcode: QUERY, rcode: NOERROR, id: 54408
;; flags: qr rd ra ; QUERY: 1, ANSWER: 3, AUTHORITY: 0, ADDITIONAL: 0
;; QUESTION SECTION:
;; tasks.proxy. IN A

;; ANSWER SECTION:
tasks.proxy. 600 IN A 10.0.0.4
tasks.proxy. 600 IN A 10.0.0.3
tasks.proxy. 600 IN A 10.0.0.5

;; AUTHORITY SECTION:

;; ADDITIONAL SECTION:

;; Query time: 0 msec
;; SERVER: 127.0.0.11
;; WHEN: Fri Sep 9 16:48:46 2016
;; MSG SIZE rcvd: 110
```

We got three answers, each with a different IP 10.0.0.4, 10.0.0.3, 10.0.0.5.

Knowing the IPs of all the instances solved the problem of having to synchronize data. With tasks.<SERVICE_NAME> we have all the info we need. The rest is only a bit of coding that will utilize those IPs. It is a similar mechanism used when synchronizing databases (more on that later).

We are not done yet. The fact that we can synchronize data on demand (or events) does not mean that the service is fault tolerant. What should we do if we need to create a new instance? What happens if an instance fails and Swarm reschedules it somewhere else?

Using service registry or key value store to store service state

We'll continue using *Docker Flow Proxy* as a playground to explore some of the mechanisms and decisions we might make when dealing with stateful services. Please note that, in this chapter, we are concentrating on services with a relatively small state. We'll explore other use cases in the chapters that follow.

Imagine that the proxy does not use Consul to store data and that we do not use volumes. What would happen if we were to scale it up? The new instances would be out of sync. Their state would be the same as the initial state of the first instance we created. In other words, there would be no state, even though the instances that are already running changed over time and generated data.

That is where Consul comes into play. Every time an instance of the proxy receives a request that results in the change of its state, it propagates that change to other instances, as well as to Consul. On the other hand, the first action the proxy performs when initialized is to consult Consul, and create the configuration from its data.

We can observe the state stored in Consul by sending a request for all the data with keys starting with `docker-flow`:

```
curl "http://$(docker-machine ip swarm-1):8500/v1/kv/\
docker-flow?recurse"
```

A part of the output is as follows:

```
[
...
  {
    "LockIndex": 0,
    "Key": "docker-flow/go-demo/path",
    "Flags": 0,
    "Value": "L2RlbW8=",
    "CreateIndex": 233,
    "ModifyIndex": 245
  },
...
```

```
{
  "LockIndex": 0,
  "Key": "docker-flow/go-demo/port",
  "Flags": 0,
  "Value": "ODA4MA==",
  "CreateIndex": 231,
  "ModifyIndex": 243
},
...
]
```

The preceding example shows that the path and the port we specified when we reconfigured the proxy for the go-demo service, is stored in Consul. If we instruct Swarm manager to scale the proxy service, new instances will be created. Those instances will query Consul and use the information to generate their configurations.

Let's give it a try:

```
docker service scale proxy=6
```

We increased the number of instances from three to six.

Let's take a sneak peek into the instance number six:

```
NODE=$(docker service ps proxy | grep "proxy.6" | awk '{print $4}')

eval $(docker-machine env $NODE)

ID=$(docker ps | grep "proxy.6" | awk '{print $1}')

docker exec -it $ID cat /cfg/haproxy.cfg
```

A part of the output of the exec command is as follows:

```
frontend services
    bind *:80
    bind *:443
    mode http

backend go-demo-be8080
  mode http
  server go-demo :8080
```

As you can see, the new instance recuperated all the information from Consul. As a result, its state became the same as the state of any other proxy instance running inside the cluster.

If we destroy an instance, the result will, again, be the same. Swarm will detect that an instance crashed and schedule a new one. The new instance will repeat the same process of querying Consul and create the same state as the other instances:

```
docker rm -f $(docker ps \
    | grep proxy.6 \
    | awk '{print $1}')
```

We should wait for a few moments until Swarm detects the failure and creates a new instance.

Once it's running, we can take a look at the configuration of the new instance. It will be the same as before:

```
NODE=$(docker service ps \
    -f desired-state=running proxy \
    | grep "proxy.6" \
    | awk '{print $4}')

eval $(docker-machine env $NODE)

ID=$(docker ps | grep "proxy.6" | awk '{print $1}')

docker exec -it $ID cat /cfg/haproxy.cfg
```

The explanation of *Docker Flow Proxy* inner workings is mostly for educational purposes. I wanted to show you one of the possible solutions when dealing with stateful services. The methods we discussed are applicable only when the state is relatively small. When it is bigger, as is the case with databases, we should employ different mechanisms to accomplish the same goals.

If we go one level higher, the primary requirements, or prerequisites, when running stateful services inside a cluster are as follows:

1. Ability to synchronize the state across all instances of the service.
2. Ability to recuperate the state during initialization.

If we manage to fulfill those two requirements, we are on the right path towards solving one of the major bottlenecks when operating stateful services inside the cluster.

What now?

That concludes the exploration of basic concepts behind the usage of service discovery inside a Swarm cluster.

Are we done learning about Swarm features? We are far from knowing everything there is to know about Docker Swarm. However, at this point, we have enough knowledge to go back to the end of Chapter 1, *Continuous Integration with Docker Containers* and make the next logical step. We can design a Continuous Delivery flow.

Now is the time to take a break before diving into the next chapter. As before, we'll destroy the machines we created and start fresh:

```
docker-machine rm -f swarm-1 swarm-2 swarm-3
```

5
Continuous Delivery and Deployment with Docker Containers

In software, when something is painful, the way to reduce the pain is to do it more frequently, not less.

— David Farley

At the time, we could not convert the **Continuous Integration (CI)** into the **Continuous Delivery (CD)** process because we were missing some essential knowledge. Now that we understand the basic principles and commands behind Docker Swarm, we can go back to the end of the Chapter 1, *Continuous Integration with Docker Containers*. We can define the steps that will let us perform the full CD process.

I won't go into Continuous Delivery details. Instead, I'll pitch it as a single sentence. *Continuous Delivery is a process applied to every commit in a code repository and results in every successful build being ready for deployment to production.*

CD means that anyone, at any time, can click a button, and deploy a build to production without the fear that something will go wrong. It means that the process is so robust that we have full confidence that "almost" any problem will be detected before the deployment to production. Needless to say, CD is an entirely automated process. There is no human involvement from the moment a commit is sent to a code repository, all the way until a build is ready to be deployed to production. The only manual action is that someone needs to press the button that will run a script that performs the deployment.

Continuous Deployment (CDP) is one step forward. It is Continuous Delivery without the button. *Continuous Deployment is a process applied to every commit in a code repository and results with every successful build being Deployed to production.*

No matter which process you choose, the steps are the same. The only difference is whether there is a button that deploys the release to production.

At this point, it is safe to assume that we'll use Docker whenever convenient and that we'll use Swarm clusters to run the services in production and production-like environments.

Let's start by specifying the steps that could define one possible implementation of the CD/CDP process:

1. Check out the code.
2. Run unit tests.
3. Build binaries and other required artifacts.
4. Deploy the service to the staging environment.
5. Run functional tests.
6. Deploy the service to the production-like environment.
7. Run production readiness tests.
8. Deploy the service to the production environment.
9. Run production readiness tests.

Now, let's get going and set up the environment we'll need for practicing the CD flow.

Defining the Continuous Delivery environment

A minimum requirement for a Continuous Delivery environment is two clusters. One should be dedicated to running tests, building artifacts and images, and all other CD tasks. We can use it for simulating a production cluster. The second cluster will be used for deployments to production.

Why do we need two clusters? Can't we accomplish the same with only one?

While we certainly could get away with only one cluster, having two will simplify quite a few processes and, more importantly, provide better isolation between production and non-production services and tasks.

The more we minimize the impact on the production cluster, the better. By not running non-production services and tasks inside the production cluster, we are reducing the risk. Therefore, we should have a production cluster separated from the rest of the environment.

Now let's get started and fire up those clusters.

Setting up Continuous Delivery clusters

What is a minimum number of servers required for a production-like cluster? I'd say two. If there's only one server, we would not be able to test whether networking and volumes work across nodes. So, it has to be plural. On the other hand, I don't want to push your laptop too much so we'll avoid increasing the number unless necessary.

For the production-like cluster, two nodes should be enough. We should add one more node that we'll use for running tests and building images. The production cluster should probably be a bit bigger since it will have more services running. We'll make it three nodes big. If needed, we can increase the capacity later on. As you already saw, adding nodes to a Swarm cluster is very easy.

By now, we set up a Swarm cluster quite a few times so we'll skip the explanation and just do it through a script.

 All the commands from this chapter are available in the `05-continuous-delivery.sh` (https://gist.github.com/vfarcic/5d08a87a3d4cb07db5348fec49720cbe) Gist.

Let's go back to the cloud-provisioning directory we created in the previous chapter and run the `scripts/dm-swarm.sh` (https://github.com/vfarcic/cloud-provisioning/blob/master/scripts/dm-swarm.sh) script. It will create the production nodes and join them into a cluster. The nodes will be called `swarm-1`, `swarm-2`, and `swarm-3`:

```
cd cloud-provisioning

scripts/dm-swarm.sh

eval $(docker-machine env swarm-1)

docker node ls
```

The output of the **node ls** command is as follows (IDs are removed for brevity):

```
HOSTNAME  STATUS  AVAILABILITY  MANAGER STATUS
swarm-2   Ready   Active        Reachable
swarm-1   Ready   Active        Leader
swarm-3   Ready   Active        Reachable
```

Next, we'll create the second cluster. We'll use it for running CD tasks as well as a simulation of a production environment. Three nodes should be enough, for now. We'll call them swarm-test-1, swarm-test-2, and swarm-test-3.

We'll create the cluster by executing the scripts/dm-test-swarm.sh (https://github.com/vfarcic/cloud-provisioning/blob/master/scripts/dm-test-swarm.sh) script:

```
scripts/dm-test-swarm.sh

eval $(docker-machine env swarm-test-1)

docker node ls
```

The output of the node ls command is as follows (IDs were removed for brevity):

```
HOSTNAME       STATUS  AVAILABILITY  MANAGER STATUS
swarm-test-2   Ready   Active        Reachable
swarm-test-1   Ready   Active        Leader
swarm-test-3   Ready   Active        Reachable
```

The only thing left, for now, is to create Docker registry services. We'll create one in each cluster. That way, there will be no direct relation between them, and they will be able to operate independently one from another. For registries running on separate clusters to share the same data, we'll mount the same host volume to both services. That way, an image pushed from one cluster will be available from the other, and vice versa. Please note that the volumes we're creating are still a workaround. Later on, we'll explore better ways to mount volumes.

Let's start with the production cluster.

We've already run the registry in the Chapter 1, *Continuous Integration with Docker Containers* . Back then, we had a single node, and we used Docker Compose to deploy services. Registry was not an option.

A note to Windows users

Git Bash has a habit of altering file system paths. To stop this, execute the following before running the code block:
export MSYS_NO_PATHCONV=1

This time, we'll run the registry as a Swarm service:

```
eval $(docker-machine env swarm-1)

docker service create --name registry \
    -p 5000:5000 \
    --reserve-memory 100m \
    --mount "type=bind,source=$PWD,target=/var/lib/registry" \
    registry:2.5.0
```

We exposed port 5000 and reserved 100 MB of memory. We used the --mount argument to expose a volume. This argument is, somewhat, similar to the Docker Engine argument --volume or the volumes argument in Docker compose files. The only significant difference is in the format. In this case, we specified that the current host directory source=$PWD should be mounted inside the container target=/var/lib/registry.

Please note that, from now on, we'll always run specific versions. While, until now, the latest was alright as a demonstration, now we're trying to simulate CD processes we'll run in "real" clusters. We should always be explicit which version of a service we want to run. That way, we can be sure that the same service is tested and deployed to production. Otherwise, we could run into a situation where one version was deployed and tested in a production-like environment, but a different one was deployed to production.

The benefits behind specific versions are even more apparent when we use images from Docker Hub. For example, if we just run the latest release of the registry, there is no guarantee that, later on, when we run it in the second cluster, the latest release will not be updated. We could, easily, end up getting different releases of the registry in different clusters. That could lead to some really hard-to-detect bugs.

I won't bother you more with versioning. I'm sure you know what's it for and when to use it.

Let's get back to the registry service. We should create it inside the second cluster as well:

```
eval $(docker-machine env swarm-test-1)

docker service create --name registry \
    -p 5000:5000 \
    --reserve-memory 100m \
    --mount "type=bind,source=$PWD,target=/var/lib/registry" \
    registry:2.5.0
```

Now we have the `registry` service running inside both clusters.

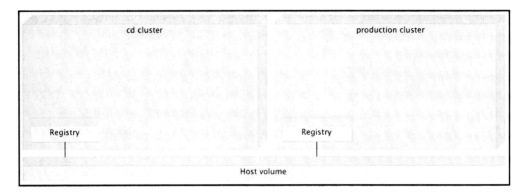

Figure 5-1: CD and production clusters with the registry service

At the moment, we do not know in which servers the registries are running. All we know is that there is an instance of the service in each cluster. Normally, we'd have to configure Docker Engine to treat the registry service as insecure and allow the traffic. To do that, we'd need to know the IP of the server the registry is running in. However, since we ran it as a Swarm service and exposed port `5000`, the routing mesh will make sure that the port is open in every node of the cluster and forward requests to the service. That allows us to treat the registry as localhost. We can pull and push images from any node as if the registry is running in each of them. Moreover, Docker Engines default behavior is to allow only localhost traffic to the registry. That means that we do not need to change its configuration.

Using node labels to constrain services

Labels are defined as key-value sets. We'll use the key `env` (short for environment). At the moment, we don't need to label the nodes used for CD tasks since we are not yet running them as services. We'll change that in one of the chapters that follow. For now, we only need to label the nodes that will be used to run our services in the production-like environment.

We'll use the nodes `swarm-test-2` and `swarm-test-3` as our production-like environment so we'll label them with the key `env` and the value `prod-like`.

Let's start with the node `swarm-test-2`:

```
docker node update \
    --label-add env=prod-like \
    swarm-test-2
```

We can confirm that the label was indeed added by inspecting the node:

```
docker node inspect --pretty swarm-test-2
```

The output of the node `inspect` command is as follows:

```
ID:                 vq5hj3lt7dskh54mr1jw4zunb
Labels:
 - env = prod-like
Hostname:           swarm-test-2
Joined at:          2017-01-21 23:01:40.557959238 +0000 utc
Status:
 State:             Ready
 Availability:      Active
 Address:           192.168.99.104
Manager Status:
 Address:           192.168.99.104:2377
 Raft Status:       Reachable
 Leader:            No
Platform:
 Operating System: linux
 Architecture:      x86_64
Resources:
 CPUs:              1
 Memory:            492.5 MiB
Plugins:
 Network:           bridge, host, macvlan, null, overlay
 Volume:            local
Engine Version:     1.13.0
Engine Labels:
 - provider = virtualbox
```

As you can see, one of the labels is `env` with the value `prod-like`.

Let's add the same label to the second node:

```
docker node update \
    --label-add env=prod-like \
    swarm-test-3
```

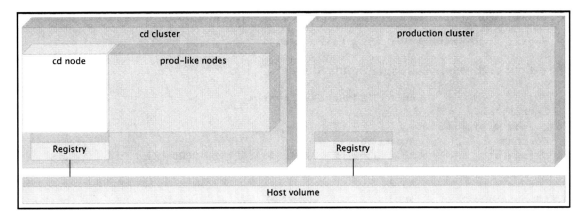

Figure 5-2: CD cluster with labeled nodes

Now that we have a few nodes labeled as production-like, we can create services that will run only on those servers.

Let's create a service with the `alpine` image and constrain it to one of the `prod-like` nodes:

```
docker service create --name util \
    --constraint 'node.labels.env == prod-like' \
    alpine sleep 1000000000
```

We can list the processes of the `util` service and confirm that it is running on one of the `prod-like` nodes:

```
docker service ps util
```

The output of the `service ps` command is as follows (IDs are removed for brevity):

```
NAME     IMAGE    NODE          DESIRED STATE   CURRENT STATE
util.1   alpine   swarm-test-2  Running         Running about a minute ago
```

As you can see, the service is running inside the `swarm-test-2` node which is labeled as `env=prod-like`.

That, in itself, does not prove that labels work. After all, two out of three nodes are labeled as production-like, so there was a 66% chance that the service would run on one of them if labels did not work. So, let's spice it up a bit.

We'll increase the number of instances to six:

```
docker service scale util=6
```

Let us take a look at the util processes:

```
docker service ps util
```

The output is as follows (IDs are removed for brevity):

```
NAME     IMAGE    NODE           DESIRED STATE  CURRENT STATE
util.1   alpine   swarm-test-2   Running        Running 15 minutes ago
util.2   alpine   swarm-test-2   Running        Running 21 seconds ago
util.3   alpine   swarm-test-3   Running        Running 21 seconds ago
util.4   alpine   swarm-test-3   Running        Running 21 seconds ago
util.5   alpine   swarm-test-2   Running        Running 21 seconds ago
util.6   alpine   swarm-test-3   Running        Running 21 seconds ago
```

As you can see, all six instances are running on nodes labeled env=prod-like (nodes swarm-test-2 and swarm-test-3).

We can observe a similar result if we would run the service in the global mode:

```
docker service create --name util-2 \
    --mode global \
    --constraint 'node.labels.env == prod-like' \
    alpine sleep 1000000000
```

Let's take a look at the util-2 processes:

```
docker service ps util-2
```

The output is as follows (IDs are removed for brevity):

```
NAME       IMAGE          NODE         DESIRED STATE CURRENT STATE
util-2...  alpine:latest swarm-test-3 Running       Running 3 seconds ago
util-2...  alpine:latest swarm-test-2 Running       Running 2 seconds ago
```

Since we told Docker that we want the service to be global, the desired state is Running on all nodes. However, since we specified the constraint node.labels.env == prod-like, replicas are running only on the nodes that match it. In other words, the service is running only on nodes swarm-test-2 and swarm-test-3. If we would add the label to the node swarm-test-1, Swarm would run the service on that node as well.

Before we move on, let's remove the `util` services:

```
docker service rm util util-2
```

Now that we know how to constrain services to particular nodes, we must create a service before proceeding with the Continuous Delivery steps.

Creating services

Before we continue exploring the Continuous Delivery steps, we should discuss a deployment change introduced with Docker Swarm. We thought that each release means a new deployment. That is not true with Docker Swarm. Instead of deploying each release, we are now updating services. After building Docker images, all we have to do is update the service that is already running. In most cases, all there is to do is to run the `docker service update --image <IMAGE> <SERVICE_NAME>` command. The service already has all the information it needs and all we have to do is to change the image to the new release.

For service update to work, we need to have a service. We need to create it and make sure that it has all the information it needs. In other words, we create a service once and update it with each release. That greatly simplifies the release process.

Since a service is created only once, the **Return On Investment** (ROI) is too low for us to automate this step. Remember, we want to automate processes that are done many times. Things that are done once and never again are not worth automating. One of those things is the creation of services. We are still running all the commands manually so consider this as a note for the next chapter that will automate the whole process.

Let us create the services that form the *go-demo* application. We'll need the `proxy`, the `go-demo` service, and the accompanying database. As before, we'll have to create the `go-demo` and the `proxy` networks. Since we already did that a couple of times, we'll run all the commands through the `scripts/dm-test-swarm-services.sh` (https://github.com/v farcic/cloud-provisioning/blob/master/scripts/dm-test-swarm-services.sh) script. It creates the services in almost the same way as before. The only difference is that it uses the `prod-like` label to restrict services only to the nodes that should be utilized for production-like deployments.

```
scripts/dm-test-swarm-services.sh

eval $(docker-machine env swarm-test-1)

docker service ls
```

The output of the `service ls` command is as follows (IDs are removed for brevity):

```
NAME         MODE           REPLICAS IMAGE
proxy        replicated 2/2          vfarcic/docker-flow-proxy:latest
go-demo      replicated 2/2          vfarcic/go-demo:1.0
go-demo-db   replicated 1/1          mongo:3.2.10
registry     replicated 1/1          registry:2.5.0
```

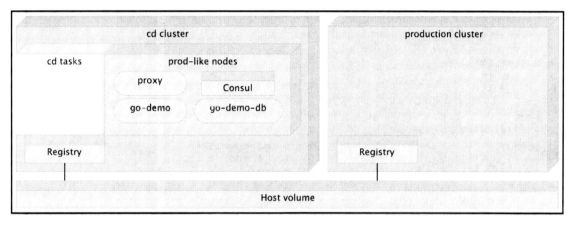

Figure 5-3: CD cluster with services running in nodes labeled as prod-like

Please note that the proxy reconfiguration port was set to 8090 on the localhost. We had to differentiate it from the port 8080 that we'll use when running the go-demo service in the staging environment.

On one hand, we want the services in the production-like cluster to resemble those in the production cluster. On the other hand, we do not want to waste resources in replication of the full production environment. For that reason, we are running two instances (replicas) of the proxy and go-demo services. Running only one would deviate too much from the idea that services should be scaled in production. Two of each gives us the ability to test that scaled services work as expected. Even if we run many more instances in production, two is just enough to replicate scaled behavior. Since we still did not manage to set up database replication, MongoDB is, for now, running as only one instance.

We can confirm that all services were indeed created and integrated successfully by sending a request to go-demo:

```
curl -i "$(docker-machine ip swarm-test-1)/demo/hello"
```

We'll also create the same services in the production cluster. The only difference will be in the number of replicas (we'll have more) and that we won't constrain them. Since there is no significant difference from what we did before, we'll use `scripts/dm-swarm-services.sh` (https://github.com/vfarcic/cloud-provisioning/blob/master/scripts/dm-swarm-services.sh) script to speed up the process:

```
scripts/dm-swarm-services.sh

eval $(docker-machine env swarm-1)

docker service ls
```

The output of the `service ls` is as follows (IDs are removed for brevity):

```
NAME         MODE        REPLICAS  IMAGE
go-demo-db   replicated  1/1       mongo:3.2.10
go-demo      replicated  3/3       vfarcic/go-demo:1.0
registry     replicated  1/1       registry:2.5.0
proxy        replicated  3/3       vfarcic/docker-flow-proxy:latest
```

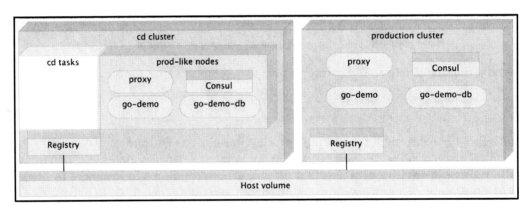

Figure 5-4: CD and production clusters with services

Now that we have the services created in both clusters, we can start working on the Continuous Delivery steps.

Walking through Continuous Delivery steps

We already know all the steps required for the Continuous Delivery process. We did each of them at least once. We got introduced to some of them in the `Chapter 1`, *Continuous Integration with Docker Containers*. After all, Continuous Delivery is Continuous Integration "extended". It's what Continuous Integration would be if it would have a clear objective.

We ran the rest of the steps throughout the chapters that lead to this point. We know how to create, and, more importantly, update a service inside a Swarm cluster. Therefore, I won't go into many details. Consider this sub-chapter a refreshment of everything we did by now.

We'll start by checking out the code of a service we want to move through the CD flow:

```
git clone https://github.com/vfarcic/go-demo.git

cd go-demo
```

Next, we should run the `unit` tests and compile the service binary:

```
eval $(docker-machine env swarm-test-1)

docker-compose \
    -f docker-compose-test-local.yml \
    run --rm unit
```

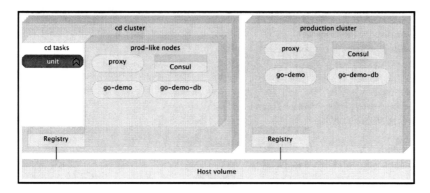

Figure 5-5: Unit tests run inside the swarm-test-1 node

Please note that we used the `swarm-test-1` node. Even though it belongs to the Swarm cluster, we used it in the "traditional" mode.

With the binary compiled, we can build Docker images:

```
docker-compose \
    -f docker-compose-test-local.yml \
    build app
```

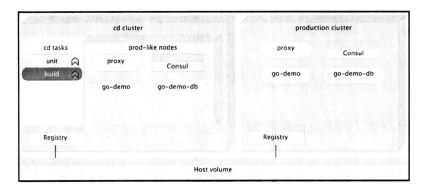

Figure 5-6: Build run inside the swarm-test-1 node

With the image built, we can run `staging` dependencies, functional tests, and tear-down everything once we're done:

```
docker-compose \
    -f docker-compose-test-local.yml \
    up -d staging-dep

docker-compose \
    -f docker-compose-test-local.yml \
    run --rm staging

docker-compose \
    -f docker-compose-test-local.yml \
    down
```

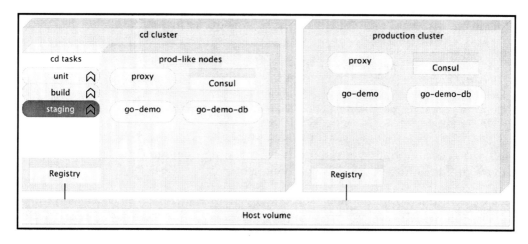

Figure 5-7: Staging or functional tests run inside the swarm-test-1 node

Now that we are confident that the new release is likely to work as expected, we can push the result to the registry:

```
docker tag go-demo localhost:5000/go-demo:1.1
```

```
docker push localhost:5000/go-demo:1.1
```

We ran the unit tests, built the binary, built the images, ran functional tests, and pushed the images to the registry. The release is very likely to work as expected. However, the only true validation is whether the release works correctly in production. There is no more reliable or worthy criteria than that. On the other hand, we want to reach production with as much confidence as we can. We'll balance those two needs by using the swarm-test cluster that is as close to production as we can reasonably get.

Right now, the go-demo service is running the release 1.0 inside the swarm-test cluster. We can confirm that by observing the output of the service ps command:

```
docker service ps go-demo -f desired-state=running
```

The output is as follows (IDs are removed for brevity):

```
NAME        IMAGE                   NODE          DESIRED STATE
go-demo.1 vfarcic/go-demo:1.0 swarm-test-2 Running
go-demo.2 vfarcic/go-demo:1.0 swarm-test-3 Running
----------------------------------------
CURRENT STATE
Running about an hour ago
Running about an hour ago
```

Let's update the currently running release to the version we just built that is 1.1:

```
docker service update \
    --image=localhost:5000/go-demo:1.1 \
    go-demo

docker service ps go-demo -f desired-state=running
```

Please note that the service was initially created with the `--update-delay 5s` argument. That means that each update will last for five seconds on each replica set (plus a few moments to pull the image and initialize containers).

After a few moments (approximately 6 seconds), the output of the `service ps` command should be as follows (IDs are removed for brevity):

```
NAME       IMAGE                        NODE         DESIRED STATE
go-demo.1 localhost:5000/go-demo:1.1 swarm-test-3 Running
go-demo.2 localhost:5000/go-demo:1.1 swarm-test-2 Running
-----------------------------------
CURRENT STATE ERROR PORTS
Running 8 seconds ago
Running 2 seconds ago
```

If the output on your laptop is different, please wait for a few moments and repeat the `service ps` command.

As you can see, the image changed to `localhost:5000/go-demo:1.1` indicating that the new release is indeed up and running.

Please note that, since the service was created with the `--constraint 'node.labels.env == prod-like'` argument, new releases are still running only in the nodes marked as `prod-like`. That shows one of the big advantages Docker Swarm provides. We create a service with all the arguments that define its complete behavior. From there on, all we have to do is update the image with each release. Things will get more complicated later on when we start scaling and doing a few other operations. However, the logic is still essentially the same. Most of the arguments we need are defined only once through the service creation command.

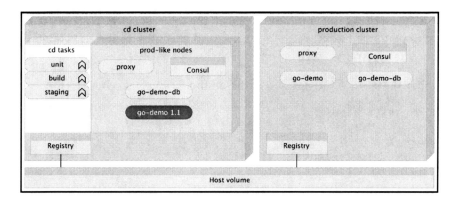

Figure 5-8: The service is updated inside the prod-like nodes in the CD cluster

Now we are ready to run some production tests. We are still not confident enough to run them against the production environment. First, we want to see whether they will pass when executed against the production-like cluster.

We'll run production tests like other types we've already run. Our Docker client is still pointing to the `swarm-test-1` node so anything we run with Docker Compose will continue being executed inside that server.

Let's take a quick look the definition of the production service inside the `docker-compose-test-local.yml` (`https://github.com/vfarcic/go-demo/blob/master/docker-compose-test-local.yml`) file:

```
production:
  extends:
    service: unit
  environment:
    - HOST_IP=${HOST_IP}
  network_mode: host
  command: bash -c "go get -d -v -t && go test --tags integration -v"
```

The `production` service `extends` the `unit` service. That means that it inherits all the properties of the `unit` service, allowing us to avoid repeating ourselves.

Further on, we are adding the environment variable `HOST_IP`. The tests we are about to run will use that variable to deduce the address of the service under test `go-demo`.

Finally, we are overwriting the command used in the `unit` service. The new command downloads *go* dependencies `go get -d -v -t` and executes all the tests tagged as integration `go test --tags integration -v`.

Let's see whether the service indeed works inside the `swarm-test` cluster:

```
export HOST_IP=localhost

docker-compose \
    -f docker-compose-test-local.yml \
    run --rm production
```

We specified that the IP of the service under test is localhost. Since the node where tests are running `swarm-test-1` belongs to the cluster, the ingress network will forward the request to the `proxy` service which, in turn, will forward it to the `go-demo` service.

The last lines of the output are as follows:

```
PASS
ok      _/usr/src/myapp 0.019s
```

All integration tests passed, and the whole operation took less than 0.2 seconds.

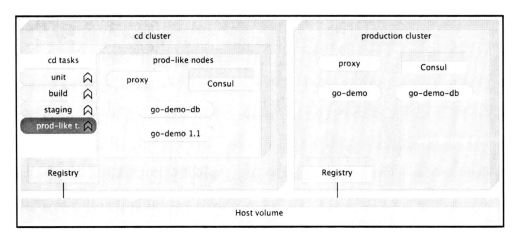

Figure 5-9: Production tests are run against the updated service inside the CD cluster

From now on, we should be fairly confident that the release is ready for production. We ran the pre-deployment unit tests, built the images, ran staging tests, updated the production-like cluster, and ran a set of integration tests.

Our Continuous Delivery steps are officially done. The release is ready and waiting for someone to make a decision to update the service running in production. In other words, at this point, the Continuous Delivery is finished, and we would be waiting for someone to press the button to update the service in the production cluster.

There is no reason to stop now. We have all the knowledge we would need to convert this process from Continuous Delivery to Continuous Deployment. All we have to do is repeat the last few commands inside the production cluster.

Walking the extra mile from Continuous Delivery to Continuous Deployment

If we do have a comprehensive set of tests that give us confidence that each commit to the code repository is working as expected and if there is a repeatable and reliable Deployment process, there is no real reason for not taking that extra mile and automatically deploying each release to production.

You might choose not to do Continuous Deployment. Maybe your process requires us to cherry pick features. Maybe our marketing department does not want new features to be available before their campaign starts. There are plenty of reasons why one would choose to stop at Continuous Delivery. Nevertheless, from the technical perspective, the process is the same. The only difference is that Continuous Delivery requires us to press the button that deploys the selected release to production while Continuous Deployment does the deployment as part of the same automated flow. In other words, the steps we are about to run are the same, with or without a button in between.

This will probably be the shortest sub-chapter in the book. We are only a few commands short of converting the Continuous Delivery process into Continuous Deployment. We need to update the service in the production cluster (swarm) and go back to the `swarm-test-1` node and execute another round of tests.

Since we already did all that, there is no strong reason to go into details. We'll just do it:

```
eval $(docker-machine env swarm-1)

docker service update \
    --image=localhost:5000/go-demo:1.1 \
    go-demo
```

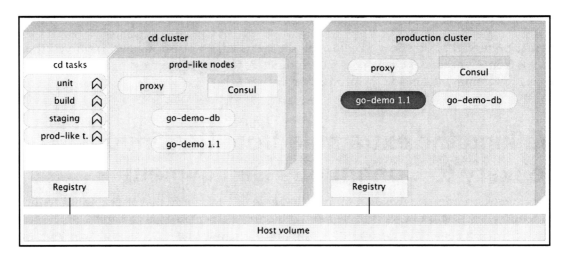

Figure 5-10: The service is updated inside the production cluster

Now that the service is updated inside the production cluster, we can execute the last round of tests:

```
eval $(docker-machine env swarm-test-1)

export HOST_IP=$(docker-machine ip swarm-1)

docker-compose \
    -f docker-compose-test-local.yml \
    run --rm production
```

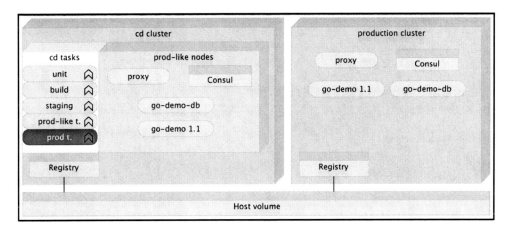

Figure 5-11: Production tests are run against the updated service inside the production cluster

We updated the release running inside the production cluster and ran another round of integration tests. Nothing failed, indicating that the new release is, indeed, running in production correctly.

What now?

Are we done with Continuous Deployment? The answer is no. We did not create the automated Continuous Deployment flow, but defined the steps that will help us run the process automatically. For the process to be fully automated and executed on each commit, we need to use one of the CD tools.

We'll use Jenkins to transform manual steps into a fully automated Continuous Deployment flow. For the whole process to work, we'll need to set up Jenkins master, a few agents, and a deployment pipeline job.

Now is the time to take a break before diving into the next chapter. As before, we'll destroy the machines we created and start fresh:

```
docker-machine rm -f \
    swarm-1 swarm-2 swarm-3 \
    swarm-test-1 swarm-test-2 swarm-test-3
```

6
Automating Continuous Deployment Flow with Jenkins

The most powerful tool we have as developers is automation.
-Scott Hanselman

We already have all the commands required for a fully automated Continuous Deployment flow. Now we need a tool that will monitor changes in our code repository and trigger those commands every time a commit is detected.

There is a plethora of CI/CD tools on the market. We'll choose Jenkins. That does not mean that it is the only choice nor that it is the best one for all use cases. I won't compare different tools nor provide more details behind the decision to use Jenkins. That would require a chapter on its own or even a whole book. Instead, we'll start by discussing Jenkins architecture.

Jenkins architecture

Jenkins is a monolithic application based on a combination of a master and agents.

Jenkins master can be described as an orchestrator. It monitors sources, triggers jobs when predefined conditions are met, stores logs and artifacts, and performs a myriad of other tasks related to CI/CD orchestration. It does not run actual tasks but makes sure that they are executed.

Jenkins agent, on the other hand, does the actual work. When master triggers a job execution, the actual work is performed by an agent.

We cannot scale Jenkins master. At least not in the same way as we scaled the `go-demo` service. We can create multiple Jenkins masters, but they cannot share the same file systems. Since Jenkins uses files to store its state, creating multiple instances would result in completely separate applications. Since the main reasons behind scaling are fault tolerance and performance benefits, none of those goals would be accomplished by scaling Jenkins master.

If Jenkins cannot be scaled, how do we meet performance requirements? We increase the capacity by adding agents. A single master can handle many agents. In most cases, an agent is a whole server (physical or virtual). It is not uncommon for a single master to have tens or even hundreds of agents (servers). In turn, each of those agents runs multiple executors that run tasks.

Traditionally, Jenkins master and agents would run on a dedicated server. That, in itself, poses a few problems. If Jenkins is running on a dedicated server, what happens when it fails? Remember, everything fails sooner or later.

For many organizations, Jenkins is mission critical. If it's not operational, new releases are not made, scheduled tasks are not run, software is not deployed, and so on. Typically, Jenkins failure would be fixed by moving the software together with the files that form its state to a healthy server. If that is done manually, and it usually is, the downtime can be substantial.

Throughout this chapter, we'll leverage the knowledge we obtained by now and try to make Jenkins fault tolerant. We might not be able to accomplish zero-downtime but, at least, we'll do our best to reduce it as much as possible. We'll also explore ways to apply what we learned to create a master and Jenkins agents in (almost) fully automated way. We'll try to make the master fault tolerant and agents scalable and dynamic.

Enough talk! Let's move towards more practical parts of the chapter.

Production environment setup

We'll start by recreating the production cluster we used in the previous chapters.

All the commands from this chapter are available in the `06-jenkins.sh` (https://gist.gi
thub.com/vfarcic/9f9995f90c6b8ce136376e38afb14588) Gist:

```
cd cloud-provisioning

git pull

scripts/dm-swarm.sh
```

We entered the `cloud-provisioning` repository we cloned earlier and pulled the latest
code. Then we executed the `scripts/dm-swarm.sh` (https://github.com/vfarcic/clou
d-provisioning/blob/master/scripts/dm-swarm.sh) script that created the production
cluster. It is the same script we used in the previous chapter.

Let's confirm that the cluster was indeed created correctly:

```
eval $(docker-machine env swarm-1)

docker node ls
```

The output of the `node ls` command is as follows (IDs are removed for brevity):

```
HOSTNAME   STATUS   AVAILABILITY   MANAGER STATUS
swarm-2    Ready    Active         Reachable
swarm-1    Ready    Active         Leader
swarm-3    Ready    Active         Reachable
```

Now that the production cluster is up and running, we can create the Jenkins service.

Jenkins service

Traditionally, we would run Jenkins in its own server. Even if we'd choose to share server's
resources with other applications, the Deployment would still be static. We'd run a Jenkins
instance (with or without Docker) and hope that it never fails. The problem with this
approach is in the fact that every application fails sooner or later. Either the process will
stop, or the whole node will die. Either way, Jenkins, like any other application, will stop
working at some moment.

The problem is that Jenkins has become a critical application in many organizations. If we move the execution or, to be more precise, triggering of all automation into Jenkins, we create a strong dependency. If Jenkins is not running, our code is not built, it is not tested, and it is not deployed. Sure, when it fails, you can bring it up again. If the server on which it is running stops working, you can deploy it somewhere else. The downtime, assuming it happens during working hours, will not be long. An hour, maybe two, or even more time will pass since the moment it stops working, someone finds out, notifies someone else, that someone restarts the application or provisions a new server. Is that a long time? It depends on the size of your organization. The more people depend on something, the bigger the cost when that something doesn't work. Even if such a downtime and the cost it produces is not critical, we already have all the knowledge and the tools to avoid it. All we have to do is create another service and let Swarm take care of the rest.

A note to Windows users
Git Bash has a habit of altering file system paths. To stop this, execute the following before running the code block:
`export MSYS_NO_PATHCONV=1`

Let's create a Jenkins service. Run the following commands from within the `cloud-provisioning` directory:

```
mkdir -p docker/jenkins

docker service create --name jenkins \
    -p 8082:8080 \
    -p 50000:50000 \
    -e JENKINS_OPTS="--prefix=/jenkins" \
    --mount "type=bind,source=$PWD/docker/jenkins,target=/var/ \
    jenkins_home"--reserve-memory 300m \
    jenkins:2.7.4-alpine

docker service ps jenkins
```

A note to Linux (example: Ubuntu) users
Docker Machine mounts users directory from the host inside the VMs it creates. That allows us to share the files. However, that feature does not work in Docker Machine running on Linux. The easiest workaround is, for now, to remove the `--mount` argument. Later on, when we reach persistent storage, you'll see how to mount volumes more effectively. The good news is that the problem will be fixed soon. Please see the *issue #1376* (`https://github.com/docker/machine/issues/1376`) for the discussion. Once the *pull request #2122* (`https://github.com/docker/machine/pull/2122`) is merged, you will be able to use automatic mounting on Linux.

Jenkins stores its state in the file system. Therefore, we started by creating a directory `mkdir` on the host. It will be used as Jenkins home. Since we are inside one of the subdirectories of our host's user, the `docker/jenkins` directory is mounted on all the machines we created.

Next, we created the service. It exposes the internal port `8080` as `8082` as well as the port `50000`. The first one is used to access Jenkins UI and the second for master/agent communication. We also defined the URL prefix `as/jenkins` and mounted the `jenkins` home directory. Finally, we reserved `300m` of memory.

Once the image is downloaded, the output of the `service ps` command is as follows (IDs are removed for brevity):

```
NAME        IMAGE                  NODE      DESIRED STATE CURRENT STATE
jenkins.1 jenkins:2.7.4-alpine swarm-1 Running       Running 52 seconds ago
```

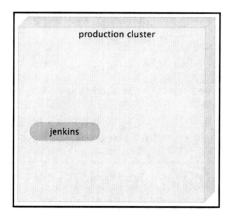

Figure 6-1: Production cluster with the Jenkins service

Jenkins 2 changed the setup process. While the previous versions allowed us to run it without any mandatory configuration, the new Jenkins forces us to go through some steps manually. Unfortunately, at the time of this writing, there is no good API to help us automate the process. While there are some *tricks* we could use, the benefits are not high enough when compared with the additional complexity they introduce. After all, we'll setup Jenkins only once, so there is no big incentive to automate the process (at least until a configuration API is created).

Let's open the UI:

```
open "http://$(docker-machine ip swarm-1):8082/jenkins"
```

A note to Windows users

Git Bash might not be able to use the open command. If that's the case, execute `docker-machine ip <SERVER_NAME>` to find out the IP of the machine and open the URL directly in your browser of choice. For example, the command above should be replaced with the command that follows:

`docker-machine ip swarm-1`

If the output would be `1.2.3.4`, you should open `http://1.2.3.4:8082/jenkins` in your browser.

The first thing you will notice is that you are required to introduce the **Administrator password**. Quite a few enterprise users requested security hardening. As a result, Jenkins cannot be accessed, anymore, without initializing a session. If you are new to Jenkins, or, at least, *version 2*, you might wonder what the password is. It is output to logs (in our case `stdout`) as well as to the file `secrets/initialAdminPassword`, which will be removed at the end of the setup process.

Let's see the content of the `secrets/initialAdminPassword` file:

```
cat docker/jenkins/secrets/initialAdminPassword
```

The output will be a `long` string that represents the temporary password. Please copy it, go back to the UI, paste it to the **Administrator password** field, and click the **Continue** button:

Unlock Jenkins

To ensure Jenkins is securely set up by the administrator, a password has been written to the log (not sure where to find it?) and this file on the server:

`/var/jenkins_home/secrets/initialAdminPassword`

Please copy the password from either location and paste it below.

Administrator password

```
································
```

Continue

Figure 6-2: Unlock Jenkins screen

Once you unlock Jenkins, you will be presented with a choice to Install suggested plugins or select those that fit your needs. The recommended plugins fit most commonly used scenarios so we'll go with that option.

Please click the **Install suggested plugins** button.

Once the plugins are downloaded and installed, we are presented with a screen that allows us to Create the first admin user. Please use `admin` as both the **Username** and the **Password**. Fill free to fill the rest of the fields with any value. Once you're done, click the `Save and Finish` button:

Figure 6-3: Create First Admin User screen

Jenkins is ready. All that's left, for now, is to click the `Start using Jenkins` button.

Now we can test whether Jenkins failover works.

Jenkins failover

Let's stop the service and observe Swarm in action. To do that, we need to find out the node it is running in, point our Docker client to it, and remove the container:

```
NODE=$(docker service ps \
    -f desired-state=running jenkins \
    | tail -n +2 | awk '{print $4}')

eval $(docker-machine env $NODE)

docker rm -f $(docker ps -qa \
    -f label=com.docker.swarm.service.name=jenkins)
```

We listed Jenkins processes and applied the filter that will return only the one with the desired state running `docker service ps -f desired-state=running jenkins`. The output was piped to the tail command that removed the header `tail -n +2` and, later on, piped again to the `awk` command that limited the output to the fourth column `awk '{print $4}'` that contains the node the process is running in. The final result was stored in the NODE variable.

Later on, we used the eval command to create environment variables that will be used by our Docker client to operate the remote engine. Finally, we retrieved the image ID and removed the container with the combination of the `ps` and `rm` commands.

As we already learned in the previous chapters, if a container fails, Swarm will run it again somewhere inside the cluster. When we created the service, we told Swarm that the desired state is to have one instance running and Swarm is doing its best to make sure our expectations are fulfilled.

Let us confirm that the service is, indeed, running:

```
docker service ps jenkins
```

If Swarm decided to re-run Jenkins on a different node, it might take a few moments until the image is pulled. After a while, the output of the `service ps` command should be as follows:

```
NAME         IMAGE          NODE    DESIRED STATE CURRENT STATE                     ERROR
jenkins.1    jenkins:alpine swarm-3 Running       Running less than a second ago
_ jenkins.1  jenkins:alpine swarm-1 Shutdown      Failed 5 seconds ago              "task: non-zero exit (137)"
```

We can do a final confirmation by reopening the the UI:

```
open "http://$(docker-machine ip swarm-1):8082/jenkins"
```

A note to Windows users
Git Bash might not be able to use the open command. If that's the case, execute `docker-machine ip <SERVER_NAME>` to find out the IP of the machine and open the URL directly in your browser of choice. For example, the command above should be replaced with the command that follows:
`docker-machine ip swarm-1`
If the output would be `1.2.3.4`, you should open
`http://1.2.3.4:8082/jenkins` in your browser.

Since Jenkins does not allow unauthenticated users, you'll have to login. Please use `admin` as both the User and the Password.

You'll notice that, this time, we did not have to repeat the setup process. Even though a fresh new Jenkins image is run on a different node, the state is still preserved thanks to the host directory we mounted.

We managed to make Jenkins fault tolerant, but we did not manage to make it run without any downtime. Due to its architecture, Jenkins master cannot be scaled. As a result, when we simulated a failure by removing the container, there was no second instance to absorb the traffic. Even though Swarm re-scheduled it on a different node, there was some downtime. During a short period, the service was not accessible. While that is not a perfect situation, we managed to reduce downtime to a minimum. We made it fault tolerant, but could not make it run without downtime. Considering its architecture, we did the best we could.

Now is the time to hook up Jenkins agents that will run our Continuous Deployment flow.

Jenkins agent

There are quite a few ways to run Jenkins agents. The problem with most of them is that they force us to add agents separately through Jenkins UI. Instead of adding agents one by one, we'll try to leverage Docker Swarms ability to scale services.

One way we can accomplish the quest for making scalable agents is the Jenkins Swarm Plugin (`https://wiki.jenkins-ci.org/display/JENKINS/Swarm+Plugin`). Before you start making wrong conclusions, I must state that this plugin has nothing to do with Docker Swarm. The only thing they share is the word Swarm.

The Jenkins Swarm Plugin (`https://wiki.jenkins-ci.org/display/JENKINS/Swarm+Plugin`) allows us to auto-discover nearby masters and join them automatically. We'll use it only for the second feature. We'll create a Docker Swarm service that will act as a Jenkins agent and join the master automatically.

First things first. We need to install the plugin.

Please open the Plugin Manager screen as shown in the following code:

```
open "http://$(docker-machine ip
swarm-1):8082/jenkins/pluginManager/available"
```

A note to Windows users

Git Bash might not be able to use the open command. If that's the case, execute `docker-machine ip <SERVER_NAME>` to find out the IP of the machine and open the URL directly in your browser of choice. For example, the command above should be replaced with the command that follows:

`docker-machine ip swarm-1`

If the output would be `1.2.3.4`, you should open `http://1.2.3.4:8082/jenkins/pluginManager/available` in your browser.

Next, we need to search for the *Self-Organizing Swarm Plug-in Modules plugin*. The easiest way to do that is by typing the plugin name inside the **Filter** field located in the top-right corner of the screen. Once you locate the plugin, please select it and click the `Install without restart` button.

Now that the plugin is installed, we can set up our second cluster that will consist of three nodes. As before, we'll call it `swarm-test`. We'll use the script `scripts/dm-test-swarm-2.sh` (https://github.com/vfarcic/cloud-provisioning/blob/master/scripts/dm-test-swarm-2.sh) to run all the commands required to create the machines and join them into the cluster.

```
scripts/dm-test-swarm-2.sh

eval $(docker-machine env swarm-test-1)

docker node ls
```

The output of the `node ls` command is as follows (IDs are removed for brevity):

```
HOSTNAME       STATUS  AVAILABILITY  MANAGER STATUS
swarm-test-2   Ready   Active        Reachable
swarm-test-1   Ready   Active        Leader
swarm-test-3   Ready   Active        Reachable
```

The only significant difference between the script we just ran and the one we used before dm-test-swarm.sh is that this one adds a few labels. The first node is labeled jenkins-agent, while the other two are labeled prod-like. The reason behind those labels is that we're trying to differentiate nodes that will be used to run tasks like building and testing jenkins-agent from those that will be used to run services in the environment that simulate production prod-like.

Let's inspect the swarm-test-1 node:

```
eval $(docker-machine env swarm-test-1)

docker node inspect swarm-test-1 --pretty
```

The output is as follows:

```
ID:                     3rznbsuvvkw4wf7f4qa32cla3
Labels:
 - env = jenkins-agent
Hostname:               swarm-test-1
Joined at:              2017-01-22 08:30:26.757026595 +0000 utc
Status:
 State:         Ready
 Availability:      Active
Manager Status:
 Address:           192.168.99.103:2377
 Raft Status:       Reachable
 Leader:            Yes
Platform:
 Operating System:      linux
 Architecture:      x86_64
Resources:
 CPUs:          1
 Memory:            492.5 MiB
Plugins:
  Network:          bridge, host, null, overlay
  Volume:           local
Engine Version:         1.13.0
Engine Labels:
 - provider = virtualbox
```

As you can see, this node has the label with the key env and the value jenkins-agent. If you inspect the other two nodes, you will see that they are also labeled but, this time, with the value prod-like:

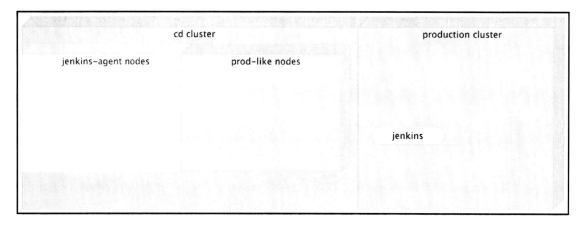

Figure 6-4: Create First Admin User screen

Now that the swarm-test cluster is set up, we are ready to create the Jenkins agent service. However, before we do that, let's take a quick look at the definition of the image we are going to use. The vfarcic/jenkins-swarm-agent Dockerfile (https://github.com/v farcic/docker-jenkins-slave-dind/blob/master/Dockerfile) is as follows:

```
FROM docker:1.12.1

MAINTAINER Viktor Farcic <viktor@farcic.com>

ENV SWARM_CLIENT_VERSION 2.2
ENV DOCKER_COMPOSE_VERSION 1.8.0
ENV COMMAND_OPTIONS ""

RUN adduser -G root -D jenkins
RUN apk --update add openjdk8-jre python py-pip git

RUN wget -q
https://repo.jenkins-ci.org/releases/org/jenkins-ci/plugins/swarm-client/ \
${SWARM_CLIENT_VERSION}/swarm-client-${SWARM_CLIENT_VERSION}-jar-with- \
dependencies.jar -P /home/jenkins/
RUN pip install docker-compose

COPY run.sh /run.sh
RUN chmod +x /run.sh

CMD ["/run.sh"]
```

It uses `docker` as the base image followed by a few environment variables that define versions of the software that will be installed. Since Jenkins runs as a `jenkins user`, we added it as well. That is followed by the installation of OpenJDK, Python, and pip. JDK is required for the Jenkins Swarm client and the rest for Docker Compose. With all the prerequisites set, we download the Swarm JAR and use pip to install Docker Compose.

Finally, we copy the `run.sh` (`https://github.com/vfarcic/docker-jenkins-slave-dind /blob/master/run.sh`) script, set its permissions to execute, and define the runtime command to run it. The script uses Java to run the Jenkins Swarm client.

Before we proceed with the Jenkins agents service, we'll need to create the `/workspace` directory in each of the hosts where the agents will run. At the moment, that is only the `swarm-test-1` node. Soon you'll see why we need this directory:

```
docker-machine ssh swarm-test-1

sudo mkdir /workspace && sudo chmod 777 /workspace && exit
```

We entered the node `swarm-test-1`, created the directory, gave it full permissions, and exited the machine.

Equipped with the understanding of the `vfarcic/jenkins-swarm-agent` image (or, at least, what it contains), we can move on and create the service:

A note to Windows users
For mounts used in the next command to work, you have to stop Git Bash from altering file system paths. Set this environment variable as follows:
`export MSYS_NO_PATHCONV=1`

```
export USER=admin

export PASSWORD=admin

docker service create --name jenkins-agent \
    -e COMMAND_OPTIONS="-master \
    http://$(docker-machine ip swarm-1):8082/jenkins \
    -username $USER -password $PASSWORD \
    -labels 'docker' -executors 5" \
    --mode global \
    --constraint 'node.labels.env == jenkins-agent' \
    --mount \
    "type=bind,source=/var/run/docker.sock,target=/var/run/docker.sock" \
    --mount \
    "type=bind,source=$HOME/.docker/machine/machines,target=/machines" \
    --mount "type=bind,source=/workspace,target=/workspace" \
    vfarcic/jenkins-swarm-agent
```

The `service create` command is, this time, a bit longer than what we're used to. The `COMMAND_OPTIONS` environment variable contains all the information the agent needs to connect to the master. We specified the address of the `master -master http://$(docker-machine ip swarm-1):8082/jenkins`, defined the `username` and `password -username $USER -password $PASSWORD`, labeled the agent `-labels 'docker'`, and set the number of executors `-executors 5`.

Further on, we declared the service to be global and constrained it to the `jenkins-agent` nodes. That means that it will run on every node that has the matching label. At the moment, that is only one server. Soon we'll see the benefits such a setup provides.

We mounted Docker socket. As a result, any command sent to the Docker client running inside the container will run against Docker Engine on the host (in this case Docker Machine). As a result, we'll avoid pitfalls that could be created by running `Docker inside Docker` or `DinD`. For more information, please read the article Using Docker-in-Docker for your CI or testing environment? Think twice (`http://jpetazzo.github.io/2015/09/03/do-not-use-docker-in-docker-for-ci/`).

We also mounted the host (laptop) directory that contains the keys. That will allow us to send requests to engines running inside the other cluster. The final mount exposes the host directory `/workspace` inside the container. All builds running inside Jenkins agents will use that directory:

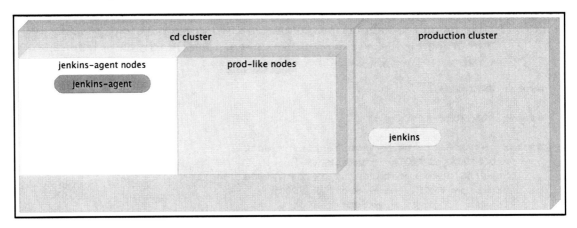

Figure 6-5: Jenkins agent run as a global service

Let's take a look at the service processes:

```
docker service ps jenkins-agent
```

The output is as follows (IDs are removed for brevity):

```
NAME               IMAGE                              NODE          DESIRED STATE  CURRENT STATE        ERROR  PORTS
jenkins-agent...   vfarcic/jenkins-swarm-agent:latest  swarm-test-1  Running        Running 2 minutes ago
```

As you can see, the service is global, so the desired state is for it to run on every node. However, since we restricted it to the nodes with the label `jenkins-agent`, containers are running only inside those that have the matching label. In other words, the service is running only on `jenkins-agent` nodes.

Let's open the Jenkins screen that displays registered agents:

```
open "http://$(docker-machine ip swarm-1):8082/jenkins/computer/"
```

A note to Windows users
Git Bash might not be able to use the open command. If that's the case, execute `docker-machine ip <SERVER_NAME>` to find out the IP of the machine and open the URL directly in your browser of choice. For example, the command above should be replaced with the command that follows:
`docker-machine ip swarm-1`
If the output would be `1.2.3.4`, you should open `http://1.2.3.4:8082/jenkins/computer` in your browser.

As you can see, two agents are registered. The master agent is running by default with every Jenkins instance. On my machine, the agent running as the `jenkins-agent` service is identified as `e0961f7c1801-d9bf7835`:

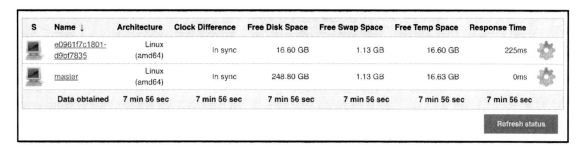

S	Name ↓	Architecture	Clock Difference	Free Disk Space	Free Swap Space	Free Temp Space	Response Time
	e0961f7c1801-d9bf7835	Linux (amd64)	In sync	16.60 GB	1.13 GB	16.60 GB	225ms
	master	Linux (amd64)	In sync	248.80 GB	1.13 GB	16.63 GB	0ms
	Data obtained	7 min 56 sec	7 min 56 sec	7 min 56 sec	7 min 56 sec	7 min 56 sec	7 min 56 sec

Figure 6-6: Jenkins Swarm agent added to the master

Since we used labels to restrict the service to the `swarm-test-1` node, at the moment we have only one agent registered (besides the master that, in most cases, should not be used).

The agent is configured to use five executors. That means that five builds can be executed in parallel. Please note that, in this case, the number of executors is artificially high. Each machine has only one CPU. Without any additional information, I would probably set the number of executors to be the same as the number of CPUs. That would be only the basic calculation that would change with time. If the tasks we're running through those executors are CPU demanding, we might lower the number of executors. However, for the purpose of this exercise, five executors should be *OK*. We have only one service, so we won't run builds in parallel.

Let's imagine that this is the real system with more builds running in parallel than the number of executors. In such a situation, some would be queued waiting for an executor to finish and free its resources. If this was a temporary case, we wouldn't need to do anything. The executing builds would end, free the resources, and run the queued builds. However, if this is a reoccurring situation, the number of queued builds would probably start increasing and everything would slow down. Since we already established that the speed is the critical element of Continuous Integration, Delivery, and Deployment processes, when things start to get in the way, we need to do something. In this case, that something is the increase of available executors and, consequently, the number of agents.

Let's imagine that we hit the limit and need to increase the number of agents. Knowing how global Swarm services work, all we have to do is create a new node:

```
docker-machine create -d virtualbox swarm-test-4

docker-machine ssh swarm-test-4

sudo mkdir /workspace && sudo chmod 777 /workspace && exit

TOKEN=$(docker swarm join-token -q worker)

eval $(docker-machine env swarm-test-4)

docker swarm join \
    --token $TOKEN \
    --advertise-addr $(docker-machine ip swarm-test-4) \
    $(docker-machine ip swarm-test-1):2377
```

We created the `swarm-test-4` node and, inside it, the `/workspace` directory. Then we got the token and joined the newly created service to the cluster as a worker.

Let's confirm that the new node is, indeed, added to the cluster:

```
eval $(docker-machine env swarm-test-1)

docker node ls
```

The output of the `node ls` command is as follows (IDs are removed for brevity):

```
HOSTNAME       STATUS  AVAILABILITY  MANAGER STATUS
swarm-test-3   Ready   Active        Reachable
swarm-test-2   Ready   Active        Reachable
swarm-test-1   Ready   Active        Leader
swarm-test-4   Ready   Active
```

Is the Jenkins agent running inside the newly created node? Let's take a look:

```
docker service ps jenkins-agent
```

The output of the `service ps` command is as follows (IDs are removed for brevity):

```
NAME               IMAGE                              NODE
jenkins-agent...   vfarcic/jenkins-swarm-agent:latest swarm-test-1
------------------------------------------
DESIRED STATE  CURRENT STATE ERROR PORTS
Running        Running
```

Since the node is not labeled as `jenkins-agent`, the agent is not running inside the `swarm-test-4` server.

Let's add the label:

```
docker node update \
    --label-add env=jenkins-agent \
    swarm-test-4

docker service ps jenkins-agent
```

This time, the output is a bit different (IDs are removed for brevity):

```
NAME           IMAGE                              NODE         DESIRED STATE CURRENT STATE     ERROR PORTS
jenkins-agent... vfarcic/jenkins-swarm-agent:latest swarm-test-4 Running       Running 1 second ago
jenkins-agent... vfarcic/jenkins-swarm-agent:latest swarm-test-1 Running       Running 4 minutes ago
```

Swarm detected the new label, run the container, and changed the state to running.

Let's go back to the Jenkins screen that lists the connected agents:

```
open "http://$(docker-machine ip swarm-1):8082/jenkins/computer"
```

A note to Windows users

Git Bash might not be able to use the open command. If that's the case, execute `docker-machine ip <SERVER_NAME>` to find out the IP of the machine and open the URL directly in your browser of choice. For example, the command above should be replaced with the command that follows:

`docker-machine ip swarm-1`

If the output would be `1.2.3.4`, you should open `http://1.2.3.4:8082/jenkins/computer` in your browser.

As you can see, the new agent **b76e943ffe6c-d9bf7835** was added to the list:

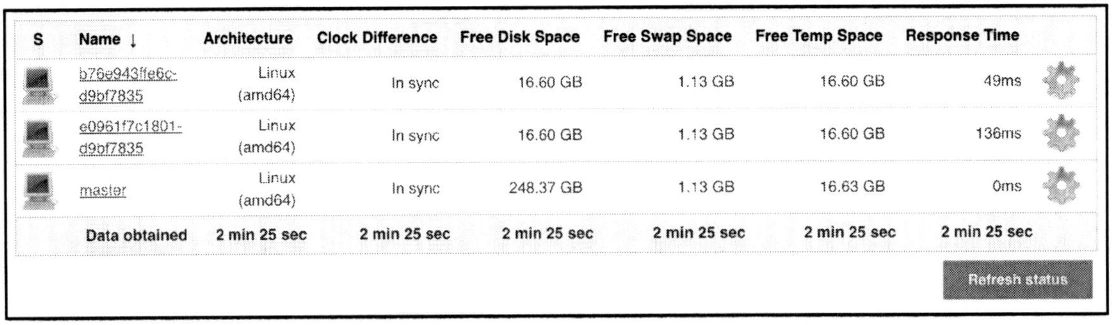

S	Name ↓	Architecture	Clock Difference	Free Disk Space	Free Swap Space	Free Temp Space	Response Time	
🖥	b76e943ffe6c-d9bf7835	Linux (amd64)	In sync	16.60 GB	1.13 GB	16.60 GB	49ms	⚙
🖥	e0961f7c1801-d9bf7835	Linux (amd64)	In sync	16.60 GB	1.13 GB	16.60 GB	136ms	⚙
🖥	master	Linux (amd64)	In sync	248.37 GB	1.13 GB	16.63 GB	0ms	⚙
	Data obtained	2 min 25 sec	2 min 25 sec	2 min 25 sec	2 min 25 sec	2 min 25 sec	2 min 25 sec	

Refresh status

Figure 6-7: The second Jenkins Swarm agent added to the master

This was very easy, wasn't it? Usually, we'd need not only to create a new server but also to run the agent and add it to Jenkins configuration through the UI. By combining *Jenkins Swarm* plugin and *Docker Swarm* global services, we managed to automate most of the steps. All we have to do is create a new node and add it to the Swarm cluster.

Before we proceed and automate the Continuous Deployment flow through Jenkins, we should create the services in production and production-like environments.

Creating services in production and production-like environments

Since a service is created only once and updated whenever some of its aspects change (example:new image with the new release), there is no strong incentive to add service creation to the Continuous Deployment flow. All we'd get is increased complexity without any tangible benefit. Therefore, we'll create all the services manually and, later on, discuss how to automate the flow that will be triggered with each new release.

We already created `go-demo`, `go-demo-db`, `proxy`, `jenkins`, and `registry` services quite a few times so we'll skip the explanation and run `scripts/dm-swarm-services-2.sh` (ht tps://github.com/vfarcic/cloud-provisioning/blob/master/scripts/dm-swarm-ser vices.sh) that will recreate the situation we had in the previous chapters:

```
scripts/dm-swarm-services-2.sh

eval $(docker-machine env swarm-1)

docker service ls
```

The output of the `service ls` command is as follows (IDs are removed for brevity):

```
NAME        MODE        REPLICAS  IMAGE
go-demo     replicated  3/3       vfarcic/go-demo:1.0
jenkins     replicated  1/1       jenkins:2.7.4-alpine
go-demo-db  replicated  1/1       mongo:3.2.10
registry    replicated  1/1       registry:2.5.0
proxy       replicated  3/3       vfarcic/docker-flow-proxy:latest
```

All the services are running. The only difference between the script we ran now and the one we used before `scripts/dm-swarm-services.sh` (https://github.com/vfarcic/cloud -provisioning/blob/master/scripts/dm-swarm-services.sh) is that, this time, we added `registry` to the mix.

Now that the production environment is up and running, let's create the same set of services inside the `swarm-test` cluster. Since this cluster is shared between services running in the production-like environment as well as Jenkins agents, we'll constrain services to `prod-like` nodes.

As with the production cluster, we'll run the services through a script. This time we'll use `scripts/dm-test-swarm-services-2.sh` (https://github.com/vfarcic/cloud-provi sioning/blob/master/scripts/dm-test-swarm-services-2.sh):

```
scripts/dm-test-swarm-services-2.sh

eval $(docker-machine env swarm-test-1)

docker service ls
```

The output of the `service ls` command is as follows (IDs are removed for brevity):

```
NAME            MODE        REPLICAS  IMAGE
jenkins-agent   global      2/2       vfarcic/jenkins-swarm-agent:latest
registry        replicated  1/1       registry:2.5.0
go-demo         replicated  2/2       vfarcic/go-demo:1.0
proxy           replicated  2/2       vfarcic/docker-flow-proxy:latest
go-demo-db      replicated  1/1       mongo:3.2.10
```

Now that the services are running in both the production and production-like environments, we can proceed with the discussion about the approach we'll take for the CD flow automation with Jenkins.

Automating Continuous Deployment flow with Jenkins

Jenkins is based on plugins. Almost every feature is a plugin. If we need to use Git, there is a plugin for it. If we want to use Active Directory for authentication, there is a plugin. You get the point. Almost everything is a plugin. Moreover, most plugins were created and are maintained by the community. When we are in doubt how to accomplish something, the *plugins directory* (https://wiki.jenkins-ci.org/display/JENKINS/Plugins) is usually the first place we start looking.

With more than 1200 plugins available, it's no wonder that, given such a huge variety, most users are compelled to use a plugin for almost any type of task. Jenkins old-timers would create a Freestyle job that, for example, clones the code and builds the binaries. It would be followed by another job that would run unit tests, another for running functional tests, and so on. All those Freestyle jobs would be connected. When the first is finished, it would invoke the second, the second would call the third, and so on. Freestyle jobs foment heavy plugins usage.

We would choose one appropriate for a given task, fill in some fields, and click save. Such an approach allows us to automate the steps without the need for the knowledge of how different tools work. Need to execute some Gradle tasks? Just choose the Gradle plugin, fill in a few fields, and off you go.

Such an approach based on heavy usage of plugins can be disastrous. Understanding automation and the tools behind it is essential. Moreover, the usage of *Freestyle* jobs breaks one of the fundamental principles in our industry. Everything should be stored in a code repository, be prone to code reviews, versioned, and so on. There is no good reason why coding practices should not apply to the automation code.

We'll take a different approach.

I am a huge believer that the steps that form a CI/CD Pipeline should be specified outside the tools like Jenkins. We should be able to define all the commands without CI/CD tools and, once we're comfortable that everything works as expected, proceed by translating those commands to the CI/CD friendly format. In other words, automation comes first, and CI/CD tools later.

Fortunately, not long ago, Jenkins introduced a new concept called *Jenkins Pipeline*. Unlike *Freestyle* jobs that were defined through Jenkins UI, *Pipeline* allows us to define CD flow as code. Since we already have a well-defined set of commands, converting them into *Jenkins Pipeline* should be relatively straightforward.

Let's give it a try.

Creating Jenkins Pipeline jobs

We'll start by defining a few environment variables. The reason behind declaring those variables is that we want to have a single place where critical information is stored. That way, when something changes (example:entry point to the cluster) we can modify a variable or two, and the changes will be propagated throughout all jobs.

Off we go. First, we need to open Jenkins global configuration screen:

```
open "http://$(docker-machine ip swarm-1):8082/jenkins/configure"
```

A note to Windows users:

Git Bash might not be able to use the open command. If that's the case, execute `docker-machine ip <SERVER_NAME>` to find out the IP of the machine and open the URL directly in your browser of choice. For example, the command above should be replaced with the command that follows:

`docker-machine ip swarm-1` If the output would be `1.2.3.4`, you should open `http://1.2.3.4:8082/jenkins/configure` in your browser.

Once inside the configuration screen, please click the **Environment variables** checkbox followed with the **Add** button. You will be presented with the fields **Name** and **Value**. The first variable we'll add will hold the production IP. However, before we type it, we need to find it out. The routing mesh redirects requests from any node to the destination service or, to be more precise, to the service that exposes the same port as the request. Therefore, we can use any server in the production cluster `swarm` as our entry point.

To get the IP of one of the nodes, we can use the `docker-machine ip` command:

```
docker-machine ip swarm-1
```

The result will differ from one case to another. On my laptop, the output is as follows:

```
192.168.99.107
```

Please copy the IP and go back to the Jenkins configuration screen. Type `PROD_IP` as **Name** and paste the IP into the Value field. It is worth noting that we just introduced a single point of failure. If the `swarm-1` node fails, all our jobs that use this variable will fail as well. The good news is that we can fix that quickly by changing the value of this environment variable. The bad news is that we can do better, but not with Docker machines. If, for example, we were to use AWS, we'd be able to utilize Elastic IP. However, we have not reached the AWS chapter yet, so changing the variable is our best option.

Next, we should add another variable that will represent the name of the production node. We'll see the usage of this variable later. For now, please create a new variable with `PROD_NAME` as **Name** and **swarm-1** as value.

We'll need similar variables for our production-like cluster `swarm-test`. Please enter variables `PROD_LIKE_IP` with the IP of the `swarm-test-1` **node** `docker-machine ip swarm-test-1` and `PROD_LIKE_NAME` with the value `swarm-test-1`:

Figure 6-8: Jenkins global configuration screen with defined environment variables

Once done with the **Environment variables**, please click the **Save** button.

Now that the environment variables are defined, we can proceed and create a Jenkins Pipeline job that will automate the execution of the CD steps we practiced.

To create the new job, please click the New Item link located in the left-hand menu. Type `go-demo` as the item name, select Pipeline, and click the **OK** button.

A Jenkins Pipeline definition contains three primary levels; node, stage, and step. We'll define the go-demo Pipeline code by going through these levels one by one.

Defining Pipeline nodes

In the Jenkins Pipeline DSL, a *node* is a step that does two things, typically by enlisting help from available executors on agents.

A node schedules the steps contained within it by adding them to the Jenkins build queue. That way, as soon as an executor slot is free on a node, the appropriate steps will be run.

It also creates a workspace, meaning a file directory specific to a particular job, where resource-intensive processing can occur without negatively impacting your Pipeline performance. Workspaces created by a node are automatically removed after all the steps contained inside the node declaration finish executing. It is a best practice to do all material work, such as building or running shell scripts, within nodes, because node blocks in a stage tell Jenkins that the steps within them are resource-intensive enough to be scheduled, request help from the agent pool, and lock a workspace only as long as they need it.

If that definition of the node confuses you, think of it as a location where the steps will run. It specifies a server (agent) that will execute tasks. That specification can be the name of the server (generally a bad idea, due to tight coupling of node configuration to agent), or a set of labels that must match those set inside an agent. If you recall the command we used to start the Jenkins Swarm agent service, you'll remember that we used `-labels docker` as one of the command options. Since Docker Engine and Compose are the only executables we need, that was the only label we needed as our node specification.

Please type the following code into the **Pipeline script** field of the **go-demo** job configuration and press the **Save** button:

```
node("docker") {
}
```

We just wrote the first iteration of the Pipeline. Let's run it.

Please click the **Build Now** button.

The job started running and displayed the message stating that **This Pipeline has run successfully, but does not define any stages**. We'll correct that in a moment. For now, let's take a look at the logs:

Figure 6-9: The first build of the Jenkins Pipeline job

You can access the logs by clicking the icon in the shape of a ball next to the build number in this case **#1**. Builds can be accessed from the *Build History* widget located in the left-hand side of the screen.

The output is as follows:

```
Started by user admin
[Pipeline] node
Running on be61529c010a-d9bf7835 in /workspace/go-demo
[Pipeline] {
[Pipeline] }
[Pipeline] // node
[Pipeline] End of Pipeline
Finished: SUCCESS
```

Not much happened in this build. Jenkins parsed the node definition and decided to use the agent `be61529c010a-d9bf7835` (one of the two Jenkins Swarm service instances) and run the steps inside the directory `/workspace/go-demo`. The directory structure is simple. All files generated by a build are located in a directory that matches the job name. In this case, the directory is `go-demo`.

Since we did not specify any step inside the node, the Pipeline finished executing almost immediately and the result was a success. Let's spice it up a bit with stages.

Defining Pipeline stages

A **stage** is a logically distinct part of the execution of any task, with parameters for locking, ordering, and labeling its part of a process relative to other parts of the same process. Pipeline syntax is often comprised of stages. Each stage step can have one or more build steps within it. It is a best practice to work within stages because they help with organization by lending logical divisions to Pipelines, and because the Jenkins Pipeline visualization feature displays stages as unique segments of the Pipeline.

What would be the stages of the flow we practiced with manual commands? We could divide the commands we defined into the following groups:

1. Pull the latest code from the repository.
2. Run unit tests and build the service and Docker images.
3. Deploy to staging environment and run tests.
4. Tag Docker images and push them to the registry.
5. Use the latest image to update the service running in production-like environment and run tests.
6. Use the latest image to update the service running in production environment and run tests.

When those groups of tasks are translated into Pipeline stages, the code inside the node is as follows:

```
stage("Pull") {
}

stage("Unit") {
}

stage("Staging") {
}
```

```
stage("Publish") {
}

stage("Prod-like") {
}

stage("Production") {
}
```

We should combine the node we defined earlier with those stages. To be more precise, they should all be defined inside the node block.

Please replace the existing Pipeline definition by copying and pasting the code from `scripts/go-demo-stages.groovy` (`https://github.com/vfarcic/cloud-provisionin g/blob/master/scripts/go-demo-stages.groovy`). You can access the job configuration by clicking the **go-demo** link inside breadcrumbs located in the top part of the screen. Once inside the main job page, please click the **Configure** button located in the left-hand menu. Once you are done writing or pasting the new Pipeline definition, save it and re-run the job by clicking the **Build Now** button.

We still do not execute any actions. However, this time, the **Stage View** screen is much more informative. It displays the stages we defined earlier:

Figure 6-10: The Jenkins Pipeline Stage View screen

Now we are ready to define the steps that will be executed inside each of the stages.

Defining Pipeline steps

Before we start writing the steps, I must, briefly, mention that there are a couple of different approaches people use to define Jenkins jobs. Some prefer to utilize Jenkins plugins to their maximum. When taken to an extreme, such approach results in every action being executed through a plugin. Do you need to run some Gradle tasks? There is a Gradle plugin (or two). Do you need to do something with Docker? There are roughly a dozen Docker plugins. How about configuration management with Ansible? There is a plugin as well.

I do not think that heavy reliance on plugins is a good thing. I believe that we should be capable of creating most, if not all the automation without Jenkins. After all, does it even make sense to use a plugin that would save us from writing a single line of command? I don't believe it does. That doesn't mean that we should not use plugins. We should, but only when they bring a real and tangible additional value. An example would be the Git plugin. It evaluates whether the code should be cloned or pulled. It manages authentication. It provides a few auto-populated environment variables we can use in conjunction with other steps.

Should we use the Git plugin always? We shouldn't. Let's say that all we have to do is perform a simple pull inside an already cloned repository, that we do not need authentication, and that there will be no usage of some of the pull information in later steps (example: commit ID). In such a case, the simplest solution possible might be the best choice. What is the easiest way to pull the code from a Git repository? Most likely that's git `pull` command executed through Shell.

Only once we know what we're doing and the process is done in a CI/CD tool agnostic way, we should proceed and tie it all together through Jenkins (or whatever is your tool of choice). That way we understand the process and have a firm handle on what should be done, not only from a pure automation perspective, but also as a choice of tools, processes, and architecture as well. All pieces need to work together in an organic and efficient way. If we manage to accomplish that, Jenkins acts as glue that ties it all together, and not as a base we start with.

Let's define the steps required for the first stage. The objective is very simple. Get the code from the Git repository. To make things slightly more complicated, we might need to clone or pull the code. The first build will have nothing so we must clone. All consecutive builds should only perform a pull into the already cloned code. While writing a script that performs that logic is relatively straightforward, this will be a good case of using a Jenkins plugin. To be more precise, we'll use Jenkins Pipeline step git that uses one of the Git plugins in the background.

The `Pull` stage stage of the Pipeline is as follows:

```
stage("Pull") { \
  git "https://github.com/vfarcic/go-demo.git" \
}
```

The git step is one of the many available through Pipelines **Domain Specific Language (DSL)**. It clones the code. If that action was already done, the code will be pulled instead. You can find more information in the *Pipeline Steps Reference* (https://jenkins.io/doc/pipeline/steps/) page.

Please note that in the real world situation we would create a webhook inside the code repository. It would trigger this job whenever a new commit is made. For now, we'll simulate a web hook by triggering the job execution manually.

Feel free to replace the existing Pipeline definition by copying and pasting the code from `scripts/go-demo-pull.groovy` (https://github.com/vfarcic/cloud-provisioning/blob/master/scripts/go-demo-pull.groovy). Once you're done, please run the job and observe the build log.

Let's move on.

The code that follows is the translation of the commands we used in the previous chapters to run unit tests and build a new Docker image:

```
withEnv([
  "COMPOSE_FILE=docker-compose-test-local.yml"
]) {

  stage("Unit") {
    sh "docker-compose run --rm unit"
    sh "docker-compose build app"
  }

}
```

We enveloped the whole stage inside the `withEnv` block that defines the `COMPOSE_FILE` variable. That way, we won't need to repeat the `-f docker-compose-test-local.yml` argument every time we execute `docker-compose`. Please note that all the other stages we'll define soon should also be inside the `withEnv` block.

The steps inside the Unit stage are the same as those we practiced while we run the flow manually. The only difference is that, this time, we put the commands inside the `sh DSL` step. It's purpose is simple. It runs a shell command.

We'll skip running the job and proceed to the next stage:

```
stage("Staging") {
try {
    sh "docker-compose up -d staging-dep"
    sh "docker-compose run --rm staging"
} catch(e) {
    error "Staging failed"
  } finally {
    sh "docker-compose down"
  }
}
```

The Staging stage is a bit more complex. The commands are inside the try/catch/finally block. The reasons for such an approach is in the way Jenkins behaves when something fails. If one of the steps in the previous stage Unit should fail, the whole Pipeline build would be aborted. That suits us well when there are no additional actions to perform. However, in the case of the Staging steps, we want to remove all the dependency containers and free the resources for something else. In other words, docker-compose down should be executed no matter the outcome of the Staging tests. If you are a programmer, you probably already know that the finally statement is always executed regardless of whether the try statement produced an error or not. In our case, the finally statement will bring down all the containers that constitute this Docker Compose project.

Off we go to the Publish stage:

```
stage("Publish") {
  sh "docker tag go-demo \
    localhost:5000/go-demo:2.${env.BUILD_NUMBER}"
  sh "docker push \
    localhost:5000/go-demo:2.${env.BUILD_NUMBER}"
}
```

There's no mystery around this stage. We are repeating the same commands we executed in previous chapters. The image is tagged and pushed to the registry.

Please note that we are using BUILD_NUMBER to provide a unique release number to the tag. It is one of Jenkins built-in environment variables that holds the value of the currently executing build ID.

The `Prod-like` stage will introduce an additional caveat. It is as follows:

```
stage("Prod-like") {
  withEnv([
     "DOCKER_TLS_VERIFY=1",
     "DOCKER_HOST=tcp://${env.PROD_LIKE_IP}:2376",
     "DOCKER_CERT_PATH=/machines/${env.PROD_LIKE_NAME}"
  ]) {
     sh "docker service update \
        --image localhost:5000/go-demo:2.${env.BUILD_NUMBER} \
        go-demo"
  }
  withEnv(["HOST_IP=localhost"]) {
     for (i = 0; i <10; i++) {
       sh "docker-compose run --rm production"
     }
  }
}
```

Since we are using rolling updates to replace the old with the new release, we have to run tests throughout the whole process. We could create a script that would verify whether all instances are updated but I wanted to keep it simple (this time). Instead, we are running the tests ten times. You might need to tweak it a bit for your needs depending on the average duration of your tests and the time required to update all instances. For demonstration purposes, ten rounds of testing in the `production-like` environment should be enough.

To summarize, in this stage we are updating the service with the new release and running ten rounds of tests during the update process.

Please note that we declared a few more environment variables. Specifically, we defined all those required for the Docker client to connect to the Docker Engine running on a remote host.

We're almost done. Now that the service is tested in the `production-like` environment, we can deploy it to the production cluster.

The `Prod` stage is almost the same as `Prod-like`:

```
stage("Production") {
  withEnv([
    "DOCKER_TLS_VERIFY=1",
    "DOCKER_HOST=tcp://${env.PROD_IP}:2376",
    "DOCKER_CERT_PATH=/machines/${env.PROD_NAME}"
  ]) {
    sh "docker service update \
    --image localhost:5000/go-demo:2.${env.BUILD_NUMBER} \
    go-demo"
  }
  withEnv(["HOST_IP=${env.PROD_IP}"]) {
    for (i = 0; i <10; i++) {
      sh "docker-compose run --rm production"
    }
  }
}
```

The only difference is that, this time, the `DOCKER_HOST` and `PROD_IP` variables point to one of the servers of the production cluster. The rest is the same as the `Prod-like` stage.

Feel free to replace the existing Pipeline definition with the code from `scripts/go-demo.groovy`. Once you're done, please run the job and observe the build log.

After a short while, the job will finish executing, and the new release will be running in the production cluster:

Stage View						
	Pull	Unit	Staging	Publish	Prod-like	Production
	6s	1min 42s	1min 6s	1s	20s	23s
Oct 06 18:53	1s	5min 8s	3min 20s	3s	1min 8s	1min 9s
Oct 06 18:43	19s	81ms	50ms	70ms	51ms	50ms
Oct 06 18:38	74ms	70ms	234ms	52ms	404ms	47ms
Oct 06 18:30						

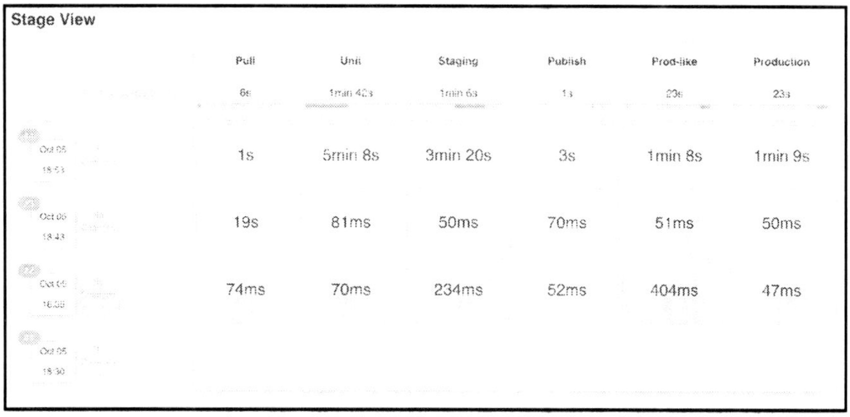

Figure 6-11: The Jenkins Pipeline Stage View screen

We can confirm that the service update with the new release was indeed successful by executing the `service ps` command:

```
eval $(docker-machine env swarm-1)

docker service ps go-demo
```

The output of the `service ps` command is as follows (IDs are removed for brevity):

```
NAME         IMAGE                         NODE     DESIRED STATE  CURRENT STATE              ERROR
go-demo.1    localhost:5000/go-demo:2.4    swarm-1  Running        Running 48 seconds ago
 _ go-demo.1  vfarcic/go-demo:1.0          swarm-3  Shutdown       Shutdown about a minute ago
go-demo.2    localhost:5000/go-demo:2.4    swarm-2  Running        Running about a minute ago
 _ go-demo.2  vfarcic/go-demo:1.0          swarm-3  Shutdown       Shutdown about a minute ago
go-demo.3    localhost:5000/go-demo:2.4    swarm-2  Running        Running 2 minutes ago
 _ go-demo.3  vfarcic/go-demo:1.0          swarm-2  Shutdown       Shutdown about a minute ago
```

That's it! We have a full Continuous Deployment Pipeline alive and kicking. If we'd add a webhook to the GitHub repository that hosts the code, the Pipeline would run every time a new commit is made. As a result, the new release would be deployed to production unless one of the steps in the Pipeline fails.

What now?

The ability to use the code to define the steps of a Continuous Deployment flow gives us more flexibility than we had before with *Freestyle* jobs. Docker Compose allowed us to run any type of tasks without the need to set up any special infrastructure. Anything can run as long as it is inside a container. Finally, Docker Swarm simplified the Deployment to production-like and production environments considerably.

We only scratched the surface of using Jenkins Pipeline to automate our Continuous Deployment flow. There are quite a few improvements we could do. For example, we might use the *Pipeline Shared Groovy Libraries Plugin* (`https://wiki.jenkins-ci.org/display/JE NKINS/Pipeline+Shared+Groovy+Libraries+Plugin`) and move steps, or even whole stages into functions and reduce code repetition. We could also create a *Jenkinsfile* (`https ://jenkins.io/doc/book/pipeline/jenkinsfile/`) that would move the Pipeline definition from Jenkins into the service repository thus keeping everything related to a single service in one place. We could, also, run production tests continuously (not only when making a new release) and ensure that we are notified if a service is not working or if it does not perform as expected.

We'll leave those and other possible improvements for some other time. While not perfect nor optimum, the go-demo Pipeline should be good enough for now.

It is the time to take a break before diving into the next chapter. As before, we'll destroy the machines we created and start fresh:

```
docker-machine rm -f \
    swarm-1 swarm-2 swarm-3 \
    swarm-test-1 swarm-test-2 \
    swarm-test-3 swarm-test-4
```

7
Exploring Docker Remote API

You can mass-produce hardware; you cannot mass-produce software - you cannot mass-produce the human mind.

–Michio Kaku

Up until now, we used Docker through its client. Whenever we needed something, the only thing we had to do is execute a `docker` command (example: `docker service create`). In most cases, that is enough when we are limiting ourselves to operating our cluster from a command line.

What happens if we want to accomplish a functionality beyond what the client offers? What if we'd like to operate Docker from inside our applications? Can we get statistics from all the containers running on the whole cluster?

One possible answer to those and quite a few other questions lies in the adoption of tools beyond those offered by Docker Inc. We'll explore quite a few of those in the chapters that follow.

Another approach would be to use Docker Remote API. After all, if we choose one of the products of the Docker ecosystem, chances are they will use the API. Docker Compose uses it to issue commands to Docker engines. Even the client uses it to communicate with the remote engine. You might find it useful as well.

By default, Docker daemon listens on `unix:///var/run/docker.sock` and the client must have root access to interact with the daemon. If a group named `docker` exists on your system, Docker applies ownership of the socket to the group. That does not mean that the socket is the only way to access the API. There are indeed quite a few others, and I encourage you to experiment with different combinations. For the purpose of this chapter, we'll stick with the socket since it is the easiest way to send API requests.

Setting up the environment

As in the previous chapters, we'll start with the creation of a cluster we'll use to experiment.

 All the commands from this chapter are available in the `07-api.sh` (`http s://gist.github.com/vfarcic/bab7f89f1cbd14f9895a9e0dc7293102`) Gist.

Please enter the `cloud-provisioning` directory where we pulled the repository. Since I might have updated it since the last time you used it, we'll issue a pull. Finally, we'll run the already familiar `script/ dm-swarm.sh` that will create a new Swarm cluster:

```
cd cloud-provisioning

git pull

scripts/dm-swarm.sh
```

The cluster is up and running.

VMs created with *Docker Machine* are based on *Boot2Docker*. It is a lightweight Linux distribution made specifically to run Docker containers. It runs entirely from RAM, is a small 38 MB download, and boots in ~5s. It is based on *Tiny Core Linux* (`http://tinycoreli nux.net/`). What distinguishes it from more popular Linux distributions is its size. It is stripped down to a bare minimum. This approach serves us well. If we adopt containers, there is no real need for most of the kernel modules usually seen in distributions like Ubuntu and RedHat.

This is in line with the minimalistic approach we strive for when working with containers. I already discussed the reasons for using `Alpine` as the base image we use for our containers. The main one is its size (only a few MB). After all, why would we ship our containers with things we don't need? The same can be said for the hosts OS. Less is better, as long as all our needs are fulfilled.

There is a caveat. *Boot2Docker* is currently designed and tuned for development. Using it for any kind of production workloads at this time is highly discouraged. That does not diminish its value, but makes a clear distinction what it's good for, and what it's not.

The reason behind this short introduction to *Boot2Docker* and Tiny Core Linux lies in the next steps. We're about to install a few programs, and we need to know the package management tool for the distribution we're using. Tiny Core Linux uses `tce-load`.

In the previous chapters, we executed most of the commands from your OS (MacOS, Linux, or Windows). This time, we'll run them inside one of the Docker Machine VMs. The reason lies in `jq` (`https://stedolan.github.io/jq/`) we'll use to format JSON output we'll be receiving from the API. It is available on most platforms, but I thought it would be better to avoid possible problems by putting you inside the VM. The second and more important reason lies in the choice to send requests to the API through the Docker socket that is available on the machines.

Without further ado, we'll proceed with installations of `curl` and `jq`:

```
docker-machine ssh swarm-1

tce-load -wi curl wget

wget https://github.com/stedolan/jq/releases/download/jq-1.5/jq-linux64

sudo mv jq-linux64 /usr/local/bin/jq

sudo chmod +x /usr/local/bin/jq
```

We entered the `swarm-1` machine and used `tce-load` to install `curl` and `wget`. Since `jq` is not available through `tce-load`, we used `wget` to download the binary. Finally, we moved `jq` to the bin directory and added execute permissions.

Now we're ready to start exploring Docker Remote API.

Operating Docker Swarm through the Docker Remote API

We won't go through the whole API. The official *documentation* (`https://docs.docker.com/engine/reference/api/docker_remote_api_v1.24/`) is well written and provides enough details. Instead, we'll go through some basic examples focused around Docker Swarm. We'll see how we can use the API by repeating some of the client commands we practiced earlier. The goal of this chapter is to get just enough knowledge to be able to use the API in your applications as well as a glue between different services we'll explore in the next chapters. Later on, we'll try to leverage this knowledge to create a monitoring system that stores the information about the cluster in a database and performs some actions.

Let's discuss a very simple example of a possible use case for the API.

If a node fails, Swarm will make sure that the containers that were running inside it are rescheduled. However, that does not mean that is enough. We might want to send an email stating that a node failed. Upon receiving such an email, someone would perform an investigation of the cause of the failed node and probably take some corrective actions. Those tasks are not urgent since Swarm mitigated the problem. However, something not being urgent does not mean that it should not be done.

The chapters that follow will try to make our cluster more robust, and the API will play a crucial role in that. For now, let's have a brief overview.

We'll start with a simple example. Let's see which nodes form our cluster:

```
curl \
    --unix-socket /var/run/docker.sock \
    http:/nodes | jq '.'
```

The output displays three nodes with detailed information for each. Showing all the information of all the nodes is too much for the book so let's limit the output to one of the nodes. All we have to do is append the name of the node to the previous command:

```
curl \
    --unix-socket /var/run/docker.sock \
    http:/nodes/swarm-1 | jq '.'
```

The output is as follows:

```
[
  {
    "ID": "2vxiqun3wvh1l1g43utk2v5a7",
    "Version": {
      "Index": 23
    },
    "CreatedAt": "2017-01-23T20:30:00.402618571Z",
    "UpdatedAt": "2017-01-23T20:30:04.026051022Z",
    "Spec": {
      "Labels": {
        "env": "prod"
      },
      "Role": "manager",
      "Availability": "active"
    },
    "Description": {
      "Hostname": "swarm-1",
      "Platform": {
        "Architecture": "x86_64",
        "OS": "linux"
      },
```

```
      "Resources": {
        "NanoCPUs": 1000000000,
        "MemoryBytes": 1044131840
      },
      "Engine": {
        "EngineVersion": "1.13.0",
        "Labels": {
          "provider": "virtualbox"
        },
        "Plugins": [
          {
            "Type": "Network",
            "Name": "bridge"
          },
          {
            "Type": "Network",
            "Name": "host"
          },
          {
            "Type": "Network",
            "Name": "macvlan"
          },
          {
            "Type": "Network",
            "Name": "null"
          },
          {
            "Type": "Network",
            "Name": "overlay"
          },
          {
            "Type": "Volume",
            "Name": "local"
          }
        ]
      }
    },
  "Status": {
    "State": "ready",
    "Addr": "127.0.0.1"
  },
  "ManagerStatus": {
    "Leader": true,
    "Reachability": "reachable",
      "Addr": "192.168.99.100:2377"
  }
},
```

The output, above, is truncated and only includes the "Leader" node. Your output will contain three sets of nodes that start with ID. We won't go into details of what each of the fields means. You should already be familiar with most of them.

Please consult *Docker Remote API v1.24: Nodes* (`https://docs.docker.com/engine/referen ce/api/docker_remote_api_v1.24/#/nodes`) for more information.

The API is not limited only to queries. We can use it to perform any of the operations available through the Docker client (and a few more). For example, we can create a new service:

```
curl -XPOST \
      -d '{
  "Name": "go-demo-db",
  "TaskTemplate": {
    "ContainerSpec": {
      "Image": "mongo:3.2.10"
    }
  }
}' \
    --unix-socket /var/run/docker.sock \
    http:/services/create | jq '.'
```

We sent a POST request to create a service named go-demo-db. The image of the service is mongo:3.2.10. As a result, the API responded with the service ID:

```
{
  "ID": "7157kfo9cp2vhed4bidrc8hfi"
}
```

Please consult *Docker Remote API v1.24: Create a service* (`https://docs.docker.com/engine /reference/api/docker_remote_api_v1.24/#create-a-service`) for more information.

We can confirm that the operation was indeed successful by listing all the services:

```
curl \
    --unix-socket /var/run/docker.sock \
    http:/services | jq '.'
```

The output is as follows:

```
[
  {
    "ID": "s73ez21cmshwu8okipejehvo0",
    "Version": {
      "Index": 26
    },
    "CreatedAt": "2017-01-23T20:47:27.247329291Z",
    "UpdatedAt": "2017-01-23T20:47:27.247329291Z",
    "Spec": {
      "Name": "go-demo-db",
      "TaskTemplate": {
        "ContainerSpec": {
          "Image":
"mongo:3.2.10@sha256:532a19da83ee0e4e2a2ec6bc4212fc4af26357c040675d5c2\
629a4e4c4563cef"
        },
        "ForceUpdate": 0
      },
      "Mode": {
        "Replicated": {
          "Replicas": 1
        }
      }
    },
    "Endpoint": {
      "Spec": {}
    },
    "UpdateStatus": {
      "StartedAt": "0001-01-01T00:00:00Z",
      "CompletedAt": "0001-01-01T00:00:00Z"
    }
  }
]
```

We got a list of services (at the moment only one) with some of their properties. We can see when was the service created, the number of replicas, and so on. Please consult *Docker Remote API v1.24: List services* (https://docs.docker.com/engine/reference/api/docker _remote_api_v1.24/#/list-services) for more information.

Similarly, we can retrieve the information of a single instance:

```
curl \
    --unix-socket /var/run/docker.sock \
    http:/services/go-demo-db | jq '.'
```

The output is almost the same as when we listed all services. The only significant difference is that, this time, we got a single result, while the list of services returned an array enclosed in [and]:

```
{
  "ID": "s73ez21cmshwu8okipejehvo0",
  "Version": {
    "Index": 26
  },
  "CreatedAt": "2017-01-23T20:47:27.247329291Z",
  "UpdatedAt": "2017-01-23T20:47:27.247329291Z",
  "Spec": {
    "Name": "go-demo-db",
    "TaskTemplate": {
      "ContainerSpec": {
        "Image":
"mongo:3.2.10@sha256:532a19da83ee0e4e2a2ec6bc4212fc4af26357c040675d5c2
629a4e4c4563cef"
      },
      "ForceUpdate": 0
    },
    "Mode": {
      "Replicated": {
        "Replicas": 1
      }
    }
  },
  "Endpoint": {
    "Spec": {}
  },
  "UpdateStatus": {
    "StartedAt": "0001-01-01T00:00:00Z",
    "CompletedAt": "0001-01-01T00:00:00Z"
  }
}
```

Please consult *Docker Remote API v1.24: Inspect one or more services* (https://docs.docker.c om/engine/reference/api/docker_remote_api_v1.24/#inspect-one-or-more-service s) for more information.

Let's spice it up a bit and scale to three replicas. We can accomplish that by updating the service. However, before we send an update request, we need the version and ID of the service. That information is available in the output of the service request we sent a moment ago. However, since we are trying to do things in a way that is easy to automate, we might be better off putting those values in environment variables.

We can use jq to filter the output and return a particular value.

The command that returns the version of the service is as follows:

```
VERSION=$(curl \
    --unix-socket /var/run/docker.sock \
    http:/services/go-demo-db | \
    jq '.Version.Index')

echo $VERSION
```

The output of the variable `$VERSION` is as follows:

```
27
```

Similarly, we should retrieve the service `ID` as well:

```
ID=$(curl \
    --unix-socket /var/run/docker.sock \
    http:/services/go-demo-db | \
    jq --raw-output '.ID')

echo $ID
```

The output is as follows:

```
7157kfo9cp2vhed4bidrc8hfi
```

Now we have all the information we need to update the service. We'll change the number of replicas to three:

```
curl -XPOST \
    -d '{
  "Name": "go-demo-db",
  "TaskTemplate": {
    "ContainerSpec": {
      "Image": "mongo:3.2.10"
    }
  },
  "Mode": {
    "Replicated": {
      "Replicas": 3
    }
  }
}' \
    --unix-socket /var/run/docker.sock \
    http:/services/$ID/update?version=$VERSION
```

Please consult *Docker Remote API v1.24: Update a service* (https://docs.docker.com/engine/reference/api/docker_remote_api_v1.24/#update-a-service) for more information.

Next, we can list the `tasks` and confirm whether the service was indeed scaled to three instances:

```
curl \
    --unix-socket /var/run/docker.sock \
    http:/tasks | jq '.'
```

The output is as follows:

```
[
  {
    "ID": "c0nev776zyuoaul51n5w9xc85",
    "Version": {
      "Index": 32
    },
    "CreatedAt": "2017-01-23T20:47:27.255828694Z",
    "UpdatedAt": "2017-01-23T20:47:51.329755266Z",
    "Spec": {
      "ContainerSpec": {
        "Image":
"mongo:3.2.10@sha256:532a19da83ee0e4e2a2ec6bc4212fc4af26357c040675d5c2\
629a4e4c4563cef"
      },
      "ForceUpdate": 0
    },
    "ServiceID": "s73ez21cmshwu8okipejehvo0",
    "Slot": 1,
    "NodeID": "2vxiqun3wvh1l1g43utk2v5a7",
    "Status": {
      "Timestamp": "2017-01-23T20:47:51.295994806Z",
      "State": "running",
      "Message": "started",
      "ContainerStatus": {
        "ContainerID":
"20112c904386733c6748bc186e84255640c9dc279fd3530b771616a1ef767957",
        "PID": 4238
      },
      "PortStatus": {}
    },
    "DesiredState": "running"
  },
  {
    "ID": "ptbp594sh5k2qey6lexafr31d",
    "Version": {
      "Index": 37
    },
    "CreatedAt": "2017-01-23T21:16:55.680872244Z",
    "UpdatedAt": "2017-01-23T21:16:55.960585822Z",
```

```
    "Spec": {
      "ContainerSpec": {
        "Image":
"mongo:3.2.10@sha256:532a19da83ee0e4e2a2ec6bc4212fc4af26357c040675d5c2\
629a4e4c4563cef"
      },
      "ForceUpdate": 0
    },
    "ServiceID": "s73ez21cmshwu8okipejehvo0",
        "Slot": 2,
     "NodeID": "skj5sjemrvnusdop3ovcv6q7h",
     "Status": {
        "Timestamp": "2017-01-23T21:16:55.882919942Z",
        "State": "preparing",
        "Message": "preparing",
        "ContainerStatus": {},
        "PortStatus": {}
     },
     "DesiredState": "running"
},
{
    "ID": "rqa04bpvdcddkeia2x1d6r95r",
    "Version": {
      "Index": 37
   },
   "CreatedAt": "2017-01-23T21:16:55.6812298Z",
   "UpdatedAt": "2017-01-23T21:16:55.960175605Z",
     "Spec": {
       "ContainerSpec": {
         "Image":
"mongo:3.2.10@sha256:532a19da83ee0e4e2a2ec6bc4212fc4af26357c040675d5c2\
629a4e4c4563cef"
      },
      "ForceUpdate": 0
   },
      "ServiceID": "s73ez21cmshwu8okipejehvo0",
      "Slot": 3,
      "NodeID": "lbgy0xih6n0w3nmzih0gnfvhd",
      "Status": {
       "Timestamp": "2017-01-23T21:16:55.881446699Z",
       "State": "preparing",
       "Message": "preparing",
       "ContainerStatus": {},
       "PortStatus": {}
     },
     "DesiredState": "running"
   }
]
```

As you can see, three tasks were returned, each representing one replica of the `go-demo-db` service.

Please consult *Docker Remote API v1.24: List tasks* (`https://docs.docker.com/engine/refe rence/api/docker_remote_api_v1.24/#list-tasks`) for more information.

All the API requests we made so far were related to nodes and services. In some cases, we might need to go lower and use the API on a container level. For example, we might want to get statistics related to a single container.

Before we proceed, please make sure that the state of all the tasks is running. Feel free to repeat the `http:/tasks` request to confirm the state. If it's not running, please wait for a while and check it again.

To get stats of a container, first we need to find out on which node it is running:

```
exit

eval $(docker-machine env swarm-1)

NODE=$(docker service ps \
    -f desired-state=running \
    go-demo-db \
    | tail -n 1 \
    | awk '{print $4}')

echo $NODE
```

We exited the `swarm-1` machine and used eval to create environment variables that instructed the Docker client running on our host to use the engine running on `swarm-1`. Please note that those environment variables are telling the client to use the same API we've been exploring throughout this chapter.

Further on, we retrieved the node where one of the containers forming the `go-demo-db` service is running. We already used a similar command a couple of times, so there's no need explaining it in more detail.

The output of the $NODE variable is as follows:

```
swarm-2
```

On my laptop, the container we're looking for is running inside the `swarm-2` node. In your case, it might be a different one.

Now we can enter the node and get the `ID` of the container:

```
docker-machine ssh $NODE

ID=$(docker ps -qa | tail -n 1)

echo $ID
```

The output of the `ID` variable is as follows:

```
f8f345042cf7
```

Finally, we are ready to get the statistics. The command is as follows:

```
curl \
    --unix-socket /var/run/docker.sock \
    http:/containers/$ID/stats
```

As soon as the request is sent, you will see a constant stream of statistics. Please press *CTRL + C* to stop the stream when you get tired looking at it.

Streaming stats might be a very useful feature if we would like to implement our own monitoring solution. In many other cases, we might want to disable streaming and retrieve only a single recordset. We can accomplish that by setting the `stream` parameter to `false`.

The command that returns a single stats recordset is as follows:

```
curl \
    --unix-socket /var/run/docker.sock \
    http:/containers/$ID/stats?stream=false
```

The output is still too big to be presented in the book, so you have to inspect it from your screen.

We won't go into details of what each field from stats means. You'll have to wait until we reach the monitoring chapter for deeper exploration. For now, the important thing to note is that you can retrieve them for each container inside your cluster.

As an exercise, create a script that retrieves all the containers running on the node. Iterate through each to get stats of all the containers running inside that VM.

Please consult *Docker Remote API v1.24: Get container stats based on resource usage* (`https://d ocs.docker.com/engine/reference/api/docker_remote_api_v1.24/#get-container-s tats-based-on-resource-usage`) for more information.

We are almost finished with the exploration of basic API requests related to Swarm services so let's remove the service we created:

```
curl -XDELETE \
    --unix-socket /var/run/docker.sock \
    http:/services/go-demo-db

curl \
    --unix-socket /var/run/docker.sock \
    http:/services
```

We sent the `DELETE` request to remove the `go-demo-db` service followed with the request to retrieve all services. The output of the later is as follows:

```
[]
```

Our service is no more. We removed it from the cluster and, since that was the only one we created, the request to retrieve the list of services returned an empty array `[]`.

Please consult *Docker Remote API v1.24: Remove a service* (`https://docs.docker.com/engin e/reference/api/docker_remote_api_v1.24/#remove-a-service`) for more information.

Finally, let's get out of the machine:

```
exit
```

Now that you have a basic understanding of the API, we can explore one possible use case.

Using Docker Remote API to automate proxy configuration

Up until now, we were sending reconfigure and remove requests to our proxy. That greatly simplified the configuration. Instead of changing HAProxy config ourselves, we let the service reconfigure itself. We used Consul to persist the state of the proxy. Can we improve the existing design by leveraging Docker Remote API? I think we can.

Instead of sending reconfigure and remove requests, we can have a service that would monitor the cluster state through the API. Such a tool could detect new and removed services and send the same request to the `proxy` like the one we would send manually.

We can go even further. Since the API allows us to retrieve any information related to the cluster, we don't need to store it in Consul anymore. Whenever a new instance of the service is created, it can retrieve all the information it needs from the API.

All in all, we can use the API to fully automate changes to the `proxy` configuration as well as its state. We can create a new service that will monitor the cluster state. We can also modify the `proxy` to consult that service during its initialization.

I thought to save you some time by taking the liberty to create such a service. The project behind it is called *Docker Flow Swarm Listener* (`https://github.com/vfarcic/docker-flow -swarm-listener`).

Let's see it in action.

Combining the Swarm listener with the proxy

The *Docker Flow Swarm Listener* (`https://github.com/vfarcic/docker-flow-swarm-list ener`) project leverages Docker Remote API. It has many usages but, for now, we'll limit ourselves to the features that can help make our proxy configuration fully hands-free.

We'll start by creating two networks:

```
eval $(docker-machine env swarm-1)

docker network create --driver overlay proxy

docker network create --driver overlay go-demo
```

We created those two networks so many times that there is no reason to go over their usefulness. The only difference is that this time, we'll have one more service to attach to the `proxy` network.

Next, we'll create the `swarm-listener` (`https://github.com/vfarcic/docker-flow-swa rm-listener`) service. It will act as a companion to the Docker Flow Proxy. Its purpose is to monitor Swarm services and send requests to the proxy whenever a service is created or destroyed.

A note to Windows users
Git Bash has a habit of altering file system paths. To stop this, execute the following:
`export MSYS_NO_PATHCONV=1`

Let's create the `swarm-listener` service:

```
docker service create --name swarm-listener \
    --network proxy \
    --mount \
    "type=bind,source=/var/run/docker.sock,target=/var/run/\
    docker.sock" \
-e DF_NOTIF_CREATE_SERVICE_URL=http://proxy:8080/v1/
    docker-flow-proxy/reconfigure \
-e DF_NOTIF_REMOVE_SERVICE_URL=http://proxy:8080/v1/
    docker-flow-proxy/remove \
    --constraint 'node.role==manager' \
    vfarcic/docker-flow-swarm-listener
```

The service is attached to the `proxy` network, mounts the Docker socket, and declares the environment variables `DF_NOTIF_CREATE_SERVICE_URL` and `DF_NOTIF_REMOVE_SERVICE_URL`. We'll see the purpose of those variables soon. The service is constrained to the manager nodes.

The next step is to create the `proxy` service:

```
docker service create --name proxy \
    -p 80:80 \
    -p 443:443 \
    --network proxy \
    -e MODE=swarm \
    -e LISTENER_ADDRESS=swarm-listener \
    vfarcic/docker-flow-proxy
```

We opened ports *80* and *443*. External requests will be routed through them towards destination services. Please note that this time, we did not open port 8080. Since the `proxy` will be receiving notifications from the `swarm-listener`, there is no need for having 8080 available for manual notifications.

The `proxy` is attached to the `proxy` network and has the mode set to swarm. The `proxy` must belong to the same network as the listener. They will exchange information whenever a service is created or removed as well as when a new instance of the `proxy` is created.

Automatically reconfiguring the proxy

Let's create the already familiar demo services:

```
docker service create --name go-demo-db \
  --network go-demo \
  mongo:3.2.10
```

```
docker service create --name go-demo \
  -e DB=go-demo-db \
  --network go-demo \
  --network proxy \
  --label com.df.notify=true \
  --label com.df.distribute=true \
  --label com.df.servicePath=/demo \
  --label com.df.port=8080 \
  vfarcic/go-demo:1.0
```

Please note the labels. We did not have them in the previous chapters. Things changed and now they are a crucial part of the service definition. The com.df.notify=true tells the swarm-listener service whether to send notifications whenever a service is created or removed. Since we don't want to add the go-demo-db service to the proxy, the label is defined only for the go-demo service. The rest of the labels match the query arguments we would use if we'd reconfigure the proxy manually. The only difference is that the labels are prefixed with com.df. For the list of the query arguments, please see the *Reconfigure* (https ://github.com/vfarcic/docker-flow-proxy#reconfigure) section of the project.

Now we should wait until all the services are running. You can see their status by executing the command that follows:

```
docker service ls
```

Once all the replicas are set to 1/1, we can see the effect of the com.df labels by sending a request to the go-demo service through the proxy:

```
curl -i "$(docker-machine ip swarm-1)/demo/hello"
```

The output is as follows:

```
HTTP/1.1 200 OK
Date: Thu, 13 Oct 2016 18:26:18 GMT
Content-Length: 14
Content-Type: text/plain; charset=utf-8

hello, world!
```

We sent a request to the proxy (the only service listening to the port 80) and got back the response from the go-demo service. The proxy was configured automatically as soon as the go-demo service was created.

The way the process works is as follows:

Docker Flow Swarm Listener is running inside one of the Swarm manager nodes and queries Docker API in search of newly created services. Once it finds a new service, it looks for its labels. If the service contains the label `com.df.notify` (it can hold any value), the rest of the labels with keys starting with `com.df.` are retrieved. All those labels are used to form request parameters. Those parameters are appended to the address specified as the `DF_NOTIF_CREATE_SERVICE_URL` environment variable defined in the `swarm-listener` service. Finally, a request is sent. In this particular case, the request was made to reconfigure the `proxy` with the service `go-demo` (the name of the service), using `/demo` as the path, and running on the port `8080`. The distribute label is not necessary in this example since we're running only a single instance of the `proxy`. However, in production, we should run at least two `proxy` instances (for fault tolerance) and the distribute argument means that reconfiguration should be applied to all.

Please see the *Reconfigure* (`https://github.com/vfarcic/docker-flow-proxy#reconfigure`) section for the list of all the arguments that can be used with the proxy.

Removing a service from the proxy

Since `swarm-listener` is monitoring `docker` services, if a service is removed, related entries in the `proxy` configuration will be removed as well:

```
docker service rm go-demo
```

If you were to check the Swarm Listener logs in the same way you would check logs for any other container service, you'd see an entry similar to the one that follows:

```
Sending service removed notification to http://proxy:8080/v1/
docker-flow-proxy/remove?serviceName=go-demo
```

A moment later, a new entry would appear in the `proxy` logs:

```
Processing request /v1/docker-flow-proxy/remove?serviceName=go-demo
Processing remove request /v1/docker-flow-proxy/remove
Removing go-demo configuration
Removing the go-demo configuration files
Reloading the proxy
```

From this moment on, the service `go-demo` is not available through the proxy.

Swarm Listener detected that the service was removed, sent a notification to the `proxy` which, in turn, changed its configuration and reloaded the underlying HAProxy.

What now?

Apart from the potential utility of having a proxy that is configured automatically whenever a service is created or removed, `swarm-listener` shows how useful it is to leverage the Docker Remote API. If you have your own needs that are not fully covered with Docker or one of the tools in its ecosystem, it is relatively easy to write your own service on top of the API. The truth is that, at the time this chapter was written, the Swarm Mode is only a couple of months old, and there aren't many third party tools that can be used to fine tune or extend its behavior. Even if you find all the tools that do more or less what you need, it's still a good idea to write a bit of code yourself and switch from more or less to exactly what you need.

I encourage you to fire up your favorite editor and write a service in your programming language of choice. You can monitor services and send yourself an email whenever a member of your team creates or removes one. Or you can integrate statistics with your favorite monitoring tool.

If you are out of ideas for your own service and you're not afraid of *Go* (https://golang.org/), you might try extending *Docker Flow Swarm Listener* (https://github.com/vfarcic/docker-flow-swarm-listener). Fork it, add a new feature, and make a pull request.

Remember, learning is golden. If the only outcome is that you learned something, that's already pretty good. If it turns up to be useful, even better.

We reached the end of the chapter, and you already know the drill. We'll destroy the machines we created and start anew.

```
docker-machine rm -f swarm-1 swarm-2 swarm-3
```

8
Using Docker Stack and Compose YAML Files to Deploy Swarm Services

Copy and paste is a design error.
–David Parnas

The most common question I receive during my Docker-related talks and workshops is usually related to Swarm and Compose.

Someone: How can I use Docker Compose with Docker Swarm?

Me: You can't! You can convert your Compose files into a Bundle that does not support all Swarm features. If you want to use Swarm to its fullest, be prepared for `docker service create` commands that contain a never ending list of arguments.

Such an answer was usually followed with disappointment. Docker Compose showed us the advantages of specifying everything in a YAML file as opposed to trying to remember all the arguments we have to pass to docker commands. It allowed us to store service definitions in a repository thus providing a reproducible and well-documented process for managing them. Docker Compose replaced bash scripts, and we loved it. Then, Docker v1.12 came along and put a difficult choice in front of us. Should we adopt Swarm and discard Compose? Since summer 2016, Swarm and Compose were not in love anymore. It was a painful divorce.

But, after almost half a year of separation, they are back together, and we can witness their second honeymoon. Kind of… We do not need Docker Compose binary for Swarm services, but we can use its YAML files.

Docker Engine v1.13 introduced support for Compose YAML files within the stack command. At the same time, *Docker Compose v1.10* introduced a new *version 3* of its format. Together, they allow us to manage our Swarm services using already familiar Docker Compose YAML format.

I will assume you are already familiar with Docker Compose and won't go into details of everything we can do with it. Instead, we'll go through an example of creating a few Swarm services.

We'll explore how to create *Docker Flow Proxy* (`http://proxy.dockerflow.com/`) service through *Docker Compose* files and the `docker stack deploy` command.

Swarm cluster setup

To setup an example Swarm cluster using Docker Machine, please run the commands that follow.

All the commands from this chapter are available in the `07-docker-stack.sh` (`https://g ist.github.com/vfarcic/57422c77223d40e97320900fcf76a550`) Gist:

```
cd cloud-provisioning

git pull

scripts/dm-swarm.sh
```

Now we're ready to deploy the `docker-flow-proxy` service.

Creating Swarm services through Docker stack commands

We'll start by creating a network:

> **A note to Windows users**
> You might experience a problem with volumes not being mapped correctly. If you see an `Invalid volume specification` error, please export the environment variable `COMPOSE_CONVERT_WINDOWS_PATHS` set to `0`:
> `export COMPOSE_CONVERT_WINDOWS_PATHS=0`
> Please make sure that the variable is exported before you run `docker-compose` or `docker stack deploy`.

```
eval $(docker-machine env swarm-1)

docker network create --driver overlay proxy
```

The `proxy` network will be dedicated to the `proxy` container and services that will be attached to it.

We'll use `docker-compose-stack.yml` (https://github.com/vfarcic/docker-flow-proxy/blob/master/docker-compose-stack.yml) from the `vfarcic/docker-flow-proxy` (https://github.com/vfarcic/docker-flow-proxy) repository to create `docker-flow-proxy` and `docker-flow-swarm-listener` services.

The content of the `docker-compose-stack.yml` file is as follows:

```
version: "3"

services:

  proxy:
    image: vfarcic/docker-flow-proxy
    ports:
      - 80:80
      - 443:443
    networks:
      - proxy
    environment:
      - LISTENER_ADDRESS=swarm-listener
      - MODE=swarm
    deploy:
      replicas: 2
```

```
    swarm-listener:
      image: vfarcic/docker-flow-swarm-listener
      networks:
        - proxy
      volumes:
        - /var/run/docker.sock:/var/run/docker.sock
      environment:
        - DF_NOTIFY_CREATE_SERVICE_URL=http://proxy:8080/v1/\
docker-flow-proxy/reconfigure
        - DF_NOTIFY_REMOVE_SERVICE_URL=http://proxy:8080/v1/\
docker-flow-proxy/remove
      deploy:
        placement:
          constraints: [node.role == manager]

networks:
  proxy:
    external: true
```

The format is written in *version 3* (mandatory for `docker stack deploy`).

It contains two services; `proxy` and `swarm-listener`. Since you are already familiar with the `proxy`, I won't go into the meaning of each argument.

When compared with previous Compose versions, most of the new arguments are defined within deploy. You can think of that section as a placeholder for Swarm-specific arguments. In this case, we are specifying that the `proxy` service should have two replicas while the `swarm-listener` service should be constrained to manager roles. Everything else defined for those two services is using the same format as in earlier Compose versions.

At the bottom of the YAML file is the list of networks which are referenced within services. If a service does not specify any, the default network will be created automatically. In this case, we opted for manual creation of a network since services from other stacks should be able to communicate with the `proxy`. Therefore, we created a network manually and defined it as external in the YAML file.

Let's create the stack based on the YAML file we explored:

```
curl -o docker-compose-stack.yml \
    https://raw.githubusercontent.com/\
vfarcic/docker-flow-proxy/master/docker-compose-stack.yml

docker stack deploy \
    -c docker-compose-stack.yml proxy
```

The first command downloaded the Compose file `docker-compose-stack.yml` (https ://github.com/vfarcic/docker-flow-proxy/blob/master/docker-compose-stack.yml) from the `vfarcic/docker-flow-proxy` (https://github.com/vfarcic/docker-flow-pr oxy) repository. The second command created the services that form the stack.

The tasks of the stack can be seen through the `stack ps` command:

```
docker stack ps proxy
```

The output is as follows (IDs are removed for brevity):

```
NAME                        IMAGE                                        NODE
proxy_proxy.1               vfarcic/docker-flow-proxy:latest             node-2
proxy_swarm-listener.1 vfarcic/docker-flow-swarm-listener:latest node-1
proxy_proxy.2               vfarcic/docker-flow-proxy:latest             node-3
--------------------------------------------------------------
DESIRED STATE CURRENT STATE            ERROR PORTS
Running       Running 2 minutes ago
Running       Running 2 minutes ago
Running       Running 2 minutes ago
```

We are running two replicas of the `proxy` (for high-availability in the case of a failure) and one of the `swarm-listener`.

Deploying more stacks

Let's deploy another stack.

This time we'll use Docker stack defined in the Compose file `docker-compose-stack.yml` (https://github.com/vfarcic/go-demo/blob/master/docker-compose-stack.yml) located in the `vfarcic/go-demo` (https://github.com/vfarcic/go-demo/) repository. It is as follows:

```
version: '3'

services:

  main:
    image: vfarcic/go-demo
    environment:
      - DB=db
    networks:
      - proxy
      - default
```

```
    deploy:
      replicas: 3
      labels:
        - com.df.notify=true
        - com.df.distribute=true
        - com.df.servicePath=/demo
        - com.df.port=8080

  db:
    image: mongo
    networks:
      - default

networks:
  default:
    external: false
  proxy:
    external: true
```

The stack defines two services (`main` and `db`). They will communicate with each other through the default network that will be created automatically by the stack (no need for `docker network create` command). Since the main service is an API, it should be accessible through the `proxy`, so we're attaching `proxy` network as well.

The important thing to note is that we used the deploy section to define `Swarm-specific` arguments. In this case, the main service defines that there should be three replicas and a few labels. As with the previous stack, we won't go into details of each service. If you'd like to go into more depth of the labels used with the main service, please visit the *Running Docker Flow Proxy In Swarm Mode With Automatic Reconfiguration* (`http://proxy.dockerflo w.com/swarm-mode-auto/`) tutorial.

Let's deploy the stack:

```
curl -o docker-compose-go-demo.yml \
    https://raw.githubusercontent.com/\
vfarcic/go-demo/master/docker-compose-stack.yml

docker stack deploy \
    -c docker-compose-go-demo.yml go-demo

docker stack ps go-demo
```

We downloaded the stack definition, executed `stack deploy` command that created the services and run the `stack ps` command that lists the tasks that belong to the `go-demo` stack. The output is as follows (IDs and Error ports columns are removed for brevity):

```
NAME              IMAGE                      NODE      DESIRED STATE
go-demo_main.1    vfarcic/go-demo:latest     node-2    Running
go-demo_db.1      mongo:latest               node-2    Running
go-demo_main.2    vfarcic/go-demo:latest     node-2    Running
go-demo_main.3    vfarcic/go-demo:latest     node-2    Running

-------------------------------------------------------------
CURRENT STATE
Running 7 seconds ago
Running 21 seconds ago
Running 19 seconds ago
Running 20 seconds ago
```

Since Mongo database is much bigger than the main service, it takes more time to pull it, resulting in a few failures. The `go-demo` service is designed to fail if it cannot connect to its database. Once the `db` service is running, the main service should stop failing, and we'll see three replicas with the current state `Running`.

After a few moments, the `swarm-listener` service will detect the main service from the `go-demo` stack and send the `proxy` a request to reconfigure itself. We can see the result by sending an HTTP request to the `proxy`:

```
curl -i "http://$(docker-machine ip swarm-1)/demo/hello"
```

The output is as follows:

```
HTTP/1.1 200 OK
Date: Thu, 19 Jan 2017 23:57:05 GMT
Content-Length: 14
Content-Type: text/plain; charset=utf-8

hello, world!
```

The `proxy` was reconfigured and forwards all requests with the base path `/demo` to the main service from the `go-demo` stack.

To stack or not to stack

Docker stack is a great addition to the Swarm Mode. We do not have to deal with `docker service create` commands that tend to have a never ending list of arguments. With services specified in Compose YAML files, we can replace those long commands with a simple `docker stack deploy`. If those YAML files are stored in code repositories, we can apply the same practices to service deployments as to any other area of software engineering. We can track changes, do code reviews, share with others, and so on.

The addition of the Docker `stack` command and its ability to use Compose files is a very welcome addition to the Docker ecosystem.

Throughout the rest of the book, we'll use `docker service create` commands when exploring new services and `docker stack deploy` to create those we are already familiar with. If you have trouble converting `docker service create` commands into stacks, please take a look at the `vfarcic/docker-flow-stacks` (`https://github.com/vfarcic /docker-flow-stacks`) repository. It contains the stacks from some of the services we'll use. I expect you to contribute with the stacks you use. Please fork the repository and make a pull request. If you have trouble making a stack, please open an issue

Cleanup

Please remove Docker Machine VMs we created. You might need those resources for some other tasks:

```
exit

docker-machine rm -f swarm-1 swarm-2 swarm-3
```

9
Defining Logging Strategy

Most software today is very much like an Egyptian pyramid with millions of bricks piled on top of each other, with no structural integrity, but just done by brute force and thousands of slaves.

—Alan Kay

We've reached the point where we have a fully operating Swarm cluster and a defined Continuous Deployment Pipeline that'll update our services on each commit. Now we can spend time coding and pushing commits to our repository knowing that the rest of the process is automated. We can, finally, spend our time on tasks that bring real value to the organization we're working for. We can dedicate our time to producing new features for the services we're working on. However, when something goes wrong, we need to stop churning new features and investigate the problem.

The first thing we tend to do when we detect an issue is to check logs. They are, by no means, not the only source of data we can use for debugging problem. We'll also need a lot of metrics (more on that in the next chapter). However, even if logs are not the only thing we should look at, they are often a good start.

A note to The DevOps 2.0 Toolkit readers
The text that follows is identical to the one published in *The DevOps 2.0 Toolkit*. If it is still fresh in your mind, feel free to jump to the *Setting up LogStash and ElasticSearch as the logging Database* (#logging-es) sub-chapter. Since I wrote the *2.0*, I discovered a few better ways to treat logs, especially inside a Swarm cluster.

Our exploration of DevOps practices and tools led us towards clustering and scaling. As a result, we developed a system that allows us to deploy services to a cluster, in an easy and efficient way. The result is an ever increasing number of containers running inside a cluster consisting of, potentially, many servers.

Monitoring one server is easy. Monitoring many services on a single server poses some difficulties. Monitoring many services on many servers requires a whole new way of thinking and a new set of tools. As you start embracing microservices, containers, and clusters, the number of created services and their instances will begin increasing rapidly. The same holds true for servers that form the cluster. We cannot, anymore, log into a node and look at logs. There are too many to look at. On top of that, they are distributed among many servers. While yesterday we had two instances of a service deployed on a single server, tomorrow we might have eight instances deployed to six servers.

We need historical and (near) real time information about our system. That information can be in the form of logs, hardware utilization, health checking, network traffic, and many other things. The need to store historical data is not new and has been in use for a long time. However, the direction that information travels has changed over time. While, in the past, most solutions were based on centralized data collectors, today, due to the very dynamic nature of services and servers, we tend to have them decentralized.

What we need for cluster logging and monitoring is a combination of decentralized data collectors that are sending information to a centralized parsing service and data storage. There are plenty of products specially designed to fulfill this requirement, ranging from on-premise to cloud solutions, and everything in between. *FluentD* (http://www.fluentd.org/), *Loggly* (https://www.loggly.com/), *GrayLog* (https://www.graylog.org/), *Splunk* (http://www.splunk.com/), and *DataDog* (https://www.datadoghq.com/) are only a few of the solutions we can employ. I chose to show you the concepts through the ELK stack (*ElasticSearch* (https://www.elastic.co/products/elasticsearch), *LogStash* (https://www.elastic.co/products/logstash), and *Kibana* (https://www.elastic.co/products/kibana)). The stack has the advantage of being free, well documented, efficient, and widely used. *ElasticSearch* (https://www.elastic.co/products/elasticsearch) established itself as one of the best databases for real-time search and analytics. It is distributed, scalable, highly available, and provides a sophisticated API. *LogStash* (https://www.elastic.co/products/logstash) allows us to centralize data processing. It can be easily extended to custom data formats and offers a lot of plugins that can fulfill almost any need. Finally, *Kibana* (https://www.elastic.co/products/kibana) is an analytics and visualization platform with intuitive interface sitting on top of ElasticSearch.

The fact that we'll use the ELK stack does not mean that it is better than the other solutions. It all depends on specific use cases and particular needs. I'll walk you through the principles of centralized logging and monitoring using the ELK stack. Once those principles are understood, you should have no problem applying them to a different stack if you choose to do so.

We switched the order of things and chose the tools before discussing the need for centralized logging. Let's remedy that.

The need for centralized logging

In most cases, log messages are written to files. That is not to say that files are the only, nor the most efficient way of storing logs. However, since most teams are using file-based logs in one form or another, for the time being, I'll assume that is your case as well. If it is, we identified the first thing we should fix. Containers expect us to send logs to `stdout` and `stderr`. Only log entries forwarded to the standard output are retrievable with `docker logs` command. Moreover, tools designed to work with container logs will expect just that. They'll assume that entries are not written to a file but sent to the output. Even without containers, I believe that `stdout` and `stderr` are where our services should log things. However, that's a story for some other time. For now, we'll concentrate on containers and assume that you are outputting your logs to `stdout` and `stderr`. If you're not, most logging libraries will allow you to change your logging destination to standard output and error.

Most of the time, we do not care what is written in logs. When things are working well, there is not much need to spend valuable time browsing through them. A log is not a novel we read to pass the time with, nor it is a technical book we read as a way to improve our knowledge. Logs are there to provide valuable info when something, somewhere, went wrong.

The situation seems to be simple. We write information to logs that we ignore most of the time, and when something goes wrong, we consult them and find the cause of the problem in no time. At least, that's what many are hoping for. The reality is far more complicated than that. In all but the most trivial systems, the debugging process is much more challenging. Applications and services are almost always interconnected, and it is often not easy to know which one caused the problem. While it might manifest in one application, investigation often shows that the cause is in another. For example, a service might have failed to instantiate. After some time spent browsing its logs, we might discover that the cause is in the database. The service could not connect to it and failed to launch. We got the symptom, but not the cause. We need to switch to the database log to find it out. With this simple example, we've already gotten to the point where looking at one log is not enough.

With distributed services running on a cluster, the situation complicates exponentially. Which instance of the service is failing? Which server is it running on? What are the upstream services that initiated the request? What are the memory and hard disk usage in the node where the culprit resides? As you might have guessed, finding, gathering, and filtering the information needed for the successful discovery of the cause is often very complicated. The bigger the system, the harder it gets. Even with monolithic applications, things can easily get out of hand.

If a microservices approach is adopted, those problems are multiplied. Centralized logging is a must for all but the simplest and smallest systems. Instead, many of us, when things go wrong, start running from one server to another and jumping from one file to the other. Like a chicken with its head cut off - running around with no direction. We tend to accept the chaos logging creates, and consider it part of our profession.

What do we look for in centralized logging? As it happens, many things, but the most important are as follows:

- A way to parse data and send them to a central database in near real-time
- The capacity of the database to handle near real-time data querying and analytics
- A visual representation of the data through filtered tables, dashboards, and so on

We already chose the tools that will be able to fulfill all those requirements (and more). The ELK stack (ElasticSearch, LogStash, and Kibana) can do all that. As in the case of all other tools we explored, this stack can easily be extended to satisfy the particular needs we'll set in front of us.

Now that we have a vague idea what we want to accomplish, and have the tools to do that, let us explore a few of the logging strategies we can use. We'll start with the most commonly used scenario and, slowly, move towards more complicated and more efficient ways to define our logging strategy.

Without further ado, let's create the environments we'll use to experiment with centralized logging and, later on, monitoring.

Setting up ElasticSearch as the logging database

As in quite a few cases before, we'll start by creating the already familiar nodes (swarm-1, swarm-2, and swarm-3):

```
cd cloud-provisioning

git pull

scripts/dm-swarm.sh
```

All the commands from this chapter are available in the
`08-logging.sh` (`https://gist.github.com/vfarcic/c89b73ebd32dbf
8f849531a842739c4d`) Gist.

The first service we'll create is *Elastic Search* (`https://hub.docker.com/_/elasticsearch`).
Since we'll need it to be accessible from a few other services, we'll also create a network
called `elk`:

```
eval $(docker-machine env swarm-1)

docker network create --driver overlay elk

docker service create \
    --name elasticsearch \
    --network elk \
    --reserve-memory 500m \
    elasticsearch:2.4
```

After a few moments, the `elasticsearch` service will be up and running.

We can check the status using the `service ps` command:

```
docker service ps elasticsearch
```

The output is as follows (IDs and ERROR PORTS columns are removed for brevity):

```
NAME             IMAGE              NODE     DESIRED STATE
elasticsearch.1  elasticsearch:2.4  swarm-1  Running
----------------------------------------------------------
CURRENT STATE
Running 19 seconds ago
```

If `elasticsearch` is still not running, please wait a few moments before proceeding.
Now that we have a database where we can store our logs, the next step is to create a
service that will parse log entries and forward the results to ElasticSearch.

Setting up LogStash as the logs parser and forwarder

We did *E* from the *ELK* stack. Now let's move to *L. LogStash* requires a configuration file. We'll use one that is already available inside the `vfarcic/cloud-provisioning` (`https://github.com/vfarcic/cloud-provisioning`) repository. We'll create a new directory, copy the `conf/logstash.conf` (`https://github.com/vfarcic/cloud-provisioning/blob/master/conf/logstash.conf`) configuration, and use it inside the `logstash` service:

```
mkdir -p docker/logstash

cp conf/logstash.conf \
    docker/logstash/logstash.conf

cat docker/logstash/logstash.conf
```

The content of the `logstash.conf` file is as follows:

```
input {
  syslog { port => 51415 }
}

output {
  elasticsearch {
    hosts => ["elasticsearch:9200"]
  }
  # Remove in production
  stdout {
    codec => rubydebug
  }
}
```

This is a very simple *LogStash* configuration. If will listen on port `51415` for `syslog` entries.

Each entry will be sent to two outputs; `elasticsearch` and `stdout`. Since both `logstash` and `elasticsearch` will be attached to the same network, all we had to do is put the service name as the host.

The second output will send everything to `stdout`. Please note that this entry should be removed before running *LogStash* in production. It creates an unnecessary overhead that, if there are many services, can be substantial. The only reason we have it is to show you how logs are passing through LogStash. In production, you'll have no need to look at its output. Instead, you'll use Kibana to explore the logs from the whole system.

Let's move on and create the second service:

A note to Windows users

For mounts used in the next command to work, you have to stop Git Bash from altering file system paths. Set this environment variable:
`export MSYS_NO_PATHCONV=1`

```
docker service create --name logstash \
    --mount "type=bind,source=$PWD/docker/logstash,target=/conf" \
    --network elk \
    -e LOGSPOUT=ignore \
    --reserve-memory 100m \
    logstash:2.4 logstash -f /conf/logstash.conf
```

We created a service called `logstash` and mounted the host volume `docker/logstash` as `/conf` inside the container. That way we'll have the configuration file currently residing on the host available inside the container.

Please note that mounting a volume is not the best way to put the configuration inside the container. Instead, we should have built our own image with the configuration inside. We should have created a Dockerfile. It could be as follows:

```
FROM logstash

RUN mkdir /config/
COPY conf/logstash.conf /config/

CMD ["-f", "/config/logstash.conf"]
```

This configuration file should not change often (if ever), so the option of creating a new image based on `logstash` is much better than mounting a volume. However, for simplicity reasons, we used the mount. Just remember to build your own image once you start applying what you learned from this chapter.

We also defined the environment variable `LOGSPOUT`. It is not relevant right now. We'll comment on it later on.

The `logStash` service should be up and running by now. Let's double check it:

```
docker service ps logstash
```

The output should be as follows:

```
NAME        IMAGE         NODE     DESIRED STATE CURRENT STATE
logstash.1 logstash:2.4 swarm-1 Running         Running 2 seconds ago
```

If the current state is still not running, please wait a few moments and repeat the `service ps` command. We can proceed only after `logstash` is operational.

Now we can confirm that `logstash` was initialized correctly. We'll need to find out which node it is running in, get the `ID` of the container, and output the logs:

```
LOGSTASH_NODE=$(docker service ps logstash | tail -n +2 | awk '{print $4}')

eval $(docker-machine env $LOGSTASH_NODE)

LOGSTASH_ID=$(docker ps -q \
    --filter label=com.docker.swarm.service.name=logstash)

docker logs $LOGSTASH_ID
```

The output of the previous command `logs` is as follows:

```
{:timestamp=>"2016-10-19T23:08:06.358000+0000", :message=>"Pipeline \
main started"}
```

`Pipeline main started` means that LogStash is running and waiting for input.

Before we set up a solution that will ship logs from all the containers inside the cluster, we'll make an intermediary step and confirm that LogStash can indeed accept `syslog` entries on port `51415`. We'll create a temporary service called `logger-test`:

```
eval $(docker-machine env swarm-1)

docker service create \
    --name logger-test \
    --network elk \
    --restart-condition none \
    debian \
    logger -n logstash -P 51415 hello world
```

The service is attached to the `elk` network so that it can communicate with the `logstash` service.

We had to specify `restart-condition` as `none`. Otherwise, when the process is finished, the container would stop, Swarm would detect it as a failure and reschedule it. In other words, without the restart condition set to none, Swarm would enter into an endless loop trying to reschedule containers that almost immediately stop.

The command we're executing sends a `syslog` message `logger`, to `logstash` running on port `51415`. The message is `hello world`.

```
eval $(docker-machine env $LOGSTASH_NODE)

docker logs $LOGSTASH_ID
```

The output is as follows:

```
{
    "message" => "<5>Oct 19 23:11:47 <someone>: hello world\u0000",
    "@version" => "1",
    "@timestamp" => "2016-10-19T23:11:47.882Z",
        "host" => "10.0.0.7",
        "tags" => [
        [0] "_grokparsefailure_sysloginput"
        ],
            "priority" => 0,
            "severity" => 0,
            "facility" => 0,
    "facility_label" => "kernel",
    "severity_label" => "Emergency"
}
```

First Swarm had to download the debian image and, once the logger message was sent, LogStash had to start accepting entries. It takes a bit of time until LogStash processes the first entry. All subsequent entries will be processed almost instantly. If your output is not similar to the one above, please wait a moment and repeat the logs command.

As you can see, LogStash received the message hello world. It also recorded a few other fields like the timestamp and host. Ignore the error message _grokparsefailure_sysloginput. We could configure LogStash to parse logger messages correctly but, since we won't be using it anymore, it would be a waste of time. Soon we'll see a much better way to forward logs.

LogStash acted as a parser of the message and forwarded it to ElasticSearch. At the moment, you'll have to take my word for it. Soon we'll see how are those messages stored and how we can explore them.

We'll remove the logger-test service. Its purpose was only to demonstrate that we have a LogStash instance that accepts syslog messages:

```
eval $(docker-machine env swarm-1)

docker service rm logger-test
```

Sending messages by invoking logger is great but is not what we're trying to accomplish.

The goal is to forward the logs from all the containers running anywhere inside the cluster.

Forwarding logs from all containers running anywhere inside a Swarm cluster

How can we forward logs from all the containers no matter where they're running? One possible solution would be to *configure logging drivers* (https://docs.docker.com/engine /admin/logging/overview/). We could use the --log-driver argument to specify a driver for each service. The driver could be syslog or any other supported option. That would solve our log shipping problem. However, using the argument for each service is tedious and, more importantly, we could easily forget to specify it for a service or two and discover the omission only after we encounter a problem and are in need of logs. Let's see if there is another option to accomplish the same result.

We could specify a log driver as a configuration option of the Docker daemon on each node. That would certainly make the setup easier. After all, there are probably fewer servers than services. If we were to choose between setting a driver when creating a service or as the daemon configuration, I'd choose the latter. However, we managed to get thus far without changing the default daemon configuration and I'd prefer if we can continue working without involving any special provisioning tools. Luckily, we still did not exhaust all our options.

We can ship logs from all our containers with the project called logspout (https://github .com/gliderlabs/logspout)

LogSpout is a log router for Docker containers that runs inside Docker. It attaches to all containers on a host, then routes their logs wherever we want. It also has an extensible module system. It's a mostly stateless log appliance. It's not meant for managing log files or looking at history. It is just a tool to get your logs out to live somewhere else, where they belong.

If you go through the project documentation, you'll notice that there are no instructions on how to run it as a Docker service. That should not matter since, by this time, you can consider yourself an expert in creating services.

What do we need from a service that should forward logs from all the containers running inside all the nodes that form a cluster? Since we want to forward them to LogStash that is already attached to the `elk` network, we should attach LogSpout to it as well. We need it to ship logs from all the nodes so the service should be global. It needs to know that the destination is the service called `logstash` and that it listens on port `51415`. Finally, one of the requirement for LogSpout is that the Docker socket from the host is mounted inside the service containers. That's what it'll use to monitor the logs.

The command that creates the service that fulfills all those objectives and requirements is as follows:

A note to Windows users
For mounts used in the next command to work, you have to stop Git Bash from altering file system paths. Set this environment variable:
`export MSYS_NO_PATHCONV=1`

```
docker service create --name logspout \
    --network elk \
    --mode global \
    --mount \
"type=bind,source=/var/run/docker.sock,target=/var/run/\
    docker.sock" \
    -e SYSLOG_FORMAT=rfc3164 \
    gliderlabs/logspout syslog://logstash:51415
```

We created a service called `logspout`, attached it to the `elk` network, set it to be global, and mounted the Docker socket. The command that will be executed once containers are created is `syslog://logstash:51415`. This tells LogSpout that we want to use `syslog` protocol to send logs to `logstash` running on port `51415`.

This project is an example of the usefulness behind the Docker Remote API. The `logspout` containers will use it to retrieve the list of all currently running containers and stream their logs. This is already the second product inside our cluster that uses the API (the first being *Docker Flow Swarm Listener* (`https://github.com/vfarcic/docker-flow-swarm-listener`)).

Let's see the status of the service we just created:

```
docker service ps logspout
```

The output is as follows (IDs & ERROR PORTS column are removed for brevity):

```
NAME          IMAGE                          NODE     DESIRED STATE
logspout...   gliderlabs/logspout:latest     swarm-3 Running
logspout...   gliderlabs/logspout:latest     swarm-2 Running
logspout...   gliderlabs/logspout:latest     swarm-1 Running
------------------------------------------------------------
CURRENT STATE
Running 11 seconds ago
Running 10 seconds ago
Running 10 seconds ago
```

The service is running in global mode resulting in an instance inside each node. Let's test whether the `logspout` service is indeed sending all the logs to LogStash. All we have to do is create a service that generates some logs and observe them from the output of LogStash . We'll use the registry to test the setup we have made so far:

```
docker service create --name registry \
    -p 5000:5000 \
    --reserve-memory 100m \
    registry
```

Before we check the LogStash logs, we should wait until the registry is running:

```
docker service ps registry
```

If the current state is still not running, please wait a few moments.

Now we can take a look at `logstash` logs and confirm that `logspout` sent it log entries generated by the `registry`:

```
eval $(docker-machine env $LOGSTASH_NODE)

docker logs $LOGSTASH_ID
```

One of the entries from the output is as follows:

```
{
    "message" => "time=\"2016-10-19T23:14:19Z\" level=info \
msg=\"listening on [::]:5000\" go.version=go1.6.3 \
instance.id=87c31e30-a747-4f70-b7c2-396dd80eb47b version=v2.5.1 \n",
          "@version" => "1",
      "@timestamp" => "2016-10-19T23:14:19.000Z",
           "host" => "10.0.0.7",
           "priority" => 14,
     "timestamp8601" => "2016-10-19T23:14:19Z",
        "logsource" => "c51c177bd308",
            "program" => "registry.1.abszmuwq8k3d7comu5041z2mc",
```

```
            "pid" => "4833",
       "severity" => 6,
       "facility" => 1,
      "timestamp" => "2016-10-19T23:14:19Z",
  "facility_label" => "user-level",
  "severity_label" => "Informational"
}
```

As before when we tested LogStash input with logger, we have the message, `timestamp`, `host`, and a few other `syslog` fields. We also got `logsource` that holds the `ID` of the container that produced the log as well as program that holds the container name. Both will be useful when debugging which service and container produced a bug.

If you go back to the command we used to create the `logstash` service, you'll notice the environment variable `LOGSPOUT=ignore`. It tells LogSpout that the service or, to be more precise, all containers that form the service, should be ignored. If we did not define it, LogSpout would forward all `logstash` logs to `logstash` thus creating an infinite loop. As we already discussed, in production we should not output LogStash entries to `stdout`. We did it only to get a better understanding of how it works. If `stdout` output is removed from the logstash configuration, there would be no need for the environment variable `LOGSPOUT=ignore`. As a result `logstash` logs would also be stored in ElasticSearch.

Now that we are shipping all the logs to LogStash and from there to ElasticSearch, we should explore the ways to consult them.

Exploring logs

Having all the logs in a central database is a good start, but it does not allow us to explore them in an easy and user-friendly way. We cannot expect developers to start issuing requests to the ElasticSearch API whenever they want to explore what went wrong. We need a UI that allows us to visualize and filter logs. We need *K* from the *ELK* stack.

A note to Windows users
You might experience a problem with volumes not being mapped correctly with Docker Compose. If you may see an *Invalid volume specification* error, please export the environment variable `COMPOSE_CONVERT_WINDOWS_PATHS` set to 0:
`export COMPOSE_CONVERT_WINDOWS_PATHS=0`
Please make sure that the variable is exported every time you run `docker-compose` or `docker stack deploy`.

Let's create one more service. This time, it'll be Kibana. Besides the need for this service to communicate with `logspout` and `elasticsearch` services, we want to expose it through the proxy, so we'll create swarm-listener and `proxy` services as well. Let's get to it:

```
docker network create --driver overlay proxy

curl -o docker-compose-stack.yml \
    https://raw.githubusercontent.com/\
vfarcic/docker-flow-proxy/master/docker-compose-stack.yml

docker stack deploy \
    -c docker-compose-stack.yml proxy
```

We created the `proxy` network, downloaded Compose file with the service definitions, and deployed the proxy stack which consists of `swarm-listener` and `proxy` services. They are the same commands as those we executed in the Chapter 8, *Using Docker Stack and Compose YAML Files to Deploy Swarm Services*, so there's no need to explain them again.

The only thing missing before we create the `kibana` service is to wait until both swarm-listener and proxy are up and running.

Please execute `docker service ls` command to confirm that both services have their replicas running.

Now we're ready to create the `kibana` service:

A note to Windows users

For mounts used in the next command to work, you have to stop Git Bash from altering file system paths. Set this environment variable:
`export MSYS_NO_PATHCONV=1`

```
docker service create --name kibana \
    --network elk \
    --network proxy \
-e ELASTICSEARCH_URL=http://elasticsearch:9200 \
    --reserve-memory 50m \
    --label com.df.notify=true \
    --label com.df.distribute=true \
    --label com.df.servicePath=/app/kibana,/bundles,/elasticsearch \
    --label com.df.port=5601 \
    kibana:4.6
```

We attached it to both the elk and `proxy` networks. The first is needed so that it can communicate with the `elasticsearch` service, while the second is required for communication with the proxy. We also set up the `ELASTICSEARCH_URL` environment variable that tells Kibana the address of the database, and reserved `50m` of memory. Finally, we defined a few labels that will be used by the `swarm-listener` to notify the proxy about the services existence. This time, the `com.df.servicePath` label has three paths that match those used by Kibana.

Le's confirm that `kibana` is running before opening its UI:

```
docker service ps kibana
```

The UI can be opened through the command that follows:

```
open "http://$(docker-machine ip swarm-1)/app/kibana"
```

A note to Windows users
Git Bash might not be able to use the open command. If that's the case, execute `docker-machine ip <SERVER_NAME>` to find out the IP of the machine and open the URL directly in your browser of choice. For example, the command above should be replaced with the command that follows:
`docker-machine ip swarm-1`
If the output would be `1.2.3.4`, you should open `http://1.2.3.4:8082/jenkins` in your browser.

You should see the screen that lets you configure ElasticSearch indexes.

Now we can explore the logs by clicking the **Discover** button from the top menu.

Kibana, by default, displays the logs generated during the last fifteen minutes. Depending on the time that passed since we produced the logs, fifteen minutes might be less than the actual time that passed. We'll increase the duration to twenty-four hours.

Please select @timestamp **as Time-field name** and click the **Create** button to generate LogStash indexes in ElasticSearch:

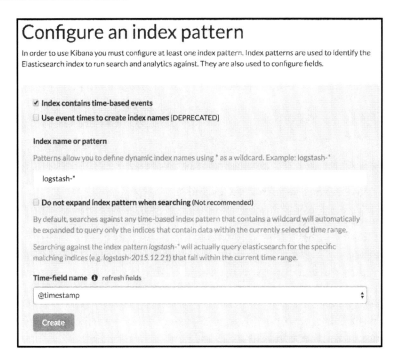

Figure 8-1: Configure an index pattern Kibana screen

Please click the **Last 15 minutes** from the top-right menu. You'll see a plethora of options we can use to filter the results based on time.

Please click the **Last 24 hours** link and observe that the time from the top-right menu changed accordingly. Now click the **Last 24 hours** button to hide the filters.

More information can be found in the *Setting the Time Filter* (`https://www.elastic.co/gui
de/en/kibana/current/discover.html#set-time-filter`) section of the documentation
for Kibana :

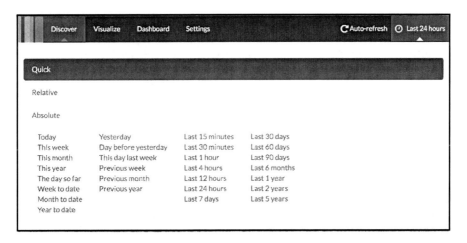

Figure 8-2: Time filters in Kibanas Discover screen

At the moment, the central part of the screen displays all the logs that match the given
`time-span`. Most of the time, on a "real" production system, we would not be interested in
all the logs produced inside the cluster. Instead, we'd filter them based on some criteria.

Let's say we want to see all the logs generated by the `proxy` service. We often don't need to
know the exact name of the program that generated them. This is true because Swarm adds
an instance number and a hashtag into container names, and we are often unsure what the
exact name is, or which instance produced a problem. Instead, we'll filter the logs to display
all those that have a program containing the word `proxy`.

Please type `program: "proxy_proxy"` in the Search field located in the upper part of the
screen and press enter. The result will be that only logs that contain `proxy_proxy` in the
program name field are displayed in the main part of the screen. Similarly, we can change
the search to the previous state and list all the logs that match the given time frame. All we
have to do is type `*` in the Search field and press Enter.

More information can be found in the *Searching Your Data* (`https://www.elastic.co/guide/en/kibana/current/discover.html#search`) section of documentation for Kibanas .

The list of all fields that match the current query is located in the left-hand menu. We can see the top values of one of those fields by clicking on it. For example, we can click on the *program* field and see all the programs that produced logs during the specified time. We can use those values as another way to filter the results. Please click the + sign next to `proxy.1.4psvagyv4bky2lftjg4a` (in your case the hash will be different). We just accomplished the same result as if we typed `program:` `"proxy.1.4psvagyv4bky2lftjg4a:` in the **Search** field.

More information can be found in the *Filtering by Field* (`https://www.elastic.co/guide/en/kibana/current/discover.html#field-filter`) section of documentation for Kibana .

The main body of the screen displays the selected fields in each row, with the option to drill down and show all the information. The truth is that the default fields (**Time** and **_source**) are not very helpful so we'll change them.

Please click the **Add** button next to **program** in the left-hand menu. You'll see that the **program** column was added to the **Time** column. Let's add a few more. Please repeat the process with the **host**, and **@timestamp** fields as well.

To see more information about a particular entry, please click the arrow pointing to the right. A table with all the fields will appear below it, and you will be able to explore all the details related to the particular logs entry.

More information can be found in the *Filtering by Field* (`https://www.elastic.co/guide/en/kibana/current/discover.html#document-data`) section of documentation for Kibana .

The only thing left in this short tour around Kibana is to save the filter we just created. Please click the **Save Search** button in the top menu to save what we created by now. Type a name for your search and click the **Save** button. Your filters are now saved and can be accessed through the **Load Saved Search** button located in the top menu:

Figure 8-3: Discover screen in Kibana

That's it. Now you know the basics how to explore your logs stored in ElasticSearch. If you're wondering what can be done with **Visualize** and **Dashboard** screens, I'll only state that they are not very useful for logs. They become much more interesting, however, if we start adding other types of information like resource usage (example: memory, CPU, network traffic, and so on).

Discussing other logging solutions

Is ELK the solution you should choose for your logging purposes? That a hard question to answer. There are a plethora of similar tools in the market, and it would be close to impossible to give a universal answer.

Do you prefer a free solution? If you do, then ELK (*ElasticSearch* (`https://www.elastic.co/products/elasticsearch`), *LogStash* (`https://www.elastic.co/products/logstash`), and *Kibana* (`https://www.elastic.co/products/kibana`)) is an excellent choice. If you're looking for an equally cheap (free) alternative, *FluentD* (`http://www.fluentd.org/`) is something worth trying out. Many other solutions might fit your needs. A simple Google search will reveal a plethora of options.

Are you more interested in a solution provided as a service? Would you like someone else taking care of your logging infrastructure? If you do, many services offer, for a fee, to host your logs in their database and provide nice interfaces you can use to explore them. I won't list examples since I decided to base this book fully on open source solutions you can run yourself. Again, Google is your friend if you'd prefer a service maintained by someone else.

What now?

We touched only the surface of what the ELK stack can do. ElasticSearch is a very powerful database that can be scaled easily and store vast amounts of data. LogStash provides almost unlimited possibilities that allow us to use virtually any data source as input (in our case `syslog`), transform it into any form we find useful, and output to many different destinations (in our case ElasticSearch). When a need occurs, you can use Kibana to go through the logs generated by your system. Finally, the tool that made all that happen is LogSpout. It ensured that all the logs produced by any of the containers running inside our cluster are collected and shipped to LogStash.

This goal of the chapter was to explore a potential solution to deal with massive quantities of logs and give you a base understanding how to collect them from services running inside a Swarm cluster. Do you know everything you should know about logging? You probably don't. However, I hope you have a good base to explore the subject in more details.

Even if you choose to use a different set of tools, the process will still be the same. Use a tool to collect logs from your services, ship them to some database, use a UI to explore them when needed.

Now we have logs that provide only part of the information we'll need to find a cause of an issue. Logs by themselves are often not enough. We need metrics from the system. Maybe our services use more memory than our cluster provides. Maybe the system takes too much time to respond. Or maybe we have a memory leak in one of our services. Those things would be very hard to find out through logs.

We need to know not only current metrics of the system but also how it behaved in the past. Even if we do have those metrics, we need a process that will notify us of problems. Looking at logs and metrics provides a lot of information we can use to debug issues, but we wouldn't know that a problem exists in the first place. We need a process that will notify us when something goes wrong or, even better, before the actual problem happens. Even with such a system in place, we should go even further and try to prevent problems from happening. Such prevention can often be automated. After all, why should we fix all the problems manually when some of them can be fixed automatically by the system itself? The ultimate goal is to make a self-healing system and involve humans only when unexpected things happen.

Metrics, notifications, self-healing systems, and other pending tasks in front of us are too much for a single chapter so we'll do one step at a time. For now, we're finished with logs and will jump into a discussion about different ways to collect metrics and use them to monitor our cluster and services running inside it.

As always, we'll end with a destructive note:

```
docker-machine rm -f swarm-1 swarm-2 swarm-3
```

10
Collecting Metrics and Monitoring the Cluster

Let us change our traditional attitude to the construction of programs. Instead of imagining that our main task is to instruct a computer what to do, let us concentrate rather on explaining to human beings what we want a computer to do.

–Donald Knuth

We managed to add centralized logging to our cluster. Logs from any container running inside any of the nodes are shipped to a central location. They are stored in Elasticsearch and available through Kibana. However, the fact that we have easy access to all the logs does not mean that we have all the information we would need to debug a problem or prevent it from happening in the first place. We need to complement our logs with the rest of the information about the system. We need much more than what logs alone can provide.

The requirements of a cluster monitoring system

With everything we've done until now, not to mention the tasks we'll do throughout the rest of the book, we are simultaneously decreasing and increasing the complexity of our system. Scaling a service is easier and less complex with Docker Swarm than it would be with containers alone. The fact is that Docker already simplified a lot the process we had before. Add to that the new networking with service discovery baked in, and the result is almost too simple to be true. On the other hand, there is complexity hidden below the surface. One of the ways such complexity manifests itself can be easily observed if we try to combine dynamic tools we have used so far, with those created in (and for) a different era.

Take *Nagios* (`https://www.nagios.org/`) as an example. I won't say that we could not use it to monitor our system (we certainly can). What I will state is that it would clash with the new system architecture we've designed so far. Our system has gotten much more complex than it was. The number of replicas is fluctuating. While today we have four instances of a service, tomorrow morning there could be six, only to fall to three in the afternoon. They are distributed across multiple nodes of the cluster, and being moved around. Servers are being created and destroyed. Our cluster and everything inside it is truly dynamic and elastic.

The dynamic nature of the system we are building would not fit into Nagios, which expects services and servers to be relatively static. It expects us to define things in advance. The problem with such an approach is that we do not have the information in advance. Swarm does. Even if we get the information we need, it will change soon.

The system we're building is highly dynamic, and the tools we should use to monitor such a system need to be able to cope with this dynamism.

It's more than that. Most of the "traditional" tools tend to treat the whole system as a black box. That, on the one hand, has a certain number of advantages. The main one is that it allows us to decouple our services from the rest of the system. In many (but not all) cases, white box monitoring means that we need to add to our services monitoring libraries and write some code around them so that they can expose the internals of our services.

Think twice before choosing to add something to your service that is not strictly its job. When we adopt a microservices approach, we should strive towards services being functionally limited to their primary goal. If it's a shopping cart, it should be an API that will allow us to add and remove items. Adding libraries and code that will extend such a service so that it can register itself in a service discovery store, or expose its metrics to the monitoring tool, produces too much coupling. Once we do that, our future options will be very limited, and making a change in the system might require considerable time and effort.

We already managed to avoid coupling service discovery with our services. The `go-demo` service does not have any knowledge of service discovery and yet, our system has all the information it needs. There are many other examples where organizations fall into a trap and start coupling their services with the system around them. In this case, our main preoccupation is whether we can accomplish the same with monitoring. Can we avoid coupling creation of metrics with the code we write for our services?

Then again, being able to do white box monitoring provides a lot of benefits black box does not have. For one, understanding the internals of a service allows us to operate with a much finer level of detail. It gives us knowledge that we could not obtain if we were to treat the system as a black box.

In a world of distributed systems designed for high availability and fast response time, it is not enough to be limited to health checks and CPU, memory, and disk usage monitoring. We already have Swarm that makes sure the services are healthy and we could easily make scripts that check essential resource usage. We need much more than that. We need white box monitoring that does not introduce unnecessary coupling. We need intelligent alerting that will notify us when something is wrong, or even automatically fix the problem. Ideally, we would have alerts and automated corrections executed before the problems even happen.

Some of the requirements we'd need from a monitoring system would be as follows:

- *A decentralized way of generating metrics* that will be able to cope with the highly dynamic nature of our cluster
- *A multi-dimensional data model* that can be queried across as many dimensions as needed
- *An efficient query language* that will allow us to exploit our monitoring data model and create effective alerting and visualization
- *Simplicity* that will allow (almost) anyone to utilize the system without extensive training

In this chapter, we'll continue the work we started in the previous. We'll explore ways to export a different set of metrics, a way to collect them, query them, and expose them through dashboards.

Before we do all that, we should make some choices. Which tools shall we use for our monitoring solution?

Choosing the right database to store system metrics

In *The DevOps 2.0 Toolkit*, I argued against "traditional" monitoring tools like *Nagios* (`https://www.nagios.org/`) and *Icinga* (`https://www.icinga.org/`). Instead, we chose to use Elasticsearch for both the logs and the system metrics. In the previous chapter, I reiterated the choice for using Elasticsearch as the logging solution. Can we extend its usage by storing metrics? Yes, we can. Should we do that? Should we use it as a place to store system metrics? Are there better solutions?

The biggest problem with Elasticsearch, if used as a database to store system metrics, is that it is not a time series type of database. Logs benefit greatly from Elasticsearch ability to perform free text search and store data in an unstructured way. However, for system metrics, we might take advantage of a different type of data storage. We need a time series database.

Time series databases are designed around optimized ways to store and retrieve time series data. One of their greatest benefits is that they store information in a very compact format allowing them to host a vast amount of data. If you compare storage needs for time-based data in other types of databases (Elasticsearch included), you'll discover that time series databases are much more efficient. In other words, if your data are time-based metrics, use a database designed for such data.

The biggest problem with most (if not all) time series databases is distributed storage. Running them with replication is not possible, or a challenge at best. To put it bluntly, such databases are designed to run a single instance. Luckily we often do not need to store long term data in such databases and can clean them up periodically. If long term storage is a must, the solution would be to export aggregated data into some other type of database like Elasticsearch which, by the way, shines when it comes to replication and sharding. However, before you go "crazy" and start exporting data, make sure that you truly need to do something like that. Time series databases can easily store a vast amount of information in a single instance. The chances are that you won't need to scale them for capacity reasons. On the other hand, if a database fails, Swarm will reschedule it, and you'll lose only a few seconds of information. Such a scenario should not be a disaster since we are dealing with aggregated data, not individual transactions.

One of the most prominent time series databases is *InfluxDB* (`https://www.influxdata.com/`). *Prometheus* (`https://prometheus.io/`) is a commonly used alternative. We'll skip the comparison of these two products except to note that we'll use the latter. Both are worthy candidates for your monitoring solution with Prometheus having a potential advantage we should not ignore. The community plan is to expose Docker metrics natively in Prometheus format. At the time of this writing, there is no fixed date when that'll happen, but we'll do our best to design the system around that plan. If you'd like to monitor the progress yourself, please watch *Docker issue 27307* (`https://github.com/docker/docker/issues/27307`). We'll use Prometheus in such a way that we'll be able to switch to Docker native metrics once they are available.

Let's convert words into actions and create the cluster that we'll use throughout this chapter.

Creating the cluster

This time we'll create more services than before so we'll need a bit bigger cluster. It's not that the services will be very demanding but that our VMs have only one CPU and 1GB memory each. Such machines are not something to brag about. This time, we'll create a cluster that consists of five machines. Apart from increasing the capacity of the cluster, everything else will be the same as before, so there's no good reason to go through the process again. We'll simply execute `scripts/dm-swarm-5.sh` (`https://github.com/vfar cic/cloud-provisioning/blob/master/scripts/dm-swarm-5.sh`):

 All the commands from this chapter are available in the `09-monitoring.sh` (`https://gist.github.com/vfarcic/271fe5ab7eb6a 3307b9f062eadcc3127`) **Gist.**

```
cd cloud-provisioning

git pull

scripts/dm-swarm-5.sh

eval $(docker-machine env swarm-1)

docker node ls
```

The output of the `docker node ls` command is as follows (IDs are removed for brevity):

```
HOSTNAME   STATUS   AVAILABILITY   MANAGER STATUS
swarm-4    Ready    Active
swarm-2    Ready    Active         Reachable
swarm-1    Ready    Active         Leader
swarm-5    Ready    Active
swarm-3    Ready    Active         Reachable
```

We created a Swarm cluster with five nodes, three of them acting as managers and the rest as workers.

Now we can create the services we used before. Since this is also something we practiced quite a few times, we'll create stacks from Compose files `vfarcic/docker-flow-proxy/docker-compose-stack.yml` (https://github.com/vfarcic/docker-flow-proxy/blob/master/docker-compose-stack.yml) and `vfarcic/go-demo/docker-compose-stack.yml` (https://github.com/vfarcic/go-demo/blob/master/docker-compose-stack.yml):

A note to Windows users
You might experience a problem with volumes not being mapped correctly with Docker Compose. If you see an *Invalid volume specification* error, please export the environment variable `COMPOSE_CONVERT_WINDOWS_PATHS` set to 0:
`export COMPOSE_CONVERT_WINDOWS_PATHS=0`
Please make sure that the variable is exported every time you run `docker-compose` or `docker stack deploy`.

```
docker network create --driver overlay proxy

curl -o proxy-stack.yml \
    https://raw.githubusercontent.com/\
vfarcic/docker-flow-proxy/master/docker-compose-stack.yml

docker stack deploy \
    -c proxy-stack.yml proxy

curl -o go-demo-stack.yml \
    https://raw.githubusercontent.com/\
vfarcic/go-demo/master/docker-compose-stack.yml

docker stack deploy \
    -c go-demo-stack.yml go-demo

docker service create --name util \
    --network proxy \
    --mode global \
    alpine sleep 1000000000

docker service ls
```

After a while, the output of the `docker service ls` command is as follows (IDs are removed for brevity):

```
NAME              REPLICAS IMAGE                              COMMAND
swarm-listener    1/1      vfarcic/docker-flow-swarm-listener
go-demo           3/3      vfarcic/go-demo:1.2
util              global   alpine                             sleep 1000000000
go-demo-db        1/1      mongo:3.2.10
proxy             3/3      vfarcic/docker-flow-proxy
```

We used stacks downloaded from GitHub repositories to create all the services except util. Right now, our cluster is hosting the demo services `go-demo` and `go-demo-db`, the `proxy`, the `swarm-listener`, and the globally scheduled util service that we'll use to experiment with monitoring metrics.

We're ready to start generating some metrics.

Prometheus metrics

Prometheus stores all data as time series. It is a stream of timestamped values that belong to the same metric and the same labels. The labels provide multiple dimensions to the metrics.

For example, if we'd like to export data based on HTTP requests from the `proxy`, we might create a metric called `proxy_http_requests_total`. Such a metric could have labels with the `request` method, `status`, and `path`. These three could be specified as follows:

```
{method="GET", url="/demo/person", status="200"}
{method="PUT", url="/demo/person", status="200"}
{method="GET", url="/demo/person", status="403"}
```

Finally, we need a value of the metric, which, in our example, would be the total number of requests.

When we combine metric names with the labels and values, the example result could be as follows:

```
proxy_http_requests_total{method="GET", url="/demo/person", status="200"}
654
proxy_http_requests_total{method="PUT", url="/demo/person", status="200"}
143
proxy_http_requests_total{method="GET", url="/demo/person", status="403"}
13
```

Through these three metrics, we can see that there were 654 successful GET requests, 143 successful PUT requests, and 13 failed GET requests HTTP 403.

Now that the format is more or less clear, we can discuss different ways to generate metrics and feed them to Prometheus.

Prometheus is based on a *pull* mechanism that scrapes metrics from the configured targets. There are two ways we can generate Prometheus-friendly data. One is to instrument our own services. Prometheus offers client libraries for *Go* (https://github.com/prometheus/client_golang), *Python* (https://github.com/prometheus/client_python), *Ruby* (https://github.com/prometheus/client_ruby), and *Java* (https://github.com/prometheus/client_java). On top of those, there are quite a few unofficial libraries available for other languages. Exposing metrics of our services is called instrumentation. Instrumenting your code is, in a way, similar to logging.

Even though instrumentation is the preferred way of providing data that will be stored in Prometheus, I advise against it. That is, unless the same data cannot be obtained by different means. The reasons for such a suggestion lie in my preference for keeping microservices decoupled from the rest of the system. If we managed to keep service discovery outside our services, maybe we can do the same with metrics.

When our service cannot be instrumented or, even better, when we do not want to instrument it, we can utilize Prometheus exporters. Their purpose is to collect already existing metrics and convert them to Prometheus format. As you'll see, our system already exposes quite a lot of metrics. Since it would be unrealistic to expect all our solutions to provide metrics in Prometheus format, we'll use exporters to do the transformation.

When scraping (pulling) data is not enough, we can change direction and push them. Even though scraping is the preferred way for Prometheus to get metrics, there are cases when such an approach is not appropriate. An example would be short-lived batch jobs. They might be so short lived that Prometheus might not be able to pull the data before the job is finished and destroyed. In such cases, the batch job can push data to the *Push Gateway* (https://github.com/prometheus/pushgateway) from which Prometheus can scrape metrics.

For the list of currently supported exporters, please consult the *Exporters and Integrations* (https://prometheus.io/docs/instrumenting/exporters/) section of the Prometheus documentation.

Now, after a short introduction to metrics, we're ready to create services that will host the exporters.

Exporting system wide metrics

We'll start with the *Node Exporter* (`https://github.com/prometheus/node_exporter`) service. It'll export different types of metrics related to our servers:

A note to Windows users

For mounts used in the next command to work, you have to stop Git Bash from altering file system paths. Set this environment variable:
`export MSYS_NO_PATHCONV=1`
This chapter contains many `docker service create` commands that use mounts. Before you execute those commands, please ensure that the environment variable `MSYS_NO_PATHCONV` exists and is set to 1:
`echo $MSYS_NO_PATHCONV`

```
docker service create \
    --name node-exporter \
    --mode global \
    --network proxy \
    --mount "type=bind,source=/proc,target=/host/proc" \
    --mount "type=bind,source=/sys,target=/host/sys" \
    --mount "type=bind,source=/,target=/rootfs" \
    prom/node-exporter:0.12.0 \
    -collector.procfs /host/proc \
    -collector.sysfs /host/proc \
    -collector.filesystem.ignored-mount-points \
    "^/(sys|proc|dev|host|etc)($|/)"
```

Since we need the `node-exporter` to be available on each server, we specified that the service should be global. Normally, we'd attach it to a separate network dedicated to monitoring tools (example:monitoring). However, Docker machines running locally might have problems with more than two networks. Since we already created the `go-demo` and `proxy` networks through `scripts/dm-swarm-services-3.sh` (`https://github.com/vfarcic/cloud-provisioning/blob/master/scripts/dm-swarm-services-3.sh`) we've reached the safe limit. For that reason, we'll use the existing `proxy` network for monitoring services as well. When operating the "real" cluster, you should create a separate network for monitoring services.

We mounted a few volumes as well.

The `/proc` directory is very special in that it is also a virtual filesystem. It's sometimes referred to as a process information pseudo-file system. It doesn't contain "real" files but runtime system information (example: system memory, devices mounted, hardware configuration, and so on).

For this reason, it can be regarded as a control and information center for the kernel. In fact, quite a lot of system utilities are simply calls to files in this directory. For example, `lsmod` is the same as `cat /proc/modules` while `lspci` is a synonym for `cat /proc/pci`. By altering files located in that directory, you can even `read/change` kernel parameters `sysctl` while the system is running. The `node-exporter` service will use it to find all the processes running inside our system.

Modern Linux distributions include a `/sys` directory as a virtual filesystem (`sysfs`, comparable to `/proc`, which is a `procfs`), which stores and allows modification of the devices connected to the system, whereas many traditional UNIX and Unix-like operating systems use `/sys` as a symbolic link to the kernel source tree.

The `sys` directory is a virtual file system provided by Linux. It provides a set of virtual files by exporting information about various kernel subsystems, hardware devices and associated device drivers from the kernel's device model to user space. By exposing it as a volume, the service will be able to gather information about the kernel.

Finally, we defined the image `prom/node-exporter` and passed a few command arguments. We specified the target volumes for `/proc` and `/sys` followed with the instruction to ignore mount points inside the container.

Please visit the *Node Exporter project* (`https://github.com/prometheus/node_exporter`) for more information.

By this time, the service should be running inside the cluster. Let's confirm that:

```
docker service ps node-exporter
```

The output of the `service ps` command is as follows (IDs are removed for brevity):

```
NAME                IMAGE                          NODE     DESIRED STATE
node-exporter...    prom/node-exporter:0.12.0      swarm-5  Running
node-exporter...    prom/node-exporter:0.12.0      swarm-4  Running
node-exporter...    prom/node-exporter:0.12.0      swarm-3  Running
node-exporter...    prom/node-exporter:0.12.0      swarm-2  Running
node-exporter...    prom/node-exporter:0.12.0      swarm-1  Running
-------------------------------------------------------
CURRENT STATE           ERROR PORTS
Running 6 seconds ago
Running 7 seconds ago
Running 7 seconds ago
Running 7 seconds ago
Running 7 seconds ago
```

Let's have a quick look at the metrics provided by the `node-exporter` service. We'll use the `util` service to retrieve the metrics:

```
UTIL_ID=$(docker ps -q --filter \
    label=com.docker.swarm.service.name=util)

docker exec -it $UTIL_ID \
    apk add --update curl drill

docker exec -it $UTIL_ID \
    curl http://node-exporter:9100/metrics
```

A sample of the `curl` output is as follows:

```
# HELP go_gc_duration_seconds A summary of the GC invocation durations.
# TYPE go_gc_duration_seconds summary
go_gc_duration_seconds{quantile="0"} 0
go_gc_duration_seconds{quantile="0.25"} 0
go_gc_duration_seconds{quantile="0.5"} 0
go_gc_duration_seconds{quantile="0.75"} 0
go_gc_duration_seconds{quantile="1"} 0
go_gc_duration_seconds_sum 0
go_gc_duration_seconds_count 0
...
```

As you can see, the metrics are in the Prometheus-friendly format. Please explore the *Node Exporter collectors* (https://github.com/prometheus/node_exporter#collectors) for more information about the meaning of each metric. For now, you should know that most of the node information you would need is available and will be, later on, scraped by Prometheus.

Since we sent a request through Docker networking, we got a load-balanced response and cannot be sure which node produced the output. When we reach the Prometheus configuration, we'll have to be more specific and skip networks load balancing.

Now that we have the information about servers, we should add metrics specific to containers. We'll use `cAdvisor` also known as **container Advisor**.

The `cAdvisor` provides container users an understanding of the resource usage and performance characteristics of their running containers. It is a running daemon that collects, aggregates, processes, and exports information about running containers. Specifically, for each container it keeps resource isolation parameters, historical resource usage, histograms of complete historical resource usage and network statistics. This data is exported container and machine-wide. It has native support for Docker containers.

Let's create the service:

```
docker service create --name cadvisor \
    -p 8080:8080 \
    --mode global \
    --network proxy \
    --mount "type=bind,source=/,target=/rootfs" \
    --mount "type=bind,source=/var/run,target=/var/run" \
    --mount "type=bind,source=/sys,target=/sys" \
    --mount "type=bind,source=/var/lib/docker,target=/var/lib/docker" \
    google/cadvisor:v0.24.1
```

Just as with the `node-exporter`, the `cadvisor` service is global and attached to the `proxy` network. It mounts a few directories that allows it to monitor Docker stats and events on the host. Since `cAdvisor` comes with a web UI, we opened port `8080` that will allow us to open it in a browser.

Before we proceed, we should confirm that the service is indeed running:

```
docker service ps cadvisor
```

The output of the `service ps` is as follows (IDs are removed for brevity):

```
NAME        IMAGE                       NODE      DESIRED STATE
cadvisor... google/cadvisor:v0.24.1     swarm-3   Running
cadvisor... google/cadvisor:v0.24.1     swarm-2   Running
cadvisor... google/cadvisor:v0.24.1     swarm-1   Running
cadvisor... google/cadvisor:v0.24.1     swarm-5   Running
cadvisor... google/cadvisor:v0.24.1     swarm-4   Running
-----------------------------------------------------------
CURRENT STATE            ERROR PORTS
Running 3 seconds ago
Running 3 seconds ago
Running 3 seconds ago
Running 8 seconds ago
Running 3 seconds ago
```

Now we can open the UI:

A note to Windows users

Git Bash might not be able to use the open command. If that's the case, execute `docker-machine ip <SERVER_NAME>` to find out the IP of the machine and open the URL directly in your browser of choice. For example, the command below should be replaced with the command that follows:

`docker-machine ip swarm-1`

If the output would be `1.2.3.4`, you should open `http://1.2.3.4:8080` in your browser.

```
open "http://$(docker-machine ip swarm-1):8080"
```

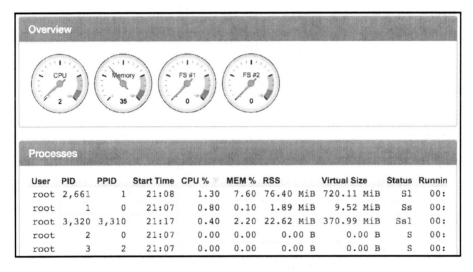

Figure 9-1: cAdvisor UI

Feel free to scroll down and explore different graphs and metrics provided by `cAdvisor`. If they are not enough, information about running containers can be obtained by clicking the Docker Containers link at the top of the screen.

Even though it might seem impressive on the first look, the UI is, more or less, useless for anything but a single server. Since it is designed as a tool to monitor a single node, it does not have much usage inside a Swarm cluster.

For one, the page and all the requests it makes are load-balanced by the ingress network. That means not only that we do not know which server returned the UI, but requests that return data used by metrics and graphs are load balanced as well. In other words, different data from all the servers is mixed, giving us a very inaccurate picture. We could skip using the service and run the image with `docker run` command (repeated for each server). However, even though that would allow us to see a particular server, the solution would still be insufficient since we would be forced to go from one server to another. Our goal is different. We need to gather and visualize data from the whole cluster, not individual servers. Therefore, the UI must go.

As a side note, certain types of metrics overlap between the `node-exporter` and `cadvisor` services. You might be tempted to choose only one of those. However, their focus is different, and the full picture can be accomplished only with the combination of the two. Since we established that the UI is useless when hosted inside a Swarm cluster, there is no good reason to expose port `8080`. Therefore, we should remove it from the service. You might be tempted to remove the service and create it again without exposing the port. There is no need for such an action. Instead, we can eliminate the port by updating the service:

```
docker service update \
    --publish-rm 8080 cadvisor

docker service inspect cadvisor --pretty
```

By examining the output of the `service inspect` command, you'll notice that the port is not opened (it does not exist).

Now that the `cadvisor` service is running, and we do not generate noise from the useless UI, we can take a quick look at the metrics `cAdvisor` exports:

```
docker exec -it $UTIL_ID \
    curl http://cadvisor:8080/metrics
```

A sample of the `curl` output is as follows:

```
# TYPE container_cpu_system_seconds_total counter
container_cpu_system_seconds_total{id="/"} 22.91
container_cpu_system_seconds_total{id="/docker"} 0.32
```

We're making excellent progress. We are exporting server and container metrics. We might continue adding metrics indefinitely and extend this chapter to an unbearable size. I'll leave the creation of services that will provide additional info as an exercise you should perform later on. Right now we'll move onto Prometheus. After all, having metrics is not of much use without being able to query and visualize them.

Scraping, querying, and visualizing Prometheus metrics

Prometheus server is designed to pull the metrics from instrumented services. However, since we wanted to avoid unnecessary coupling, we used exporters that provide the metrics we need. Those exporters are already running as Swarm services, and now we are ready to exploit them through Prometheus.

To instantiate the Prometheus service, we should create a configuration file with the exporters running in our cluster. Before we do that, we need to retrieve the IPs of all the instances of an exporter service. If you recall the `Chapter 4`, *Service Discovery inside a Swarm Cluster*, we can retrieve all the IPs by appending the tasks. prefix to the service name.

To retrieve the list of all the replicas of the `node-exporter` service, we could, for example, drill it from one of the instances of the `util` service:

```
docker exec -it $UTIL_ID \
    drill tasks.node-exporter
```

The relevant part of the output is as follows:

```
;; ANSWER SECTION:
tasks.node-exporter.    600 IN  A   10.0.0.21
tasks.node-exporter.    600 IN  A   10.0.0.23
tasks.node-exporter.    600 IN  A   10.0.0.22
tasks.node-exporter.    600 IN  A   10.0.0.19
tasks.node-exporter.    600 IN  A   10.0.0.20
```

We retrieved the IPs of all currently running replicas of the service.

The list of the IPs themselves is not enough. We need to tell Prometheus that it should use them in a dynamic fashion. It should consult tasks.<SERVICE_NAME> every time it wants to pull new data. Fortunately, Prometheus can be configured through `dns_sd_configs` to use an address as service discovery. For more information about the available options, please consult the *Configuration* (`https://prometheus.io/docs/operating/configuration/`) section of the documentation.

Equipped with the knowledge of the existence of the `dns_sd_configs` option, we can move forward and define a Prometheus configuration. We'll use the one I prepared for this chapter. It is located in `conf/prometheus.yml` (`https://github.com/vfarcic/cloud-pr ovisioning/blob/master/conf/prometheus.yml`)

Let us quickly go through it:

```
cat conf/prometheus.yml
```

The output is as follows:

```
global:
  scrape_interval: 5s

scrape_configs:
  - job_name: 'node'
    dns_sd_configs:
      - names: ['tasks.node-exporter']
        type: A
        port: 9100
  - job_name: 'cadvisor'
    dns_sd_configs:
      - names: ['tasks.cadvisor']
        type: A
        port: 8080
  - job_name: 'prometheus'
    static_configs:
      - targets: ['prometheus:9090']
```

We defined three jobs. The first two `node` and `cadvisor` are using the `dns_sd_configs` (DNS service discovery configs) option. Both have the tasks.<SERVICE_NAME> defined as the name, are of type A (you'll notice the type from the `drill` output), and have the internal ports defined. The last one `prometheus` will provide the internal metrics.

Please note that we set `scrape_interval` to five seconds. In production, you might want more granular data and change it to, for example, one-second interval. Beware! The shorter the interval, the higher the cost. The more often we scrape metrics, the more resources will be required to do that, as well as to query those results, and even store the data. Try to find a balance between data granularity and resource usage. Creating the Prometheus service is easy (as is almost any other Swarm service).

We'll start by creating a directory where we'll persist Prometheus data:

```
mkdir -p docker/prometheus
```

Now we can create the service:

```
docker service create \
    --name prometheus \
    --network proxy \
    -p 9090:9090 \
    --mount "type=bind,source=$PWD/conf/prometheus.yml, \
```

```
        target=/etc/prometheus/prometheus.yml"
        --mount "type=bind,source=$PWD/docker/\
        prometheus,target=/prometheus"
        prom/prometheus:v1.2.1
    docker service ps prometheus
```

We created the `docker/prometheus` directory where we'll persist Prometheus state.

The service is quite ordinary. It is attached to the `proxy` network, exposes the port `9090`, and mounts the configuration file and the state directory.

The output of the `service ps` command is as follows (IDs and ERROR columns are removed for brevity):

```
NAME            IMAGE                       NODE      DESIRED STATE
prometheus.1    prom/prometheus:v1.2.1      swarm-3   Running
----------------------------------------------
CURRENT STATE
Running 59 seconds ago
```

Please note that it would be pointless to scale this service. Prometheus is designed to work as a single instance. In most cases, that's not a problem since it can easily store and process a vast amount of data. If it fails, Swarm will reschedule it somewhere else and, in that case, we would lose only a few seconds of data.

Let's open its UI and explore what can be done with it:

A note to Windows users
Git Bash might not be able to use the open command. If that's the case, execute `docker-machine ip <SERVER_NAME>` to find out the IP of the machine and open the URL directly in your browser of choice. For example, the command below should be replaced with the command that follows:
`docker-machine ip swarm-1`
If the output would be `1.2.3.4`, you should open `http://1.2.3.4:9090` in your browser.

```
open "http://$(docker-machine ip swarm-1):9090"
```

The first thing we should do is check whether it registered all the exported targets.

Please click the **Status** button in the top menu and select **Targets**. You should see that five **cadvisor** targets match the five servers that form the cluster. Similarly, there are five **node** targets. Finally, one **prometheus** target is registered as well:

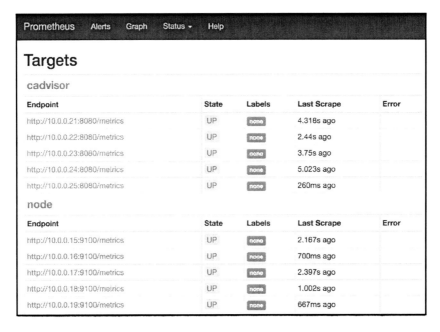

Figure 9-2: Targets registered in Prometheus

Now that we confirmed that all the targets are indeed registered and that Prometheus started scraping metrics they provide, we can explore ways to retrieve data and visualize them through `ad-hoc` queries.

Please click the *Graph* button from the top menu, select `node_memory_MemAvailable` from the `- insert metric at cursor -` list, and click the **Execute** button.

You should see a table with the list of metrics and a value associated with each. Many prefer a visual representation of the data which can be obtained by clicking the **Graph** tab located above the list. Please click it.

You should see the available memory for each of the five servers. It is displayed as evolution over the specified period which can be adjusted with the fields and buttons located above the graph. Not much time passed since we created the `prometheus` service so you should probably reduce the period to five or fifteen minutes.

The same result can be accomplished by typing the query (or in this case the name of the metric) in the **Expression** field. Later on, we'll do a bit more complicated queries that cannot be defined by selecting a single metric from the `-insert metric at cursor` - list:

Figure 9-3: Prometheus graph with available memory

Now might be a good time to discuss one of the main shortcomings of the system we set up so far. We do not have the information that would allow us to relate data with a particular server easily. Since the list of addresses is retrieved through Docker networking which creates a virtual IP for each replica, the addresses are not those of the servers. There is no easy way around this (as far as I know) so we are left with two options. One would be to run the exporters as "normal" containers (example: `docker run`) instead of as services. The advantage of such an approach is that we could set network type as `host` and get the IP of the server. The problem with such an approach is that we'd need to run exporters separately for each server.

That wouldn't be so bad except for the fact that each time we add a new server to the cluster, we'd need to run all the exporters again. To make things more complicated, it would also mean that we'd need to change the Prometheus configuration as well, or add a separate service registry only for that purpose.

The alternative is to wait. The inability to retrieve a host IP from a service replica is a known limitation. It is recorded in several places, one of them being *issue 25526* (`https://github.com/docker/docker/issues/25526`). At the same time, the community has already decided to expose Prometheus metrics natively from Docker Engine. That would remove the need for some, if not all, of the exporters we created as services. I'm confident that one of those two will happen soon. Until then, you'll have to make a decision to ignore the fact that IPs are virtual or replace services with containers run separately on each server in the cluster. No matter the choice you make, I'll show you, later on, how to find the relation between virtual IPs and hosts.

Let's go back to querying Prometheus metrics.

The example with `node_memory_MemAvailable` used only the metric and, as a result, we got all its time series.

Let's spice it up a bit and create a graph that will return idle CPU. The query would be `node_cpu{mode="idle"}`. Using `mode="idle"` will limit the `node_cpu` metric only to data labeled as idle. Try it out and you'll discover that the graph should consist of five almost straight lines going upwards. That does not look correct.

Let's create a bit more accurate picture by introducing the `irate` function. It calculates the per-second instant rate of increase of the time series. That is based on the last two data points. To use the `irate` function, we also need to specify the measurement duration. The modified query is as follows:

```
irate(node_cpu{mode="idle"}[5m])
```

Since we are scraping metrics from the `cadvisor` service, we can query different container metrics as well. For example, we can see the memory usage of each container.

Please execute the query that follows:

```
container_memory_usage_bytes
```

Please execute the query and see the result for yourself. You should see the idle CPU rate per node measured over 5 minute intervals:

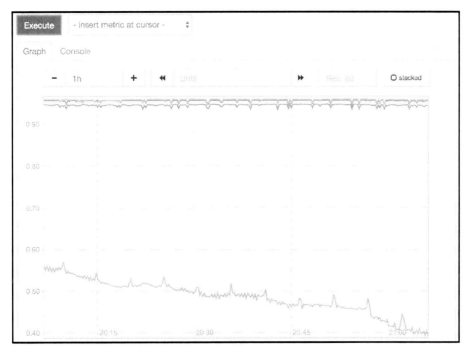

Figure 9-4: Prometheus graph with CPU idle rate

If you explore the results through the graph, you'll discover that cAdvisor uses the most memory (around 800M on my machine). That does not look correct. The service should have a much smaller footprint. If you look at its labels, you'll notice that the ID is /. That's the cumulative result of the total memory of all containers passing through cAdvisor. We should exclude it from the results with the != operator.

Please execute the query that follows:

```
container_memory_usage_bytes{id!="/"}
```

This time, the result makes much more sense. The service that uses the most memory is Prometheus itself.

The previous query used label id to filter data. When combined with the != operator, it excluded all metrics that have the id set to /.

Even with such a small cluster, the number of containers might be too big for a single graph so we might want to see the results limited to a single service. That can be accomplished by filtering the data with the `container_label_com_docker_swarm_service_name`.

Let's see the memory usage of all `cadvisor` replicas:

```
container_memory_usage_bytes{container_label_com_docker_swarm_service_\
name="cadvisor"}
```

All this looks great but is not very useful as a monitoring system. Prometheus is geared more towards `ad-hoc` queries than as a tool we can use to create dashboards that would give us a view of the whole system. For that, we need to add one more service to the mix.

Using Grafana to create dashboards

Prometheus offers a dashboard builder called *PromDash* (`https://github.com/prometheus/promdash`). However, it is deprecated for Grafana, so we won't consider it as worthy of running inside our cluster.

Grafana (`http://grafana.org/`) is one of the leading tools for querying and visualization of time series metrics. It features interactive and editable graphs and supports multiple data sources. Graphite, Elasticsearch, InfluxDB, OpenTSDB, KairosDB, and, most importantly, Prometheus are supported out of the box. If that's not enough, additional data sources can be added through plugins. Grafana is truly a rich UI that has established itself as a market leader. Best of all, it's free.

Let's create a `grafana` service:

```
docker service create \
    --name grafana \
    --network proxy \
    -p 3000:3000 \
    grafana/grafana:3.1.1
```

A few moments later, the status of the replica should be running:

```
docker service ps grafana
```

The output of the `service ps` command is as follows (IDs are removed for brevity):

```
NAME       IMAGE                 NODE     DESIRED STATE  CURRENT STATE
grafana.1  grafana/grafana3.1.1  swarm-1  Running        Running 24 seconds
ago
```

Now that the service is running, we can open the UI:

A note to Windows users

Git Bash might not be able to use the `open` command. If that's the case, execute `docker-machine ip <SERVER_NAME>` to find out the IP of the machine and open the URL directly in your browser of choice. For example, the command below should be replaced with the command that follows:

`docker-machine ip swarm-1`

If the output would be `1.2.3.4`, you should open `http://1.2.3.4:3000` in your browser.

```
open "http://$(docker-machine ip swarm-1):3000"
```

You will be presented with the login screen. The default username and password are **admin**. Go ahead and log in.

The username and password, as well as many other settings, can be adjusted through configuration files and environment variables. Since we are running Grafana inside a Docker container, environment variables are a better option. For more info, please visit the *Configuration* (`http://docs.grafana.org/installation/configuration/`) section of the official documentation.

The first thing we should do is add Prometheus as a data source.

Please click the *Grafana* logo located in the top-left part of the screen, select **Data Sources**, and click the **+ Add data source** button.

We'll name it `Prometheus` and choose the same for the Type. Enter `http://prometheus:9090` as the `Url` and click the **Add** button. That's it. From now on, we can visualize and query any metric stored in Prometheus.

Let's create the first dashboard.

Please click the *Grafana* logo, select **Dashboards**, and click **+ New**. In the top-left part of the screen, there is a green vertical button. Click it, select **Add Panel**, and choose **Graph**. You'll see the default graph with test metrics. It's not very useful unless you'd like to admire pretty lines going up and down. We'll change the Panel data source from default to Prometheus. Enter `irate(node_cpu{mode="idle"}[5m])` as Query. A few moments later you should see a graph with CPU usage.

By default, graphs display six hours of data. In this case, that might be *OK* if you are a slow reader and it took you that much time to create the prometheus service and read the text that followed. I will assume that you have only half an hour worth of data and want to change the graph's timeline.

Please click the **Last 6 hours** button located in the top-right corner of the screen, followed by the **Last 30 minutes** link. The graph should be similar to *Figure 9-5:*

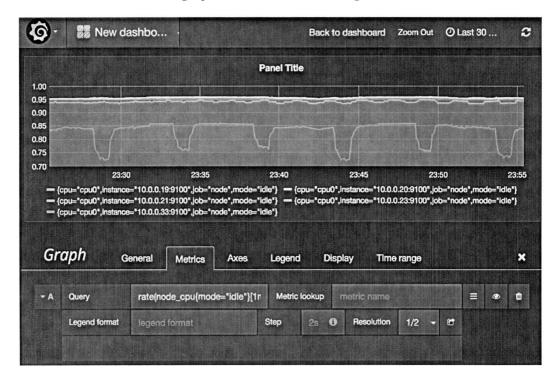

Figure 9-5: Grafana graph with CPU rate fetched from Prometheus

There are quite a few things you can customize to make a graph fit your needs. I'll leave that to you. Go ahead and play with the new toy. Explore different options it offers.
If you are lazy as I am, you might want to skip creating all the graphs and dashboards you might need and just leverage someone else's effort. Fortunately, the Grafana community is very active and has quite a few dashboards made by its members.

Please open the *dashboards* (`https://grafana.net/dashboards`) section in *grafana.net* (`http s://grafana.net`). You'll see a few filters on the left-hand side as well as the general **search** field. We can, for example, search for `node exporter`.

I encourage you to explore all the offered **node exporter** dashboards at some later time. For now, we'll select the *Node Exporter Server Metrics* (`https://grafana.net/dashboards/405`). Inside the page, you'll see the **Download Dashboard** button. Use it to download the JSON file with dashboard definition.

Let's get back to our `grafana` service:

A note to Windows users
Git Bash might not be able to use the `open` command. If that's the case, execute `docker-machine ip <SERVER_NAME>` to find out the IP of the machine and open the URL directly in your browser of choice. For example, the command below should be replaced with the command that follows:
`docker-machine ip swarm-1`
If the output would be `1.2.3.4`, you should open `http://1.2.3.4:3000` in your browser.

```
open "http://$(docker-machine ip swarm-1):3000"
```

Open, one more time, the **Dashboards** option is hidden behind the Grafana logo and select **Import**. Click the **Upload .json file** button and open the file you just downloaded. We'll leave the **Name** intact and choose **Prometheus** as datasource. Finally, click the **Save & Open** button to finish.

The magic happened, and we got quite a few graphs belonging to one of the nodes. However, the graphs are mostly empty since the default duration is seven days and we have only an hour or so worth of data. Change the time range to, let's say, one hour. The graphs should start making sense.

Let's spice it up a bit and add more servers to the mix. Please click the IP/port of the selected node and choose a few more. You should see metrics from each of the nodes:

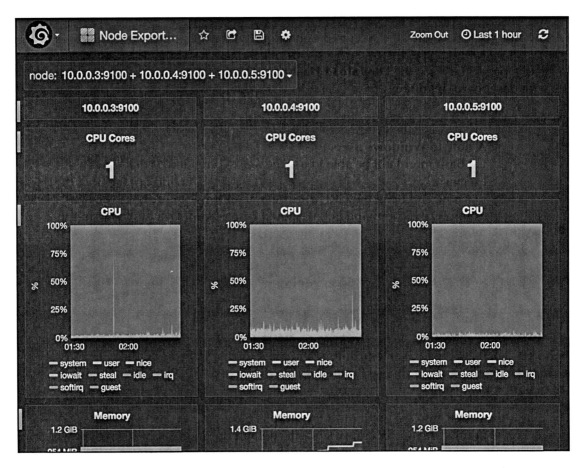

Figure 9-6: Grafana dashboard with metrics from selected nodes from Prometheus

While this dashboard is useful when we want to compare metrics between the selected nodes, I think it is not so useful if we'd like to focus on a single node. In that case, the *Node Exporter Server Stats* (https://grafana.net/dashboards/704) dashboard might be a better option. Please follow the same steps to import it into the grafana service.

You can still change the node presented in the dashboard (IP in the top-left corner of the screen). However, unlike the other dashboard, this one displays only one node at the time.

Both dashboards are very useful depending on the case. If we need to compare multiple nodes then the *Node Exporter Server Metrics* (`https://grafana.net/dashboards/405`) might be a better option. On the other hand, when we want to concentrate on a specific server, the *Node Exporter Server Stats* (`https://grafana.net/dashboards/704`) dashboard is probably a better option. You should go back and import the rest of the *Node Exporter* dashboards and try them as well. You might find them more useful than those I suggested.

Sooner or later, you'll want to create your own dashboards that fit your needs better. Even in that case, I still advise you to start by importing one of those made by the community and modifying it instead of starting from scratch. That is, until you get more familiar with Prometheus and Grafana, refer to the following image:

Figure 9-7: Grafana dashboard with a single node metrics from Prometheus

The next dashboard we'll create will need logs from Elasticsearch so let's set up logging as well.

We won't go into details of the logging services since we already explored them in the Chapter 9, *Defining Logging Strategy*:

```
docker service create \
    --name elasticsearch \
    --network proxy \
    --reserve-memory 300m \
    -p 9200:9200 \
    elasticsearch:2.4
```

Before we proceed with a LogStash service, we should confirm that elasticsearch is running:

```
docker service ps elasticsearch
```

The output of the service ps command should be similar to the one that follows (IDs & Error Ports column are removed for brevity):

```
NAME              IMAGE              NODE     DESIRED STATE CURRENT STATE
elasticsearch.1 elasticsearch:2.4 swarm-2 Running       Running 1 seconds
ago
```

Now we can create a logstash service:

```
docker service create \
    --name logstash \
    --mount "type=bind,source=$PWD/conf,target=/conf" \
    --network proxy \
    -e LOGSPOUT=ignore \
    logstash:2.4 \
    logstash -f /conf/logstash.conf
```

Let's confirm it's running before moving onto the last logging service:

```
docker service ps logstash
```

The output of the service ps command should be similar to the one that follows (IDs and ERROR PORTS columns are removed for brevity):

```
NAME         IMAGE         NODE     DESIRED STATE CURRENT STATE
logstash.1 logstash:2.4 swarm-2 Running       Running 2 minutes ago
```

Finally, we'll create a `logspout` service as well:

```
docker service create \
    --name logspout \
    --network proxy \
    --mode global \
    --mount "type=bind,source=/var/run/docker.sock,\
    target=/var/run/docker.sock" \
    -e SYSLOG_FORMAT=rfc3164 \
    gliderlabs/logspout \
    syslog://logstash:51415
```

... and confirm it's running:

```
docker service ps logspout
```

The output of the `service ps` command should be similar to the one that follows (IDs and ERROR PORTS columns are removed for brevity):

```
NAME            IMAGE                        NODE    DESIRED STATE CURRENT STATE
logspout...     gliderlabs/logspout:latest   swarm-1 Running       Running 9
seconds ago
logspout...     gliderlabs/logspout:latest   swarm-5 Running       Running 9
seconds ago
logspout...     gliderlabs/logspout:latest   swarm-4 Running       Running 9
seconds ago
logspout...     gliderlabs/logspout:latest   swarm-3 Running       Running 9
seconds ago
logspout...     gliderlabs/logspout:latest   swarm-2 Running       Running 10
seconds ago
```

Now that logging is operational, we should add Elasticsearch as one more Grafana data source:

> **A note to Windows users**
> Git Bash might not be able to use the open command. If that's the case,
> execute `docker-machine ip <SERVER_NAME>` to find out
> the IP of the machine and open the URL directly in your browser of choice.
> For example, the command below should be replaced with the command
> that follows:
> `docker-machine ip swarm-1`
> If the output would be `1.2.3.4`, you should open
> `http://1.2.3.4:3000` in your browser.

```
open "http://$(docker-machine ip swarm-1):3000"
```

Please click on the Grafana logo, and select **Data Sources**. A new screen will open with the currently defined sources (at the moment only Prometheus). Click the **+ Add data source** button.

We'll use `Elasticsearch` as both the **name** and the **type**. The Url should be `http://e lasticsearch:9200` and the value of the **Index name** should be set to `"logstash-*"`. Click the **Add** button when finished.

Now we can create or, to be more precise, import our third dashboard. This time, we'll import a dashboard that will be primarily focused on Swarm services.

Please open the Docker Swarm & Container Overview (`https://grafana.net/dashboards /609`) dashboard page, download it, and import it into Grafana. In the **Import Dashboard** screen for Grafana , you will be asked to set one **Prometheus** and two **Elasticsearch** data sources. After you click the **Save & Open** button, you will be presented with a dashboard full of metrics related to Docker Swarm and containers in general.

You will notice that some of the graphs from the dashboard are empty. That's not an error but an indication that our services are not prepared to be monitored. Let's update them with some additional information that the dashboard expects.

Exploring Docker Swarm and container overview dashboard in Grafana

One of the things missing from the dashboard are host names. If you select the **Hostnames** list, you'll notice that it is empty. The reason behind that lies in the `node-exporter` service. Since it is running inside containers, it is oblivious of the name of the underlying host.

We already commented that IPs from the `node-exporter` are not very valuable since they represent addresses of network endpoints. What we truly need are either "real" host IPs or host names. Since we cannot get the real IPs from Docker services, the alternative is to use host names instead. However, the official `Node Exporter` container does not provide that so we'll need to resort to an alternative.

We'll change our `node-exporter` service with the image created by GitHub user `bvis`. The project can be found in the `bvis/docker-node-exporter` (`https://github.com/bvis/docker-node-exporter`) GitHub repository. Therefore, we'll remove the `node-exporter` service and create a new one based on the `basi/node-exporter` (`https://hub.docker.com/r/basi/node-exporter/`) image:

```
docker service rm node-exporter

docker service create \
    --name node-exporter \
    --mode global \
    --network proxy \
    --mount "type=bind,source=/proc,target=/host/proc" \
    --mount "type=bind,source=/sys,target=/host/sys" \
    --mount "type=bind,source=/,target=/rootfs" \
    --mount "type=bind,source=/etc/hostname,target=/etc/\
    host_hostname" \
    -e HOST_HOSTNAME=/etc/host_hostname \
    basi/node-exporter:v0.1.1 \
    -collector.procfs /host/proc \
    -collector.sysfs /host/proc \
    -collector.filesystem.ignored-mount-points \
    "^/(sys|proc|dev|host|etc)($|/)" \
    -collector.textfile.directory /etc/node-exporter/ \
    -collectors.enabled="conntrack,diskstats,\
    entropy,filefd,filesystem,loadavg,\
    mdadm,meminfo,netdev,netstat,stat,textfile,time,vmstat,ipvs"
```

Apart from using a different image `basi/node-exporter`, we mounted the `/etc/hostname` directory from which the container can retrieve the name of the underlying host. We also added the environment variable `HOST_HOSTNAME` as well as a few additional collectors.

We won't go into details of the command since it is similar to the one we used previously. The meaning of the additional arguments can be found in the project's README (`https://github.com/bvis/docker-node-exporter`) file.

The important thing to note is that the new `node-exporter` service will include the `hostname` together with the virtual IP created by Docker networking. We'll be able to use that to establish the relation between the two.

Instead of creating the new service, we could have updated the one that was running before. I decided against that so that you can see the complete command in case you choose to use node metrics in your production cluster.

Please go back to the **Grafana** dashboard that is already opened in your browser and refresh the screen *Ctrl+R* or *Cmd+R*. You'll notice that some of the graphs that were empty are now colorful with metrics coming from the new `node-exporter`.

The **Hostnames** list holds all the nodes with their IPs on the left side and their host names on the right. We can now select any combination of the **hosts** and the **CPU Usage by Node**, **Free Disk by Node**, **Available Memory by Node**, and **Disk I/O by Node** graphs will be updated accordingly, as shown in the following image:

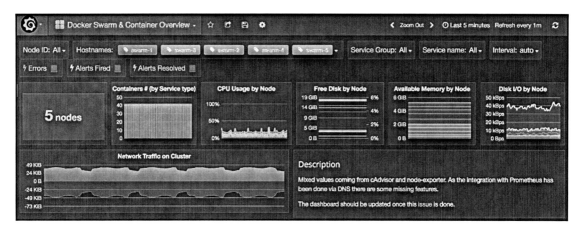

Figure 9-8: Docker Swarm Grafana dashboard with node metrics

Not only have we obtained part of the data required for the dashboard, but we also established the relation between virtual IPs and host names. Now you will be able to find out the relation between virtual IPs used in other dashboards and `hostnames`. In particular, if you monitor **Node Exporter** dashboards and detect a problem that should be fixed, you can go back to the Swarm dashboard and find out the host that requires your attention.

The solution with host names is still not the best one but should be a decent workaround *until issue 27307* (`https://github.com/docker/docker/issues/27307`) is fixed. The choice is yours. With the ability to relate virtual IPs with host names, I chose to stick with Docker services instead resorting to non-Swarm solutions.

The next thing that needs fixing are service groups.

If you open the **Service Group** list, you'll notice that it is empty. The reason behind that lies in the way the dashboard is configured. It expects that we distinguish services through the container label `com.docker.stack.namespace`. Since we did not specify any, the list contains only the **All** option.

Which groups should we have? The answer to that question varies from one use case to another. With time, you'll define the groups that best fit your organization. For now, we'll split our services into databases, backend, and infrastructure. We'll put go-demo-db into the db group, go-demo into backend, and all the rest into infra. Even though elasticsearch is a database, it is part of our infrastructure services, so we'll treat it as such.

We can add labels to existing services. There is no need to remove them and create new ones. Instead, we'll execute docker service update commands to add com.docker.stack.namespace labels by leveraging the --container-label-add argument.

The first service we'll put into a group is go-demo_db:

```
docker service update \
    --container-label-add \
    com.docker.stack.namespace=db \
    go-demo_db
```

Let's confirm that the label was indeed added:

```
docker service inspect go-demo_db \
    --format \
    "{{.Spec.TaskTemplate.ContainerSpec.Labels}}"
```

The --format argument allowed us to avoid lengthy output and display only what interests us.

The output of the service inspect command is as follows:

```
map[com.docker.stack.namespace:db]
```

As you can see, the com.docker.stack.namespace label was added and holds the value db.

We should do the same with the go-demo service and put it to the backend group:

```
docker service update \
    --container-label-add \
    com.docker.stack.namespace=backend \
    go-demo_main
```

The last group is `infra`. Since quite a few services should belong to it, we'll update them all with a single command:

```
for s in \
    proxy_proxy \
    logspout \
    logstash \
    util \
    prometheus \
    elasticsearch
do
    docker service update \
        --container-label-add \
        com.docker.stack.namespace=infra \
        $s
done
```

We iterated over the names of all the services and executed the `service update` command for each.

Please note that the `service update` command reschedules replicas. That means that the containers will be stopped and run again with new parameters. It might take a while until all services are fully operational. Please list the services with `docker service ls` and confirm that they are all running before proceeding. Once all the replicas are up, we should go back to the Grafana dashboard and refresh the screen (*Ctrl+R* or *cmd+R*).

This time, when you open the **Service Group** list, you'll notice that the three groups we created are now available. Go ahead, and select a group or two. You'll see that the graphs related to services are changing accordingly.

We can also filter the result by `Service Name` and limit the metrics displayed in some of the graphs to a selected set of services.

If you scroll down towards the middle of the dashboard, you'll notice that network graphs related to the `proxy` have too many services while those that exclude `proxy` are empty. We can correct that through the **Proxy** selector. It allows us to define which services should be treated as a `proxy`. Please open the list and select `proxy`.

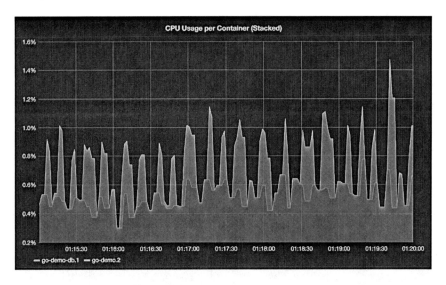

Figure 9-10: Grafana dashboard with network traffic graphs

The two network graphs related to a `proxy` are now limited to the `proxy` service or, to be more concrete, the service we identified as such. The bottom now contains metrics from all other services. Separating monitoring of the external and internal traffic is useful. Through the proxy graphs, you can see the traffic coming from and going to external sources while the other two are reserved for internal communication between services.

Let's generate a bit of traffic and confirm that the change is reflected in proxy graphs. We'll generate a hundred requests:

```
for i in {1..100}
do
    curl "$(docker-machine ip swarm-1)/demo/hello"
done
```

If you go back to `proxy` network graphs, you should see a spike in traffic. Please note that the dashboard refreshes data every minute. If the spike is still not visible, you might need to wait, click the **Refresh** button located in the top-right corner of the screen, or change the refresh frequency, refer the following image:

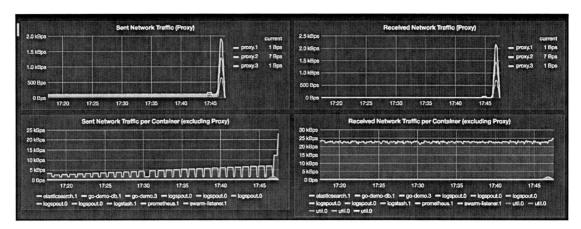

Figure 9-10: Grafana dashboard with network traffic graphs

We'll move on towards the next option in the dashboard menu and click the **Errors** checkbox. This checkbox is connected to Elasticsearch. Since there are no logged errors, the graphs stayed the same.

Let's generate a few errors and see how they visualize in the dashboard.

The `go-demo` service has an API that will allow us to create random errors. On average, one out of ten requests will produce an error. We'll need them to demonstrate one of the integrations between Prometheus metrics and data from Elasticsearch:

```
for i in {1..100}
do
    curl "$(docker-machine ip swarm-1)/demo/random-error"
done
```

A sample of the output should be as follows:

```
Everything is still OK
Everything is still OK
ERROR: Something, somewhere, went wrong!
Everything is still OK
Everything is still OK
```

If you go back to the dashboard, you'll notice red lines representing the point of time when the errors occurred. When such a thing happens, you can investigate system metrics and try to deduce whether the errors were caused by some hardware failure, saturated network, or some other reason. If all that fails, you should go to your Kibana UI, browse through logs and try to deduce the cause from them.Refer to the following image:

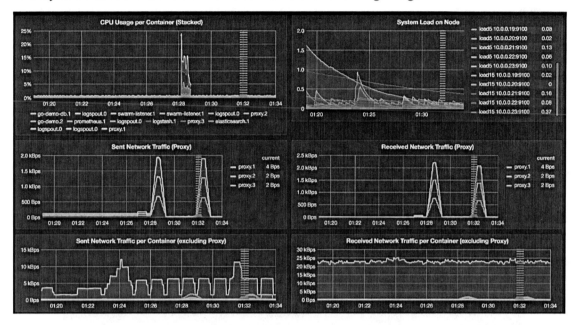

Figure 9-11: Grafana dashboard with network traffic graphs

It is important that your system does not report false positives as errors. If you notice that there is an error reported through logs, but there's nothing to do, it would be better to change the code, so that particular case is not treated as an error. Otherwise, with false positives, you'll start seeing too many errors and start ignoring them. As a result, when a real error occurs, the chances are that you will not notice it.

We'll skip the **Alerts Fired** and **Alerts Resolved** options since they are related to *X-Pack* (ht tps://www.elastic.co/products/x-pack), which is a commercial product. Since the book is aimed at open source solutions, we'll skip it. That does not mean that you should not consider purchasing it. Quite the contrary. Under certain circumstances, *X-Pack* is a valuable addition to the tool set.

That concludes our quick exploration of the **Docker Swarm & Container Overview** dashboard options. The graphs themselves should be self-explanatory. Take a few moments to explore them yourself.

Adjusting services through dashboard metrics

Our services are not static. Swarm will reschedule them with each release, when a replica fails, when a node becomes unhealthy, or as a result of a myriad of other causes. We should do our best to provide Swarm as much information as we can. The better we describe our desired service state, the better will Swarm do its job.

We won't go into all the information we can provide through `docker service create` and `docker service update` commands. Instead, we'll concentrate on the `--reserve-memory` argument. Later on, you can apply similar logic to `--reserve-cpu`, `--limit-cpu`, `--limit-memory`, and other arguments.

We'll observe the memory metrics in Grafana and update our services accordingly.

Please click on the **Memory Usage per Container (Stacked)** graph in Grafana and choose **View**. You'll see a screen with a zoomed graph that displays the memory consumption of the top twenty containers. Let's filter the metrics by selecting **prometheus** from the **Service Name** list.

Prometheus uses approximately 175 MB of memory. Let's add that information to the service:

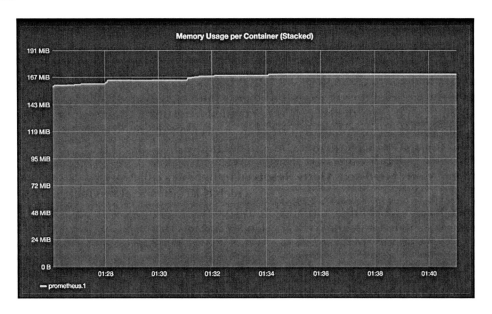

Figure 9-12: Grafana graph with containers memory consumption filtered with Prometheus service

```
docker service update \
    --reserve-memory 200m \
    prometheus
```

We updated the `prometheus` service by reserving `200m` of memory. We can assume that its memory usage will increase with time, so we reserved a bit more than what it currently needs.

Please note that `--reserve-memory` does not truly reserve memory, but gives a hint to Swarm how much we expect the service should use. With that information, Swarm will make a better distribution of services inside the cluster.

Let's confirm that Swarm rescheduled the service:

```
docker service ps prometheus
```

The output of the `service ps` command is as follows (IDs and Error columns are removed for brevity):

```
NAME                IMAGE                      NODE     DESIRED STATE
prometheus.1        prom/prometheus:v1.2.1 swarm-3 Running
_ prometheus.1      prom/prometheus:v1.2.1 swarm-1 Shutdown
_ prometheus.1      prom/prometheus:v1.2.1 swarm-5 Shutdown
----------------------------------------------------
CURRENT STATE
Running 5 minutes ago
Shutdown 6 minutes ago
Shutdown 5 hours ago
```

We can also confirm that the `--reserve-memory` argument is indeed applied:

```
docker service inspect prometheus --pretty
```

The output is as follows:

```
ID:         6yez6se1oejvfhkvyuqg0ljfy
Name:       prometheus
Mode:       Replicated
 Replicas:  1
Update status:
 State:      completed
 Started:    10 minutes ago
 Completed: 9 minutes ago
 Message:    update completed
Placement:
UpdateConfig:
 Parallelism:  1
 On failure:   pause
```

```
ContainerSpec:
 Image:        prom/prometheus:v1.2.1
 Mounts:
  Target = /etc/prometheus/prometheus.yml
  Source = /Users/vfarcic/IdeaProjects/cloud-
provisioning/conf/prometheus.yml
  ReadOnly = false
  Type = bind
  Target = /prometheus
  Source = /Users/vfarcic/IdeaProjects/cloud-provisioning/docker/prometheus
  ReadOnly = false
  Type = bind
 Resources:
  Reservations:
   Memory:    200 MiB
 Networks: 51rht5mtx58tg5gxdzo2rzirw
 Ports:
  Protocol = tcp
  TargetPort = 9090
  PublishedPort = 9090
```

As you can observe from the `Resources` section, the service now has `200 MiB` reserved. We should repeat a similar set of actions for `logstash`, `go-demo`, `go-demo-db`, `elasticsearch`, and `proxy` services.

The results might be different on your laptop. In my case, the commands that reserve memory based on Grafana metrics are as follows:

```
docker service update \
    --reserve-memory 250m logstash

docker service update \
    --reserve-memory 10m go-demo_main

docker service update \
    --reserve-memory 100m go-demo_db

docker service update \
    --reserve-memory 300m elasticsearch

docker service update \
    --reserve-memory 10m proxy_proxy
```

After each update, Swarm will reschedule containers that belong to the service. As a result, it'll place them inside a cluster in such a way that none is saturated with memory consumption. You should extend the process with CPU and other metrics and repeat it periodically.

Please note that increasing memory and CPU limits and reservations is not always the right thing to do. In quite a few cases, you might want to scale services so that resource utilization is distributed among multiple replicas.

We used ready-to-go dashboards throughout this chapter. I think that they are an excellent starting point and provide a good learning experience. With time, you will discover what works best for your organization and probably start modifying those dashboards or create new ones specifically tailored to your needs. Hopefully, you will contribute them back to the community.

Please let me know if you create a dashboard that complements those we used in this chapter or even replaces them. I'd be happy to feature them in the book.

Before we move on to the next chapter, let us discuss some of the monitoring best practices.

Monitoring best practices

You might be tempted to put as much information in a dashboard as you can. There are so many metrics, so why not visualize them? Right? Wrong! Too much data makes important information hard to find. It makes us ignore what we see since too much of it is noise.

What you really need is to have a quick glance of the central dashboard and deduce in an instant whether there is anything that might require your attention. If there is something to be fixed or adjusted, you can use more specialized Grafana dashboards or ad-hoc queries in Prometheus to drill into details.

Create the central dashboard with just enough information to fit a screen and provide a good overview of the system. Further on, create additional dashboards with more details. They should be organized similar to how we organize code. There is usually a main function that is an entry point towards more specific classes. When we start coding, we tend to open the main function and drill down from it until we reach a piece of code that will occupy our attention. Dashboards should be similar. We start with a dashboard that provides critical and very generic information. Such a dashboard should be our home and provide just enough metrics to deduce whether there is a reason to go deeper into more specific dashboards.

A single dashboard should have no more than six graphs. That's usually just the size that fits a single screen. You are not supposed to scroll up and down to see all the graphs while in the central dashboard. Everything essential or critical should be visible.

Each graph should be limited to no more than six plots. In many cases, more than that only produces noise that is hard to decipher.

Do allow different teams to have different dashboards, especially those that are considered as primary or main. Trying to create a dashboard that fits everyone's needs is a bad practice. Each team has different priorities that should be fulfilled with different metrics visualizations.

Do the dashboards we used in this chapter fulfill those rules? They don't. They have too many graphs with too many plots. That begs the question: Why did we use them? The answer is simple. I wanted to show you a quick and dirty way to get a monitoring system up-and-running in no time. I also wanted to show you as many different graphs as I could without overloading your brain. See for yourself which graphs do not provide value and remove them. Keep those that are truly useful and modify those that provide partial value. Create your own dashboards. See what works best for you.

What now?

Put the monitoring system into practice. Don't try to make it perfect from the first attempt. You'll fail if you do. Iterate over dashboards. Start small, grow with time. If you are a bigger organization, let each team create their own set of dashboards and share what worked well, as well as what failed to provide enough value.

Monitoring is not a simple thing to do unless you want to spend all your time in front of a dashboard. The solution should be designed in such a way that you need only a glance to discover whether a part of the system requires your attention.

Now let us destroy everything we did. The next chapter will be a new subject with a new set of challenges and solutions:

```
docker-machine rm -f swarm-1 \
    swarm-2 swarm-3 swarm-4 swarm-5
```

11
Embracing Destruction: Pets versus Cattle

Any roles involved in a project that do not directly contribute toward the goal of putting valuable software in the hands of users as quickly as possible should be carefully considered.

-Stein Inge Morisbak

We should discuss the high-level strategies before we start exploring tools and processes that will help us create and operate a "real" Swarm cluster. How are we going to treat our servers? Are they going to be pets or cattle?

How do you know whether you are treating your servers as pets or cattle? Ask yourself the following question. What will happen if several of your servers went offline right now? If they are pets, such a situation will cause a significant disruption for your users. If they are cattle, such an outcome will go unnoticed. Since you are running multiple instances of a service distributed across multiple nodes, failure of a single server (or a couple of them), would not result in a failure of all replicas. The only immediate effect would be that some services would run fewer instances and would have a higher load. Failed replicas would be rescheduled so the original number would soon be restored. In parallel, failed nodes would be replaced with new VMs. The only adverse effect of a failure of a couple of servers would be increased response time due to lower capacity. After a couple of minutes, everything would get back to normal with failed replicas rescheduled, and failed nodes replaced with new VMs. And the best thing is, it would all happen without manual interaction. If that's how your cluster is operating right now, you are treating your servers as cattle. Otherwise, you have pets in your data center.

Traditional systems administration is based on physical servers. To add a new machine to a data center, we need to purchase it upfront, wait until it arrives from the vendor, configure it in our office, move it to the data center location, and plug it in. The whole process can take a considerable amount of time. It is not uncommon for weeks, or even months to pass until we get a new fully provisioned server operating inside a data center.

Considering such a big waiting period and the costs, it is only natural that we do our best to keep servers as healthy as possible. If one of them starts behaving badly, we will do everything in our power to fix it as quickly as possible. What else can we do? Wait for weeks or months until a replacement arrives? Of course not. SSH into the faulty machine, find out what's wrong, and fix it. If a process died, bring it up again. If a hard disk broke, replace it. If a server is overloaded, add more memory.

It is only natural that, in such circumstances, we develop an emotional attachment to each of our servers. It starts with a name. Each new server gets one. There is Garfield, Mordor, Spiderman, and Sabrina. We might even decide on a theme. Maybe all our servers will get a name based on comic book superheroes. Or perhaps you prefer mythical creatures? How about ex-boyfriends and ex-girlfriends? Once we give a server a name, we start treating it as a pet. How do you feel? Do you need something? What's wrong? Should I take you to a veterinary? Each pet server is unique, hand raised, and cared for.

The change started with virtualization. The ability to create and destroy virtual machines allowed us to take a different approach to computing. Virtualization enabled us to stop treating our servers as pets. If virtualized servers are created and destroyed on a whim, it is pointless to give them names. There is no emotional attachment since their lifespan can be very short. Instead of *Garfield*, now we have *vm262.ecme.com*. Tomorrow, when we try to log into it, we might discover that it was replaced with *vm435.ecme.com*.

With virtualization, we started treating our servers as cattle. They do not have names, but numbers. We don't deal with them individually but as a herd. If a specimen is sick, we kill it. Curing it is slow and runs a risk of infecting the rest of the herd. If a server starts manifesting problems, terminate it immediately, and replace it with a new one.

The problem with this approach lies in habits we have accumulated over the years working with physical hardware. The switch from pets to cattle requires a mental change. It requires unlearning obsolete practices before switching to new ways of working.

Even though on-premise virtualization opened doors to quite a few new possibilities, many continued treating virtualized servers in the same way as they were treating physical nodes. Old habits die hard. Even though our servers became a herd, we keep treating each as pets. Part of the reason for the difficulty making a switch towards more elastic and dynamic computing lies in physical limitations of our data center. New VMs can be created only if there are available resources. Once we reach the limit, a VM has to be destroyed for a new one to be created. Our physical servers are still a valuable commodity. VMs gave us elasticity that is still bound by limitations imposed by the total of the computing power we possess.

We treat our valuable possessions with care since they are not cheap or easy to replace. We take good care of them since they should last for a long time. On the other hand, we have an entirely different approach to cheap things that are easy to replace. If a glass breaks, you probably don't try to glue the pieces together. You throw them to trash. There are plenty of other glasses in a cupboard, and all we have to do when their number becomes too small is buy a new set the next time we visit a shopping mall. Today we do not even need to go to a shopping mall but can order a new set online, and it will be delivered to our doorstep the same day. We should apply the same logic to servers.

Cloud computing made a big difference. Servers are no longer a valuable possession but a commodity. We can replace a node at any time without any additional cost. We can add a dozen servers to our cluster in a matter of minutes. We can remove them when we don't need them and reduce the cost.

Cloud computing is fundamentally different from "traditional" data centers. When utilized to its full potential, no server is indispensable or unique. The worst thing we can do is transition to the cloud without changing our processes and architecture. If we simply move our on-premise servers to the cloud without changing the processes we use to maintain them, the only thing we'll accomplish is higher cost.

With cloud computing, the notion of a server, its value, and the time required to get it, changed drastically. Such a significant change needs to be followed with a new set of processes and tools that execute them. Fault tolerance is the goal, speed is the key, and automation is a must.

What now?

Up until this point, we used Docker Machine to create servers locally and join them into a cluster. The intention was to teach you the fundamentals of creating and operating a Swarm cluster without spending money on hosting providers. Now that we reached the point where you are comfortable with how Docker Swarm Mode works, the time has come to move to "real" servers. We'll continue being "cheap" by using small instances that are either free or very inexpensive, and create just enough servers to demonstrate the process. The goal of the chapters that follow will be to walk you through a few setups, compare them, and choose the one we'll apply to our production. The only things you should change are VM instance types and the number of servers. Everything else can be the same as in the examples we'll work with.

We already saw how to accomplish fault tolerance by utilizing Docker Swarm as the service scheduler. The chapters that follow will try to achieve the required speed and automation on the infrastructure level. We'll use different tools and processes to automate the creation of a cluster in a few cloud computing providers. The first in line is **Amazon Web Services (AWS)**.

struction: Pets vs Cattle

12
Creating and Managing a Docker Swarm Cluster in Amazon Web Services

In fast moving markets, adaptation is significantly more important than optimization.
–Larry Constantine

The time has finally come to set up a Swarm cluster that is closer to what we should have in production. The reason I added the word "closer" lies in a few subjects that we'll explore in later chapters. Later on, once we go through a few hosting providers, we'll work on the missing pieces (example: persistent storage).

For now, we'll limit ourselves to the creation of a production-like cluster and exploration of different tools we can choose from.

Since AWS holds by far the biggest share of the hosting market, it is the natural choice as the first provider we'll explore.

I'm sure that AWS does not need much of an introduction. Even if you haven't used it, I'm sure you are aware of its existence and a general gist.

Amazon Web Services (**AWS**) were created in 2006 with the offering of IT infrastructure services. The type of services AWS offered later on became commonly known as cloud computing. With the cloud, companies and individuals alike no longer need to plan for and procure servers and other IT infrastructure weeks or months in advance. Instead, they can instantly spin up hundreds or even thousands of servers in minutes.

I will assume that you already have an AWS account. If that's not the case, please head over to Amazon Web Services and sign-up. Even if you already made up a firm decision to use a different cloud computing provider or in-house servers, I highly recommend going through this chapter. You will be introduced to a few tools you might not have in your tool belt and be able to compare AWS with other solutions.

Before we jump into practical exercises, we'll need to install the AWS CLI, get the access keys and decide the region and the zone where we'll run the cluster.

Installing AWS CLI and setting up the environment variables

The first thing we should do is get the AWS credentials.

Please open the *Amazon EC2 Console* (`https://console.aws.amazon.com/ec2/`), click on your name from the top-right menu, and select **My Security Credentials**. You will see the screen with different types of credentials. Expand the **Access Keys (Access Key ID** and **Secret Access Key)** section and click the **Create New Access Key** button. Expand the **Show Access Key** section to see the keys.

You will not be able to view the keys later on, so this is the only chance you'll have to Download Key File.

 All the commands from this chapter are available in the `11-aws.sh` (`http s://gist.github.com/vfarcic/03931d011324431f211c4523941979f8`) Gist.

We'll place the keys as environment variables that will be used by the tools we'll explore in this chapter:

```
export AWS_ACCESS_KEY_ID=[...]

export AWS_SECRET_ACCESS_KEY=[...]
```

Please replace `[...]` with the actual values.

We'll need to install AWS **Command Line Interface (CLI)** (`https://aws.amazon.com/cli /`)and gather info about your account.

A note to Windows users

I found the most convienent way to get awscli installed on Windows is to use *Chocolatey* (`https://chocolatey.org/`). Download and install Chocolatey, then run `choco install awscli` from an Administrator Command Prompt. Later in the chapter, Chocolatey will be used to install `jq`, `packer`, and terraform.

If you haven't already, please open the *Installing the AWS Command Line Interface* (`http://docs.aws.amazon.com/cli/latest/userguide/installing.html`) page and follow the installation method best suited for your OS.

Once you're done, we should confirm that the installation was successful by outputting the version:

```
aws --version
```

The output (from my laptop) is as follows:

```
aws-cli/1.11.15 Python/2.7.10 Darwin/16.0.0 botocore/1.4.72
```

A note to Windows users

You might need to reopen your *GitBash* terminal for the changes to the environment variable `path` to take effect.

Now that the CLI is installed, we can get the region and the availability zones our cluster will run in.

Amazon EC2 is hosted in multiple locations worldwide. These locations are composed of regions and availability zones. Each region is a separate geographic area composed of multiple isolated locations known as availability zones. Amazon EC2 provides you the ability to place resources, such as instances, and data in multiple locations.

You can see the currently available regions from the *Available Regions* (`http://docs.aws.amazon.com/AWSEC2/latest/UserGuide/using-regions-availability-zones.html#concepts-available-regions`) section of the *Regions and Availability Zones* (`http://docs.aws.amazon.com/AWSEC2/latest/UserGuide/using-regions-availability-zones.html`) page.

Throughout this chapter, I will be using `us-east-1` (US East (N. Virginia)) region. Feel free to change it to the region closest to your location.

Please put the region inside the environment variable `AWS_DEFAULT_REGION`:

```
export AWS_DEFAULT_REGION=us-east-1
```

With the region selected, we can decide which availability zone we'll select to run our cluster.

Each region is completely independent and consists of multiple availability zones. Zones within a region are isolated and connected through low-latency links.

As a general rule, you should place all your nodes of a cluster inside one region and benefit from low-latency links. Those nodes should be distributed across multiple availability zones so that failure of one of them does not imply failure of the whole cluster. If you have a need to operate across multiple regions, the best option is to set up multiple clusters (one for each region). Otherwise, if you'd set up a single cluster that spans multiple regions, you might experience latency problems.

A note to first time AWS users

If this is the first time you are executing `aws`, you will receive a message asking you to configure credentials. Please run the `aws configure` command and follow the instructions. You will be asked for credentials. Use those we generated earlier. Feel free to answer the rest of the questions with the enter key.

Let's use the AWS CLI to see the available zones within the selected region:

```
aws ec2 describe-availability-zones \
    --region $AWS_DEFAULT_REGION
```

Since I selected `us-east-1` as the region, the output is as follows:

```
{
    "AvailabilityZones": [
        {
            "State": "available",
            "RegionName": "us-east-1",
            "Messages": [],
            "ZoneName": "us-east-1a"
        },
        {
            "State": "available",
            "RegionName": "us-east-1",
            "Messages": [],
            "ZoneName": "us-east-1b"
        },
```

```
        {
            "State": "available",
            "RegionName": "us-east-1",
            "Messages": [],
            "ZoneName": "us-east-1d"
        },
        {
            "State": "available",
            "RegionName": "us-east-1",
            "Messages": [],
            "ZoneName": "us-east-1e"
        }
    ]
}
```

As you can see, there are four zones (a, b, d, and e) available for the us-east-1 region. In your case, depending on the selected region, the output might be different.

Please choose the zones and put them inside environment variables, one for each of the five servers that will form our cluster:

AWS_ZONE[1]=b

AWS_ZONE[2]=d

AWS_ZONE[3]=e

AWS_ZONE[4]=b

AWS_ZONE[5]=d

Feel free to choose any combination of availability zones. In my case, I made a decision to distribute the cluster across zones b, d, and e.

Now we are all set with the prerequisites that will allow us to create the first Swarm cluster in AWS. Since we used Docker Machine throughout the most of the book, it will be our first choice.

Setting up a Swarm cluster with Docker Machine and AWS CLI

We'll continue using the vfarcic/cloud-provisioning (https://github.com/vfarcic/cloud-provisioning) repository. It contains configurations and scripts that'll help us out. You already have it cloned. To be on the safe side, we'll pull the latest version:

```
cd cloud-provisioning

git pull
```

Let's create the first EC2 instance:

```
docker-machine create \
    --driver amazonec2 \
    --amazonec2-zone ${AWS_ZONE[1]} \
    --amazonec2-tags "Type,manager" \
    swarm-1
```

We specified that the *Docker Machine* should use the amazonec2 driver to create an instance in the zone we defined as the environment variable AWS_ZONE_1.

We made a tag with the key type and the value manager. Tag are mostly for informational purposes.

Finally, we specified the name of the instance to be swarm-1.

The output is as follows:

```
Running pre-create checks...
Creating machine...
(swarm-1) Launching instance...
Waiting for machine to be running, this may take a few minutes...
Detecting operating system of created instance...
Waiting for SSH to be available...
Detecting the provisioner...
Provisioning with ubuntu(systemd)...
Installing Docker...
Copying certs to the local machine directory...
Copying certs to the remote machine...
Setting Docker configuration on the remote daemon...
Checking connection to Docker...
Docker is up and running!
To see how to connect your Docker Client to the Docker Engine running on
this\ virtual machine, run: docker-machine env swarm-1
```

Docker machine launched an AWS EC2 instance, provisioned it with Ubuntu, and installed and configured Docker Engine.

Now we can initialize the cluster. We should use private IPs for all communication between nodes. Unfortunately, the command `docker-machine ip` returns only the public IP, so we'll have to resort to a different method to get the private IP.
We can use the `aws ec2 describe-instances` command to retrieve all the information about our EC2 instances. We also filter only running instances by adding `Name=instance-state-name,Values=running`. Doing so excludes instances that are being terminated or that are terminated:

```
aws ec2 describe-instances \
    --filter "Name=tag:Name,Values=swarm-1" \
    "Name=instance-state-name,Values=running"
```

The `describe-instances` command lists all the EC2 instances. We combined it with `--filter` to limit the output to the instance tagged with the name `swarm-1`.

The relevant sample of the output is as follows:

```
{
"Reservations": [
  {
    . . .
    "Instances": [
      {
        . . .
        "PrivateIpAddress": "172.31.51.25",
        . . .
```

Even though we got all the information related to the `swarm-1` EC2 instance, we still need to limit the output to the `PrivateIpAddress` value. We'll use `jq` (`https://stedolan.gith ub.io/jq/`)to filter the output and get what we need. Please download and install the distribution suited for your OS:

A note to Windows users
Using Chocolatey, install `jq` from an Administrator Command Prompt via `choco install jq`.

```
MANAGER_IP=$(aws ec2 describe-instances \
    --filter "Name=tag:Name,Values=swarm-1" \
    "Name=instance-state-name,Values=running" \
    | jq -r ".Reservations[0].Instances[0].PrivateIpAddress")
```

We used `jq` to retrieve the first element of the Reservations array. Within it, we got the first entry of the Instances, followed with the `PrivateIpAddress`. The `-r` returns the value in its raw format (in this case without double quotes that surround the IP). The result of the command is stored in the environment variable `MANAGER_IP`.

To be on the safe side, we can echo the value of the newly created variable:

```
echo $MANAGER_IP
```

The output is as follows:

```
172.31.51.25
```

Now we can execute the `swarm init` command in the same way as we did in the previous chapters:

```
eval $(docker-machine env swarm-1)

docker swarm init \
    --advertise-addr $MANAGER_IP
```

Let's confirm that the cluster is indeed initialized:

```
docker node ls
```

The output is as follows (IDs are removed for brevity):

```
HOSTNAME   STATUS   AVAILABILITY   MANAGER STATUS
swarm-1    Ready    Active         Leader
```

Apart from creating an EC2 instance, `docker-machine` created a security group as well.

A security group acts as a virtual firewall that controls the traffic. When you launch an instance, you associate one or more security groups with the instance. You add rules to each security group that allows traffic to or from its associated instances.

At the time of this writing, Docker Machine was not yet adapted to support Swarm Mode out of the box. As a result, it created an AWS security group named `docker-machine` and opened only the ingress (inbound) ports `22` and `2376`. Egress (output) is opened for all ports.

For Swarm Mode to function correctly, the ingress ports that should be opened are as follows:

- TCP port 2377 for cluster management communications
- TCP and UDP port 7946 for communication among nodes
- TCP and UDP port 4789 for overlay network traffic

To modify the security group, we need to get its ID. We can see the info of a security group with the `aws ec2 describe-security-groups` command:

```
aws ec2 describe-security-groups \
    --filter "Name=group-name,Values=docker-machine"
```

The part of the output is as follows:

```
...
            "GroupName": "docker-machine",
            "VpcId": "vpc-7bbc391c",
            "OwnerId": "036548781187",
            "GroupId": "sg-f57bf388"
        }
    ]
}
```

The command that will assign the ID to the SECURITY_GROUP_ID environment variable is as follows:

```
SECURITY_GROUP_ID=$(aws ec2 \
    describe-security-groups \
    --filter \
    "Name=group-name,Values=docker-machine" |\
    jq -r '.SecurityGroups[0].GroupId')
```

We requested the information about the security group `docker-machine` and filtered the JSON output to get the `GroupId` key located in the first element of the `SecurityGroups` array.

Now we can use the `aws ec2 authorize-security-group-ingress` command to open TCP ports 2377, 7946, and 4789:

```
for p in 2377 7946 4789; do \
    aws ec2 authorize-security-group-ingress \
        --group-id $SECURITY_GROUP_ID \
        --protocol tcp \
        --port $p \
        --source-group $SECURITY_GROUP_ID
done
```

We should execute a similar command to open UDP ports `7946` and `4789`:

```
for p in 7946 4789; do \
    aws ec2 authorize-security-group-ingress \
        --group-id $SECURITY_GROUP_ID \
        --protocol udp \
        --port $p \
        --source-group $SECURITY_GROUP_ID
done
```

Please note that, in all the cases, we specified that the `source-group` should be the same as the security group. That means that the ports will be opened only to instances that belong to the same group. In other words, those ports will not be available to the public. Since they will be used only for internal communication within the cluster, there is no reason to put our security at risk by exposing those ports further.

Please repeat the `aws ec2 describe-security-groups` command to confirm that the ports were indeed opened:

```
aws ec2 describe-security-groups \
    --filter \
    "Name=group-name,Values=docker-machine"
```

Now we can add more nodes to the cluster. We'll start by creating two new instances and joining them as managers:

```
MANAGER_TOKEN=$(docker swarm join-token -q manager)

for i in 2 3; do
    docker-machine create \
        --driver amazonec2 \
        --amazonec2-zone ${AWS_ZONE[$i]} \
        --amazonec2-tags "Type,manager" \
        swarm-$i

    IP=$(aws ec2 describe-instances \
        --filter "Name=tag:Name,Values=swarm-$i" \
        "Name=instance-state-name,Values=running" \
        | jq -r ".Reservations[0].Instances[0].PrivateIpAddress")

eval $(docker-machine env swarm-$i)

    docker swarm join \
        --token $MANAGER_TOKEN \
        --advertise-addr $IP \
        $MANAGER_IP:2377
done
```

There's no need to explain the commands we just executed since they are the combination of those we used before.

We'll add a few worker nodes as well:

```
WORKER_TOKEN=$(docker swarm join-token -q worker)

for i in 4 5; do
  docker-machine create \
    --driver amazonec2 \
    --amazonec2-zone ${AWS_ZONE[$i]} \
    --amazonec2-tags "type,worker" \
    swarm-$i

  IP=$(aws ec2 describe-instances \
    --filter "Name=tag:Name,Values=swarm-$i" \
    "Name=instance-state-name,Values=running" \
    | jq -r ".Reservations[0].Instances[0].PrivateIpAddress")

  eval $(docker-machine env swarm-$i)

  docker swarm join \
    --token $WORKER_TOKEN \
    --advertise-addr $IP \
    $MANAGER_IP:2377
done
```

Let's confirm that all five nodes are indeed forming the cluster:

```
eval $(docker-machine env swarm-1)

docker node ls
```

The output is as follows (IDs are removed for brevity):

```
HOSTNAME  STATUS  AVAILABILITY  MANAGER STATUS
swarm-4   Ready   Active
swarm-2   Ready   Active        Reachable
swarm-3   Ready   Active        Reachable
swarm-5   Ready   Active
swarm-1   Ready   Active        Leader
```

That's it. Our cluster is ready. The only thing left is to deploy a few services and confirm that the cluster is working as expected.

Since we already created the services quite a few times, we'll speed up the process with the `vfarcic/docker-flow-proxy/docker-compose-stack.yml` (https://github.com/vfarcic/docker-flow-proxy/blob/master/docker-compose-stack.yml) and `vfarcic/go-demo/docker-compose-stack.yml` (https://github.com/vfarcic/go-demo/blob/master/docker-compose-stack.yml) Compose stacks. They'll create the `proxy`, `swarm-listener`, `go-demo-db`, and `go-demo` services:

```
docker-machine ssh swarm-1

sudo docker network create --driver overlay proxy

curl -o proxy-stack.yml \
    https://raw.githubusercontent.com/ \
vfarcic/docker-flow-proxy/master/docker-compose-stack.yml

sudo docker stack deploy \
    -c proxy-stack.yml proxy

curl -o go-demo-stack.yml \
    https://raw.githubusercontent.com/ \
vfarcic/go-demo/master/docker-compose-stack.yml

sudo docker stack deploy \
    -c go-demo-stack.yml go-demo

exit

docker service ls
```

Non-Windows users do not need to enter the `swarm-1` machine and can accomplish the same result by deploying the stacks directly from their laptops.

It'll take a few moments until all the images are downloaded. After a while, the output of the `service ls` command should be as follows (IDs are removed for brevity):

```
NAME                    MODE         REPLICA  IMAGE
go-demo_db              replicated   1/1      mongo:latest
go-demo_main            replicated   3/3      vfarcic/go-demo:latest
proxy_swarm-listener    replicated   1/1      vfarcic/docker-flow-
swarmlistener:latest
proxy_proxy             replicated   2/2      vfarcic/docker-flow-proxy:latest
```

Let's confirm that the `go-demo` service is accessible:

```
curl "$(docker-machine ip swarm-1)/demo/hello"
```

The output is as follows:

```
curl: (7) Failed to connect to 54.157.196.113 port 80: Operation timed out
```

That's embarrassing. Even though all the services are running and we used the same commands as in the previous chapters, we cannot access the `proxy` and, through it, the `go-demo` service.

The explanation is quite simple. We never opened ports `80` and `443`. By default, all incoming traffic to AWS EC2 instances is closed, and we opened only the ports required for Swarm to operate properly. They are open inside EC2 instances attached to the `docker-machine security` group, but not outside our AWS VPC.

We'll use the `aws ec2 authorize-security-group-ingress` command to open the ports `80` and `443`. This time we'll specify `cidr` instead `source-group` as the source:

```
for p in 80 443; do
    aws ec2 authorize-security-group-ingress \
        --group-id $SECURITY_GROUP_ID \
        --protocol tcp \
        --port $p \
        --cidr "0.0.0.0/0"
done
```

The `aws ec2 authorize-security-group-ingress` command was executed twice; once for port `80` and the second time for `443`.

Let's send the request one more time:

```
curl "$(docker-machine ip swarm-1)/demo/hello"
```

This time the output is as expected. We got our response:

```
hello, world!
```

We set up the whole Swarm cluster in AWS using Docker Machine and AWS CLI. Is that everything we need? That depends on the requirements we might define for our cluster. We should probably add a few Elastic IP addresses.

An Elastic IP address is a static IP address designed for dynamic cloud computing. It is associated with your AWS account. With an Elastic IP address, you can mask the failure of an instance or software by rapidly remapping the address to another instance in your account. An Elastic IP address is a public IP address which is reachable from the Internet. If your instance does not have a public IP address, you can associate an Elastic IP address with it to enable communication with the Internet; for example, to connect to your instance from your local computer.

In other words, we should probably set at least two Elastic IPs and map them to two of the EC2 instances in the cluster. Those two (or more) IPs would be set as our DNS records. That way, when an instance fails, and we replace it with a new one, we can remap the Elastic IP without affecting our users.

There are quite a few other improvements we could do. However, that would put us in an awkward position. We would be using a tool that is not meant for setting up a complicated cluster.

The creation of VMs was quite slow. Docker Machine spent too much time provisioning it with Ubuntu and installing Docker Engine. We can reduce that time by creating our own **Amazon Machine Image** (AMI) with Docker Engine pre-installed. However, with such an action, the main reason for using Docker Machine would be gone. Its primary usefulness is simplicity. Once we start complicating the setup with other AWS resources, we'll realize that the simplicity is being replaced with too many ad-hoc commands.

Running `docker-machine` and `aws` commands works great when we are dealing with a small cluster, especially when we want to create something fast and potentially not very durable. The biggest problem is that everything we've done so far has been ad-hoc commands. Chances are that we would not be able to reproduce the same steps the second time. Our infrastructure is not documented, so our team would not know what constitutes our cluster.

My recommendation is to use `docker-machine` and `aws` as a quick and dirty way to create a cluster mostly for demo purposes. It can be useful for production as well, as long as the cluster is relatively small.

We should look at alternatives if we'd like to set up a complicated, bigger, and potentially more permanent solution.

Let us delete the cluster we created and explore the alternatives with a clean slate:

```
for i in 1 2 3 4 5; do
    docker-machine rm -f swarm-$i
done
```

The only thing left is to remove the security group `docker-machine` created:

```
aws ec2 delete-security-group \
    --group-id $SECURITY_GROUP_ID
```

The last command might fail if the instances are not yet terminated. If that's the case, please wait a few moments and repeat the command.

Let us move on and explore *Docker for AWS*.

Setting up a Swarm cluster with Docker for AWS

Before we create a Swarm cluster using *Docker for AWS*, we'll need to generate a Key Pair that we'll use to SSH into the EC2 instances.

To create a new `key-pair`, please execute the command that follows:

```
aws ec2 create-key-pair \
    --key-name devops21 \
    | jq -r '.KeyMaterial' >devops21.pem
```

We executed `aws ec2 create-key-pair` command and passed `devops21` as the name. The output was filtered with `jq` so that only the actual value is returned. Finally, we sent the output to the `devops21.pem` file.

If someone gets a hold of your key file, your instances would be exposed. Therefore, we should move the key somewhere safe.

A common location for SSH keys on Linux/OSX systems is `$HOME/.ssh`. If you are a Windows user, feel free to change the command that follows to any destination you think is appropriate:

```
mv devops21.pem $HOME/.ssh/devops21.pem
```

We should also change permissions by giving the current user only the read access and removing all permissions from other users or groups. Feel free to skip the command that follows if you are a Windows user:

```
chmod 400 $HOME/.ssh/devops21.pem
```

Finally, we'll put the path to the key inside the environment variable `KEY_PATH`:

```
export KEY_PATH=$HOME/.ssh/devops21.pem
```

Now we are ready to create a Swarm stack using *Docker for AWS*.

Please open the *Docker for AWS Release Notes* (`https://docs.docker.com/docker-for-aws /release-notes/`) page and click the **Deploy Docker Community Edition for AWS** button.

After you log into the *AWS Console*, you will be presented with the **Select Template** screen. It is a generic **CloudFormation** screen with the **Docker for AWS** template already selected:

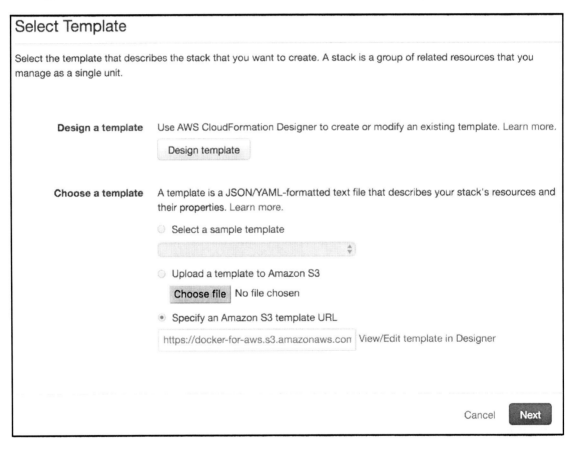

Figure 11-1: Docker For AWS Select Template screen

There's not much to do here, so please click the **Next** button.

The next screen allows us to specify details of the stack we are about to launch. The fields should be self-explanatory. The only modification we'll make is the reduction of Swarm workers from *5* to *1*. The exercises in this section won't need more than four servers, so three managers and one worker should suffice. We'll leave instance types with their default values `t2.micro`. By creating only four micro nodes, the whole exercise should have almost negligible cost, and you won't be able to complain to your friends that you went bankrupt because of me. The total cost will probably be smaller than the price of a can of soda or a cup of coffee you're drinking while reading this.

The **Which SSH key to use?** field should hold the `devops21` key we just created. Please select it:

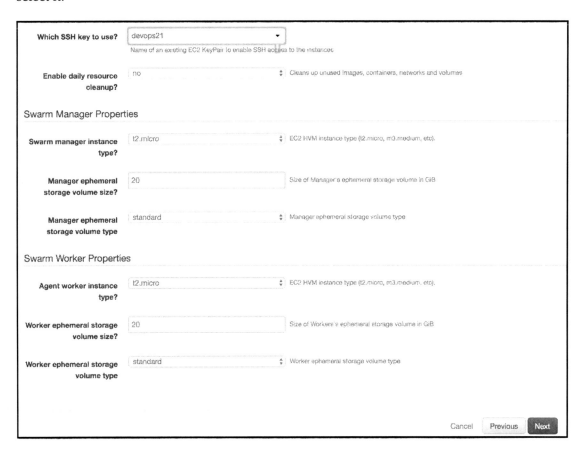

Figure 11-2: Docker For AWS Specify Details screen

Click the **Next** button.

We won't change anything from the **Options** screen. Later on, when you get comfortable with *Docker for AWS*, you might want to go back to this screen and fiddle with the additional options. For now, we'll just ignore its existence:

Figure 11-3: Docker For AWS Options screen

Click the **Next** button.

We reached the last screen. Feel free to review the information about the stack. Once you're done, click the **I acknowledge that AWS CloudFormation might create IAM resources**. checkbox followed by the **Create** button:

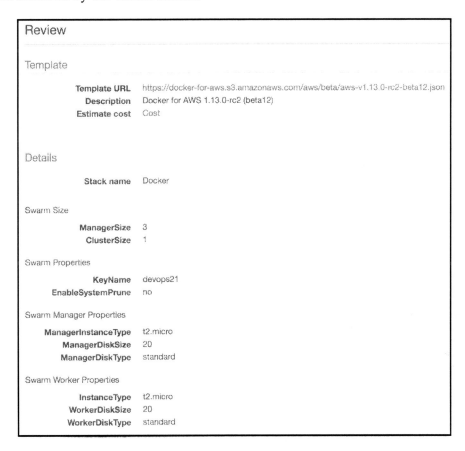

Figure 11-4: Docker For AWS Review Screen

You will see the screen that allows you to create a new stack. Please click the **refresh** button located in the top-right corner. You'll see the *Docker* stack with the status
CREATE_IN_PROGRESS.

It will take a while until all the resources are created. If you'd like to see the progress, please select the *Docker* stack and click the **restore** button located in the bottom-right part of the screen. You'll see the list of all the events generated by the *Docker for AWS* template. Feel free to explore the content of the tabs while waiting for the stack creation to finish:

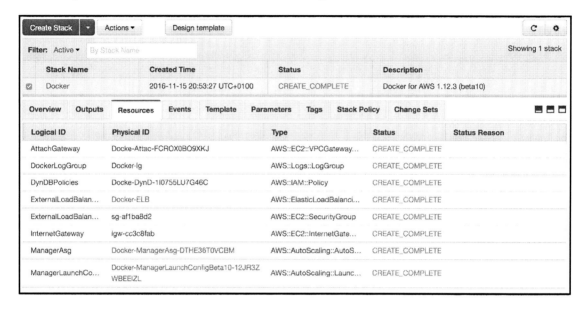

Figure 11-5: Docker For AWS stack status screen

We can proceed once the *Docker* stack status is CREATE_COMPLETE.

Our cluster is ready. We can enter one of the manager instances and explore the cluster in more detail.

To find information about Swarm manager instances, please click the **Outputs** tab:

Figure 11-6: Docker For AWS Stack outputs screen

You'll see two rows.

We'll store the value of the **DefaultDNSTarget** in an environment variable. It'll come in handy soon:

```
DNS=[ . . . ]
```

Please replace [. . .] with the actual DefaultDNSTarget value.

If this were a "real" production cluster, you'd use it to update your DNS entries. It is the public entry to your system.

Click the link next to the **Managers** column. You will be presented with the **EC2 Instances** screen that contains the results filtered by manager nodes. The workers are hidden:

Figure 11-7: Docker For AWS EC2 instances filtered by manager nodes

Select one of the managers and find its **Public IP**. As with the DNS, we'll store it as an environment variable:

```
MANAGER_IP=[...]
```

Please replace `[...]` with the actual Public IP value.

We are, finally, ready to SSH into one of the managers and explore the cluster we just created:

```
ssh -i $KEY_PATH docker@$MANAGER_IP
```

Once inside the server, you will be presented with a welcome message. The OS specifically made for this stack is very minimalistic, and the message reflects that:

```
Welcome to Docker!
~ $
```

As usual, we'll start by listing the nodes that form the cluster:

```
docker node ls
```

The output is as follows (IDs are removed for brevity):

```
HOSTNAME                      STATUS  AVAILABILITY  MANAGER STATUS
ip-10-0-17-154.ec2.internal   Ready   Active        Reachable
ip-10-0-15-215.ec2.internal   Ready   Active        Reachable
ip-10-0-31-44.ec2.internal    Ready   Active
ip-10-0-15-214.ec2.internal   Ready   Active        Leader
```

The only thing left is to create a few services that will confirm that the cluster works as expected.

We'll deploy the same `vfarcic/docker-flow-proxy/docker-compose-stack.yml` (https://github.com/vfarcic/docker-flow-proxy/blob/master/docker-compose-stack.yml) and `vfarcic/go-demo/docker-compose-stack.yml` (https://github.com/vfarcic/go-demo/blob/master/docker-compose-stack.yml) stacks we used with the cluster we created with Docker Machine:

```
sudo docker network create --driver overlay proxy

curl -o proxy-stack.yml \
    https://raw.githubusercontent.com/ \
vfarcic/docker-flow-proxy/master/docker-compose-stack.yml

docker stack deploy \
    -c proxy-stack.yml proxy

curl -o go-demo-stack.yml \
    https://raw.githubusercontent.com/ \
vfarcic/go-demo/master/docker-compose-stack.yml

docker stack deploy \
    -c go-demo-stack.yml go-demo
```

We downloaded the Compose file and deployed the stacks.

Let's confirm that the services are indeed up and running:

```
docker service ls
```

After a while, the output should be as follows (IDs are removed for brevity):

```
NAME                  MODE         REPLICAS
proxy_proxy           replicated   2/2
go-demo_main          replicated   3/3
proxy_swarm-listener  replicated   1/1
go-demo_db            replicated   1/1
-------------------------------------------
IMAGE
vfarcic/docker-flow-proxy:latest
vfarcic/go-demo:latest
vfarcic/docker-flow-swarm-listener:latest
mongo:latest
```

Let's get out of the server and confirm that the `go-demo` service is accessible to the public:

```
exit

curl $DNS/demo/hello
```

As expected, we received the response confirming that the cluster is operational and accessible:

```
hello, world!
```

What happens if our servers become too crowded and we need to expand the capacity? How can we increase (or decrease) the number of nodes that form our cluster? The answer lies in AWS **Auto Scaling Groups**. Please click the **Auto Scaling Groups** link from the **AUTO SCALING** group in the left-hand menu of the EC2 console and select the row with the group name that starts with `Docker-NodeAsg`:

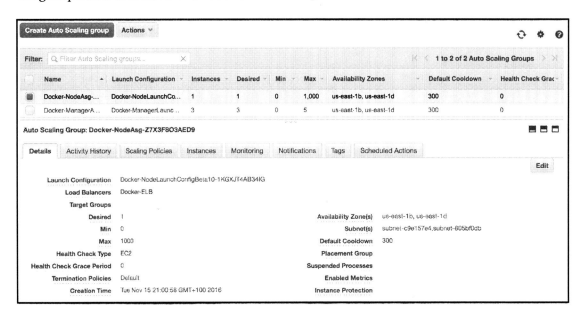

Figure 11-8: Docker For AWS Auto Scaling Groups

To scale or de-scale the number of nodes, all we have to do is click the **Edit** button from the **Actions** menu, change the value of the **Desired** field from 1 to *2*, and click the **Save** button. The number of **Desired** instances will immediately change to *2*. However, it might take a while until the actual number of instances aligns with the desire. Let's go back to one of the manager servers and confirm that the desire we expressed is indeed fulfilled:

```
ssh -i $KEY_PATH docker@$MANAGER_IP

docker node ls
```

It might take a while until the new instance is created and joined to the cluster. The end result should be as follows (IDs are removed for brevity):

```
HOSTNAME                         STATUS   AVAILABILITY   MANAGER STATUS
ip-10-0-17-154.ec2.internal      Ready    Active         Reachable
ip-10-0-15-215.ec2.internal      Ready    Active         Reachable
ip-10-0-31-44.ec2.internal       Ready    Active
ip-10-0-15-214.ec2.internal      Ready    Active         Leader
ip-10-0-11-174.ec2.internal      Ready    Active
```

What happens in case one of the servers fails? After all, everything fails sooner or later. We can test that by removing one of the nodes.

Please click the **Instances** link from the left-hand menu of the EC2 console, select one of the `Docker-worker` nodes, click **Actions**, and change the **Instance State to Terminate**. Confirm the termination by clicking the **Yes, Terminate** button:

```
docker node ls
```

After a while, the output of the node `ls` command should be as follows (IDs are removed for brevity):

```
HOSTNAME                         STATUS   AVAILABILITY   MANAGER STATUS
ip-10-0-17-154.ec2.internal      Ready    Active         Reachable
ip-10-0-15-215.ec2.internal      Ready    Active         Reachable
ip-10-0-31-44.ec2.internal       Ready    Active
ip-10-0-15-214.ec2.internal      Ready    Active         Leader
ip-10-0-11-174.ec2.internal      Down     Active
```

Once the auto scaling group realizes that the node is down, it'll start the process of creating a new one and joining it to the cluster:

```
docker node ls
```

Before long, the output of the node `ls` command should be as follows (IDs are removed for brevity):

```
HOSTNAME                         STATUS   AVAILABILITY   MANAGER STATUS
ip-10-0-17-154.ec2.internal      Ready    Active         Reachable
ip-10-0-15-215.ec2.internal      Ready    Active         Reachable
ip-10-0-2-22.ec2.internal        Ready    Active
ip-10-0-31-44.ec2.internal       Ready    Active
ip-10-0-15-214.ec2.internal      Ready    Active         Leader
ip-10-0-11-174.ec2.internal      Down     Active
```

The server we terminated is still marked as Down, and a new one is created and added to the cluster in its place.

There's much more to the *Docker for AWS* stack than we explored. I hope that what you learned during this brief exploration gave you enough base information to expand the knowledge by yourself.

Instead of exploring more details about the stack, we'll see how we can accomplish the same result without the UI. By this time you should know me well enough to understand that I prefer automatable and reproducible ways of running tasks. I broke my "no UIs unless necessary" rule only to give you a better understanding how the *Docker for AWS* stack works. A fully automated way to do the same is coming up next.

Before we proceed, we'll delete the stack and, with it, remove the cluster. That will be the last time you'll see any UI in this chapter.

Please click the **Services** link from the top menu, followed by the **CloudFormation** link. Select the Docker stack, and click the **Delete Stack** option from the **Actions** menu:

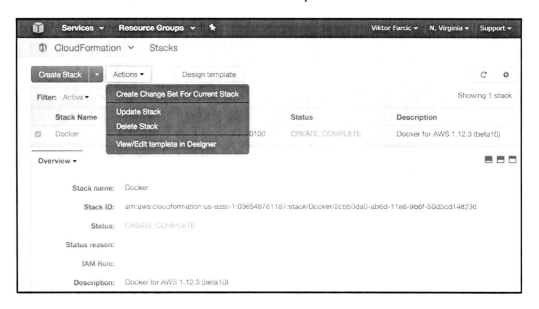

Figure 11-9: Docker For AWS Delete Stack screen

Confirm the destruction by clicking the **Yes**, **Delete** button that appears after you click **Delete Stack**.

Automatically setting up a Swarm cluster with Docker for AWS

Creating a *Docker for AWS* stack from the UI was a great exercise. It helped us understand better how things work. However, our mission is to automate as many processes as possible. With automation, we gain speed, reliability, and higher quality. When we run some manual tasks, like going through a UI and selecting different options, we are increasing the chance that something will go wrong due to human error. We are slow. We are much slower than machines when we need to execute repeatable steps.

Due to my mistrust in manual operations of repeatable tasks, it's only natural to seek a more automated way to create a *Docker for AWS* stack. All we did through the AWS console was to fill in a few fields which, in the background, generate parameters which are later used to execute a `CloudFormation` process. We can do the same without a UI.

We'll start by defining a few environment variables. They will be the same as those you already created in this chapter. Feel free to skip the next set of commands if you still have the same terminal session open:

```
export AWS_DEFAULT_REGION=us-east-1

export AWS_ACCESS_KEY_ID=[...]

export AWS_SECRET_ACCESS_KEY=[...]
```

Please change `us-east-1` to the region of your choice and replace `[...]` with the actual values.

If you recall the first screen that allowed us to select a template, you'll remember that there was a field with pre-populated URL of a **CloudFormation** template. At the time of this writing, the template is `Docker.tmpl` (`https://editions-us-east-1.s3.amazonaws.com/aws/stable/Docker.tmpl`) Please note that the address differs from one region to another. I'll be using `us-east-1` edition.

We can inspect the template by retrieving its content with `curl`:

```
curl https://editions-us-east-1.s3.amazonaws.com/aws/stable/Docker.tmpl
```

Please spend some time exploring the output. Even if you are not familiar with `CloudFormation` syntax, you should recognize the AWS resources.

The part of the template that we are most interested in is Metadata:

```
curl https://editions-us-east-1.s3.amazonaws.com/aws/stable/ \
Docker.tmpl  \
    | jq '.Metadata'
```

The output is as follows:

```
{
  "AWS::CloudFormation::Interface": {
    "ParameterGroups": [
      {
        "Label": {
          "default": "Swarm Size"
        },
        "Parameters": [
         "ManagerSize",
         "ClusterSize"
        ]
      },
      {
        "Label": {
        "default": "Swarm Properties"
        },
        "Parameters": [
         "KeyName",
         "EnableSystemPrune",
         "EnableCloudWatchLogs"
        ]
      },
      {
        "Label": {
          "default": "Swarm Manager Properties"
        },
        "Parameters": [
         "ManagerInstanceType",
         "ManagerDiskSize",
         "ManagerDiskType"
        ]
      },
      {
        "Label": {
          "default": "Swarm Worker Properties"
        },
        "Parameters": [
```

```
                    "InstanceType",
                    "WorkerDiskSize",
                    "WorkerDiskType"
                ]
        }
    ],
        "ParameterLabels": {
            "ClusterSize": {
                "default": "Number of Swarm worker nodes?"
            },
        "EnableCloudWatchLogs": {
            "default": "Use Cloudwatch for container logging?"
        },
        "EnableSystemPrune": {
            "default": "Enable daily resource cleanup?"
        },
        "InstanceType": {
            "default": "Agent worker instance type?"
        },
        "KeyName": {
            "default": "Which SSH key to use?"
        },
        "ManagerDiskSize": {
            "default": "Manager ephemeral storage volume size?"
        },
        "ManagerDiskType": {
            "default": "Manager ephemeral storage volume type"
        },
        "ManagerInstanceType": {
            "default": "Swarm manager instance type?"
        },
        "ManagerSize": {
            "default": "Number of Swarm managers?"
        },
        "WorkerDiskSize": {
            "default": "Worker ephemeral storage volume size?"
        },
        "WorkerDiskType": {
            "default": "Worker ephemeral storage volume type"
        }
        }
    }
  }
}
```

We can use the `ParameterLabels` to customize the result of the template.

The command that would create the same stack like the one we generated using the AWS console is as follows:

```
aws cloudformation create-stack \
    --template-url https://editions-us-east \
    -1.s3.amazonaws.com/aws/stable/Docker.tmpl \
    --stack-name swarm \
    --capabilities CAPABILITY_IAM \
    --parameters \
    ParameterKey=KeyName,ParameterValue=devops21 \
    ParameterKey=InstanceType,ParameterValue=t2.micro \
    ParameterKey=ManagerInstanceType,ParameterValue=t2.micro \
    ParameterKey=ManagerSize,ParameterValue=3 \
    ParameterKey=ClusterSize,ParameterValue=1
```

The command should be self-explanatory. We used `aws` to create a `CloudFormation` stack with all the required parameters.

We can monitor the status of the stack resources by executing the `cloudformation describe-stack-resources` command:

```
aws cloudformation describe-stack-resources \
    --stack-name swarm
```

After a while, three manager instances should be created:

```
aws ec2 describe-instances \
    --filters "Name=tag:Name,Values=swarm-Manager" \
    "Name=instance-state-name,Values=running"
```

Now we can enter one of the managers and start creating services. I'll skip the examples that create services and validate that they are working correctly. The end-result is the same cluster as the one we created previously with AWS console.

Feel free to explore the cluster on your own and `delete` the stack once you're finished:

```
aws cloudformation delete-stack \
    --stack-name swarm
```

For anything but small clusters, *Docker for AWS* is a much better option than using the combination with `docker-machine` and `aws` commands. It is a more robust and reliable solution. However, it comes with its downsides.

Docker for AWS is still young and prone to frequent changes. Moreover, it is still so new that the documentation is close to non-existent.

By being an out-of-the-box solution, it is very easy to use and requires little effort. That is both a blessing and a curse. It is a good choice if what you need is, more or less, what *Docker for AWS* offers. However, if your needs are different, you might experience quite a few problems when trying to adapt the template to your needs. The solution is based on a custom OS, `CloudFormation` template, and containers built specifically for this purpose. Changing anything but the template is highly discouraged.

Overall, I think that *Docker for AWS* has a very bright future and is, in most cases, a better solution than `docker-machine`. If those two were the only choices, my vote would be to use *Docker for AWS*. Fortunately, there are many other options we can choose from; much more than could fit into a single chapter. You might be reading the printed edition of the book, and I don't feel comfortable sacrificing too many trees. Therefore, I'll present only one more set of tools we can use to create a Swarm (or any other type of) cluster.

Setting up a Swarm cluster with Packer and Terraform

This time we'll use a set of tools completely unrelated to Docker. It'll be *Packer*(https://www.packer.io/)and *Terraform* (https://www.terraform.io/). Both are coming from *HashiCorp* (https://www.hashicorp.com/).

A note to Windows users
Using Chocolatey, install packer from an administrator command prompt via `choco install packer`. For terraform, execute `choco install terraform` in an administrator command prompt.

Packer allows us to create machine images. With Terraform we can create, change, and improve cluster infrastructure. Both tools support almost all the major providers. They can be used with Amazon EC2, CloudStack, DigitalOcean, Google Compute Engine (GCE), Microsoft Azure, VMware, VirtualBox, and quite a few others. The ability to be infrastructure agnostic allows us to avoid vendor lock-in. With a minimal change in configuration, we can easily transfer our cluster from one provider to another. Swarm is designed to work seamlessly no matter which hosting provider we use, as long as the infrastructure is properly defined. With Packer and Terraform we can define infrastructure in such a way that transitioning from one to another is as painless as possible.

Using Packer to create Amazon Machine Images

The `vfarcic/cloud-provisioning` (https://github.com/vfarcic/cloud-provisioning) repository already has the Packer and Terraform configurations we'll use. They are located in the `terraform/aws` directory:

```
cd terraform/aws
```

The first step is to use Packer to create an **Amazon Machine Image (AMI)**. To do that, we'll need AWS access keys set as environment variables. They will be the same as those you already created in this chapter. Feel free to skip the next set of commands if you still have the same terminal session open:

```
export AWS_ACCESS_KEY_ID=[...]

export AWS_SECRET_ACCESS_KEY=[...]

export AWS_DEFAULT_REGION=us-east-1
```

Please replace `[...]` with the actual values.

We'll instantiate all Swarm nodes from the same AMI. It'll be based on Ubuntu and have the latest Docker engine installed.

The JSON definition of the image we are about to build is in `terraform/aws/packer-ubuntu-docker.json` (https://github.com/vfarcic/cloud-provisioning/blob/master/terraform/aws/packer-ubuntu-docker.json):

```
cat packer-ubuntu-docker.json
```

The configuration consists of two sections: `builders` and `provisioners`:

```
{
    "builders": [{
    ...
    }],
    "provisioners": [{
    ...
    }]
}
```

The builders section defines all the information Packer needs to build an image. The `provisioners` section describes the commands that will be used to install and configure software for the machines created by builders. The only required section is builders.

Builders are responsible for creating machines and generating images from them for various platforms. For example, there are separate builders for EC2, VMware, VirtualBox, and so on. Packer comes with many builders by default, and can also be extended to add new builders.

The `builders` section we'll use is as follows:

```
"builders": [{
  "type": "amazon-ebs",
  "region": "us-east-1",
  "source_ami_filter": {
    "filters": {
      "virtualization-type": "hvm",
      "name": "*ubuntu-xenial-16.04-amd64-server-*",
      "root-device-type": "ebs"
    },
    "owners": ["099720109477"],
    "most_recent": true
  },
  "instance_type": "t2.micro",
  "ssh_username": "ubuntu",
  "ami_name": "devops21",
  "force_deregister": true
}],
```

Each type of builder has specific arguments that can be used. We specified that the `type` is `amazon-ebs`. Besides `amazon-ebs`, we can also use `amazon-instance` and `amazon-chroot` builders for AMIs. In most cases, `amazon-ebs` is what we should use. Please visit the *Amazon AMI Builder* (`https://www.packer.io/docs/builders/amazon.html`) page for more info.

Please note that, when using `amazon-ebs` type, we have to provide AWS keys. We could have specified them through the **access_key** and **secret_key** fields. However, there is an alternative. If those fields are not specified, Packer will try to get the values from environment variables `AWS_ACCESS_KEY_ID` and `AWS_SECRET_ACCESS_KEY`. Since we already exported them, there's no need to repeat ourselves by setting them inside the Packer configuration. Moreover, those keys should be secret. Putting them inside the config would risk exposure.

The region is critical since an AMI can be created only within one region. If we wanted to share the same machine across multiple regions, each would need to be specified as a separate builder.

We could have specified `source_ami` with the ID of the initial AMI that would serve as a base for the newly created machine. However, since AMIs are unique to a particular region, that would make it unusable if we decide to change the region. Instead, we took a different approach and specified the `source_ami_filter` which will populate the `source_ami` field. It'll filter AMIs and find an Ubuntu `16.04` image with `hvm` virtualization type with Root Device Type set to `ebs`. The owners field will limit the results to a trusted AMI provider. Since the filter would fail if more than one AMI is returned, the `most_recent` field will limit the result by selecting the newest image.

The `instance_type` field defines which EC2 instance type will be used to build the AMI. Please note that this will not prevent us from instantiating VMs based on this image using any other instance type supported, in this case, by Ubuntu.

Unlike other fields we used, the `ssh_username` is not specific to the `amazon-ebs` builder. It specifies the user Packer will use while creating the image. Just like the instance type, it will not prevent us from specifying any other user when instantiating VMs based on this image.

The `ami_name` field is the name we'll give to this AMI.

In case we already created an AMI with the same, the `force_deregister` field will remove it before creating the new one.

Please visit the *AMI Builder (EBS Backed)* (`https://www.packer.io/docs/builders/amazon -ebs.html`) page for more information.

The second section is provisioners. It contains an array of all the provisioners that Packer should use to install and configure software within running machines before turning them into Machine Images.

There are quite a few provisioner types we can use. If you read *The DevOps 2.0 Toolkit*, you know that I advocated Ansible as the provisioner of choice. Should we use it here as well? In most cases, when building images meant to run Docker containers, I opt for a simple shell. The reasons for a change from Ansible to Shell lies in the different objectives provisioners should fulfill when running on live servers, as opposed to building images.

Unlike Shell, Ansible (and most other provisioners) are idempotent. They verify the actual state and execute one action or another depending on what should be done for the desired state to be fulfilled. That's a great approach since we can run Ansible as many times as we want and the result will always be the same. For example, if we specify that we want to have JDK 8, Ansible will SSH into a destination server, discover that the JDK is not present and install it. The next time we run it, it'll discover that the JDK is already there and do nothing.

Such an approach allows us to run Ansible playbooks as often as we want and it'll always result in JDK being installed. If we'd try to accomplish the same through a Shell script, we'd need to write lengthy `if/else` statements. If JDK is installed, do nothing, if it's not installed, install it, if it's installed, but the version is not correct, upgrade it, and so on.

So, why not use it with Packer? The answer is simple. We do not need idempotency since we'll run it only once while creating an image. We won't use it on running instances. Do you remember the "pets vs cattle" discussion? Our VMs will be instantiated from an image that already has everything we need. If the state of that VM changes, we'll terminate it and create a new one.

If we need to do an upgrade or install additional software, we won't do it inside the running instance, but create a new image, destroy running instances, and instantiate new ones based on the updated image.

Is idempotency the only reason we would use Ansible? Definitely not! It is a very handy tool when we need to define a complicated server setup. However, in our case the setup is simple. We need Docker Engine and not much more. Almost everything will be running inside containers. Writing a few Shell commands to install Docker is easier and faster than defining Ansible playbooks. It would probably take the same number of commands to install Ansible as to install Docker.

To make a Long story short, we'll use `shell` as our provisioner of choice for building AMIs.

The `provisioners` section we'll use is as follows:

```
"provisioners": [{
  "type": "shell",
  "inline": [
    "sleep 15",
    "sudo apt-get update",
    "sudo apt-get install -y apt-transport-https ca-certificates \
nfs-common",
    "sudo apt-key adv --keyserver hkp://ha.pool.sks-keyservers.net: \
80 --recv-keys 58118E89F3A912897C070ADBF76221572C52609D",
    "echo 'deb https://apt.dockerproject.org/repo ubuntu-xenial \
main' | sudo tee /etc/apt/sources.list.d/docker.list",
    "sudo apt-get update",
    "sudo apt-get install -y docker-engine",
    "sudo usermod -aG docker ubuntu"
  ]
}]
```

The `shell type` is followed by a set of commands. They are the same as the commands we can find in the *Install Docker on Ubuntu* (`https://docs.docker.com/engine/installation /linux/ubuntulinux/`) page.

Now that we have a general idea how Packer configuration works, we can proceed and build an image:

```
packer build -machine-readable \
    packer-ubuntu-docker.json \
    | tee packer-ubuntu-docker.log
```

We ran the `packer` build of the `packer-ubuntu-docker.json` with the `machine-readable` output sent to the `packer-ubuntu-docker.log` file. Machine readable output will allow us to parse it easily and retrieve the ID of the AMI we just created.

The final lines of the output are as follows:

```
...
1480105510,,ui,say,Build 'amazon-ebs' finished.
1480105510,,ui,say,\n==> Builds finished. The artifacts of successful
builds are:
1480105510,amazon-ebs,artifact-count,1
1480105510,amazon-ebs,artifact,0,builder-id,mitchellh.amazonebs
1480105510,amazon-ebs,artifact,0,id,us-east-1:ami-02ebd915
1480105510,amazon-ebs,artifact,0,string,AMIs were \
created: \n\nus-east-1: ami-02ebd915
1480105510,amazon-ebs,artifact,0,files-count,0
1480105510,amazon-ebs,artifact,0,end
1480105510,,ui,say,--> amazon-ebs: AMIs were created: \n\nus-east-1:
ami-02ebd915
```

Apart from the confirmation that the build was successful, the relevant part of the output is the line id, `us-east-1:ami-02ebd915`. It contains the AMI ID we'll need to instantiate VMs based on the image.

You might want to store the `packer-ubuntu-docker.log` in your code repository in case you need to get the ID from a different server.

The flow of the process we executed can be described through *figure 11-10:*

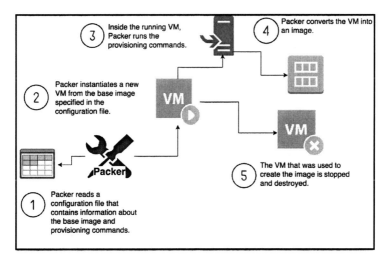

Figure 11-10: The flow of the Packer process

Now we are ready to create a Swarm cluster with VMs based on the image we built.

Using Terraform to create a Swarm cluster in AWS

We'll start by redefining the environment variables we used with Packer in case you start this section in a new terminal session:

```
cd terraform/aws

export AWS_ACCESS_KEY_ID=[...]

export AWS_SECRET_ACCESS_KEY=[...]

export AWS_DEFAULT_REGION=us-east-1
```

Please replace [...] with the actual values.

Terraform does not force us to have any particular file structure. We can define everything in a single file. However, that does not mean that we should. Terraform configs can get big, and separation of logical sections into separate files is often a good idea. In our case, we'll have three tf files. The terraform/aws/variables.tf (https://github.com/vfarcic/cloud-provisioning/blob/master/terraform/aws/variables.tf) holds all the variables.

If we need to change any parameter, we'll know where to find it. The terraform/aws/common.tf (https://github.com/vfarcic/cloud-provisioning/blob/master/terraform/aws/common.tf) file contains definitions of the elements that might be potentially reusable on other occasions. Finally, the terraform/aws/swarm.tf (https://github.com/vfarcic/cloud-provisioning/blob/master/terraform/aws/swarm.tf) file has the Swarm-specific resources.

We'll explore each of the Terraform configuration files separately.

The content of the terraform/aws/variables.tf (https://github.com/vfarcic/cloud-provisioning/blob/master/terraform/aws/variables.tf) file is as follows:

```
variable "swarm_manager_token" {
  default = ""
}
variable "swarm_worker_token" {
  default = ""
}
variable "swarm_ami_id" {
  default = "unknown"
}
variable "swarm_manager_ip" {
  default = ""
}
variable "swarm_managers" {
  default = 3
}
variable "swarm_workers" {
  default = 2
}
variable "swarm_instance_type" {
  default = "t2.micro"
}
variable "swarm_init" {
  default = false
}
```

The `swarm_manager_token` and `swarm_worker_token` will be required to join the nodes to the cluster. The `swarm_ami_id` will hold the ID of the image we created with Packer. The `swarm_manager_ip` variable is the IP of one of the managers that we'll need to provide for the nodes to join the cluster. The `swarm_managers` and `swarm_workers` define how many nodes we want of each. The `swarm_instance_type` is the type of the instance we want to create. If defaults to the smallest and cheapest (often free) instance. Feel free to change it to a more potent type later on if you start using this Terraform config to create a "real" cluster. >Finally, the `swarm_init` variable allows us to specify whether this is the first run and the node should initialize the cluster. We'll see its usage very soon.

The content of the `terraform/aws/common.tf` (https://github.com/vfarcic/cloud-pr ovisioning/blob/master/terraform/aws/common.tf) file is as follows:

```
resource "aws_security_group" "docker" {
  name = "docker"
  ingress {
    from_port   = 22
    to_port     = 22
    protocol    = "tcp"
    cidr_blocks = ["0.0.0.0/0"]
  }
  ingress {
    from_port = 80
    to_port   = 80
    protocol  = "tcp"
    cidr_blocks = ["0.0.0.0/0"]
  }
  ingress {
    from_port = 443
    to_port   = 443
    protocol  = "tcp"
    cidr_blocks = ["0.0.0.0/0"]
  }
  ingress {
    from_port = 2377
    to_port   = 2377
    protocol  = "tcp"
    self      = true
  }
  ingress {
    from_port = 7946
    to_port   = 7946
    protocol  = "tcp"
    self      = true
  }
  ingress {
```

```
        from_port = 7946
        to_port   = 7946
        protocol  = "udp"
        self      = true
    }
    ingress {
        from_port = 4789
        to_port   = 4789
        protocol  = "tcp"
        self      = true
    }
    ingress {
        from_port = 4789
        to_port   = 4789
        protocol  = "udp"
        self      = true
    }
    egress {
        from_port   = 0
        to_port     = 0
        protocol    = "-1"
        cidr_blocks = ["0.0.0.0/0"]
    }
}
```

Each resource is defined with a type (example: `aws_security_group`) and a name (example: `docker`). The type determines which resource should be created and must be one of those currently supported.

The first resource `aws_security_group` contains the list of all ingress ports that should be opened. Port `22` is required for SSH. Ports `80` and `443` will be used for HTTP and HTTPS access to the `proxy`. The rest of the ports will be used for Swarms internal communication. TCP port `2377` is for cluster management communications, TCP and UDP port `7946` for communication among nodes, and TCP and UDP port `4789` for overlay network traffic. Those are the same ports we had to open when we created the cluster using Docker Machine. Please note that all but ports `22`, `80` and `443` are assigned to self. That means that they will be available only to other servers that belong to the same group. Any outside access will be blocked.

The last entry in the `aws_security_group` is `egress` allowing communication from the cluster to the outside world without any restrictions.

Please consult the `AWS_SECURITY_GROUP` (`https://www.terraform.io/docs/providers/aws/d/security_group.html`) page for more info.

Now comes the "real deal". The `terraform/aws/swarm.tf` (`https://github.com/vfarci`
`c/cloud-provisioning/blob/master/terraform/aws/swarm.tf`) file contains the
definition of all the instances we'll create. Since the content of this file is a bit bigger than the
others, we'll examine each resource separately.

The first resource in line is the `aws_instance` type named `swarm-manager`. Its purpose is
to create Swarm manager nodes:

```
resource "aws_instance" "swarm-manager" {
  ami = "${var.swarm_ami_id}"
  instance_type = "${var.swarm_instance_type}"
  count = "${var.swarm_managers}"
  tags {
    Name = "swarm-manager"
  }
  vpc_security_group_ids = [
    "${aws_security_group.docker.id}"
  ]
  key_name = "devops21"
  connection {
    user = "ubuntu"
    private_key = "${file("devops21.pem")}"
  }
  provisioner "remote-exec" {
    inline = [
      "if ${var.swarm_init}; then docker swarm init \
--advertise-addr ${self.private_ip}; fi",
      "if ! ${var.swarm_init}; then docker swarm join \
--token ${var.swarm_manager_token} --advertise-addr \
${self.private_ip} ${var.swarm_manager_ip}:2377; fi"
    ]
  }
}
```

The resource contains the `ami` that references the image we created with Packer. The actual
value is a variable that we'll define at runtime. The `instance_type` specifies the type of the
instance we want to create. The default value is fetched from the variable
`swarm_instance_type`. By default, it is set to `t2.micro`. Just as any other variable, it can
be overwritten at runtime.

The count field defines how many managers we want to create. The first time we run
`terraform`, the value should be 1 since we want to start with one manager that will
initialize the cluster. Afterward, the value should be whatever is defined in variables. We'll
see the use case of both combinations soon.

The tags are for informational purposes only.

The `vpc_security_group_ids` field contains the list of all groups we want to attach to the server. In our case, we are using only the group docker defined in `terraform/aws/common.tf`.

The `key_name` is the name of the key we have stored in AWS. We created the `devops21` key at the beginning of the chapter. Please double check that you did not remove it. Without it, you won't be able to SSH into the machine.

The connection field defines the SSH connection details. The user will be `ubuntu`. Instead of a password, we'll use the `devops21.pem` key.

Finally, the provisioner is defined. The idea is to do as much provisioning as possible during the creation of the images. That way, instances are created much faster since the only action is to create a VM out of an image. However, there is often a part of provisioning that cannot be done when creating an image. The `swarm init` command is one of those. We cannot initialize the first Swarm node until we get the IP of the server. In other words, the server needs to be running (and therefore has an IP) before the `swarm init command` is executed.

Since the first node has to initialize the cluster while any other should join, we're using if statements to distinguish one case from the other. If the variable `swarm_init` is true, the docker swarm init command will be executed. On the other hand, if the variable `swarm_init` is set to false, the command will be docker swarm join. In that case, we are using another variable `swarm_manager_ip` to tell the node which manager to use to join the cluster.

Please note that the IP is obtained using the special syntax `self.private_ip`. We are referencing oneself and getting the `private_ip`. There are many other attributes we can get from a resource.

Please consult the *AWS_INSTANCE* (`https://www.terraform.io/docs/providers/aws/r/instance.html`) page for more info.

Let's take a look at the `aws_instance` resource named `swarm-worker`:

```
resource "aws_instance" "swarm-worker" {
  count = "${var.swarm_workers}"
  ami = "${var.swarm_ami_id}"
  instance_type = "${var.swarm_instance_type}"
  tags {
    Name = "swarm-worker"
  }
  vpc_security_group_ids = [
    "${aws_security_group.docker.id}"
```

```
    ]
    key_name = "devops21"
    connection {
      user = "ubuntu"
      private_key = "${file("devops21.pem")}"
    }
    provisioner "remote-exec" {
      inline = [
      "docker swarm join --token ${var.swarm_worker_token} \
--advertise-addr ${self.private_ip} ${var.swarm_manager_ip}:2377"
      ]
    }
  }
```

The `swarm-worker` resource is almost identical to `swarm-manager`. The only difference is in the count field that uses the `swarm_workers` variable and the provisioner. Since a worker cannot initialize a cluster, there was no need for if statements, so the only command we want to execute is `docker swarm join`

Terraform uses a naming convention that allows us to specify values as environment variables by adding the `TF_VAR_` prefix. For example, we can specify the value of the variable `swarm_ami_id` by setting the environment variable `TF_VAR_swarm_ami_id`. The alternative is to use the `-var` argument. I prefer environment variables since they allow me to specify them once instead of adding `-var` to every command.

The last part of the `terraform/aws/swarm.tf` (`https://github.com/vfarcic/cloud-pro visioning/blob/master/terraform/aws/swarm.tf`) specification are outputs.

When building potentially complex infrastructure, Terraform stores hundreds or thousands of attribute values for all resources. But, as a user, we may only be interested in a few values of importance, such as manager IPs. Outputs are a way to tell Terraform what data is relevant. This data is outputted when apply is called, and can be queried using the `terraform output` command.

The outputs we defined are as follows:

```
    output "swarm_manager_1_public_ip" {
      value = "${aws_instance.swarm-manager.0.public_ip}"
    }

    output "swarm_manager_1_private_ip" {
      value = "${aws_instance.swarm-manager.0.private_ip}"
    }
    output "swarm_manager_2_public_ip" {
      value = "${aws_instance.swarm-manager.1.public_ip}"
    }
```

```
output "swarm_manager_2_private_ip" {
  value = "${aws_instance.swarm-manager.1.private_ip}"
}

output "swarm_manager_3_public_ip" {
  value = "${aws_instance.swarm-manager.2.public_ip}"
}

output "swarm_manager_3_private_ip" {
  value = "${aws_instance.swarm-manager.2.private_ip}"
}
```

They are public and private IPs of the managers. Since there are only a few (if any) reasons to know worker IPs, we did not define them as outputs. Please consult the *Output Configuration* (https://www.terraform.io/docs/configuration/outputs.html) page for more info. Since we'll use the AMI we created with Packer, we need to retrieve the ID from the `packer-ubuntu-docker.log`. The command that follows parses the output and extracts the ID:

```
export TF_VAR_swarm_ami_id=$( \
    grep 'artifact,0,id' \
    packer-ubuntu-docker.log \
    | cut -d: -f2)
```

Before we create our cluster and the infrastructure around it, we should ask Terraform to show us the execution plan:

```
terraform plan
```

The result is an extensive list of resources and their properties. Since the output is too big to be printed, I'll limit the output only to the resource types and names:

```
...
+ aws_instance.swarm-manager.0
...
+ aws_instance.swarm-manager.1
...
+ aws_instance.swarm-manager.2
...
+ aws_instance.swarm-worker.0
...
+ aws_instance.swarm-worker.1
...
+ aws_security_group.docker
...
Plan: 6 to add, 0 to change, 0 to destroy.
```

Since this is the first execution, all the resources would be created if we were to execute terraform apply. We would get five EC2 instances; three managers and two workers. That would be accompanied by one security group.

If you see the complete output, you'll notice that some of the property values are set to `<computed>`. That means that Terraform cannot know what will be the actual values until it creates the resources. A good example are IPs. They do not exist until the EC2 instance is created.

We can also output the plan using the `graph` command:

```
terraform graph
```

The output is as follows:

```
digraph {
    compound = "true"
    newrank = "true"
    subgraph "root" {
       "[root] aws_instance.swarm-manager" [label = \
"aws_instance.swarm-manager",shape = "box"]
       "[root] aws_instance.swarm-worker" [label = \
"aws_instance.swarm-worker", shape= "box"]
       "[root] aws_security_group.docker" [label = \
"aws_security_group.docker", shape = "box"]
       "[root] provider.aws" [label = "provider.aws", shape = \
"diamond"]
       "[root] aws_instance.swarm-man ager" -> "[root] \
aws_security_group.docker"
       "[root] aws_instance.swarm-manager" -> "[root] provider.aws" \
       "[root] aws_instance.swarm-worker" -> "[root] \
aws_security_group.docker"
       "[root] aws_instance.swarm-worker" -> "[root] provider.aws" \
       "[root] aws_security_group.docker" -> "[root] provider.aws" \
    }
}
```

That, in itself, is not very useful.

The `graph` command is used to generate a visual representation of either a configuration or an execution plan. The output is in the DOT format, which can be used by GraphViz to make graphs.

Please open *Graphviz Download* (`http://www.graphviz.org/Download..php`) page and download and install the distribution compatible with your OS.

Now we can combine the `graph` command with dot:

```
terraform graph | dot -Tpng > graph.png
```

The output should be the same as in *Figure 11-11*:

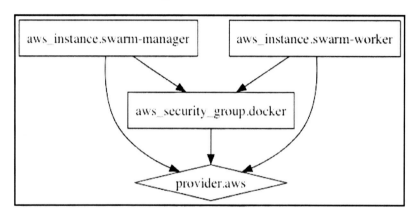

Figure 11-11: The image generated by Graphviz from the output of the terraform graph command

Visualization of the plan allows us to see the dependencies between different resources. In our case, all resources will use the `aws` provider. Both instance types will depend on the security group docker.

When dependencies are defined, we don't need to explicitly specify all the resources we need.

As an example, let's take a look at the plan Terraform will generate when we limit it to only one Swarm manager node, so that we can initialize the cluster:

```
terraform plan \
    -target aws_instance.swarm-manager \
    -var swarm_init=true \
    -var swarm_managers=1
```

The runtime variables `swarm_init` and `swarm_managers` will be used to tell Terraform that we want to initialize the cluster with one manager. The plan command takes those variables into account and outputs the execution plan.

The output, limited only to resource types and names, is as follows:

```
+ aws_instance.swarm-manager
+ aws_security_group.docker
```

Even though we specified that we only want the plan for the `swarm-manager` resource, Terraform noticed that it depends on the security group `docker`, and included it in the execution plan.

The only thing missing before we start creating the AWS resources is to copy the SSH key `devops21.pem` to the current directory. The configuration expects it to be there:

```
export KEY_PATH=$HOME/.ssh/devops21.pem

cp $KEY_PATH devops21.pem
```

Please change the `KEY_PATH` value to the correct path before copying it.

We'll start small and create only one manager instance that will initialize the cluster. As we saw from the plan, it depends on the security group, so Terraform will create it as well.

```
terraform apply \
    -target aws_instance.swarm-manager \
    -var swarm_init=true \
    -var swarm_managers=1
```

The output is too big to be presented in the book. If you look at it from your terminal, you'll notice that the security group is created first since `swarm-manager` depends on it. Please note that we did not specify the dependency explicitly. However, since the resource has it specified in the `vpc_security_group_ids` field, Terraform understood that it is the dependency.

Once the `swarm-manager` instance is created, Terraform waited until SSH access is available. After it had managed to connect to the new instance, it executed `provisioning` commands that initialized the cluster.

The final lines of the output are as follows:

```
Apply complete! Resources: 2 added, 0 changed, 0 destroyed.

The state of your infrastructure has been saved to the path
below. This state is required to modify and destroy your
infrastructure, so keep it safe. To inspect the complete state
use the `terraform show` command.

State path: terraform.tfstate
```

```
Outputs:

swarm_manager_1_private_ip = 172.31.49.214
swarm_manager_1_public_ip = 52.23.252.207
```

The outputs are defined at the bottom of the `terraform/aws/swarm.tf` (https://github
.com/vfarcic/cloud-provisioning/blob/master/terraform/aws/swarm.tf) file. Please
note that not all outputs are listed but only those of the resources that were created.

We can use the public IP of the newly created EC2 instance and SSH into it.

You might be inclined to copy the IP. There's no need for that. Terraform has a command
that can be used to retrieve any information we defined as the output.

The command that retrieves the public IP of the first, and currently the only manager is as
follows:

```
terraform output swarm_manager_1_public_ip
```

The output is as follows:

```
52.23.252.207
```

We can leverage the `output` command to construct `SSH` commands. As an example, the
command that follows will SSH into the machine and retrieve the list of Swarm nodes:

```
ssh -i devops21.pem \
    ubuntu@$(terraform output \
    swarm_manager_1_public_ip) \
    docker node ls
```

The output is as follows (IDs are removed for brevity):

```
HOSTNAME          STATUS AVAILABILITY MANAGER STATUS
ip-172-31-49-214 Ready  Active       Leader
```

From now on, we won't be limited to a single manager node that initialized the cluster. We
can create all the rest of the nodes. However, before we do that, we need to discover the
`manager` and `worker` tokens. For security reasons, it is better that they are not stored
anywhere, so we'll create environment variables:

```
export TF_VAR_swarm_manager_token=$(ssh \
    -i devops21.pem \
    ubuntu@$(terraform output \
    swarm_manager_1_public_ip) \
    docker swarm join-token -q manager)
```

```
export TF_VAR_swarm_worker_token=$(ssh \
    -i devops21.pem \
    ubuntu@$(terraform output \
    swarm_manager_1_public_ip) \
    docker swarm join-token -q worker)
```

We'll also need to set the environment variable `swarm_manager_ip`:

```
export TF_VAR_swarm_manager_ip=$(terraform \
    output swarm_manager_1_private_ip)
```

Even though we could use `aws_instance.swarm-manager.0.private_ip` inside the `terraform/aws/swarm.tf` (https://github.com/vfarcic/cloud-provisioning/blob/master/terraform/aws/swarm.tf), it is a good idea to have it defined as an environment variable. That way, if the first manager fails, we can easily change it to `swarm_manager_2_private_ip` without modifying the `tf` files.

Now, let us see the plan for the creation of all the missing resources:

```
terraform plan
```

The was no need to specify targets since, this time, we want to create all the resources that are missing.

The last line of the output is as follows:

```
...
Plan: 4 to add, 0 to change, 0 to destroy.
```

We can see that the plan is to create four new resources. Since we already have one manager running and specified that the desired number is three, two additional managers will be created together with two workers.

Let's apply the execution plan:

```
terraform apply
```

The last lines of the output are as follows:

```
...
Apply complete! Resources: 4 added, 0 changed, 4 destroyed.

The state of your infrastructure has been saved to the path
below. This state is required to modify and destroy your
infrastructure, so keep it safe. To inspect the complete state
use the `terraform show` command.
```

```
State path: terraform.tfstate

Outputs:

swarm_manager_1_private_ip = 172.31.49.214
swarm_manager_1_public_ip = 52.23.252.207
swarm_manager_2_private_ip = 172.31.61.11
swarm_manager_2_public_ip = 52.90.245.134
swarm_manager_3_private_ip = 172.31.49.221
swarm_manager_3_public_ip = 54.85.49.136
```

All four resources were created, and we got the output of the manager public and private IPs.

Let's enter into one of the managers and confirm that the cluster indeed works:

```
ssh -i devops21.pem \
    ubuntu@$(terraform \
    output swarm_manager_1_public_ip)

docker node ls
```

The output of the node ls command is as follows (IDs are removed for brevity):

```
HOSTNAME            STATUS   AVAILABILITY   MANAGER STATUS
ip-172-31-61-11     Ready    Active         Reachable
ip-172-31-49-221    Ready    Active         Reachable
ip-172-31-50-78     Ready    Active
ip-172-31-49-214    Ready    Active         Leader
ip-172-31-49-41     Ready    Active
```

All the nodes are present, and the cluster seems to be working.

To be fully confident that everything works as expected, we'll deploy a few services. Those will be the same services we were creating throughout the book, so we'll save ourselves some time and deploy the vfarcic/docker-flow-proxy/docker-compose-stack.yml (https://github.com/vfarcic/docker-flow-proxy/blob/master/docker-compose-stack.yml) and vfarcic/go-demo/docker-compose-stack.yml (https://github.com/vfarcic/go-demo/blob/master/docker-compose-stack.yml) stacks:

```
sudo docker network create --driver overlay proxy

curl -o proxy-stack.yml \
    https://raw.githubusercontent.com/ \
vfarcic/docker-flow-proxy/master/docker-compose-stack.yml

sudo docker stack deploy \
```

```
        -c proxy-stack.yml proxy

curl -o go-demo-stack.yml \
    https://raw.githubusercontent.com/ \
vfarcic/go-demo/master/docker-compose-stack.yml

sudo docker stack deploy \
    -c go-demo-stack.yml go-demo

docker service ls
```

We downloaded the script from the repository, gave it executable permissions, and executed it. At the end, we listed all the services.

After a while, the output of the `service ls` command should be as follows (IDs are removed for brevity):

```
NAME                      MODE        REPLICAS
go-demo_db                replicated  1/1
proxy_swarm-listener      replicated  1/1
proxy_proxy               replicated  2/2
go-demo_main              replicated  3/3
-------------------------------------------------
IMAGE
mongo:latest
vfarcic/docker-flow-swarm-listener:latest
vfarcic/docker-flow-proxy:latest
vfarcic/go-demo:latest
```

Finally, let's send a request to the `go-demo` service through the `proxy`. If it returns the correct response, we'll know that everything works correctly:

```
curl localhost/demo/hello
```

The output is as follows:

```
hello, world!
```

It works!

Are we finished? We probably are. As a last check, let's validate that the `proxy` is accessible from outside the security group. We can confirm that by exiting the server and sending a request from our laptop:

```
exit

curl $(terraform output \
    swarm_manager_1_public_ip)/demo/hello
```

The output is as follows:

```
hello, world!
```

Let's see what happens if we simulate a failure of an instance.

We'll delete an instance using AWS CLI. We could use Terraform to remove an instance. However, removing it with the AWS CLI will more closely simulate an unexpected failure of a node. To remove an instance, we need to find its ID. We can do that with the `terraform show` command. Let's say that we want to remove the second worker. The command to find all its information is as follows:

```
terraform state show "aws_instance.swarm-worker[1]"
```

The output is as follows:

```
id                                            = i-6a3a1964
ami                                           = ami-02ebd915
associate_public_ip_address                   = true
availability_zone                             = us-east-1b
disable_api_termination                       = false
ebs_block_device.#                            = 0
ebs_optimized                                 = false
ephemeral_block_device.#                      = 0
iam_instance_profile                          =
instance_state                                = running
instance_type                                 = t2.micro
key_name                                      = devops21
monitoring                                    = false
network_interface_id                          = eni-322fd9cc
private_dns                                    = ip-172-31-56-227.ec2.internal
private_ip                                     = 172.31.56.227
public_dns                                     =
ec2-54-174-83-184.compute-1.amazonaws.com
public_ip                                     = 54.174.83.184
root_block_device.#                           = 1
root_block_device.0.delete_on_termination     = true
root_block_device.0.iops                      = 100
root_block_device.0.volume_size               = 8
root_block_device.0.volume_type               = gp2
security_groups.#                             = 0
source_dest_check                             = true
subnet_id                                      = subnet-e71631cd
tags.%                                         = 1
tags.Name                                      = swarm-worker
tenancy                                        = default
vpc_security_group_ids.#                      = 1
vpc_security_group_ids.937984769              = sg-288e1555
```

Among other pieces of data, we got the ID. In my case, it is `i-6a3a1964`.Before running the command that follows, please change the ID to the one you got from the `terraform state show` command:

```
aws ec2 terminate-instances \
    --instance-ids i-6a3a1964
```

The output is as follows:

```
{
    "TerminatingInstances": [
        {
            "InstanceId": "i-6a3a1964",
            "CurrentState": {
                "Code": 32,
                "Name": "shutting-down"
            },
            "PreviousState": {
                "Code": 16,
                "Name": "running"
            }
        }
    ]
}
```

AWS changed the state of the instance from `running` to `shutting-down`.

Let's run the `terraform plan` command one more time:

```
terraform plan
```

The last line of the output is as follows:

```
Plan: 1 to add, 0 to change, 0 to destroy.
```

Terraform deduced that one resource `swarm-worker.1` needs to be added to reconcile the discrepancy between the state it has stored locally and the actual state of the cluster.

All we have to do to restore the cluster to the desirable state is to run `terraform apply`:

```
terraform apply
```

The last lines of the output are as follows:

```
...
Apply complete! Resources: 1 added, 0 changed, 0 destroyed.

The state of your infrastructure has been saved to the path
below. This state is required to modify and destroy your
infrastructure, so keep it safe. To inspect the complete state
use the `terraform show` command.

State path: terraform.tfstate

Outputs:

swarm_manager_1_private_ip = 172.31.60.117
swarm_manager_1_public_ip = 52.91.201.148
swarm_manager_2_private_ip = 172.31.57.177
swarm_manager_2_public_ip = 54.91.90.33
swarm_manager_3_private_ip = 172.31.48.226
swarm_manager_3_public_ip = 54.209.238.50
```

We can see that one resource was added. The terminated worker has been recreated, and the cluster continues operating at its full capacity.

The state of the cluster is stored in the `terraform.tfstate` file. If you are not running it always from the same computer, you might want to store that file in your repository together with the rest of configuration files. The alternative is to use *Remote State* (`https://www.terraform.io/docs/state/remote/index.html`)and, for example, store it in Consul.

Changing the desired state of the cluster is easy as well. All we have to to is add more resources and rerun `terraform apply`.

We are finished with the brief introduction to Terraform for AWS.

The flow of the process we executed can be described through *figure 11-12:*

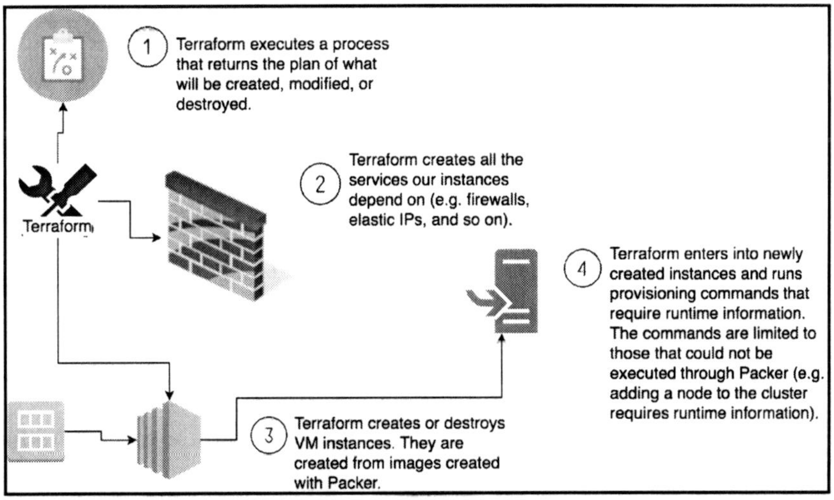

Figure 11-12: The flow of the Terraform process

Let's destroy what we did before we compare the different approaches we took to create and manage a Swarm cluster in AWS:

```
terraform destroy –force
```

The cluster is gone as if it never existed, saving us from unnecessary expenses.

Choosing the right tools to create and manage Swarm clusters in AWS

We tried three different combinations to create a Swarm cluster in AWS. We used *Docker Machine* with the *AWS CLI*, *Docker for AWS* with a CloudFormation template, and *Packer* with *Terraform*. That is, by no means, the final list of the tools we can use. The time is limited, and I promised myself that this book will be shorter than *War and Peace* so I had to draw the line somewhere. Those three combinations are, in my opinion, the best candidates as your tools of choice. Even if you do choose something else, this chapter, hopefully, gave you an insight into the direction you might want to take.

Most likely you won't use all three combinations so the million dollar question is which one should it be?

Only you can answer that question. Now you have the practical experience that should be combined with the knowledge of what you want to accomplish. Each use case is different, and no combination would be the best fit for everyone.

Nevertheless, I will provide a brief overview and some of the use-cases that might be a good fit for each combination.

To Docker Machine or not to Docker Machine?

Docker Machine is the weakest solution we explored. It is based on ad-hoc commands and provides little more than a way to create an EC2 instance and install Docker Engine. It uses *Ubuntu 15.10* as the base AMI. Not only that it is old but is a temporary release. If we choose to use Ubuntu, the correct choice is *16.04* **Long Term Support (LTS)**.

Moreover, Docker Machine still does not support Swarm Mode so we need to manually open the port before executing `docker swarm init` and `docker swarm join` commands. To do that, we need to combine Docker Machine with AWS Console, AWS CLI, or CloudFormation.

If Docker Machine would, at least, provide the minimum setup for Swarm Mode (as it did with the old Standalone Swarm), it could be a good choice for a small cluster.

As it is now, the only true benefit Docker Machine provides when working with a Swarm cluster in AWS is Docker Engine installation on a remote node and the ability to use the `docker-machine env` command to make our local Docker client seamlessly communicate with the remote cluster. Docker Engine installation is simple so that alone is not enough. On the other hand, the `docker-machine env` command should not be used in a production environment. Both benefits are too weak.

Many of the current problems with Docker Machine can be fixed with some extra arguments (example: `--amazonec2-ami`) and in combination with other tools. However, that only diminishes the primary benefit behind Docker Machine. It was supposed to be simple and work out of the box. That was partly true before *Docker 1.12*. Now, at least in AWS, it is lagging behind.

Does that mean we should discard Docker Machine when working with AWS? Not always. It is still useful when we want to create an ad-hoc cluster for demo purposes or maybe experiment with some new features. Also, if you don't want to spend time learning other tools and just want something you're familiar with, Docker Machine might be the right choice. I doubt that's your case.

The fact that you reached this far in this book tells me that you do want to explore better ways of managing a cluster.

The final recommendation is to keep Docker Machine as the tool of choice when you want to simulate a Swarm cluster locally as we did before this chapter. There are better choices for AWS.

To Docker for AWS or not to Docker for AWS?

Docker for AWS (`https://docs.docker.com/docker-for-aws/release-notes/`) is opposite from Docker Machine. It is a complete solution for your Swarm cluster. While Docker Machine does not do much more than to create EC2 instances and install Docker Engine, *Docker for AWS* sets up many of the things we might have a hard time setting up ourselves. Autoscaling groups, VPCs, subnets, and ELB are only a few of the things we get with it.

There is almost nothing we need to do to create and manage a Swarm cluster with *Docker for AWS*. Choose how many managers and how many workers you need, click the **Create Stack** button, and wait a few minutes. That's all there is to it.

There's even more. *Docker for AWS* comes with a new OS specifically designed to run containers.

Does so much praise for *Docker for AWS* inevitably mean it's the best choice? Not necessarily. It depends on your needs and the use case. If what *Docker for AWS* offers is what you need, the choice is simple. Go for it. On the other hand, if you'd like to change some of its aspects or add things that are not included, you might have a hard time. It is not easy to modify or extend it.

As an example, *Docker for AWS* will output all the logs to *Amazon CloudWatch* (`https://aws.amazon.com/cloudwatch/`). That's great as long as CloudWatch is where you want to have your logs. On the other hand, if you prefer the ELK stack, DataDog, or any other logging solution, you will discover that changing the default setup is not that trivial.

Let's see another example. What if you'd like to add persistent storage. You might mount an EFS volume on all servers, but that's not an optimum solution. You might want to experiment with RexRay or Flocker. If that's the case, you will discover that, again, it's not that simple to extend the system. You'd probably end up modifying the CloudFormation template and risk not being able to upgrade to a new *Docker for AWS* version.

Did I mention that *Docker for AWS* is still young? At the time of this writing, it is, more or less, stable, but it still has its problems.

More than problems, it lacks some features like, for example, persistent storage. All this negativity does not mean that you should give up on *Docker for AWS*. It is a great solution that will only become better with time.

The final recommendation is to use *Docker for AWS* if it provides (almost) everything you need or if you do not want to start working on your solution from scratch. The biggest show stopper would be if you already have a set of requirements that need to be fulfilled no matter the tool you'll use.

If you decide to host your cluster in AWS and you do not want to spend time learning how all its services work, read no more. *Docker for AWS* is what you need. It saves you from learning about security groups, VPCs, elastic IPs, and a myriad of other services that you might, or might not need.

To Terraform or not to Terraform?

Terraform, when combined with Packer, is an excellent choice. HashiCorp managed to make yet another tool that changes the way we configure and provision servers.

Configuration management tools have as their primary objective the task of making a server always be in the desired state. If a web server stops, it will be started again. If a configuration file is changed, it will be restored. No matter what happens to a server, its desired state will be restored. Except, when there is no fix to the issue. If a hard disk fails, there's nothing configuration management can do.

The problem with configuration management tools is that they were designed to work with physical, not virtual servers. Why would we fix a faulty virtual server when we can create a new one in a matter of seconds? Terraform understands how cloud computing works better than anyone and embraces the idea that our servers are not pets anymore. They are cattle. It'll make sure that all your resources are available. When something is wrong on a server, it will not try to fix it. Instead, it will destroy it and create a new one based on the image we choose.

Does that mean that there is no place for Puppet, Chef, Ansible, and other similar tools? Are they obsolete when operating in the cloud? Some are more outdated than others. Puppet and Chef are designed to run an agent on each server continuously monitoring its state and modifying it if things go astray. There is no place for such tools when we start treating our servers as cattle. Ansible is in a bit better position since it is more useful than others as a tool designed to configure a server instead to monitor it. As such, it could be very helpful when creating images.

We can combine Ansible with Packer. Packer would create a new VM, Ansible would provision that VM with everything we need, and leave it to Packer to create an image out of it. If the server setup is complicated, that makes a lot of sense. The question is how complex a server setup should be? With AWS, many of the resources that would traditionally run on a server are now services. We do not set up a firewall on each server but use VPC and security group services. We don't create a lot of system users since we do not log into a machine to deploy software. Swarm does that for us. We do not install web servers and runtime dependencies anymore. They are inside containers. Is there a true benefit from using configuration management tools to install a few things into VMs that will be converted into images? More often than not, the answer is no. The few things we need can be just as easily installed and configured with a few Shell commands. Configuration management of our cattle can, and often should, be done with bash.

I might have been too harsh. Ansible is still a great tool if you know when to use it and for what purpose. If you prefer it over bash to install and configure a server before it becomes an image, go for it. If you try to use it to control your nodes and create AWS resources, you're on a wrong path. Terraform does that much better. If you think that it is better to provision a running node instead instantiating images that already have everything inside, you must have much more patience than I do.

Now that we established my bias towards tools that are designed from the ground up to work with cloud (as opposed to on-premise physical servers), you might be wondering whether to use CloudFormation instead of Terraform.

The major problem with CloudFormation is that it is designed to lock you into AWS. It manages Amazon services and not much more. Personally, I think that vendor lock-in is unacceptable if there is a good alternative. If you are already using AWS services to their fullest, feel free to disregard my opinion on that subject. I prefer the freedom of choice. I'm usually trying to design systems that have as little dependency on the provider as it makes sense. I'll use a service in AWS if it's truly better or easier to setup than some other. In some cases, that's true, while in many others it isn't. AWS VPCs and security groups are a good example of services that provide a lot of value. I don't see a reason not to use them, especially since they are easy to replace if I move to a different provider.

CloudWatch would be an opposite example. ELK is a better solution than CloudWatch, it's free, and it can be ported to any provider. The same can be said, for example, for ELB. It is mostly obsolete with Docker Networking. If you need a proxy, choose HAProxy or nginx.

For you, the vendor lock-in argument might be irrelevant. You might have chosen AWS and will stick with it for some time to come. Fair enough. However, Terraform's ability to work with a myriad of hosting providers is not the only advantage it has.

When compared with CloudFormation, its configuration is easier to understand, it works well with other types of resources like *DNSimple* (https://www.terraform.io/docs/providers/dnsimple/), and its ability to display a plan before applying it can save us from a lot of painful errors. When combined with Packer, it is, in my opinion, the best combination for managing a cloud infrastructure.

Let's get back to the original discussion. Should we use *Docker for AWS* or *Terraform* with *Packer*?

Unlike Docker Machine that was easy to reject for most cases, the dilemma whether to use *Terraform* or *Docker for AWS* is harder to resolve. It might take you a while to reach with Terraform the state where the cluster has everything you need. It is not an out-of-the-box solution. You have to write the configs yourself. If you are experienced with AWS, such a feat should not cause much trouble. On the other hand, if AWS is not your strongest virtue, it might take you quite a while to define everything.

Still, I would discard learning AWS as the reason to choose one over the other. Even if you go with an out-of-the-box solution like *Docker for AWS*, you should still know AWS. Otherwise, you're running a risk of failing to react to infrastructure problems when they come. Don't think that anything can save you from understanding AWS intricacies. The question is only whether you'll learn the details before or after you create your cluster.

The final recommendation is to use Terraform with Packer if you want to have a control of all the pieces that constitute your cluster or if you already have a set of rules that need to be followed. Be ready to spend some time tuning the configs until you reach the optimum setup. Unlike with Docker for AWS, you will not have a definition of a fully functioning cluster in an hour. If that's what you want, choose Docker for AWS. On the other hand, when you do configure Terraform to do everything you need, the result will be beautiful.

The final verdict

What should we use? How do we make a decision? Fully functioning cluster made by people who know what they're doing *Docker for AWS* versus fully operational cluster made by you Terraform. Docker for AWS versus whatever you'd like to label your own solution Terraform. More things than you need (Docker for AWS) versus just the resources you want Terraform.

Making the choice is hard. *Docker for AWS* is still too young and might be an immature solution. Docker folks will continue developing it and it will almost certainly become much better in the not so distant future. Terraform gives you freedom at a price.

Personally, I will closely watch the improvements in *Docker for AWS* and reserve the right to make the verdict later. Until that time, I am slightly more inclined towards Terraform. I like building things. It's a very narrow victory that should be revisited soon.

13

Creating and Managing a Docker Swarm Cluster in DigitalOcean

Plan to throw one (implementation) away; you will, anyhow.
−Fred Brooks

We already saw a few ways to create and operate a Swarm cluster in AWS. Now we'll try to do the same in *DigitalOcean* (https://www.digitalocean.com/). We'll explore some of the tools and configurations that can be used with this hosting provider.

Unlike AWS that is known to everyone, DigitalOcean is relatively new and less well known. You might be wondering why I chose DigitalOcean before some other providers like Azure and GCE. The reason lies in the differences between AWS (and other similar providers) and DigitalOcean. The two differ in many aspects. Comparing them is like comparing David and Goliath. One is small while the other (AWS) is huge. DigitalOcean understands that it cannot compete with AWS on its own ground, so it decided to play a different game.

DigitalOcean launched in 2011 and is focused on very specific needs. Unlike AWS with its *everything-to-everyone* approach, DigitalOcean provides virtual machines. There are no bells and whistles. You do not get lost in their catalog of services since it is almost non-existent. If you need a place to host your cluster and you do not want to use services designed to lock you in, DigitalOcean might be the right choice.

DigitalOcean's main advantages are pricing, high performance, and simplicity. If that's what you're looking for, it is worth trying it out.

Let's go through these three advantages one by one.

DigitalOcean's pricing is probably the best among all cloud providers. No matter whether you are a small company in need of only a couple of servers, or a big entity that is looking for a place to instantiate hundreds or even thousands of servers, chances are that DigitalOcean will be cheaper than any other provider. That might leave you wondering about the quality. After all, cheaper things tend to sacrifice it. Is that the case with DigitalOcean?

DigitalOcean offers very high-performance machines. All disk drives are SSD, network speed is 1 Gbps, and it takes less than a minute to create and initialize droplets (their name for VMs). As a comparison, AWS EC2 instance startup time can vary between one and three minutes.

The last advantages DigitalOcean offers are their UI and API. Both are clean and easy to understand. Unlike AWS that can have a steep learning curve, you should have no trouble learning how to use them in a few hours.

Enough with the words of praise. Not everything can be great. What are the disadvantages?

DigitalOcean does not offer a plethora of services. It does a few things, and it does them well. It is a bare-bone **Infrastructure as a service (IaaS)** provider. It assumes that you will set up the services yourself. There is no load balancing, centralized logging, sophisticated analytics, hosted databases, and so on. If you need those things, you are expected to set them up yourself. Depending on your use case, that can be an advantage or a disadvantage.

A comparison between DigitalOcean and AWS is unfair since the scope of what each does is different. DigitalOcean is not trying to compete with AWS as a whole. If pressed to compare something, that would be DigitalOcean against AWS EC2. In such a case, DigitalOcean wins hands down.

I will assume that you already have a DigitalOcean account. If that's not the case, please register using: `https://m.do.co/c/ee6d08525457` . You'll get 10 in credit. That should be more than enough to run the examples in this chapter. DigitalOcean is so cheap that you will probably finish this chapter with more than 9 remaining balance.

Even if you've already made a firm decision to use a different cloud computing provider or on-premise servers, I highly recommend going through this chapter. It will help you compare DigitalOcean with your provider of choice.

Let's give DigitalOcean a spin and judge through examples whether it is a good choice to host our Swarm cluster.

You might notice that some parts of this chapter are very similar, or even the same as those you read in the other cloud computing chapters like `Chapter 12`, *Creating and Managing a Docker Swarm Cluster in Amazon Web Services*. The reason for the partial repetition is the goal to make the cloud computing chapters useful not only to those who read everything, but also those who skipped other providers and jumped right here.

Before we move into practical exercises, we'll need to get the access keys and decide the region where we'll run the cluster.

Setting up the environment variables

In the `Chapter 12`, *Creating And Managing A Docker Swarm Cluster in Amazon Web Services*, we installed AWS **Command Line Interface (CLI)** (`https://aws.amazon.com/cli/`) that helped us with some of the tasks. DigitalOcean has a similar interface called doctl. Should we install it? I don't think we need a CLI for DigitalOcean. Their API is clean and well defined, and we can accomplish everything a CLI would do with simple curl requests. DigitalOcean proves that a well designed API goes a long way and can be the only entry point into the system, saving us the trouble of dealing with middle-man applications like CLIs.

Before we start using the API, we should generate an access token that will serve as the authentication method.

Please open the *DigitalOcean tokens* screen (`https://cloud.digitalocean.com/settings/api/tokens`) and click the**Generate New Token** button. You'll be presented with the **New personal access token** popup, as shown in the following image:

Figure 12-1: DigitalOcean new personal access token screen

Type `devops21` as **Token name** and click the **Generate Token** button. You'll see the newly generated token. We'll put it into the environment variable `DIGITALOCEAN_ACCESS_TOKEN`.

All the commands from this chapter are available in the Gist `12-digital-ocean.sh` (`https://gist.github.com/vfarcic/81248d2b6551f6a1c2bcfb76026bae5e`).

Copy the token before running the command that follows:

```
export DIGITALOCEAN_ACCESS_TOKEN=[...]
```

Please replace `[...]` with the actual token.

Now we can decide which region our cluster will run in.

We can see the currently available regions by sending a request to `https://api.digitalocean.com/v2/regions`:

```
curl -X GET
    -H "Authorization: Bearer $DIGITALOCEAN_ACCESS_TOKEN"
    "https://api.digitalocean.com/v2/regions"
    | jq '.'
```

We sent an HTTP GET request to the regions API. The request contains the access token. The response is piped to jq.

A part of the output is as follows:

```
{
  "regions": [
    ...
    {
       "name": "San Francisco 2",
       "slug": "sfo2",
       "sizes": [
"512mb",
"1gb",
"2gb"
       ],
       "features": [
"private_networking",
"backups",
"ipv6",
"metadata",
"storage"
       ],
       "available": true
},
    ...
  ],
  "links": {},
  "meta": {
    "total": 12
}
}
```

As we can see from the bottom of the response, DigitalOcean currently supports twelve regions. Each contains the information about available droplet sizes and the supported features.

Throughout this chapter, I will be using **San Francisco 2 (sfo2)** region. Feel free to change it to the region closest to your location. If you choose to run the examples in a different region, please make sure that it contains the private_networking feature.

We'll put the region inside the environment variable DIGITALOCEAN_REGION:

```
export DIGITALOCEAN_REGION=sfo2
```

Now we are all set with the prerequisites that will allow us to create the first Swarm cluster in DigitalOcean. Since we used Docker Machine throughout most of the book, it will be our first choice.

Setting up a Swarm cluster with Docker Machine and DigitalOcean API

We'll continue using the `vfarcic/cloud-provisioning` (`https://github.com/vfarcic/cloud-provisioning`) repository. It contains configurations and scripts that'll help us out. You already have it cloned. To be on the safe side, we'll pull the latest version:

```
cd cloud-provisioning

git pull
```

Let's create the first droplet:

```
docker-machine create \
    --driver digitalocean  \
    --digitalocean-size 1gb  \
    --digitalocean-private-networking \
    swarm-1
```

We specified that the *Docker Machine* should use the `digitalocean` driver to create an instance in the region we defined as the environment variable `DIGITALOCEAN_REGION`. The size of the droplet is 1 GB and it has private networking enabled.

Docker Machine launched a DigitalOcean droplet, provisioned it with Ubuntu, and installed and configured Docker Engine.

As you no doubt already noticed, everyone is trying to come up with a different name for the same thing. DigitalOcean is no exception. They came up with the term *droplet*. It is a different name for a virtual private server. Same thing, different name.

Now we can initialize the cluster. We should use private IPs for all communication between nodes. Unfortunately, `docker-machine ip` command returns only the public IP, so we'll have to resort to a different method to get the private IP.

We can send a GET request to the droplets API:

```
curl -X GET \
    -H "Authorization: Bearer $DIGITALOCEAN_ACCESS_TOKEN"  \
"https://api.digitalocean.com/v2/droplets"  \
    | jq '.'
```

A part of the output is as follows:

```
{
"droplets": [
    {
            "id": 33906152,
            "name": "swarm-1",
            . . .
            "networks": {
            "v4": [
              {
                 "ip_address": "138.68.11.80",
                 "netmask": "255.255.240.0",
                 "gateway": "138.68.0.1",
                 "type": "public"
              },
              {
                 "ip_address": "10.138.64.175",
                 "netmask": "255.255.0.0",
                 "gateway": "10.138.0.1",
                 "type": "private"
              }
            ],
            "v6": []
        },
        . . .
    ],
    "links": {},
    "meta": {
       "total": 1
      }
    }
```

The `droplets` API returned all information about all the droplets we own (at the moment only one). We are interested only in the private IP of the newly created instance called swarm-1. We can get it by filtering the results to include only the droplet named swarm-1 and selecting the v4 element with the type private.

We'll use `jq` (`https://stedolan.github.io/jq/`) to filter the output and get what we need. If you haven't already, please download and install the jq distribution suited for your OS.

The command that sends the request, filters the result, and stores the private IP as an environment variable is as follows:

```
MANAGER_IP=$(curl -X GET  \
    -H "Authorization: Bearer $DIGITALOCEAN_ACCESS_TOKEN"  \
"https://api.digitalocean.com/v2/droplets"  \
    | jq -r '.droplets[]
    | select(.name=="swarm-1").networks.v4[]
    | select(.type=="private").ip_address')
```

We sent a `GET` request to the `droplets` API, used the `jq select` statement to discard all the entries except the one with the name `swarm-1`. That was followed with another select statement that returned only the private address. The output was stored as the environment variable `MANAGER_IP`.

To be on the safe side, we can echo the value of the newly created variable:

```
echo $MANAGER_IP
```

The output is as follows:

```
10.138.64.175
```

Now we can execute the `swarm init` command in the same way as we did in the previous chapters:

```
eval $(docker-machine env swarm-1)

docker swarm init \
    --advertise-addr $MANAGER_IP
```

Let's confirm that the cluster is indeed initialized:

```
docker node ls
```

The output is as follows (IDs are removed for brevity):

```
HOSTNAME STATUS   AVAILABILITY  MANAGER STATUS
swarm-1  Ready    Active        Leader
```

Now that we initialized the cluster, we can add more nodes. We'll start by creating two new instances and joining them as managers:

```
MANAGER_TOKEN=$(docker swarm join-token -q manager)

for i in 2 3; do
  docker-machine create \
    --driver digitalocean \
    --digitalocean-size 1gb \
    --digitalocean-private-networking \
    swarm-$i

  IP=$(curl -X GET \
    -H "Authorization: Bearer $DIGITALOCEAN_ACCESS_TOKEN" \
"https://api.digitalocean.com/v2/droplets" \
    | jq -r ".droplets[]
    | select(.name==\"swarm-$i\").networks.v4[]
    | select(.type==\"private\").ip_address")

eval $(docker-machine env swarm-$i)

  docker swarm join \
    --token $MANAGER_TOKEN \
    --advertise-addr $IP \
$MANAGER_IP:2377
done
```

There's no need to explain the commands we just executed since they are the combination of those we used before.

We'll add a few worker nodes as well:

```
WORKER_TOKEN=$(docker swarm join-token -q worker)

for i in 4 5; do
  docker-machine create \
    --driver digitalocean \
    --digitalocean-size 1gb \
    --digitalocean-private-networking \
  swarm-$i

  IP=$(curl -X GET \
    -H "Authorization: Bearer $DIGITALOCEAN_ACCESS_TOKEN" \
    "https://api.digitalocean.com/v2/droplets" \
    | jq -r ".droplets[]
    | select(.name==\"swarm-$i\").networks.v4[]
    | select(.type==\"\private\").ip_address")
```

```
    eval $(docker-machine env swarm-$i)

    docker swarm join \
      --token $WORKER_TOKEN \
      --advertise-addr $IP \
      $MANAGER_IP:2377
    done
```

Let's confirm that all five nodes are indeed forming the cluster:

```
    eval $(docker-machine env swarm-1)

    docker node ls
```

The output is as follows (IDs are removed for brevity):

```
    HOSTNAME  STATUS  AVAILABILITY  MANAGER STATUS
    swarm-5   Ready   Active
    swarm-1   Ready   Active        Leader
    swarm-4   Ready   Active
    swarm-2   Ready   Active        Reachable
    swarm-3   Ready   Active        Reachable
```

That's it. Our cluster is ready. The only thing left is to deploy a few services and confirm that the cluster is working as expected.

Since we already created the services quite a few times, we'll speed up the process with the vfarcic/docker-flow-proxy/docker-compose-stack.yml (https://github.com/vf arcic/docker-flow-proxy/blob/master/docker-compose-stack.yml) and vfarcic/go-demo/docker-compose-stack.yml (https://github.com/vfarcic/go-demo/blob/mast er/docker-compose-stack.yml) Compose stacks. They'll create the proxy, swarm-listener, go-demo-db, and go-demo services:

```
    docker-machine ssh swarm-1

    sudo docker network create --driver overlay proxy

    curl -o proxy-stack.yml \
        https://raw.githubusercontent.com/ \
    vfarcic/docker-flow-proxy/master/docker-compose-stack.yml

    sudo docker stack deploy \
        -c proxy-stack.yml proxy

    curl -o go-demo-stack.yml \
        https://raw.githubusercontent.com/ \
    vfarcic/go-demo/master/docker-compose-stack.yml
```

```
sudo docker stack deploy \
    -c go-demo-stack.yml go-demo

exit

docker service ls
```

Non-Windows users do not need to enter the `swarm-1` machine and can accomplish the same result by deploying the stacks directly from their laptops.

It'll take a few moments until all the images are downloaded. After a while, the output of the `service ls command` should be as follows (IDs are removed for brevity):

```
NAME            REPLICAS IMAGE                                   COMMAND
go-demo         3/3      vfarcic/go-demo:1.2
go-demo-db      1/1      mongo:3.2.10
proxy           3/3      vfarcic/docker-flow-proxy
swarm-listener  1/1      vfarcic/docker-flow-swarm-listener
```

Let's confirm that the `go-demo` service is accessible:

```
curl -i $(docker-machine ip swarm-1)/demo/hello
```

The output is as follows:

```
HTTP/1.1 200 OK
Date: Wed, 07 Dec 2016 05:05:58 GMT
Content-Length: 14
Content-Type: text/plain; charset=utf-8

hello, world!
```

We set up the whole Swarm cluster using Docker Machine and the DigitalOcean API. Is that everything we need? That depends on the requirements we might define for our cluster. We should probably add a few Floating IP addresses.

A DigitalOcean Floating IP is a publicly-accessible static IP address that can be assigned to one of your Droplets. A Floating IP can also be instantly remapped, via the DigitalOcean Control Panel or API, to one of your other Droplets in the same data center. This instant remapping capability grants you the ability to design and create **High Availability (HA)** server infrastructure setups that do not have a single point of failure, by adding redundancy to the entry point, or gateway, to your servers.

In other words, we should probably set at least two Floating IPs and map them to two of the droplets in the cluster. Those two (or more) IPs would be set as our DNS records. That way, when an instance fails, and we replace it with a new one, we can remap the Elastic IP without affecting our users.

There are quite a few other improvements we could do. However, that would put us in an awkward position. We would be using a tool that is not meant for setting up a complicated cluster.

The creation of VMs was quite slow. Docker Machine spent too much time provisioning it with Ubuntu and installing Docker Engine. We can reduce that time by creating snapshots with Docker Engine pre-installed. However, with such an action, the main reason for using Docker Machine would be gone. Its primary usefulness is simplicity. Once we start complicating the setup with other resources, we'll realize that the simplicity is being replaced with too many ad-hoc commands.

Running `docker-machine` combined with API requests works great when we are dealing with a small cluster, especially when we want to create something fast and potentially not very durable. The biggest problem is that everything we've done so far has been ad-hoc commands. Chances are that we would not be able to reproduce the same steps the second time. Our infrastructure is not documented so our team would not know what constitutes our cluster.

My recommendation is to use `docker-machine` in DigitalOcean as a quick and dirty way to create a cluster mostly for demo purposes. It can be useful for production as well, as long as the cluster is relatively small.

We should look at alternatives if we'd like to set up a more complex, bigger, and potentially more permanent solution.

Let us delete the cluster we created and explore the alternatives with a clean slate:

```
for i in 1 2 3 4 5; do
    docker-machine rm -f swarm-$i
done
```

If you read the previous chapter, at this point you are probably expecting to see a sub-chapter named *Docker for DigitalOcean*. There is no such thing. At least not at the time I'm writing this chapter. Therefore, we'll jump right into *Packer* and *Terraform*.

Setting up a Swarm cluster with Packer and Terraform

This time we'll use a set of tools completely unrelated to Docker. It'll be *Packer* (https://www.packer.io/) and *Terraform* (https://www.terraform.io/). Both are coming from *HashiCorp* (https://www.hashicorp.com/). Packer allows us to create machine images. With Terraform we can create, change, and improve cluster infrastructure. Both tools support almost all the major providers.

They can be used with Amazon EC2, CloudStack, DigitalOcean, **Google Compute Engine (GCE)**, Microsoft Azure, VMWare, VirtualBox, and quite a few others. The ability to be infrastructure agnostic allows us to avoid vendor lock-in. With a minimal change in configuration, we can easily transfer our cluster from one provider to another. Swarm is designed to work seamlessly no matter which hosting provider we use, as long as the infrastructure is properly defined. With Packer and Terraform we can define infrastructure in such a way that transitioning from one to another is as painless as possible.

Using Packer to create DigitalOcean snapshots

The vfarcic/cloud-provisioning (https://github.com/vfarcic/cloud-provisioning) repository already has the Packer and Terraform configurations we'll use. They are located in the directory terraform/do:

```
cd terraform/do
```

The first step is to use Packer to create a snapshot. To do that, we'll need our DigitalOcean API token set as the environment variable DIGITALOCEAN_API_TOKEN. It is the same token we set as the environment variable DIGITALOCEAN_ACCESS_TOKEN. Unfortunately, Docker Machine and Packer have different naming standards:

```
export DIGITALOCEAN_API_TOKEN=[...]
```

Please replace [...] with the actual token.

We'll instantiate all Swarm nodes from the same snapshot. It'll be based on Ubuntu and have the latest Docker Engine installed.

The JSON definition of the image we are about to build is in `terraform/do/packer-ubuntu-docker.json` (https://github.com/vfarcic/cloud-provisioning/blob/master/terraform/do/packer-ubuntu-docker.json):

```
cat packer-ubuntu-docker.json
```

The configuration consists of two sections: `builders` and `provisioners`:

```
{
    "builders": [{
      ...
    }],
    "provisioners": [{
      ...
    }]
}
```

The `builders` section defines all the information Packer needs to build a snapshot. The `provisioners` section describes the commands that will be used to install and configure software for the machines created by builders. The only required section is builders.

Builders are responsible for creating machines and generating images from them for various platforms. For example, there are separate builders for EC2, VMware, VirtualBox, and so on. Packer comes with many builders by default, and can also be extended to add new builders.

The builders section we'll use is as follows:

```
"builders": [{
    "type": "digitalocean",
    "region": "sfo2",
    "image": "ubuntu-16-04-x64",
    "size": "1gb",
    "private_networking": true,
    "snapshot_name": "devops21-{{timestamp}}"
}]
```

Each type of builder has specific arguments that can be used. We specified that the `type` is `digitalocean`. Please visit the **DigitalOcean Builder** page (https://www.packer.io/docs/builders/digitalocean.html) for more info.

Please note, when using the `digitalocean` type, we have to provide the token. We could have specified it through the `api_token` field. However, there is an alternative. If the field is not specified, Packer will try to get the value from the environment variable `DIGITALOCEAN_API_TOKEN`. Since we already exported it, there's no need to repeat ourselves with the token inside Packer configuration. Moreover, the token should be secret.

Putting it inside the config would risk exposure.The region is critical since a snapshot can be created only within one region. If we wanted to share the same machine across multiple regions, each would need to be specified as a separate builder.

We set the image to `ubuntu-16-04-x64`. That will be the base image which we'll use to create our own. The size of the snapshot is not directly related to the size of the droplets we'll create, so there's no need to make it big. We set it to 1 GB.

By default, DigitalOcean enables only public networking, so we defined `private_networking` as `true`. Later on, we'll set up Swarm communication to be available only through the private network.

The `snapshot_name` field is the name we'll give to this snapshot. Since there is no option to overwrite an existing snapshot, the name must be unique so we added `timestamp` to the name.

Please visit the DigitalOcean Builder page (`https://www.packer.io/docs/builders/digi talocean.html`) for more information.

The second section is provisioners. It contains an array of all the provisioners that Packer should use to install and configure software within running machines before turning them into snapshots.

There are quite a few `provisioner` types we can use. If you read *The DevOps 2.0 Toolkit* (`ht tps://www.amazon.com/dp/B01BJ4V66M`), you know that I advocated Ansible as the `provisioner` of choice. Should we use it here as well? In most cases, when building images meant to run Docker containers, I opt for a simple shell. The reasons for a change from Ansible to Shell lies in the different objectives `provisioners` should fulfill when running on live servers, as opposed to building images.

Unlike Shell, Ansible (and most other `provisioners`) are idempotent. They verify the actual state and execute one action or another depending on what should be done for the desired state to be fulfilled. That's a great approach since we can run Ansible as many times as we want and the result will always be the same. For example, if we specify that we want to have JDK 8, Ansible will SSH into a destination server, discover that the JDK is not present and install it. The next time we run it, it'll discover that the JDK is already there and do nothing. Such an approach allows us to run Ansible playbooks as often as we want and it'll always result in JDK being installed. If we tried to accomplish the same through a Shell script, we'd need to write lengthy `if/else` statements. If JDK is installed, do nothing, if it's not installed, install it, if it's installed, but the version is not correct, upgrade it, and so on.

So, why not use it with Packer? The answer is simple. We do not need idempotency since we'll run it only once while creating an image. We won't use it on running instances. Do you remember the *pets vs cattle* discussion? Our VMs will be instantiated from an image that already has everything we need. If the state of that VM changes, we'll terminate it and create a new one. If we need to do an upgrade or install additional software, we won't do it inside the running instance, but create a new image, destroy running instances, and instantiate new ones based on the updated image.

Is idempotency the only reason we would use Ansible? Definitely not! It is a very handy tool when we need to define complicated server setup. However, in our case the setup is simple. We need Docker Engine and not much more. Almost everything will be running inside containers. Writing a few Shell commands to install Docker is easier and faster than defining Ansible playbooks.

It would probably take the same number of commands to install Ansible as to install Docker.

Long story short, we'll use shell as our `provisioner` of choice for building AMIs.

The `provisioners` section we'll use is as follows:

```
"provisioners": [{
  "type": "shell",
  "inline": [
    "sudo apt-get update",
    "sudo apt-get install -y apt-transport-https ca-certificates nfs-common",
    "sudo apt-key adv --keyserver hkp://ha.pool.sks-keyservers.net:80\
--recv-keys 58118E89F3A912897C070ADBF76221572C52609D",
    "echo 'deb https://apt.dockerproject.org/repo ubuntu-xenial main'\
| sudo tee /etc/apt/sources.list.d/docker.list",
    "sudo apt-get update",
    "sudo apt-get install -y docker-engine"
  ]
}]
```

The shell type is followed by a set of commands. They are the same as the commands we can find in the Install Docker *on Ubuntu* (`https://docs.docker.com/engine/installatio n/linux/ubuntulinux/`) page.

Now that we have a general idea how Packer configuration works, we can proceed and build an image:

```
packer build -machine-readable \
    packer-ubuntu-docker.json \
    | tee packer-ubuntu-docker.log
```

We run the `packer build` of the `packer-ubuntu-docker.json` with the `machine-readable` output sent to the `packer-ubuntu-docker.log` file. Machine readable output will allow us to parse it easily and retrieve the ID of the snapshot we just created.

The final lines of the output are as follows:

```
. . .
1481087549,,ui,say,Build 'digitalocean' finished.
1481087549,,ui,say,n==> Builds finished. The artifacts of successful builds
are:
1481087549,digitalocean,artifact-count,1
1481087549,digitalocean,artifact,0,builder-id,pearkes.digitalocean
1481087549,digitalocean,artifact,0,id,sfo2:21373017
1481087549,digitalocean,artifact,0,string,A snapshot was created: \
'devops21-1481087268' (ID: 21373017) in region 'sfo2'
1481087549,digitalocean,artifact,0,files-count,0
1481087549,digitalocean,artifact,0,end
1481087549,,ui,say,--> digitalocean: A snapshot was created:\
'devops21-1481087268' (ID: 21373017) in region 'sfo2'
```

Apart from the confirmation that the build was successful, the relevant part of the output is the line `id,sfo2:21373017`. It contains the snapshot ID we'll need to instantiate VMs based on the image. You might want to store the `packer-ubuntu-docker.log` in your code repository in case you need to get the ID from a different server.

The flow of the process we executed can be described through *figure 12-2:*

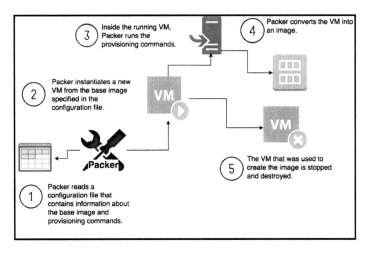

Figure 12-2: The flow of the Packer process

Now we are ready to create a Swarm cluster with VMs based on the snapshot we built.

Using Terraform to create a Swarm cluster in DigitalOcean

Terraform is the third member of the *everyone-uses-a-different-environment-variable-for-the-token* club. It expects the token to be stored as environment variable `DIGITALOCEAN_TOKEN`:

```
export DIGITALOCEAN_TOKEN=[...]
```

Please replace `[...]` with the actual token.

Terraform does not force us to have any particular file structure. We can define everything in a single file. However, that does not mean that we should. Terraform configs can get big, and separation of logical sections into separate files is often a good idea. In our case, we'll have three `tf` files. The `terraform/do/variables.tf` (https://github.com/vfarcic/cloud-provisioning/blob/master/terraform/do/variables.tf) holds all the variables. If we need to change any parameter, we'll know where to find it. The `terraform/do/common.tf` (https://github.com/vfarcic/cloud-provisioning/blob/master/terraform/do/common.tf) file contains definitions of the elements that might be potentially reusable on other occasions. Finally, the `terraform/do/swarm.tf` (https://github.com/vfarcic/cloud-provisioning/blob/master/terraform/do/swarm.tf) file has the Swarm-specific resources. We'll explore each of the Terraform configuration files separately.

The content of the `terraform/do/variables.tf` (https://github.com/vfarcic/cloud-provisioning/blob/master/terraform/do/variables.tf) file is as follows:

```
variable "swarm_manager_token" {
    default = ""
}
variable "swarm_worker_token" {
    default = ""
}
variable "swarm_snapshot_id" {
    default = "unknown"
}
variable "swarm_manager_ip" {
    default = ""
}
variable "swarm_managers" {
    default = 3
}
variable "swarm_workers" {
    default = 2
}
```

```
variable "swarm_region" {
    default = "sfo2"
}
variable "swarm_instance_size" {
    default = "1gb"
}
variable "swarm_init" {
    default = false
}
```

The `swarm_manager_token` and `swarm_worker_token` will be required to join the nodes to the cluster. The `swarm_snapshot_id` will hold the ID of the snapshot we created with Packer. The `swarm_manager_ip` variable is the IP of one of the managers that we'll need to provide for the nodes to join the cluster. The `swarm_managers` and `swarm_workers` define how many nodes we want of each. The `swarm_region` defines the region our cluster will run in while the `swarm_instance_size` is set to 1 GB. Feel free to change it to a bigger size if you start using this Terraform config to create a real cluster. Finally, the `swarm_init` variable allows us to specify whether this is the first run and the node should initialize the cluster. We'll see its usage very soon.

The content of the `terraform/do/common.tf` (https://github.com/vfarcic/cloud-pro visioning/blob/master/terraform/do/common.tf) file is as follows:

```
resource "digitalocean_ssh_key" "docker" {
  name = "devops21-do"
  public_key = "${file("devops21-do.pub")}"
}

resource "digitalocean_floating_ip" "docker_1" {
  droplet_id = "${digitalocean_droplet.swarm-manager.0.id}"
  region = "${var.swarm_region}"
}

resource "digitalocean_floating_ip" "docker_2" {
  droplet_id = "${digitalocean_droplet.swarm-manager.1.id}"
  region = "${var.swarm_region}"
}

resource "digitalocean_floating_ip" "docker_3" {
  droplet_id = "${digitalocean_droplet.swarm-manager.2.id}"
  region = "${var.swarm_region}"
}
output "floating_ip_1" {
  value = "${digitalocean_floating_ip.docker_1.ip_address}"
}
```

```
output "floating_ip_2" {
  value = "${digitalocean_floating_ip.docker_2.ip_address}"
}

output "floating_ip_3" {
  value = "${digitalocean_floating_ip.docker_3.ip_address}"
}
```

Each resource is defined with a type (For example, `digitalocean_ssh_key`) and a name (For example, `docker`). The type determines which resource should be created and must be one of those currently supported.

The first resource `digitalocean_ssh_key` allows us to manage SSH keys for droplet access. Keys created with this resource can be referenced in your droplet configuration via their ID or fingerprint. We set it as the value of the `devops21-do.pub` file that we'll create soon.

The second resource we're using is the `digitalocean_floating_ip`. It represents a publicly-accessible static IP address that can be mapped to one of our droplets. We defined three of those. They would be used in our DNS configuration. That way, when a request is made to your domain, DNS redirects it to one of the floating IPs. If one the droplets is down, DNS should use one of the other entries. That way, you'd have time to change the floating IP from the failed to a new droplet.

Please consult the *DIGITALOCEAN_SSH_KEY* (`https://www.terraform.io/docs/provide rs/do/r/ssh_key.html`) and *DIGITALOCEAN_FLOATING_IP* (`https://www.terraform.i o/docs/providers/do/r/floating_ip.html`) pages for more info.

Besides the resources, we also defined a few outputs. They represent values that will be displayed when Terraform apply is executed and can be queried easily using the output command.

When building potentially complex infrastructure, Terraform stores hundreds or thousands of attribute values for all resources. But, as a user, we may only be interested in a few values of importance, such as manager IPs. Outputs are a way to tell Terraform what data is relevant.

In our case, the outputs are the addresses of the floating IPs.

Please consult the *Output Configuration* (`https://www.terraform.io/docs/configuration /outputs.html`) page for more info.

Now comes the real deal. The `terraform/do/swarm.tf` (https://github.com/vfarcic/cloud-provisioning/blob/master/terraform/do/swarm.tf) file contains the definition of all the instances we'll create.

Since the content of this file is a bit bigger than the others, we'll examine each resource separately.

The first resource in line is the `digitalocean_droplet` type named `swarm-manager`. Its purpose is to create Swarm manager nodes:

```
resource "digitalocean_droplet" "swarm-manager" {
  image = "${var.swarm_snapshot_id}"
  size = "${var.swarm_instance_size}"
  count = "${var.swarm_managers}"
  name = "${format("swarm-manager-%02d", (count.index + 1))}"
  region = "${var.swarm_region}"
  private_networking = true
  ssh_keys = [
"${digitalocean_ssh_key.docker.id}"
  ]
  connection {
    user = "root"
    private_key = "${file("devops21-do")}"
    agent = false
  }
  provisioner "remote-exec" {
    inline = [
"if ${var.swarm_init}; then docker swarm init \
--advertise-addr ${self.ipv4_address_private}; fi",
"if ! ${var.swarm_init}; then docker swarm join \
--token ${var.swarm_manager_token} --advertise-addr
${self.ipv4_address_private} ${var.swarm_manager_ip}:2377; fi"
    ]
  }
}
```

The resource contains the image that references the snapshot we created with Packer. The actual value is a variable that we'll define at runtime. The size specifies the size of the instance we want to create. The default value is fetched from the variable `swarm_instance_size`. By default, it is set to 1 GB. Just as any other variable, it can be overwritten at runtime.

The count field defines how many managers we want to create. The first time we run terraform, the value should be 1 since we want to start with one manager that will initialize the cluster. Afterward, the value should be whatever is defined in variables. We'll see the use case of both combinations soon.

The name, the region, and the `private_networking` should be self-explanatory. The ssh-keys type is an array that, at this moment, contains only one element; the ID of the `digitalocean_ssh_key` resource we defined in the `common.tf` file.

The connection field defines the SSH connection details. The user will be root. Instead of a password, we'll use the `devops21-do` key.

Finally, the `provisioner` is defined. The idea is to do as much provisioning as possible during the creation of the images. That way, instances are created much faster since the only action is to create a VM out of an image. However, there is often a part of provisioning that cannot be done when creating an image. The `swarm init` command is one of those. We cannot initialize the first Swarm node until we get the IP of the server. In other words, the server needs to be running (and therefore has an IP) before the `swarm init` command is executed.

Since the first node has to initialize the cluster while any other should join, we're using `if` statements to distinguish one case from the other. If the variable `swarm_init` is `true`, the `docker swarm init` command will be executed. On the other hand, if the variable `swarm_init` is set to `false`, the command will be `docker swarm join`. In that case, we are using another variable `swarm_manager_ip` to tell the node which manager to use to join the cluster. Please note that the IP is obtained using the special syntax `self.ipv4_address_private`. We are referencing oneself and getting the `ipv4_address_private`. There are many other attributes we can get from a resource. Please consult the *DIGITALOCEAN_DROPLET* (`https://www.terraform.io/docs/provid ers/do/r/droplet.html`) page for more info.

Let's take a look at the `digitalocean_droplet` resource named `swarm-worker`:

```
resource "digitalocean_droplet" "swarm-worker" {
  image = "${var.swarm_snapshot_id}"
  size = "${var.swarm_instance_size}"
  count = "${var.swarm_workers}"
  name = "${format("swarm-worker-%02d", (count.index + 1))}"
  region = "${var.swarm_region}"
  private_networking = true
  ssh_keys = [
    "${digitalocean_ssh_key.docker.id}"
  ]
  connection {
    user = "root"
    private_key = "${file("devops21-do")}"
    agent = false
  }
  provisioner "remote-exec" {
```

```
    inline = [
        "docker swarm join --token ${var.swarm_worker_token} \
--advertise-addr ${self.ipv4_address_private} ${var.swarm_manager_ip}:\
2377"
    ]
  }
}
```

The `swarm-worker` resource is almost identical to `swarm-manager`. The only difference is in the count field that uses the `swarm_workers` variable and the `provisioner`. Since a worker cannot initialize a cluster, there was no need for `if` statements, so the only command we want to execute is `docker swarm join`. Terraform uses a naming convention that allows us to specify values as environment variables by adding the `TF_VAR_` prefix. For example, we can specify the value of the variable `swarm_snapshot_id` by setting the environment variable `TF_VAR_swarm_snapshot_id`. The alternative is to use the `-var` argument. I prefer environment variables since they allow me to specify them once instead of adding `-var` to every command. The last part of the `terraform/do/swarm.tf` (`https://github.com/vfarcic/cloud-provisioning/blob/master/terraform/do/swarm.tf`) specification are outputs.

The outputs we defined are as follows:

```
output "swarm_manager_1_public_ip" {
  value = "${digitalocean_droplet.swarm-manager.0.ipv4_address}"
}

output "swarm_manager_1_private_ip" {
  value = "${digitalocean_droplet.swarm-manager.0.ipv4_address_private}"
}

output "swarm_manager_2_public_ip" {
  value = "${digitalocean_droplet.swarm-manager.1.ipv4_address}"
}

output "swarm_manager_2_private_ip" {
  value = "${digitalocean_droplet.swarm-manager.1.ipv4_address_private}"
}

output "swarm_manager_3_public_ip" {
  value = "${digitalocean_droplet.swarm-manager.2.ipv4_address}"
}

output "swarm_manager_3_private_ip" {
  value = "${digitalocean_droplet.swarm-manager.2.ipv4_address_private}"
}
```

They are public and private IPs of the managers. Since there are only a few (if any) reasons to know worker IPs, we did not define them as outputs.

Since we'll use the snapshot we created with Packer, we need to retrieve the ID from the `packer-ubuntu-docker.log`. Let's take another look at the file:

```
cat packer-ubuntu-docker.log
```

The important line of the output is as follows:

```
1481087549,digitalocean,artifact,0,id,sfo2:21373017
```

The command that follows parses the output and extracts the ID:

```
export TF_VAR_swarm_snapshot_id=$( \
    grep 'artifact,0,id' \
    packer-ubuntu-docker.log \
    | cut -d: -f2)
```

Let's double-check that the command worked as expected:

```
echo $TF_VAR_swarm_snapshot_id
```

The output is as follows:

```
21373017
```

We got the ID of the snapshot. Before we start creating the resources, we need to create the SSH key `devops21-do` we referenced in the Terraform config.

We'll create the SSH key using `ssh-keygen`:

```
ssh-keygen -t rsa
```

When asked to *enter file in which to save the key*, please answer with `devops21-do`. The rest of the questions can be answered in any way you see fit. I'll leave them all empty.

The output should be similar to the one that follows:

```
Generating public/private rsa key pair.
Enter file in which to save the key (/Users/vfarcic/.ssh/id_rsa): devops21-
do
Enter passphrase (empty for no passphrase):
Enter same passphrase again:
Your identification has been saved in devops21-do.
Your public key has been saved in devops21-do.pub.
```

```
The key fingerprint is:
SHA256:a9BqjLkcC9eMnuKH+TZPE6E9S0w+cDQD4HTWEY9CuVk \
vfarcic@Viktors-MacBook-Pro-2.local
The key's randomart image is:
+---[RSA 2048]----+
|  o.=+*o         |
| o +..E=         |
| . o+= .         |
|   oX o          |
|   . X S         |
|    O B .        |
|  .o* X o        |
|  +=+B o         |
| ..=Bo.          |
+----[SHA256]-----+
```

Now that the `devops21-do` key is created, we can start using Terraform. Before we create our cluster and the infrastructure around it, we should ask Terraform to show us the execution plan.

A note to Terraform v0.8+users.

Normally, we would not need to specify targets to see the whole execution plan. However, Terraform *v0.8* introduced a bug that sometimes prevents us from outputting a plan if a resource has a reference to another, not yet created, resource. In this case, the `digitalocean_floating_ip.docker_2` and `digitalocean_floating_ip.docker_3` are such resources. The targets from the command that follows are intended to act as a workaround until the problem is fixed:

```
terraform plan \
    -target digitalocean_droplet.swarm-manager \
    -target digitalocean_droplet.swarm-worker \
```

The result is an extensive list of resources and their properties. Since the output is too big to be printed, I'll limit the output only to the resource types and names:

```
. . .
+ digitalocean_droplet.swarm-manager.0
. . .
+ digitalocean_droplet.swarm-manager.1
. . .
+ digitalocean_droplet.swarm-manager.2
. . .
+ digitalocean_droplet.swarm-worker.0
```

```
. . .
+ digitalocean_droplet.swarm-worker.1
. . .
+ digitalocean_ssh_key.docker
. . .
Plan: 6 to add, 0 to change, 0 to destroy.
```

Since this is the first execution, all the resources would be created if we were to execute `terraform apply`. We would get five droplets; three managers and two workers. That would be accompanied by three floating IPs and one SSH key.

If you see the complete output, you'll notice that some of the property values are set to `<computed>`. That means that Terraform cannot know what will be the actual values until it creates the resources. A good example is IPs. They do not exist until the droplet is created.

We can also output the plan using the `graph` command:

```
terraform graph
```

The output is as follows:

```
digraph {
    compound = "true"
    newrank = "true"
    subgraph "root" {
"[root] digitalocean_droplet.swarm-manager" [label = \
"digitalocean_droplet.swarm-manager", shape = "box"]
"[root] digitalocean_droplet.swarm-worker" [label = \
"digitalocean_droplet.swarm-worker", shape = "box"]
"[root] digitalocean_floating_ip.docker_1" [label = \
"digitalocean_floating_ip.docker_1", shape = "box"]
"[root] digitalocean_floating_ip.docker_2" [label = \
"digitalocean_floating_ip.docker_2", shape = "box"]
"[root] digitalocean_floating_ip.docker_3" [label = \
"digitalocean_floating_ip.docker_3", shape = "box"]
"[root] digitalocean_ssh_key.docker" [label = \
"digitalocean_ssh_key.docker", shape = "box"]
"[root] provider.digitalocean" [label = \
"provider.digitalocean", shape = "diamond"]
"[root] digitalocean_droplet.swarm-manager" \
-> "[root] digitalocean_ssh_key.docker"
"[root] digitalocean_droplet.swarm-manager" \
-> "[root] provider.digitalocean"
"[root] digitalocean_droplet.swarm-worker" \
-> "[root] digitalocean_ssh_key.docker"
"[root] digitalocean_droplet.swarm-worker" \
-> "[root] provider.digitalocean"
"[root] digitalocean_floating_ip.docker_1"
```

```
   -> "[root] digitalocean_droplet.swarm-manager"
"[root] digitalocean_floating_ip.docker_1" \
   -> "[root] provider.digitalocean"
"[root] digitalocean_floating_ip.docker_2" \
   -> "[root] digitalocean_droplet.swarm-manager"
"[root] digitalocean_floating_ip.docker_2" \
   -> "[root] provider.digitalocean"
"[root] digitalocean_floating_ip.docker_3" \
   -> "[root] digitalocean_droplet.swarm-manager"
"[root] digitalocean_floating_ip.docker_3" \
   -> "[root] provider.digitalocean"
"[root] digitalocean_ssh_key.docker" \
   -> "[root] provider.digitalocean"
      }
}
```

That, in itself, is not very useful.

The `graph` command is used to generate a visual representation of either a configuration or an execution plan. The output is in the DOT format, which can be used by GraphViz to make graphs.

Please open *Graphviz* Download page (`http://www.graphviz.org/Download.php`) and download and install the distribution compatible with your OS.

Now we can combine the `graph` command with `dot`:

```
terraform graph | dot -Tpng > graph.png
```

The output should be the same as in the *Figure 11-10:*

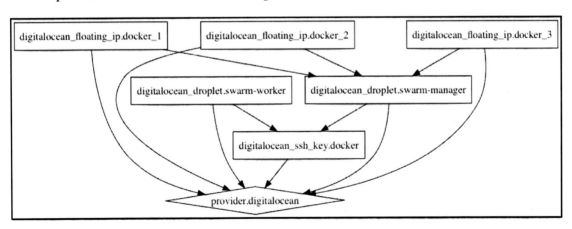

Figure 12-3: The image generated by Graphviz from the output of the terraform graph command

Visualization of the plan allows us to see the dependencies between different resources. In our case, all resources will use the `digitalocean` provider. Both instance types will depend on the SSH key docker, and the floating IPs will be attached to manager droplets.

When dependencies are defined, we don't need to specify explicitly all the resources we need.

As an example, let's take a look at the plan Terraform will generate when we limit it only to one Swarm manager node so that we can initialize the cluster:

```
terraform plan \
    -target digitalocean_droplet.swarm-manager \
    -var swarm_init=true \
    -var swarm_managers=1
```

The runtime variables `swarm_init` and `swarm_managers` will be used to tell Terraform that we want to initialize the cluster with one manager. The plan command takes those variables into account and outputs the execution plan.

The output, limited only to resource types and names, is as follows:

```
+ digitalocean_droplet.swarm-manager
...
+ digitalocean_ssh_key.docker
...
Plan: 2 to add, 0 to change, 0 to destroy.
```

Even though the specified that we want only the plan for the `swarm-manager` resource, Terraform noticed that it depends on the SSH key docker, and included it in the execution plan.

We'll start small and create only one manager instance that will initialize the cluster. As we saw from the plan, it depends on the SSH key, so Terraform will create it as well:

```
terraform apply \
    -target digitalocean_droplet.swarm-manager \
    -var swarm_init=true \
    -var swarm_managers=1
```

The output is too big to be presented fully in the book. If you look at it from your terminal, you'll notice that the SSH key is created first since `swarm-manager` depends on it. Please note that we did not specify the dependency explicitly. However, since the resource has it specified in the `ssh_keys` field, Terraform understood that it is the dependency.

Once the `swarm-manager` instance is created, Terraform waited until SSH access is available. After it had managed to connect to the new instance, it executed provisioning commands that initialized the cluster.

The final lines of the output are as follows:

```
Apply complete! Resources: 2 added, 0 changed, 0 destroyed.

. . .

Outputs:

swarm_manager_1_private_ip = 10.138.255.140
swarm_manager_1_public_ip = 138.68.57.39
```

The outputs are defined at the bottom of the `terraform/do/swarm.tf` (https://github.com/vfarcic/cloud-provisioning/blob/master/terraform/do/swarm.tf) file. Please note that not all outputs are listed but only those of the resources that were created.

We can use the public IP of the newly created droplet and SSH into it.

You might be inclined to copy the IP. There's no need for that. Terraform has a command that can be used to retrieve any information we defined as the output.

The command that retrieves the public IP of the first, and currently the only manager is as follows:

```
terraform output swarm_manager_1_public_ip
```

The output is as follows:

```
138.68.57.39
```

We can leverage the output command to construct SSH commands. As an example, the command that follows will SSH into the machine and retrieve the list of Swarm nodes:

```
ssh -i devops21-do \
    root@$(terraform output \
    swarm_manager_1_public_ip) \
    docker node ls
```

The output is as follows (IDs are removed for brevity):

```
HOSTNAME          STATUS   AVAILABILITY   MANAGER STATUS
swarm-manager-01  Ready    Active         Leader
```

From now on, we won't be limited to a single manager node that initialized the cluster. We can create all the rest of the nodes. However, before we do that, we need to discover the manager and worker tokens. For security reasons, it is better that they are not stored anywhere, so we'll create environment variables:

```
export TF_VAR_swarm_manager_token=$(ssh \
    -i devops21-do \
    root@$(terraform output \
    swarm_manager_1_public_ip) \
    docker swarm join-token -q manager)

export TF_VAR_swarm_worker_token=$(ssh \
    -i devops21-do \
    root@$(terraform output \
    swarm_manager_1_public_ip) \
    docker swarm join-token -q worker)
```

We'll also need to set the environment variable `swarm_manager_ip`:

```
export TF_VAR_swarm_manager_ip=$(terraform \
    output swarm_manager_1_private_ip)
```

Even though we could use `digitalocean_droplet.swarm-manager.0.private_ip` inside the `terraform/do/swarm.tf` (https://github.com/vfarcic/cloud-provisioning/blob/master/terraform/do/swarm.tf) it is a good idea to have it defined as an environment variable. That way, if the first manager fails, we can easily change it to `swarm_manager_2_private_ip` without modifying the `.tf` files.

Now, let us see the plan for the creation of the rest of Swarm nodes:

```
terraform plan \
    -target digitalocean_droplet.swarm-manager \
    -target digitalocean_droplet.swarm-worker
```

The relevant lines of the output are as follows:

```
...
+ digitalocean_droplet.swarm-manager.1
...
+ digitalocean_droplet.swarm-manager.2
...
+ digitalocean_droplet.swarm-worker.0
...
+ digitalocean_droplet.swarm-worker.1
...
Plan: 4 to add, 0 to change, 0 to destroy.
```

We can see that the plan is to create four new resources. Since we already have one manager running and specified that the desired number is three, two additional managers will be created together with two workers.

Let's apply the execution plan:

```
terraform apply \
    -target digitalocean_droplet.swarm-manager \
    -target digitalocean_droplet.swarm-worker
```

The last lines of the output are as follows:

```
. . .
Apply complete! Resources: 4 added, 0 changed, 0 destroyed.

. . .

Outputs:

swarm_manager_1_private_ip = 10.138.255.140
swarm_manager_1_public_ip = 138.68.57.39
swarm_manager_2_private_ip = 10.138.224.161
swarm_manager_2_public_ip = 138.68.17.88
swarm_manager_3_private_ip = 10.138.224.202
swarm_manager_3_public_ip = 138.68.29.23
```

All four resources were created, and we got the output of the manager public and private IPs.

Let's enter into one of the managers and confirm that the cluster indeed works:

```
ssh -i devops21-do \
    root@$(terraform \
    output swarm_manager_1_public_ip)

docker node ls
```

The output of the `node ls` command is as follows (IDs are removed for brevity):

```
HOSTNAME          STATUS AVAILABILITY MANAGER STATUS
swarm-manager-02 Ready  Active       Reachable
swarm-manager-01 Ready  Active       Leader
swarm-worker-02  Ready  Active
swarm-manager-03 Ready  Active       Reachable
swarm-worker-01  Ready  Active
```

All the nodes are present, and the cluster seems to be working.

To be fully confident that everything works as expected, we'll deploy a few services. Those will be the same services we were creating throughout the book, so we'll save us some time and deploy the `vfarcic/docker-flow-proxy/docker-compose-stack.yml` (https ://github.com/vfarcic/docker-flow-proxy/blob/master/docker-compose-stack.yml) and `vfarcic/go-demo/docker-compose-stack.yml` (https://github.com/vfarcic/go -demo/blob/master/docker-compose-stack.yml) stacks:

```
sudo docker network create --driver overlay proxy

curl -o proxy-stack.yml \
    https://raw.githubusercontent.com/\
vfarcic/docker-flow-proxy/master/docker-compose-stack.yml

sudo docker stack deploy \
    -c proxy-stack.yml proxy

curl -o go-demo-stack.yml \
    https://raw.githubusercontent.com/\
vfarcic/go-demo/master/docker-compose-stack.yml

sudo docker stack deploy \
    -c go-demo-stack.yml go-demo
```

We downloaded the stacks from the repositories and executed the `stack deploy` commands.

All we have to do now is wait for a few moments, execute the `service ls` command, and confirm that all the replicas are running:

```
docker service ls
```

The output of the `service ls` command should be as follows (IDs are removed for brevity):

```
NAME           REPLICAS IMAGE                                 COMMAND
go-demo-db     1/1      mongo:3.2.10
proxy          3/3      vfarcic/docker-flow-proxy
go-demo        3/3      vfarcic/go-demo:1.2
swarm-listener 1/1      vfarcic/docker-flow-swarm-listener
```

Finally, let's send a request to the `go-demo` service through the `proxy`. If it returns the correct response, we'll know that everything works correctly:

```
curl -i localhost/demo/hello
```

The output is as follows:

```
HTTP/1.1 200 OK
Date: Wed, 07 Dec 2016 06:21:01 GMT
Content-Length: 14
Content-Type: text/plain; charset=utf-8

hello, world!
```

It works!

Are we finished? We probably are. As a last check, let's validate that the proxy is accessible from outside the servers. We can confirm that by exiting the server and sending a request from our laptop:

```
exit

curl -i $(terraform output \
    swarm_manager_1_public_ip)/demo/hello
```

The output is as follows:

```
HTTP/1.1 200 OK
Date: Wed, 07 Dec 2016 06:21:33 GMT
Content-Length: 14
Content-Type: text/plain; charset=utf-8

hello, world!
```

We are still missing floating IPs. While they are not necessary for this demo, we would create them if this were a production cluster, and use them to configure our DNSes.

This time, we can create the plan without specifying the targets:

```
terraform plan
```

The relevant parts of the output are as follows:

```
...
+ digitalocean_floating_ip.docker_1
...
+ digitalocean_floating_ip.docker_2
...
+ digitalocean_floating_ip.docker_3
...
Plan: 3 to add, 0 to change, 0 to destroy.
```

As you can see, Terraform detected that all the resources except floating IPs are already created so it created the plan that would execute the creation of only three resources.

Let's apply the plan:

```
terraform apply
```

The output is as follows:

```
. . .
Apply complete! Resources: 3 added, 0 changed, 0 destroyed.

. . .

Outputs:

floating_ip_1 = 138.197.232.121
floating_ip_2 = 138.197.232.119
floating_ip_3 = 138.197.232.120
swarm_manager_1_private_ip = 10.138.255.140
swarm_manager_1_public_ip = 138.68.57.39
swarm_manager_2_private_ip = 10.138.224.161
swarm_manager_2_public_ip = 138.68.17.88
swarm_manager_3_private_ip = 10.138.224.202
swarm_manager_3_public_ip = 138.68.29.23
```

The floating IPs were created and we can see the output of their IPs.

The only thing left is to confirm that floating IPs are indeed created and configured correctly. We can do that by sending a request through one of them:

```
curl -i $(terraform output \
    floating_ip_1)/demo/hello
```

As expected, the output is status 200 OK:

```
HTTP/1.1 200 OK
Date: Wed, 07 Dec 2016 06:23:27 GMT
Content-Length: 14
Content-Type: text/plain; charset=utf-8

hello, world!
```

Let's see what happens if we simulate a failure of an instance.

We'll delete an instance using the DigitalOcean API. We could use Terraform to remove an instance. However, removing it with the API will be a closer simulation of an unexpected failure of a node.

To remove an instance, we need to find its ID. We can do that with the `terraform show` command.

Let's say that we want to remove the second worker. The command to find all its information is as follows:

```
terraform state show "digitalocean_droplet.swarm-worker[1]"
```

The output is as follows:

```
id                    = 33909722
disk                  = 30
image                 = 21373017
ipv4_address          = 138.68.57.13
ipv4_address_private  = 10.138.224.209
locked                = false
name                  = swarm-worker-02
private_networking    = true
region                = sfo2
resize_disk           = true
size                  = 1gb
ssh_keys.#            = 1
ssh_keys.0           = 5080274
status                = active
tags.#               = 0
vcpus                 = 1
```

Among other pieces of data, we got the ID. In my case, it is 33909722.

Before running the command that follows, please change the ID to the one you got from the `terraform state show` command:

```
curl -i -X DELETE \
    -H "Authorization: Bearer $DIGITALOCEAN_TOKEN" \
"https://api.digitalocean.com/v2/droplets/33909722"
```

The relevant part of the output is as follows:

```
HTTP/1.1 204 No Content
. . .
```

DigitalOcean does not provide any response content to DELETE requests, so the status 204 indicates that the operation was successful.

It will take a couple of moments until the droplet is removed entirely.

Let's run the `terraform plan` command one more time:

```
terraform plan
```

The relevant parts of the output are as follows:

```
. . .
+ digitalocean_droplet.swarm-worker.1
. . .
Plan: 1 to add, 0 to change, 0 to destroy.
```

Terraform deduced that one resource `swarm-worker.1` needs to be added to reconcile the discrepancy between the state it has stored locally and the actual state of the cluster.

All we have to do to restore the cluster to the desirable state is to run `terraform apply`:

```
terraform apply
```

The relevant parts of the output are as follows:

```
. . .
Apply complete! Resources: 1 added, 0 changed, 0 destroyed.

. . .

Outputs:

floating_ip_1 = 138.197.232.121
floating_ip_2 = 138.197.232.119
floating_ip_3 = 138.197.232.120
swarm_manager_1_private_ip = 10.138.255.140
swarm_manager_1_public_ip = 138.68.57.39
swarm_manager_2_private_ip = 10.138.224.161
swarm_manager_2_public_ip = 138.68.17.88
swarm_manager_3_private_ip = 10.138.224.202
swarm_manager_3_public_ip = 138.68.29.23
```

We can see that one resource was added. The terminated worker has been recreated, and the cluster continues operating at its full capacity.

The state of the cluster is stored in the `terraform.tfstate` file. If you are not running it always from the same computer, you might want to store that file in your repository together with the rest of your configuration files. The alternative is to use Remote State (`https://www.terraform.io/docs/state/remote/index.html`) and, for example, store it in Consul.

Changing the desired state of the cluster is easy as well. All we have to to is add more resources and rerun `terraform apply`.

We are finished with the brief introduction to Terraform for DigitalOcean.

The flow of the process we executed can be described through *Figure 12-4*:

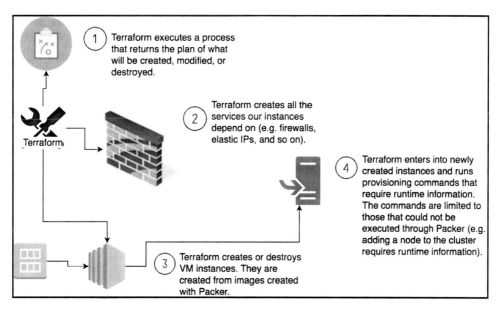

Figure 12-4: The flow of the Terraform process

Let's destroy what we did before we compare the different approaches we took to create and manage a Swarm cluster in DigitalOcean:

```
terraform destroy -force
```

The last line of the output is as follows:

```
...
Destroy complete! Resources: 9 destroyed.
```

The cluster is gone as if it never existed, saving us from unnecessary expenses.

Let's see how to remove a snapshot.

Before we remove the snapshot we created, we need to find its `ID`.

The request that will return the list of all snapshots is as follows:

```
curl -X GET \
    -H "Authorization: Bearer $DIGITALOCEAN_ACCESS_TOKEN" \
"https://api.digitalocean.com/v2/snapshots?resource_type=droplet" \
    | jq '.'
```

The output of the response is as follows:

```
{
  "snapshots": [
    {
      "id": "21373017",
      "name": "devops21-1481087268",
      "regions": [
"sfo2"
      ],
      "created_at": "2016-12-07T05:11:05Z",
      "resource_id": "33907398",
      "resource_type": "droplet",
      "min_disk_size": 30,
      "size_gigabytes": 1.32
}
  ],
  "links": {},
  "meta": {
    "total": 1
}
}
```

We'll use jq to get the snapshot ID:

```
SNAPSHOT_ID=$(curl -X GET \
    -H "Authorization: Bearer $DIGITALOCEAN_ACCESS_TOKEN" \
"https://api.digitalocean.com/v2/snapshots?resource_type=droplet" \
    | jq -r '.snapshots[].id')
```

We sent an HTTP GET request to retrieve all snapshots and used jq to retrieve only the ID. The result was stored in the environment variable SNAPSHOT_ID.

Now we can send a DELETE request that will remove the snapshot:

```
curl -X DELETE \
    -H "Authorization: Bearer $DIGITALOCEAN_ACCESS_TOKEN" \
"https://api.digitalocean.com/v2/snapshots/$SNAPSHOT_ID"
```

The relevant output of the response is as follows:

```
HTTP/1.1 204 No Content
. . .
```

The snapshot has been removed. No resources are running on the DigitalOcean account, and you will not be charged anything more than what you spent from running the exercises in this chapter.

Choosing the right tools to create and manage Swarm clusters in DigitalOcean

We tried two different combinations to create a Swarm cluster in DigitalOcean. We used *Docker Machine* with the *DigitalOcean API* and *Packer* with *Terraform*. That is, by no means, the final list of the tools we can use. The time is limited, and I promised to myself that this book will be shorter than *War and Peace*, so I had to draw the line somewhere. Those two combinations are, in my opinion, the best candidates as your tools of choice. Even if you do choose something else, this chapter, hopefully, gave you an insight into the direction you might want to take.

Most likely you won't use both combinations so the million dollar question is which one should it be?

Only you can answer that question. Now you have the practical experience that should be combined with the knowledge of what you want to accomplish. Each use case is different, and no combination would be the best fit for everyone.

Nevertheless, I will provide a brief overview and some of the use-cases that might be a good fit for each combination.

To Docker Machine or not to Docker Machine?

Docker Machine is the weaker solution we explored. It is based on ad-hoc commands and provides little more than a way to create droplets and install Docker Engine. It uses *Ubuntu 15.10* as the base snapshot. Not only that it is old but is a temporary release. If we choose to use Ubuntu, the correct choice is 16.04 **Long Term Support (LTS)**.

If Docker Machine would, at least, provide the minimum setup for Swarm Mode (as it did with the old Standalone Swarm), it could be a good choice for a small cluster.

As it is now, the only true benefit Docker Machine provides when working with a Swarm cluster in DigitalOcean is Docker Engine installation on a remote node and the ability to use the `docker-machine env` command to make our local Docker client seamlessly communicate with the remote cluster. Docker Engine installation is simple so that alone is not enough. On the other hand, `docker-machine env` command should not be used in a production environment. Both benefits are too weak.

Many of the current problems with Docker Machine can be fixed with some extra arguments (For example, `--digitalocean-image`) and in combination with other tools. However, that only diminishes the primary benefit behind Docker Machine. It was supposed to be simple and work out of the box. That was partly true before Docker 1.12. Now, at least in DigitalOcean, it is lagging behind.

Does that mean we should discard Docker Machine when working with DigitalOcean? Not always. It is still useful when we want to create an ad-hoc cluster for demo purposes or maybe experiment with some new features. Also, if you don't want to spend time learning other tools and just want something you're familiar with, Docker Machine might be the right choice. I doubt that's your case. The fact that you reached this far in this book tells me that you do want to explore better ways of managing a cluster.

The final recommendation is to keep Docker Machine as the tool of choice when you want to simulate a Swarm cluster locally as we did in the previous chapters. There are better choices for DigitalOcean.

To Terraform or not to Terraform?

Terraform, when combined with Packer, is an excellent choice. HashiCorp managed to make yet another tool that changes the way we configure and provision servers.

Configuration management tools have as their primary objective the task of making a server always be in the desired state. If a web server stops, it will be started again. If a configuration file is changed, it will be restored. No matter what happens to a server, its desired state will be restored. Except, when there is no fix to the issue. If a hard disk fails, there's nothing configuration management can do.

The problem with configuration management tools is that they were designed to work with physical, not virtual servers. Why would we fix a faulty virtual server when we can create a new one in a matter of seconds? Terraform understands how cloud computing works better than anyone and embraces the idea that our servers are not pets anymore. They are cattle. It'll make sure that all your resources are available.

When something is wrong on a server, it will not try to fix it. Instead, it will destroy it and create a new one based on the image we choose.

Does that mean that there is no place for Puppet, Chef, Ansible, and other similar tools? Are they obsolete when operating in the cloud? Some are more outdated than others. Puppet and Chef are designed to run an agent on each server, continuously monitoring its state and modifying it if things go astray. There is no place for such tools when we start treating our servers as cattle. Ansible is in a bit better position since it is more useful than others, as a tool designed to configure a server instead of monitor it. As such, it could be very helpful when creating images.

We can combine Ansible with Packer. Packer would create a new VM, Ansible would provision that VM with everything we need, and leave it to Packer to create an image out of it. If the server setup is complicated, that makes a lot of sense. We don't create a lot of system users since we do not log into a machine to deploy software. Swarm does that for us. We do not install web servers and runtime dependencies anymore. They are inside containers. Is there a true benefit from using configuration management tools to install a few things into VMs that will be converted into images? More often than not, the answer is no. The few things we need can be just as easily installed and configured with a few Shell commands. Configuration management of our cattle can, and often should, be done with bash.

I might have been too harsh. Ansible is still a great tool if you know when to use it and for what purpose. If you prefer it over bash to install and configure a server before it becomes an image, go for it. If you try to use it to control your nodes and create DigitalOcean resources, you're on a wrong path. Terraform does that much better. If you think that it is better to provision a running node instead of instantiating images that already have everything inside, you must have much more patience than I do.

The final recommendation is to use *Terraform* with *Packer* if you want to have control of all the pieces that constitute your cluster, or if you already have a set of rules that need to be followed. Be ready to spend some time tuning the configs until you reach the optimum setup. Unlike AWS that, for good or bad, forces us to deal with many types of resources, DigitalOcean is simple. You create droplets, add a few floating IPs, and that's it. You might want to install a firewall on the machines. If you do, the best way would be to do that during the creation of a snapshot with Packer. It is questionable whether a firewall is needed when using Swarm networking, but that's a discussion for some other time.

Since there is no such thing as *Docker for DigitalOcean*, Terraform is a clear winner. DigitalOcean is simple, and that simplicity is reflected through Terraform configuration.

The final verdict

Terraform wins over Docker Machine in a landsilde. If there is such a thing as *Docker for DigitalOcean*, this discussion would be longer. As it is now, the choice is easy. If you choose DigitalOcean, manage your cluster with Packer and Terraform.

To DigitalOcean or not to DigitalOcean

Generally speaking, I like products and services that are focused on very few things and do them well. DigitalOcean is one of those. It is an **Infrastructure as a Service(IaaS)** provider and nothing else. The services it provides are few in number (For example, floating IP) and limited to those that are a real necessity. If you're looking for a provider that will offer you everything you can imagine, choose **Amazon Web Services(AWS)**, Azure, GCE, or any other cloud computing provider that aims at delivering not only hosting but also numerous services on top. The fact that you reached this far in this book tells me that there are strong chances that you are interested in setting up infrastructure services yourself. If that's the case, DigitalOcean is worth a try. Doing everything often means not doing anything really well. DigitalOcean does a few things, and it does them well. What is does, it does better than most.

The real question is whether you need only an **Infrastructure as a Service (IaaS)** provider or you need **Platform as a Service (PaaS)** as well. In my opinion, containers make PaaS obsolete. It will be gradually replaced with containers managed by schedulers (For example, *Docker Swarm*) or **Containers as a Service (CaaS)**. You might not agree with me. If you do, a huge part of AWS becomes obsolete leaving it with EC2, storage, VPCs, and only a handful of other services. In such a case, DigitalOcean is a mighty competitor and an excellent choice. The few things it does, it does better than AWS at a lower price. The performance is impressive. It's enough to measure the time it requires to create a droplet and compare it with the time AWS requires to create and initiate an EC2 instance. The difference is huge. The first time I created a droplet, I thought that there's something wrong. My brain could not comprehend that it could be done in less than a minute.

Did I mention simplicity? DigitalOcean is simple, and I love simplicity. Therefore, the logical conclusion is that I love DigitalOcean. The real mastery is to make complex things easy to use. That's where both Docker and DigitalOcean shine.

14
Creating and Managing Stateful Services in a Swarm Cluster

Any sufficiently advanced technology is indistinguishable from magic.
- Arthur C. Clarke

If you're attending conferences, listening to podcasts, reading forums, or you are involved in any other form of a debate related to containers and cloud-native applications, you must have heard the mantra stateless services. It's almost like a cult. Only stateless services are worthy. Everything else is heresy. The solution to any problem is to remove the state. How do we scale this application? Make it stateless. How do we put this into a container? Make it stateless. How do we make it fault tolerant? Make it stateless. No matter the problem, the solution is to be stateless.

Are all the services we used until now stateless? They're not. Therefore, the logic dictates, we did not yet solve all the problems.

Before we start exploring stateless services, we should go back in time and discuss The twelve-factor app methodology.

Exploring the twelve-factor app methodology

Assuming that my memory still serves me well, *Heroku* (https://www.heroku.com/) became popular somewhere around 2010. It showed us how to leverage *Software-as-a-Service* principles. It freed developers from thinking too much about underlying infrastructure. It allowed them to concentrate on development and leave the rest to others.

All we had to do is push our code to Heroku. It would detect the programming language we use, create a VM and install all the dependencies, build, launch, and so on. The result would be our application running on a server.

Sure, in some cases Heroku would not manage to figure out everything by itself. When that happens, all we'd have to do is create a simple config that would give it a few extra pieces of information. Still very easy and efficient.

Startups loved it (some still do). It allowed them to concentrate on developing new features and leave everything else to Heroku. We write software, and someone else runs it. This is **Software-as-a-Service (SaaS)** at its best. The idea and the principles behind it become so popular that many decided to clone the idea and create their own Heroku-like services.

Shortly after Heroku received a broad adoption, its creators realized that many applications did not perform as expected. It's one thing to have a platform that frees developers from operations, but quite another thing to actually write code that fares well under SaaS providers. So, Heroku folks and a few others came up with *The Twelve-Factor App* (`https ://12factor.net/`) principles. If your application fulfills all twelve factors, it will work well as SaaS. Most of those factors are valid for any modern application, no matter whether it will run inside on-premise servers or through a cloud computing provider, inside PaaS, SaaS, a container, or none of the above. Every modern application should be made using The twelve-factor app methodology. Or, at least, that's what many are saying.

Let us explore each of those factors and see how well we fare against it. Maybe, just maybe, what we learned so far will make us twelve-factor compliant. We'll go through all the factors and compare them with the services we used through this book.

1. **Codebase**

   One codebase tracked in revision control, many deploys. The `go-demo` service is in a single Git repository. Every commit is deployed to testing and production environments. All other services we created are released by someone else. – Passed

2. **Dependencies**

   Explicitly declare and isolate dependencies. All the dependencies are inside Dockers images. Excluding Docker Engine, there is no system-wide dependency. Docker images fulfill this principle by default.– *Passed*

3. **Config**

Store config in the environment.

The `go-demo` service does not have any configuration file. Everything is set through environment variables. The same can be said for all other services we created. Service discovery through networking was a huge help accomplishing this, by allowing us to find services without any configuration. Please note that this principle applies only to configurations that vary between deployments. Everything else can continue being a file as long as it stays the same no matter when and where the service is deployed. - Passed

4. **Backing services**

Treat backing services as attached resources.

In our case, MongoDB is a backing service. It is attached to the primary service `go-demo` through networking. – *Passed*

5. **Build, release, run**

Strictly separate build and run stages.

In this context, everything except running services is considered the build phase. In our case, the build phase is clearly separated from run stages. Jenkins is building our services while Swarm is running them. Building and running are performed in separate clusters. – Passed

6. **Processes**

Execute the app as one or more stateless processes.

We are failing this principle big time. Even though the `go-demo` service is stateless, almost everything else (`docker-flow-proxy`, `jenkins`, `prometheus`, and so on) is not. – Failed

7. **Port binding**

Export services via port binding.

Docker networking and the `docker-flow-proxy` are taking care of port bindings. In many cases, the only service that will bind any port is the `proxy`. Everything else should be inside one or more networks and made accessible through the `proxy`. – Passed

8. **Concurrency**

   Scale out via the process model.

   This factor is directly related to statelessness. Stateless services (example: `go-demo`) are easy to scale. Some non-stateless services (example: `docker-flow-proxy`) are designed to be scalable, so they fulfill this principle as well. Many other stateful services (example: Jenkins, Prometheus, and so on) cannot be scaled horizontally. Even when they can, the process is often too complicated and prone to errors. – Failed

9. **Disposability**

   Maximize robustness with fast startup and graceful shutdown.

   Stateless services are disposable by default. They can be started and stopped at a moments notice, and they tend to be fault tolerant. In case an instance fails, Swarm will reschedule it in one of the healthy nodes. The same cannot be said for all the services we used. Jenkins and MongoDB, just to name a few, will lose their state in case of a failure. That makes them anything but disposable. – Failed

10. **Dev/prod parity**

    Keep development, staging, and production as similar as possible.

    That is one of the main benefits Docker provides. Since containers are created from immutable images, a service will be the same no matter whether it runs on our laptop, testing environment, or production. – Passed

11. **Logs**

    Treat logs as event streams.

    The *ELK* stack together with *LogSpout* fulfills this principle. All the logs from all the containers are streamed into *ElasticSearch* as long as applications inside the containers are outputting them to `stdout`. Jenkins, as we run it, is the exception since it writes some of the logs to files. However, that is configurable, so we won't fault it for that. – Passed

12. Admin processes

Run `admin/management` tasks as one-off processes. In our case, all the processes are executed as Docker containers, apparently fulfilling this factor. – Passed

We passed nine out of twelve factors. Should we aim for all twelve? Actually, the question is wrong. A better-phrased question would be whether we can aim for all twelve factors. We often can't. The world was not built yesterday, and we cannot throw away all the legacy code and start fresh. Even if we could, twelve-factor app principles have one big fallacy. They assume that there is such a thing as a system comprised completely of stateless services.

No matter which architecture style we adopt (microservices included), applications have a state! In a microservices style architecture, each service can have multiple instances, and each service instance should be designed to be stateless. What that means, is that a service instance does not store any data across operations. Hence, being stateless means that any service instance can retrieve all application state required to execute a behavior, from somewhere else. That is a significant architectural constraint of microservices style applications, as it enables resiliency, elasticity, and allows any available service instance to execute any task. Even though the state is not inside a service we are developing, it still exists and needs to be managed somehow. The fact that we did not develop the database where the state is stored does not mean that it should not follow the same principles and be scalable, fault tolerant, resilient, and so on.

So, all systems have a state, but a service can be stateless if it cleanly separates behaviors from data, and can fetch data required to perform any behavior.

Could the authors of twelve-factor app principles be so shortsighted as to assume that state does not exist? They indeed aren't. They assume that everything but the code we write will be a service maintained by someone else. Take MongoDB as an example. Its primary purpose is to store state, so it is, of course, stateful. The twelve-factor app authors assume that we are willing to let someone else manage stateful services and focus only on those we are developing.

While, in some cases, we might choose to use Mongo as a service maintained by one of the cloud providers, in many others such a choice is not the most efficient. If anything else, such services tend to be very expensive. That cost is often worth paying when we do not have the knowledge or the capacity to maintain our backing services. However, when we do, we can expect better and cheaper results if we run a database ourselves. In such a case, it is one of our services, and it is obviously stateful. The fact that we did not write all the services does not mean we are not running them and are, therefore, responsible for them.

The good news is that all three principles we failed are related to statefulness. If we manage to create services in a way that their state is preserved on shutdown and shared between all instances, we'll manage to make the whole system *cloud native*. We'll be able to run it anywhere, scale its services as needed, and make the system fault tolerant.

Creating and managing stateful services is the only major piece of the puzzle we are missing. After this chapter, you will be on your way to running any type of services inside your Swarm cluster.

We will start the practical part of this chapter by creating a Swarm cluster. We'll use AWS only as a demonstration. The principles explored here can be applied to almost any cloud computing provider as well as to on-premise servers.

Setting up a Swarm cluster and the proxy

We'll use *Packer* (`https://www.packer.io/`) and *Terraform* (`https://www.terraform.io/`) to create a Swarm cluster in AWS. For now, the configuration we'll use will be (almost) the same as the one we explored in the `Chapter 12`, *Creating and Managing a Docker Swarm Cluster in Amazon Web Services (AWS)*. We'll extend it later on when we reach more complex scenarios.

 All the commands from this chapter are available in the `13-volumes.sh` (`https://gist.github.com/vfarcic/338e8f2baf2f0c9aa 1ebd70daac31899`) Gist.

We'll continue using the `vfarcic/cloud-provisioning` (`https://github.com/vfarcic /cloud-provisioning`) repository. It contains configurations and scripts that'll help us out. You already have it cloned. To be on the safe side, we'll `pull` the latest version:

```
cd cloud-provisioning

git pull
```

Packer and Terraform configurations are in the `terraform/aws-full` (`https://github.c om/vfarcic/cloud-provisioning/tree/master/terraform/aws-full`) directory:

```
cd terraform/aws-full
```

We'll define a few environment variables that will provide Packer the information it needs when working with AWS:

```
export AWS_ACCESS_KEY_ID=[...]

export AWS_SECRET_ACCESS_KEY=[...]

export AWS_DEFAULT_REGION=us-east-1
```

Please replace [...] with the actual values. Consult the Chapter 12, *Creating And Managing A Docker Swarm Cluster in Amazon Web Services* if you lost the keys and forgot how to create them.

We are ready to create the first image we'll use in this chapter. The Packer configuration we'll use is in terraform/aws-full/packer-ubuntu-docker-compose.json (https://github.com/vfarcic/cloud-provisioning/blob/master/terraform/aws-full/packer-ubuntu-docker-compose.json). It is almost the same as the one we used before so we'll comment only the relevant differences. They are as follows:

```
    "provisioners": [{
...
    }, {
"type": "file",
"source": "docker.service",
"destination": "/tmp/docker.service"
    }, {
"type": "shell",
"inline": [
"sudo mv /tmp/docker.service /lib/systemd/system/docker.service",
"sudo chmod 644 /lib/systemd/system/docker.service",
"sudo systemctl daemon-reload",
"sudo systemctl restart docker"
    ]
    }]
```

The file provisioner copies the docker.service file into the VM. The commands from the shell provisioner will move the uploaded file to the correct directory, give it correct permissions, and restart the docker service.

The docker.service (https://github.com/vfarcic/cloud-provisioning/blob/master/terraform/aws-full/docker.service) file is as follows:

```
[Unit]
Description=Docker Application Container Engine
Documentation=https://docs.docker.com
After=network.target docker.socket
Requires=docker.socket

[Service]
Type=notify
ExecStart=/usr/bin/dockerd -H fd:// -H tcp://0.0.0.0:2375
ExecReload=/bin/kill -s HUP $MAINPID
LimitNOFILE=infinity
LimitNPROC=infinity
LimitCORE=infinity
TasksMax=infinity
TimeoutStartSec=0
Delegate=yes
KillMode=process

[Install]
WantedBy=multi-user.target
```

The Docker service configuration is almost identical to the default one. The only difference is -H tcp://0.0.0.0:2375 in ExecStart.

By default, Docker Engine does not allow remote connections. If its configuration is left unchanged, we cannot send commands from one server to another. By adding -H tcp://0.0.0.0:2375, we are telling Docker to accept requests from any address 0.0.0.0. Normally, that would be a big security risk. However, all AWS ports are closed by default. Later on, we'll open 2375 only to servers that belong to the same security group. As a result, we will be able to control any Docker Engine as long as we are inside one of our servers. As you will see soon, this will come in handy in quite a few examples that follow.

Let's build the AMI defined in packer-ubuntu-docker-compose.json:

```
packer build -machine-readable \
    packer-ubuntu-docker.json \
    | tee packer-ubuntu-docker.log
```

Now we can turn our attention to Terraform that'll create our cluster. We'll copy the SSH key `devops21.pem` that we created earlier and declare a few environment variables that will allow Terraform to access our AWS account:

```
export TF_VAR_aws_access_key=$AWS_ACCESS_KEY_ID

export TF_VAR_aws_secret_key=$AWS_SECRET_ACCESS_KEY

export TF_VAR_aws_default_region=$AWS_DEFAULT_REGION

export KEY_PATH=$HOME/.ssh/devops21.pem

cp $KEY_PATH devops21.pem

export TF_VAR_swarm_ami_id=$( \
    grep 'artifact,0,id' \
    packer-ubuntu-docker.log \
    | cut -d: -f2)
```

Terraform expects environment variables to be prefixed with TF_VAR, so we had to create new ones, even though their values are the same as those we used for Packer. The value of the environment variable KEY_PATH is only an example. You might have it stored somewhere else. If that's the case, please change the value to the correct path.

The last command filters the packer-ubuntu-docker.log and stores the AMI ID as the environment variable TF_VAR_swarm_ami_id.

Now we can create a Swarm cluster. Three VMs should suffice for the exercises that follow, so we'll only create managers. Since the commands will be the same as those we executed in the previous chapters, we'll just skip the explanation and run them:

```
terraform apply \
    -target aws_instance.swarm-manager \
    -var swarm_init=true \
    -var swarm_managers=1

export TF_VAR_swarm_manager_token=$(ssh \
    -i devops21.pem \
    ubuntu@$(terraform output \
    swarm_manager_1_public_ip) \
    docker swarm join-token -q manager)

export TF_VAR_swarm_manager_ip=$(terraform \
    output swarm_manager_1_private_ip)

terraform apply \
    -target aws_instance.swarm-manager
```

We created the first server and initialized the Swarm cluster. Later on, we retrieved the token and the IP of one of the managers and used that data to create and join two additional nodes.

To be on the safe side, we'll enter one of the managers and list the nodes that form the cluster:

```
ssh -i devops21.pem \
    ubuntu@$(terraform output \
    swarm_manager_1_public_ip) \

docker node ls
```

The output is as follows (IDs are removed for brevity):

```
HOSTNAME          STATUS AVAILABILITY MANAGER STATUS
ip-172-31-16-158 Ready  Active       Leader
ip-172-31-31-201 Ready  Active       Reachable
ip-172-31-27-205 Ready  Active       Reachable
```

Where are the workers?

We did not create any worker nodes. The reason is simple. For the exercises in this chapter, three nodes are more than enough. That should not prevent you from adding worker nodes when you start using a similar cluster setup in your organization.

To add worker nodes, please execute the commands that follow:

```
export TF_VAR_swarm_worker_token=$(ssh\ '-i devops21.pem
''ubuntu@$(terraform output ''swarm_manager_1_public_ip)'
'docker swarm join-token -q worker) terraform apply\'-
target aws_instance.swarm-worker'
```

If the output would be `1.2.3.4`, you should open `http://1.2.3.4/jenkins` in your browser.

We are almost done. The only thing left, before we move into statefulness, is to run the `docker-flow-proxy` and `docker-flow-swarm-listener` services. Since we already created them quite a few times, there's no need for an explanation so we can speed up the process by deploying the `vfarcic/docker-flow-proxy/docker-compose-stack.yml` (`https://github.com/vfarcic/docker-flow-proxy/blob/master/docker-compose-stack.yml`) stack:

```
docker network create --driver overlay proxy

curl -o proxy-stack.yml \
    https://raw.githubusercontent.com/\
vfarcic/docker-flow-proxy/master/docker-compose-stack.yml
```

```
docker stack deploy \
    -c proxy-stack.yml proxy

exit
```

Running stateful services without data persistence

We'll start the exploration of stateful services in a Swarm cluster by taking a look at what would happen if we deploy them as any other service.

A good example is Jenkins. Every job we create is an XML file. Every plugin we install is an HPI file. Every configuration change is stored as XML. You get the picture. Everything we do in Jenkins ends up being a file. All those files form its state. Without it, Jenkins would not be able to operate. Jenkins is also a good example of the problems we have with legacy applications. If we were to design it today, it would probably use a database to store its state. That would allow us to scale it since all instances would share the same state by being connected to the same database. There are quite a few other design choices we would probably make if we were to design it today from scratch. Being legacy is not necessarily a bad thing. Sure, having the experience we have today would help us avoid some of the pitfalls of the past. On the other hand, being around for a long time means that it is battle tested, has a high rate of adoption, a huge number of contributors, a big user base, and so on. Everything is a trade-off, and we cannot have it all.

We'll put aside the pros and cons of having a well established and battle-tested versus young and modern, but often unproven application. Instead, let's take a look at how Jenkins, as a representative of a stateful service, behaves when running inside the Swarm cluster we created with Terraform:

```
ssh -i devops21.pem \
    ubuntu@$(terraform output \
    swarm_manager_1_public_ip)

docker service create --name jenkins \
-e JENKINS_OPTS="--prefix=/jenkins" \
    --label com.df.notify=true \
    --label com.df.distribute=true \
    --label com.df.servicePath=/jenkins \
    --label com.df.port=8080 \
    --network proxy \
    --reserve-memory 300m \
    jenkins:2.7.4-alpine
```

We entered one of the managers and created the `jenkins` service.

Please wait a few moments until `jenkins` service is running. You can use docker `service ps jenkins` to check the current state.

Now that Jenkins is running, we should open it in a browser:

```
exit

open "http://$(terraform output swarm_manager_1_public_ip)/jenkins"
```

A note to Windows users
Git Bash might not be able to use the `open` command. If that's the case, execute `terraform output swarm_manager_1_public_ip` to find out the IP of the manager and open the URL directly in your browser of choice. For example, the command above should be replaced with the command that follows:
`terraform output swarm_manager_1_public_ip`
If the output would be `1.2.3.4`, you should open `http://1.2.3.4/jenkins` in your browser.

As you remember from the Chapter 6, *Automating Continuous Deployment Flow with Jenkins*, we need to retrieve the password from logs or its file system. However, this time, doing that is a bit more complicated. Docker Machine mounts local (laptop's) directory into every VM it creates so we could retrieve the `initialAdminPassword` without even entering VMs.

There is no such thing with AWS *at least not yet*, so we need to find out which EC2 instance hosts Jenkins, find the ID of the container, and enter into it to get the file. Such a thing would be easy to do manually but, since we are committed to automation, we'll do it the hard way.

We'll start the quest of finding the password by entering one of the managers and list service tasks:

```
ssh -i devops21.pem \
    ubuntu@$(terraform output \
    swarm_manager_1_public_ip) \

docker service ps jenkins
```

The output is as follows (IDs and ERROR coloumn are removed for brevity):

```
NAME        IMAGE                   NODE             DESIRED STATE
jenkins.1   jenkins:2.7.4-alpine   ip-172-31-16-158  Running
----------------------------------------------------------------
CURRENT STATE
Running 8 minutes ago
```

Luckily, AWS EC2 instances contain internal IP in their names. We can use that to our advantage:

```
JENKINS_IP=$(docker service ps jenkins \
    | tail -n 1 \
    | awk '{ print $4 }' \
    | cut -c 4- \
    | tr "-" ".")
```

We listed the service tasks and piped it to tail so that only the last line is returned. Then we used awk to get the fourth column. The cut command printed the result from the fourth byte effectively removing ip-. All that was piped to tr that replaced - with Finally, the result was stored in the environment variable JENKINS_IP.

If this was too freaky for you, feel free to assign the value manually (in my case it was 172.31.16.159).

Now that we know which node is hosting Jenkins, we need to retrieve the ID of the container. Since we modified the docker.service config to allow us to send commands to a remote engine, we can use the -H argument.

The command that retrieves the ID of the Jenkins container is as follows:

```
JENKINS_ID=$(docker -H tcp://$JENKINS_IP:2375 \
    ps -q \
    --filter label=com.docker.swarm.service.name=jenkins)
```

We used -H to tell the local client to connect to the remote engine running in tcp://$JENKINS_IP:2375. We listed all running containers ps in quiet mode -q so that only IDs are returned. We also applied a filter, so that only the service named Jenkins is retrieved. The result was stored in the environment variable JENKINS_ID.

Now we can use the IP and the ID to enter the container and output the password stored in the file /var/jenkins_home/secrets/initialAdminPassword.

```
docker -H tcp://$JENKINS_IP:2375 \
    exec -it $JENKINS_ID \
    cat /var/jenkins_home/secrets/initialAdminPassword
```

The output is, in my case, as follows:

```
cb7483ce39894c44a48b761c4708dc7d
```

Please copy the password, return to the Jenkins UI, and paste it.

Complete the Jenkins setup before proceeding further. You already know the drill from the `Chapter 6`, *Automating Continuous Deployment Flow with Jenkins*, so I'll let you do it in peace.

The result should be the screen similar to the one in the *figure 13-1*:

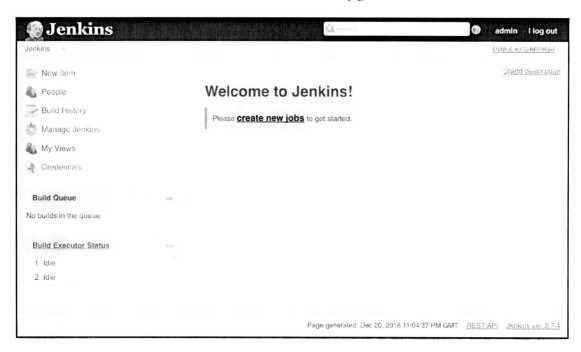

Figure 13-1: Jenkins home screen after the initial setup

Here comes the easy question which I'm sure you'll know how to answer. What would happen if, for whatever reason, Jenkins instance fails?

Let's simulate the failure and observe the outcome:

```
docker -H tcp://$JENKINS_IP:2375 \
    rm -f $JENKINS_ID
```

We used the environment variables `JENKINS_IP` and `JENKINS_ID` to send the forced remove `rm -f` command to the remote node that hosts Jenkins.

Nothing lasts forever. Sooner or later, the service would fail. If it doesn't, the node where it runs will. By removing the container, we simulated what would happen in a real-world situation.

After a while, Swarm will detect that the jenkins replica failed and instantiate a new one. We can confirm that by listing jenkins tasks:

```
docker service ps jenkins
```

The output is as follows (IDs are removed for brevity):

```
NAME           IMAGE                  NODE             DESIRED STATE CURRENT
STATE
jenkins.1    jenkins:2.7.4-alpine ip-172-31-31-201    Running       Running
about 1 min
_ jenkins.1 jenkins:2.7.4-alpine ip-172-31-16-158    Shutdown      Failed
about 1 min
-------------------------------------------------------------------
ERROR PORT
"task: non-zero exit (137)"
```

So far, so good. Swarm is doing what we want it to do. It is making sure that our services are (almost) always running.

The only thing left is to go back to the UI and refresh the screen.

The screen should look similar to the one in *figure 13-2*:

Figure 13-2: Jenkins initial setup screen

That's embarrassing. Everything we did is lost, and we are back to square one. Since Jenkins state was not persisted outside the container, when Swarm created a new one, it started with a blank slate.

How can we solve this problem? Which solutions can we employ to address the persistence issue?

Please remove the `jenkins` service before proceeding:

```
docker service rm jenkins

exit
```

Persisting stateful services on the host

Host-based persistence was very common in the early Docker days when people were running containers on predefined nodes without schedulers like Docker Swarm, Kubernetes, or Mesos. Back then, we would choose a node where we'll run a container and put it there. Upgrades were performed on the same server. In other words, we packaged applications as containers and, for the most part, treated them as any other traditional service. If a node fails... tough luck! It's a disaster with or without containers.

Since serves were prederfined, we could persist the state on the host and rely on backups when that host dies. Depending on the backup frequency, we could lose a minute, an hour, a day, or even a whole week worth of data. Life is hard.

The only positive thing about this approach is that persistence is easy. We would mount a host volume inside a container. Files are persisted outside the container so no data would be lost under "normal" circumstances. If the container is restarted as a result of a failure or an upgrade, data would still be there when we run a new container.

There are other single-host variations of the model. Data volumes, data only containers, and so on. All of them share the same drawback. They remove portability. Without portability, there is no fault tolerance, nor is there scaling. There is no Swarm.

Host-based persistence is unacceptable, so I won't waste any more of your time.

If you have a sysadmin background, you are probably wondering why I haven't mentioned **Network File System** (**NFS**). The reason is simple. I wanted you to feel the pain before diving into the obvious solution.

Persisting stateful services on a Network File System

We need to find a way to retain state outside containers that run our services.

We could mount a volume on the host. That would allow us to preserve state if a container fails and is rescheduled on the same node. The problem is that such a solution is too limited. There is no guarantee that Swarm will reschedule the service to the same node unless we constrain it. If we would do something like that, we'd prevent Swarm from ensuring service availability. When that node would fail (every node fails sooner or later), Swarm could not reschedule the service. We would be fault tolerant only as long as our servers are running.

We can solve the problem of a node failure by mounting a NFS to each of the servers. That way, every server would have access to the same data, and we could mount a Docker volume to it.

We'll use **Amazon Elastic File System (EFS)** (`https://aws.amazon.com/efs/`). Since this book is not dedicated to AWS, I'll skip the comparison of different AWS file systems and only note that the choice of EFS is based on its ability to be used across multiple availability zones.

Please open the *EFS home* (`https://console.aws.amazon.com/efs/home`) screen:

```
open "https://console.aws.amazon.com/efs/home?region=$AWS_DEFAULT_REGION"
```

 A note to Windows users
Git Bash might not be able to use the `open` command. If that's the case, please replace `$AWS_DEFAULT_REGION` with the region where your cluster is running (for example, `us-east-1`) and open it in a browser.

Click the **Create file system** button. For each of the availability zones, replace the default security group with *docker* (we created it earlier with Terraform). Click the button **Next Step** twice, followed by **Create File System**.

We should wait until Life cycle state is set to **Available** for each of the zones.

Now we are ready to mount the EFS in each of the nodes. The easiest way to do that is by clicking the **Amazon EC2 mount instructions** link. We are interested only in the command from the third point of the Mounting your file system section. Please copy it.

All that's left is to enter each of the nodes and execute the command that will mount the EFS volume:

```
ssh -i devops21.pem \
    ubuntu@$(terraform output \
    swarm_manager_1_public_ip)

sudo mkdir -p /mnt/efs
```

We entered the first manager and created /mnt/efs directory.

Paste the command you copied from the **EC2 mount instructions** screen. We'll make a tiny modification before executing it. Please change the destination path from efs to /mnt/efs and execute it.

In my case, the command is as follows (yours will be different):

```
sudo mount -t nfs4 \
    -o nfsvers=4.1,rsize=1048576,wsize=1048576,hard,timeo=600,\
    retrans=2 fs-07538d4e.efs.us-east-1.amazonaws.com:/ \
    /mnt/efs
```

We should also create a sub-directory where we'll store Jenkins state:

```
sudo mkdir -p /mnt/efs/jenkins

sudo chmod 777 /mnt/efs/jenkins

exit
```

We created the directory /mnt/efs/jenkins, gave full permissions to everyone, and exited the server. Since Swarm might decide to create the service on any of the nodes, we should repeat the same process on the rest of the servers. Please note that your mount will be different, so do not simply paste the sudo mount command that follows:

```
ssh -i devops21.pem \
    ubuntu@$(terraform output \
    swarm_manager_2_public_ip)

sudo mkdir -p /mnt/efs

sudo mount -t nfs4 \
    -o nfsvers=4.1,rsize=1048576,wsize=1048576,hard,timeo=600, \
    retrans=2 fs-07538d4e.efs.us-east-1.amazonaws.com:/ \
    /mnt/efs

exit
```

```
ssh -i devops21.pem \
    ubuntu@$(terraform output \
    swarm_manager_3_public_ip)

sudo mkdir -p /mnt/efs

sudo mount -t nfs4 \
    -o nfsvers=4.1,rsize=1048576,wsize=1048576,hard,timeo=600,\
    retrans=2 fs-07538d4e.efs.us-east-1.amazonaws.com:/ \
    /mnt/efs

exit
```

Now we can, finally, try again to create the `jenkins` service. Hopefully, this time the state will be preserved in case of a failure:

```
ssh -i devops21.pem \
    ubuntu@$(terraform output \
    swarm_manager_1_public_ip) \

docker service create --name jenkins \
-e JENKINS_OPTS="--prefix=/jenkins" \
    --mount "type=bind,source=/mnt/efs/jenkins,target=/var/jenkins_home" \
    --label com.df.notify=true \
    --label com.df.distribute=true \
    --label com.df.servicePath=/jenkins \
    --label com.df.port=8080 \
    --network proxy \
    --reserve-memory 300m \
    jenkins:2.7.4-alpine
```

The only difference between this command and the one we used before is in the `--mount` argument. It tells Docker to mount host directory `/mnt/efs/jenkins` as `/var/jenkins_home` inside the container. Since we mounted `/mnt/efs` as EFS volume on all nodes, the `jenkins` service will have access to the same files no matter which server it will run in.

Now we should wait until the service is running. Please execute the `service ps` command to see the current state:

```
docker service ps jenkins
```

Let's open Jenkins UI in a browser:

```
exit

open "http://$(terraform output swarm_manager_1_public_ip)/jenkins"
```

A note to Windows users

Git Bash might not be able to use the `open` command. If that's the case, execute `terraform output swarm_manager_1_public_ip` to find out the IP of the manager and open the URL directly in your browser of choice. For example, the preceding command should be replaced with the command that follows:

`terraform output swarm_manager_1_public_ip`

If the output would be `1.2.3.4`, you should open `http://1.2.3.4/jenkins` in your browser.

This time, since Jenkins home directory is mounted as `/mnt/efs/jenkins`, finding the password will be much easier. All we have to to is output the contents of the file `/mnt/efs/jenkins/secrets/initialAdminPassword` from one of the servers:

```
ssh -i devops21.pem \
    ubuntu@$(terraform output \
    swarm_manager_1_public_ip)

cat /mnt/efs/jenkins/secrets/initialAdminPassword
```

Please copy the password and paste it to the **Administrator password** field in the Jenkins UI. Complete the setup:

Figure 13-3: Jenkins home screen after the initial setup

We'll simulate a failure one more time and observe the results. The commands that follow are the same as those we executed previously so there should be no reason to comment them:

```
JENKINS_IP=$(docker service ps jenkins \
    | tail -n 1 \
    | awk '{ print $4 }' \
    | cut -c 4- \
    | tr "-" ".")

JENKINS_ID=$(docker -H tcp://$JENKINS_IP:2375 \
    ps -q \
    --filter label=com.docker.swarm.service.name=jenkins)

docker -H tcp://$JENKINS_IP:2375 \
    rm -f $JENKINS_ID

docker service ps jenkins
```

Please wait until Swarm instantiates a new replica and refresh the Jenkins UI screen in your browser. This time, we are presented with the login page instead of going back to the initial setup. The state was preserved, making our `jenkins` service fault tolerant. In the worst case scenario, when the service or the entire node fails, we'll have a short period of downtime until Swarm recreates the failed replica. You might be wondering: why did I force you to go through manual steps to create an EFS and mount it? Shouldn't that be done automatically through Terraform? The reason is simple. This solution is not worth automating. It has quite a few downsides.

We would need to place states from all the services into the same EFS drive. A better solution would be to create an EFS volume for each service. The problem with such an approach is that we would need to alter the Terraform config every time someone adds a new stateful service to the cluster. In that case, Terraform would not be of much help since it is not meant to have service-specific configs. It should act as a method to setup a cluster that could host any service. Even if we accept a single EFS volume for all services, we would still need to create a new sub-directory for each service. Wouldn't it be much better if we leave Terraform as a tool for creating infrastructure and Docker for all tasks related to services?

Fortunately, there are better ways to create and mount EFS volumes.

Before we explore alternatives, please remove the `jenkins` service and `exit` the server:

```
docker service rm jenkins

exit
```

There is no reason to keep the EFS volume we created earlier, so please head back to *EFS console* (https://console.aws.amazon.com/efs), select the file system, and click **Actions** followed with the **Delete file system** button. For the rest of the steps, please follow the instructions on the screen.

Data volume orchestration

There are quite a few storage orchestration solutions that integrate with Docker through its volume plugins. We won't compare them. Such an attempt would require a whole chapter, maybe even a book.

Even if you choose a different solution, the principles that will be explained shortly apply to (almost) all others. For a complete list of currently supported plugins, please visit the *Volume plugins* (https://docs.docker.com/engine/extend/legacy_plugins/#/volume-plugins) section of the *Use Docker Engine Plugins* (https://docs.docker.com/engine/extend/legacy_plugins/) documentation.

REX-Ray (https://github.com/codedellemc/rexray) is a vendor agnostic storage orchestration engine. It is built on top of the *libStorage* (http://libstorage.readthedocs.io) framework. It supports *EMC*, *Oracle VirtualBox*, and *Amazon EC2*. At the time of this writing, support for *GCE*, *Open Stack*, *Rackspace,* and *DigitalOcean* is under way.

I find it easier to grasp something when I see it in action. In that spirit, instead of debating for a long time what REX-Ray does and how it works, we'll jump right into a practical demonstration.

Persisting stateful services with REX-Ray

We'll start by setting up REX-Ray manually. If it turns out to be a good solution for our stateful services, we'll move it to Packer and Terraform configurations. Another reason for starting with a manual setup is to give you a better understanding how it works.

Let's get going.

Besides the AWS access keys and the region that we already used quite a few times, we'll also need the ID of the security group we created previously with Terraform:

```
terraform output security_group_id
```

The output should be similar to the one that follows (yours will be different):

```
sg-d9d4d1a4
```

Please copy the value. We'll need it soon.

We'll enter one of the nodes where we'll install and configure REX-Ray:

```
ssh -i devops21.pem \
    ubuntu@$(terraform output \
    swarm_manager_1_public_ip)
```

REX-Ray is fairly simple to set up. That's one of the reasons I prefer it over some other solutions:

```
curl -sSL https://dl.bintray.com/emccode/rexray/install | sh -s -- stable
```

The output is as follows:

```
REX-Ray
-------
Binary:  /usr/bin/rexray
SemVer:  0.6.3
OsArch:  Linux-x86_64
Branch:  v0.6.3
Commit:  69b1f5c2d86a2103c792bec23b5855babada1c0a
Formed:  Wed, 07 Dec 2016 23:22:14 UTC

libStorage
----------
SemVer:  0.3.5
OsArch:  Linux-x86_64
Branch:  v0.6.3
Commit:  456dd68123dd6b49da0275d9bbabd6c800583f61
Formed:  Wed, 07 Dec 2016 23:21:36 UTC
```

We installed *REX-Ray version 0.6.3*, as well as its dependency *libStorage version 0.3.5*. In your case, versions might be newer.

Next, we'll create environment variables with values required for REX-Ray configuration:

```
export AWS_ACCESS_KEY_ID=[...]

export AWS_SECRET_ACCESS_KEY=[...]

export AWS_DEFAULT_REGION=[...]

export AWS_SECURITY_GROUP=[...]
```

Please replace `[...]` with the actual values. The value of the security group should be the same as the one we previously retrieved with the `terraform output security_group_id` command.

Now we are ready to configure REX-Ray through its YML configuration file stored in `/etc/rexray/config.yml`:

```
echo "
libstorage:
  service: efs
  server:
    services:
      efs:
        driver: efs
        efs:
          accessKey:      ${AWS_ACCESS_KEY_ID}
          secretKey:      ${AWS_SECRET_ACCESS_KEY}
          securityGroups: ${AWS_SECURITY_GROUP}
          region:         ${AWS_DEFAULT_REGION}
          tag:            rexray" \
    | sudo tee /etc/rexray/config.yml
```

We set the driver to `efs` and provided it with the AWS data. The result was output to the `/etc/rexray/config.yml` file.

Now we can start the service:

```
sudo rexray service start
```

The output is as follows:

```
rexray.service - rexray
    Loaded: loaded (/etc/systemd/system/rexray.service; enabled; \
vendor preset: enabled)
    Active: active (running) since Thu 2016-12-22 19:34:51 UTC; 245ms ago
 Main PID: 7238 (rexray)
    Tasks: 4
   Memory: 10.6M
      CPU: 109ms
   CGroup: /system.slice/rexray.service/\
           _7238 /usr/bin/rexray start -f

Dec 22 19:34:51 ip-172-31-20-98 systemd[1]: Started rexray.
```

REX-Ray is running, and we can `exit` the node:

```
exit
```

Since we do not know which node will host our stateful services, we need to set up REX-Ray on every node of the cluster. Please repeat the setup steps on Swarm manager nodes 2 and 3.

Once REX-Ray is running on all the nodes, we can give it a spin. Please enter one of the managers:

```
ssh -i devops21.pem \
    ubuntu@$(terraform output \
    swarm_manager_1_public_ip)
```

REX-Ray can be used directly through the `rexray` binary we installed. For example, we can list all the volumes:

```
sudo rexray volume get
```

The output is as follows:

```
ID   Name   Status   Size
```

There's not much to see since we have not created any volumes yet. We can do that with the `rexray` volume create command. However, there is no need for such a thing. Thanks to its integration with Docker, there is not much need to use the binary directly for any operation.

Let's try one more time to create the `jenkins` service. This time, we'll use REX-Ray as the volume driver:

```
docker service create --name jenkins \
-e JENKINS_OPTS="--prefix=/jenkins" \
    --mount "type=volume,source=jenkins,target=/var/jenkins_home, \
volume-driver=rexray" \
    --label com.df.notify=true \
    --label com.df.distribute=true \
    --label com.df.servicePath=/jenkins \
    --label com.df.port=8080 \
    --network proxy \
    --reserve-memory 300m \
    jenkins:2.7.4-alpine
```

The only difference between the command we just executed and the previous attempt to create the `jenkins` service is in the `--mount` argument. The source is now simply a name `jenkins`. It represents the name of the volume. The target is still the same and represents Jenkins home inside a container. The important difference is the addition of the `volume-driver` argument. That was the instruction that Docker should use `rexray` to mount a volume.

If integration between REX-Ray and Docker worked, we should see a `jenkins` volume:

```
sudo rexray volume get
```

The output is as follows:

```
ID          Name     Status    Size
fs-0a64ba43 jenkins  attached  6144
```

This time, the output of the `rexray` volume get command is not empty. We can see the `jenkins` volume. As I already mentioned, there's not much need to use the `rexray` binary. We can accomplish many of its features directly through Docker. For example, we can execute `docker volume ls` command to list all the volumes:

```
docker volume ls
```

The output is as follows:

```
DRIVER   VOLUME NAME
rexray   jenkins
```

Listing volumes proves only that Docker and REX-Ray registered a new mount. Let's take a look at what happened in AWS:

```
exit
```

```
open "https://console.aws.amazon.com/efs/home?region=$AWS_DEFAULT_REGION"
```

A note to Windows users
Git Bash might not be able to use the `open` command. If that's the case, please replace `$AWS_DEFAULT_REGION` with the region where your cluster is running (for example, `us-east-1`) and open it in a browser.

You should see a screen similar to the one presented in *Figure 13-4*:

Figure 13-4: AWS EFS volume created and mounted with REX-Ray

As you can see, REX-Ray created a new EFS volume called `rexray/jenkins` and mounted a target in the same availability zone as the node that hosts the `jenkins` service.

The only thing missing to satisfy my paranoid nature is to kill Jenkins and confirm that REX-Ray mounted the EFS volume on a new container that will be re-scheduled by Swarm.

As before, we'll start by setting up Jenkins:

```
open "http://$(terraform output swarm_manager_1_public_ip)/jenkins"
```

A note to Windows users

Git Bash might not be able to use the `open` command. If that's the case, execute `terraform output swarm_manager_1_public_ip` to find out the IP of the manager and open the URL directly in your browser of choice. For example, the preceding command should be replaced with the command that follows:

`terraform output swarm_manager_1_public_ip`

If the output would be `1.2.3.4`, you should open `http://1.2.3.4/jenkins` in your browser.

We are faced with a recurring challenge. How to find the initial Jenkins administrator password. On the bright side, the challenge is useful as a demonstration of different ways to access content inside containers.

This time, we'll leverage REX-Ray to access data stored in the EFS volume instead of trying to find the node and the ID of the container that hosts the `jenkins` service:

```
ssh -i devops21.pem \
    ubuntu@$(terraform output \
    swarm_manager_1_public_ip)

docker run -it --rm \
    --volume-driver rexray \
    -v jenkins:/var/jenkins_home \
    alpine cat /var/jenkins_home/secrets/initialAdminPassword
```

The output should be similar to the one that follows:

```
9c5e8e51af954d7988b310d862c3d38c
```

We created a new alpine container that also used the rexray volume driver to attach to the jenkins EFS volume. The command output the contents of the `/var/jenkins_home/secrets/initialAdminPassword` file that contains the password. Since we specified the `--rm` argument, Docker removed the container after the process `cat` exited. The final result is the password output to the screen. Please copy it and paste it to the **Administrator password** field in the Jenkins UI. Complete the setup.

Now we need to go through the painful processes of finding the node that hosts Jenkins, getting the ID of the container, and executing the `docker rm` command on the remote engine. In other words, we'll run the same set of commands we executed during previous murderous attempts:

```
JENKINS_IP=$(docker service ps jenkins | tail -n 1 \
    | awk '{ print $4 }' | cut -c 4- | tr "-" ".")

JENKINS_ID=$(docker -H tcp://$JENKINS_IP:2375 \
    ps -q \
    --filter label=com.docker.swarm.service.name=jenkins)

docker -H tcp://$JENKINS_IP:2375 \
    rm -f $JENKINS_ID
```

A few moments later, Swarm will re-schedule the container, and Jenkins will be running again.

Please wait until the service current state is running:

```
docker service ps jenkins
```

Reload Jenkins UI and observe that you are redirected to the login screen instead to the initial setup. The state was preserved.

We're finished with this cluster. Now we need to remove the volume manually. Otherwise, since it was not created by Terraform, it would be preserved even after we destroy the cluster and AWS would continue charging us for it. The problem is that a volume cannot be removed as long as one or more services are using it, so we'll need to destroy `jenkins` service as well:

```
docker service rm jenkins

docker volume rm jenkins

exit

terraform destroy -force
```

Choosing the persistence method for stateful services

There are quite a few other tools we could use to persist state. Most of them fall into one of the groups we explored. Among different approaches we can take, the three most commonly taken are as follows:

1. Do not persist the state.
2. Persist the state on the host.
3. Persist the state somewhere outside the cluster.

There's no reason to debate why persisting data from stateful services is critical, so the first option is automatically discarded.

Since we are operating a cluster, we cannot rely on any given host to be always available. It might fail at any given moment. Even if a node does not fail, sooner or later a service will, and Swarm will reschedule it. When that happens, there is no guarantee that Swarm will run a new replica on the same host. Even if, against all odds, the node never fails, and the service is unbreakable, the first time we execute an update of that service (example: a new release), Swarm will, potentially, create the new replica somewhere else. All in all, we don't know where the service will run nor how long it will stay there. The only way to invalidate that statement is to use constraints that would tie a service to a particular host. However, if we do that, there would be no purpose in using Swarm nor reading this book. All in all, the state should not be persisted on a specific host.

That leaves us with the third option. The state should be persisted somewhere outside the cluster, probably on a network drive. Traditionally, sysadmins would mount a network drive on all hosts, thus making the state available to services no matter where they're running. There are quite a few problems with that approach, the main one being the need to mount a single drive and expect all stateful services to persist their state to it. We could, theoretically, mount a new drive for every single service. Such a requirement would quickly become a burden. If, for example, we used Terraform to manage our infrastructure, we'd need to update it every time there is a new service. Do you remember the first principle of twelve-factor apps? One service should have one codebase. Everything that a service needs should be in a single repository. Therefore, Terraform or any other infrastructure configuration tool should not contain any details specific to a service.

The solution to the problem is to manage volumes using similar principles as those we're using to manage services. Just as we adopted schedulers (example: Swarm) that are managing our services, we should adopt volume schedulers that should handle our mounts.

Since we adopted Docker containers as a way to run our services, a volume scheduler should be able to integrate with it and provide a seamless experience. In other words, managing volumes should be an integral part of managing services. Docker volume plugins allow us precisely that. Their purpose is to integrate third party solutions into the Docker ecosystem and make volume management transparent.

REX-Ray is one of the solutions we explored. There are many others, and I'll leave it to you to compare them and make your decision which volume scheduler works the best in your use case.

If we are presented only with the choices we explored in this chapter, REX-Ray is a clear winner. It allows us to persist data across the cluster in a transparent way. The only extra requirement is to make sure that REX-Ray is installed. After that, we mount volumes with its driver as if they are regular host volumes. Behind the scenes, REX-Ray does the heavy lifting. It creates a network drive, mounts it, and manages it.

Long story short, we'll use REX-Rey for all our stateful services. That is not entirely accurate so let me rephrase. We'll use REX-Ray for all our stateful services that do not use replication and synchronization between instances. If you are wondering what that means, all I can say is that patience is a virtue. We'll get there soon.

Now that we decided that REX-Ray will be part of our stack, it is worthwhile adding it to our Packer and Terraform configs.

Adding REX-Ray to packer and terraform

We already went through REX-Ray manual setup so it should be relatively easy to add it to Packer and Terraform configurations. We'll add to Packer the static parts that do not depend on runtime resources and the rest to Terraform. What that means is that Packer will create AMIs with REX-Ray installed and Terraform will create its configuration and start the service.

Let's take a look at the `terraform/aws-full/packer-ubuntu-docker-rexray.json` (https://github.com/vfarcic/cloud-provisioning/blob/master/terraform/aws-full/packer-ubuntu-docker-rexray.json) file:

```
cat packer-ubuntu-docker-rexray.json
```

The only difference when compared with the `terraform/aws-full/packer-ubuntu-docker.json` (https://github.com/vfarcic/cloud-provisioning/blob/master/terraform/aws-full/packer-ubuntu-docker.json) config we used before is an additional command in the shell `provisioner`:

```
"provisioners": [{
  "type": "shell",
  "inline": [
    ...
    "curl -sSL https://dl.bintray.com/emccode/rexray/install | sh -s --
stable"
    ...
  }]
```

When creating a VM which will later become an AMI, Packer will execute the same command that we ran when we installed REX-Ray manually.

Let's build the AMI:

```
packer build -machine-readable \
    packer-ubuntu-docker-rexray.json \
    | tee packer-ubuntu-docker-rexray.log

export TF_VAR_swarm_ami_id=$(\
    grep 'artifact,0,id' \
    packer-ubuntu-docker-rexray.log \
    | cut -d: -f2)
```

We built the AMI and stored the ID in the environment variable `TF_VAR_swarm_ami_id`. It'll be used by Terraform soon.

Defining the Terraform part of the REX-Ray setup is a bit more complex since its configuration needs to be dynamic and decided at runtime.

The configuration is defined in the `terraform/aws-full/rexray.tpl` (https://github.com/vfarcic/cloud-provisioning/blob/master/terraform/aws-full/rexray.tpl) template:

```
cat rexray.tpl
```

The output is as follows:

```
libstorage:
  service: efs
  server:
    services:
      efs:
        driver: efs
        efs:
          accessKey:       ${aws_access_key}
          secretKey:       ${aws_secret_key}
          region:          ${aws_default_region}
          securityGroups:  ${aws_security_group}
          tag:             rexray
```

As you can see, the AWS keys, the region, and the security groups are defined as variables. The magic happens in the terraform/aws-full/common.tf (https://github.com/vfar cic/cloud-provisioning/blob/master/terraform/aws-full/common.tf) file:

```
cat common.tf
```

The relevant part of the output is the template_file datasource. It is as follows:

```
data "template_file" "rexray" {
  template = "${file("rexray.tpl")}"

  vars {
    aws_access_key = "${var.aws_access_key}"
    aws_secret_key = "${var.aws_secret_key}"
    aws_default_region = "${var.aws_default_region}"
    aws_security_group = "${aws_security_group.docker.id}"
  }
}
```

Contents of the template are in the rexray.tpl (https://github.com/vfarcic/cloud-pr ovisioning/blob/master/terraform/aws-full/rexray.tpl) file we explored earlier. The variables from the template are defined in the vars section. The value of the last variable aws_security_group will be decided at runtime once the aws_security_group called docker is created.

Finally, the last piece of the puzzle is in the terraform/aws-full/swarm.tf (https://gi thub.com/vfarcic/cloud-provisioning/blob/master/terraform/aws-full/swarm.tf) file:

```
cat swarm.tf
```

Both `swarm-manager` and `swarm-worker` AWS instances have two extra lines in the `remote-exec provisioners`. They are as follows:

```
"if ${var.rexray}; then echo \"${data.template_file.rexray.rendered}\"\
 | sudo tee /etc/rexray/config.yml; fi",
"if ${var.rexray}; then sudo rexray service start >/dev/null 2>/dev/null;
fi"
```

Commands are inside an `if` statement. That allows us to decide at runtime whether REX-Ray should be configured and started or not. Normally, you would not need the if statement. You'll either choose to use REX-Ray, or not. However, at the beginning of this chapter we needed a cluster with REX-Ray and I did not want to maintain two almost identical copies of the configuration (one with, and the other without REX-Ray).

The important part is inside the if statement. The first line puts the content of the template into the `/etc/rexray/config.yml` (`https://github.com/vfarcic/cloud-provisioning /blob/master/terraform/aws-full/swarm.tf`) file. The second starts the service.

Now that it is evident how we defined REX-Ray inside Terraform configs, it is time to create a cluster with it automatically:

```
terraform apply \
    -target aws_instance.swarm-manager \
    -var swarm_init=true \
    -var swarm_managers=1 \
    -var rexray=true
```

The first node that initializes the Swarm cluster was created and we can proceed by adding two more manager nodes:

```
export TF_VAR_swarm_manager_token=$(ssh \
    -i devops21.pem \
    ubuntu@$(terraform output \
    swarm_manager_1_public_ip) \
    docker swarm join-token -q manager)

export TF_VAR_swarm_manager_ip=$(terraform \
    output swarm_manager_1_private_ip)

terraform apply \
    -target aws_instance.swarm-manager \
    -var rexray=true
```

We retrieved the token and the IP of the first manager and used that info to create the rest of the nodes.

Let's enter one of the servers and confirm that REX-Ray is installed:

```
ssh -i devops21.pem \
    ubuntu@$(terraform output \
    swarm_manager_1_public_ip)

rexray version
```

The output of the `rexray version` command is as follows:

```
REX-Ray
-------
Binary: /usr/bin/rexray
SemVer: 0.6.3
OsArch: Linux-x86_64
Branch: v0.6.3
Commit: 69b1f5c2d86a2103c792bec23b5855babada1c0a
Formed: Wed, 07 Dec 2016 23:22:14 UTC

libStorage
----------
SemVer: 0.3.5
OsArch: Linux-x86_64
Branch: v0.6.3
Commit: 456dd68123dd6b49da0275d9bbabd6c800583f61
Formed: Wed, 07 Dec 2016 23:21:36 UTC
```

Both REX-Ray and libStorage are installed. Finally, before we check whether it is working, let's have a quick look at the config.

```
cat /etc/rexray/config.yml
```

The output is as follows:

```
libstorage:
service: efs
server:
  services:
  efs:
    driver: efs
    efs:
      accessKey:       ##########
      secretKey:       ##########
      region:          ##########
      securityGroups:  ##########
      tag:             rexray
```

I obscured my AWS account details for obvious reasons. Nevertheless, the config looks *OK* and we can give REX-Ray a spin.

We'll deploy the `vfarcic/docker-flow-proxy/docker-compose-stack.yml` (https ://github.com/vfarcic/docker-flow-proxy/blob/master/docker-compose-stack.yml) stack and create the `jenkins` service in the same way we did while we were experimenting with REX-Ray installed manually:

```
docker network create --driver overlay proxy

curl -o proxy-stack.yml \
    https://raw.githubusercontent.com/ \
vfarcic/docker-flow-proxy/master/docker-compose-stack.yml

docker stack deploy \
    -c proxy-stack.yml proxy

docker service create --name jenkins \
-e JENKINS_OPTS="--prefix=/jenkins" \
    --mount "type=volume,source=jenkins,target=/var/jenkins_home,\
volume-driver=rexray" \
    --label com.df.notify=true \
    --label com.df.distribute=true \
    --label com.df.servicePath=/jenkins \
    --label com.df.port=8080 \
    --network proxy \
    --reserve-memory 300m \
    jenkins:2.7.4-alpine
```

It should take only a few moments until the script is finished. Now we can check the Docker volumes:

```
docker volume ls
```

The output is as follows:

```
DRIVER              VOLUME NAME
rexray              jenkins
```

As expected, the `jenkins` service created the `rexray` volume with the same name. We should wait until Jenkins is running and open it in a browser:

```
docker service ps jenkins # Wait until finished

exit

open "http://$(terraform output swarm_manager_1_public_ip)/jenkins"
```

A note to Windows users
Git Bash might not be able to use the open command. If that's the case, execute `terraform output swarm_manager_1_public_ip` to find out the IP of the manager and open the URL directly in your browser of choice. For example, the command above should be replaced with the command that follows:
`terraform output swarm_manager_1_public_ip`
If the output would be `1.2.3.4`, you should open `http://1.2.3.4/jenkins` in your browser.

The only thing left is to recuperate the initial administrative password and use it to setup Jenkins:

```
ssh -i devops21.pem \
    ubuntu@$(terraform output \
    swarm_manager_1_public_ip)

docker run -it --rm \
    --volume-driver rexray \
    -v jenkins:/var/jenkins_home \
    alpine cat /var/jenkins_home/secrets/initialAdminPassword
```

I'll leave the rest to you. Finish the setup, destroy the container, wait until Swarm reschedules it, confirm that the state is preserved, and so on and so forth. Spend some time playing with it.

Unless you developed an emotional attachment with Jenkins and REX-Ray, please remove the service and the volume. We won't need it anymore:

```
docker service rm jenkins

docker volume rm jenkins

exit
```

Prometheus, ElasticSearch, and Mongo are only a few examples of services that store the state. Should we add REX-Ray mounts for all of them? Not necessarily. Some stateful services already have a mechanism to preserve their state. Before we start attaching REX-Ray mount like there is no tomorrow, we should first check whether a service already has a data replication mechanism.

Persisting stateful services without replication

Jenkins is a good example of a stateful service that forces us to preserve its state. Moreover, it is incapable of sharing or synchronizing state between multiple instances. As a result, it cannot scale. There cannot be two Jenkins masters with the same or replicated state. Sure, you can create as many masters as you want but each will be an entirely separate service without any relation to other instances.

The most obvious negative side-effect of Jenkins inability to scale horizontally is performance. If a master is under heavy load, we cannot create a new instance and thus reduce the burden from the original.

There are only three types of services that can be scaled. They need to be stateless, stateful and capable of using shared state, or stateful and capable of synchronizing state. Jenkins is none of those and, therefore, it cannot be scaled horizontally. The only thing we can do to increase Jenkins capacity is to add more resources (for example: CPU and memory). Such an action would improve its performance but would not provide high-availability. When Jenkins fails, Swarm will re-schedule it. Still, there is a period between a failure and a new replica being fully operational.

During that time, Jenkins would not be functional. Without the ability to scale, there is no high-availability.

A big part of Jenkins workload is performed by its agents, so many organizations will not need to deal with the fact that it is not scalable.

The reason for this transgression into Jenkins statefulness is to demonstrate one of the ways stateful services can be designed. When running stateful services that do not have a synchronization mechanism, there is no better option we can employ than to mount a volume from an external drive. That does not mean that mounting a volume is the only option we can use to deploy stateful services, but that is a preferable way to treat those that cannot share or synchronize their state across multiple replicas.

Let's explore stateful services that do implement state synchronization.

Persisting stateful services with synchronization and replication

When creating stateful services, the natural reaction is to think of a way to preserve their state. While in many cases that is the correct thing to do, in some others it isn't. It depends on service's architecture.

Throughout this book, we explored at least two stateful services that can synchronize their state across all instances. Those are *Docker Flow Proxy* and *MongoDB*. In a nutshell, the ability to synchronize state means that when data inside one instance changes, it is capable of propagating that change to all other instances. The biggest problem with that process is how to guarantee that everyone has the same data without sacrificing availability. We'll leave that discussion for some other time and place. Instead, let us go through the `docker-flow-proxy` and `mongo` services and decide which changes (if any) we need to apply to accomplish high availability and performance. We'll use them as examples how to treat stateful services capable of data replication and synchronization.

Not everyone uses Mongo for storing data, nor everyone thinks that *Docker Flow Proxy* is the best choice for routing requests. The chances are that your choice of a database and the proxy is different. Even in that case, I strongly suggest you read the text that follows since it uses those two services only as examples of how you could design your replication and how to set up third-party stateful service that already has it incorporated. Most DBs use the same principles for replication and synchronization, and you should have no problem taking MongoDB examples as a blueprint for creating your database services.

Persisting docker flow proxy state

Docker Flow Proxy is a stateful service. However, that did not prevent us from scaling it. Its architecture is made in a way that, even though it is stateful, all instances have the same data. The mechanism to accomplish that has quite a few names. I prefer calling it state replication and synchronization.

When one of the instances receives a new instruction that changes its state, it should find all the other replicas and propagate the change.

The replication flow is usually as follows:

1. An instance receives a request that changes its state.
2. It finds the addresses of all the other instances of the same service.
3. It re-sends the request to all other instances of the same service.

The ability to propagate changes is not enough. When a new instance is created, a stateful service with data replication needs to be capable of requesting a complete state from one of the other instances. The first action it needs to perform when initialized is to reach the same state as other replicas. That can be accomplished through a pull mechanism. While propagation of a change of state of one instance often entails a push to all other instances, initialization of a new instance is often followed by a data pull.

The synchronization flow is often as follows:

1. A new instance of a service is created.
2. It finds the address of one of the other instances of the same service.
3. It pulls data from the other instance of the same service.

You already saw *Docker Flow Proxy* in action quite a few times. We scaled it, and we simulated a failure which resulted in re-scheduling. In both cases, all replicas always had the same state or, to be more precise, the same configuration. You saw it before, so there's no need to go into another round of a practical demonstration of proxy's capabilities.

Understanding how replication and synchronization works does not mean that we should write our services as stateful and employ those mechanisms ourselves. Quite the contrary. When appropriate, design your services to be stateless and store their state in a database. Otherwise, you might quickly run into problems and realize that you'll have to reinvent the wheel. For example, you might be faced with consensus problems that are already solved in protocols like Raft and Paxos. You might need to implement a variation of a Gossip protocol. And so on, and so forth. Concentrate on what brings value to your project and use proven solutions for everything else.

Recommending the usage of an external database instead of storing the state inside our services might sound conflicting knowing that *Docker Flow Proxy* did the opposite. It is a stateful application without any external data store (at least when running in Swarm mode). The reason is simple. The proxy was not written from scratch. It uses HAProxy in the background which, in turn, does not have the ability to store its configs (state) externally. If I were to write a proxy from scratch, it would save its state externally. I might do that one day. Until then, HAProxy is stateful and so is *Docker Flow Proxy*. From a user's perspective, that should not be an issue since it employs data replication and synchronization between all instances. The problem is for developers working on the project.

Let's take a look at another example of a stateful service with data replication.

Persisting MongoDB state

We used `go-demo` service throughout the book. It helped us understand better how Swarm works. Among other things, we scaled the service quite a few times. That was easy to do since it is stateless. We can create as many replicas as we want without having to worry about data. It is stored somewhere else.

The `go-demo` service externalizes its state to MongoDB. If you paid attention, we never scaled the database. The reason is simple. MongoDB cannot be scaled with a simple `docker service scale` command.

Unlike *Docker Flow Proxy* that was designed from the ground up to leverage Swarm's networking to find other instances before replicating data, MongoDB is network agnostic. It cannot auto-discover its replicas. To make things more complicated, only one instance can be primary meaning that only one instance can receive write requests. All that means that we cannot scale Mongo using Swarm. We need a different approach. Let's try to set up three MongoDBs with data replication by creating a replica set. We'll start with a manual process that will provide us with an understanding of the problems we might face and solutions we might employ. Later on, once we reach a satisfactory outcome, we'll try to automate the process.

We'll start by entering one of the manager nodes:

```
ssh -i devops21.pem \
    ubuntu@$(terraform output \
    swarm_manager_1_public_ip)
```

All members of a Mongo replica set need to be able to communicate with each other, so we'll create the same old `go-demo` network:

```
docker network create --driver overlay go-demo
```

If we were to create a single service with three replicas, Swarm would create a single network endpoint for the service and load balance requests among all instances. The problem with that approach is in MongoDB configuration. It needs a fixed address of every DB that will belong to the replica set.

Instead of creating three replicas of a service, we'll create three services:

```
for i in 1 2 3; do
    docker service create --name go-demo-db-rs$i \
        --reserve-memory 100m \
        --network go-demo \
        mongo:3.2.10 mongod --replSet "rs0"
done
```

The command we executed created services `go-demo-db-rs1`, `go-demo-db-rs2`, and `go-demo-db-rs3`. They all belong to the `go-demo` network so that they can communicate with each other freely. The command specified for all services `mongod --replSet "rs0"`, making them all belong to the same Mongo replica set called `rs0`. Please don't confuse Swarm replicas with Mongo replica sets. While they have a similar objective, the logic behind them is quite different.

We should wait until all the services are running:

```
docker service ls
```

The relevant part of the output is as follows (IDs are removed for brevity):

```
NAME             REPLICAS IMAGE           COMMAND
...
go-demo-db-rs2 1/1        mongo:3.2.10 mongod --replSet rs0
go-demo-db-rs1 1/1        mongo:3.2.10 mongod --replSet rs0
go-demo-db-rs3 1/1        mongo:3.2.10 mongod --replSet rs0
...
```

Now we should configure Mongo's replica set. We'll do that by creating one more `mongo` service:

```
docker service create --name go-demo-db-util \
    --reserve-memory 100m \
    --network go-demo \
    --mode global \
    mongo:3.2.10 sleep 100000
```

We made the service global so that we ensure it will run on the same node we're in. That makes the process easier than trying to figure out the IP of a node it runs in. It belongs to the same `go-demo` network so that it can access the other DB services.

We do not want to run Mongo server inside this service. The purpose of `go-demo-db-util` is to give us a Mongo client that we can use to connect to other DBs and configure them. Therefore, we replaced the default command `mongod` with a very long sleep.

To enter into one of the containers of the `go-demo-db-util` service, we need to find its ID:

```
UTIL_ID=$(docker ps -q \
    --filter label=com.docker.swarm.service.name=go-demo-db-util)
```

Now that we have the ID of the `go-demo-db-util` replica running on the same server, we can enter inside the container:

```
docker exec -it $UTIL_ID sh
```

The next step is to execute a command that will initiate Mongo's replica set:

```
mongo --host go-demo-db-rs1 --eval '
    rs.initiate({
        _id: "rs0",
        version: 1,
        members: [
            {_id: 0, host: "go-demo-db-rs1" },
            {_id: 1, host: "go-demo-db-rs2" },
            {_id: 2, host: "go-demo-db-rs3" }
        ]
    })
'
```

We used the local `mongo` client to issue the command on the server running inside `go-demo-db-rs1`. It initiated the replica set with the ID `rs0` and specified that the three services we created previously should be its members. Thanks to Docker Swarm networking, we do not need to know the IPs. It was enough to specify the names of the services.

The response is as follows:

```
MongoDB shell version: 3.2.10
connecting to: go-demo-db-rs1:27017/test
{ "ok" : 1 }
```

We should not trust the acknowledgment alone. Let's take a look at the config:

```
mongo --host go-demo-db-rs1 --eval 'rs.conf()'
```

We issued another command to the remote server running in `go-demo-db-rs1`. It retrieved the replica set configuration. Part of the output is as follows:

```
MongoDB shell version: 3.2.10
connecting to: go-demo-db-rs1:27017/test
{
        "_id" : "rs0",
        "version" : 1,
        "protocolVersion" : NumberLong(1),
        "members" : [
                {
                        "_id" : 0,
                        "host" : "go-demo-db-rs1:27017",
                        "arbiterOnly" : false,
                        "buildIndexes" : true,
                        "hidden" : false,
                        "priority" : 1,
                        "tags" : {
```

```
                    },
                    "slaveDelay" : NumberLong(0),
                    "votes" : 1
                },
                ...
        ],
        "settings" : {
                "chainingAllowed" : true,
                "heartbeatIntervalMillis" : 2000,
                "heartbeatTimeoutSecs" : 10,
                "electionTimeoutMillis" : 10000,
                "getLastErrorModes" : {

                },
                "getLastErrorDefaults" : {
                        "w" : 1,
                        "wtimeout" : 0
                },
                "replicaSetId" : ObjectId("585d643276899856d1dc5f36")
        }
}
```

We can see that the replica set has three members (two were removed for brevity).

Let's send one more command to the remote Mongo running in `go-demo-db-rs1`. This time, we'll check the status of the replica set:

```
mongo --host go-demo-db-rs1 --eval 'rs.status()'
```

Part of the output is as follows:

```
connecting to: go-demo-db-rs1:27017/test
{
        "set" : "rs0",
        "date" : ISODate("2016-12-23T17:52:36.822Z"),
        "myState" : 1,
        "term" : NumberLong(1),
        "heartbeatIntervalMillis" : NumberLong(2000),
        "members" : [
                {
                        "_id" : 0,
                        "name" : "go-demo-db-rs1:27017",
                        "health" : 1,
                        "state" : 1,
                        "stateStr" : "PRIMARY",
                        "uptime" : 254,
                        "optime" : {
                                "ts" : Timestamp(1482515517, 2),
```

```
                           "t" : NumberLong(1)
                 },
                 "optimeDate" : ISODate("2016-12-23T17:51:57Z"),
                 "infoMessage" : "could not find member to sync from",
                 "electionTime" : Timestamp(1482515517, 1),
                 "electionDate" : ISODate("2016-12-23T17:51:57Z"),
                 "configVersion" : 1,
                 "self" : true
             },
             ...
     ],
     "ok" : 1
 }
```

Info about two replicas is removed for brevity.

We can see that all the Mongo replicas are running. The `go-demo-db-rs1` service is acting as the primary, while the other two are secondary nodes.

Setting up a Mongo replica set means that data will be replicated to all its members. One is always a primary, while the rest are secondary servers. With the current configuration, we can read and write data only to the primary server. Replica set can be configured to allow read access to all the servers. Writing is always restricted to the primary.

Let us generate some sample data:

```
mongo --host go-demo-db-rs1
```

We entered into the remote Mongo running on `go-demo-db-rs1`.

The output is as follows:

```
MongoDB shell version: 3.2.10
connecting to: go-demo-db-rs1:27017/test
Welcome to the MongoDB shell.
For interactive help, type "help".
For more comprehensive documentation, see
        http://docs.mongodb.org/
Questions? Try the support group
        http://groups.google.com/group/mongodb-user
rs0:PRIMARY>
```

As you can see from the prompt, we are inside the primary database server.

We'll create a few records in the database test:

```
use test

db.books.insert(
    {
        title:"The DevOps 2.0 Toolkit"
    }
)

db.books.insert(
    {
        title:"The DevOps 2.1 Toolkit"
    }
)

db.books.find()
```

The previous command retrieved all the records from the database test.

The output is as follows:

```
{ "_id" : ObjectId("585d6491660a574f80478cb6"), "title" : \
"The DevOps 2.0 Toolkit" }
{ "_id" : ObjectId("585d6491660a574f80478cb7"), "title" : \
"The DevOps 2.1 Toolkit" }
```

Now that we have the replica set configured and a few sample records, we can simulate failure of one of the servers and observe the result:

```
exit # Mongo

exit # go-demo-db-util

RS1_IP=$(docker service ps go-demo-db-rs1 \
    | tail -n 1 \
    | awk '{ print $4 }' \
    | cut -c 4- \
    | tr "-" ".")

docker -H tcp://$RS1_IP:2375 ps
```

We exited MongoDB and the `go-demo-db-util` service replica. Then we found the IP of `go-demo-db-rs1` (primary member of the Mongo replica set) and listed all the containers running on the server.

The output is as follows (IDs and STATUS columns are removed for brevity):

```
IMAGE                              COMMAND                    CREATED
mongo:3.2.10                       "/entrypoint.sh sleep"  3 minutes ago
mongo:3.2.10                       "/entrypoint.sh mongo"  6 minutes ago
vfarcic/docker-flow-proxy:latest "/docker-entrypoint.s"  13 minutes ago
------------------------------------------------------------------------
NAMES                                        PORTS
go-demo-db-util.0.8qcsmlzioohn3j6p78hntskj1  27017/tcp
go-demo-db-rs1.1.86sg93z9oasd43dtgoax53nuw   27017/tcp
proxy.2.3tlpr1xyiu8wm70lmrffod7ui            80/tcp,443/tcp/,8080/tcp
```

Now we can find the ID of the `go-demo-db-rs1` service replica and simulate failure by removing it:

```
RS1_ID=$(docker -H tcp://$RS1_IP:2375 \
    ps -q \
    --filter label=com.docker.swarm.service.name=go-demo-db-rs1) \

docker -H tcp://$RS1_IP:2375 rm -f $RS1_ID
```

Let's take a look at the `go-demo-db-rs1` tasks:

```
docker service ps go-demo-db-rs1
```

Swarm discovered that one of the replicas failed and re-scheduled it. A new instance will be running a few moments later.

The output of the `service ps` command is as follows (IDs are removed for brevity):

```
NAME                 IMAGE          NODE                DESIRED STATE
go-demo-db-rs1.1     mongo:3.2.10 ip-172-31-16-215   Running
_ go-demo-db-rs1.1   mongo:3.2.10 ip-172-31-16-215   Shutdown
------------------------------------------------------------------------
CURRENT STATE               ERROR
Running 28 seconds ago
Failed 35 seconds ago       "task: non-zero exit (137)"
```

We'll enter the `go-demo-db-util` service replica one more time and output the status of the Mongo replica set:

```
docker exec -it $UTIL_ID sh

mongo --host go-demo-db-rs1 --eval 'rs.status()'
```

The relevant part of the output is as follows:

```
MongoDB shell version: 3.2.10
connecting to: go-demo-db-rs1:27017/test
{
        "set" : "rs0",
        "date" : ISODate("2016-12-23T17:56:08.543Z"),
        "myState" : 2,
        "term" : NumberLong(2),
        "heartbeatIntervalMillis" : NumberLong(2000),
        "members" : [
                {
                    "_id" : 0,
                    "name" : "go-demo-db-rs1:27017",
                    ...
                    "stateStr" : "SECONDARY",
                    ...
                },
                {
                    "_id" : 1,
                    "name" : "go-demo-db-rs2:27017",
                    ...
                    "stateStr" : "PRIMARY",
                    ...
                },
                {
                    "_id" : 2,
                    "name" : "go-demo-db-rs3:27017",
                    ...
                    "stateStr" : "SECONDARY",
                    ...
                }
        ],
        "ok" : 1
}
```

We can see that the `go-demo-db-rs2` become the primary Mongo replica. A simplified flow of what happened is as follows:

- Mongo replica `go-demo-db-rs1` failed
- The remaining members noticed its absence and promoted `go-demo-db-rs2` to the PRIMARY status
- In the meantime, Swarm rescheduled the failed service replica
- The primary Mongo replica noticed that the `go-demo-db-rs1` server came back online and joined the Mongo replica set as secondary

- The newly created `go-demo-db-rs1` synchronized its data from one of the other members of the Mongo replica set

One of the key elements for all this to work is Docker networking. When the rescheduled service replica came back online, it maintained the same address `go-demo-db-rs1`, and we did not need to change the configuration of the Mongo replica set.

If we used VMs and, in the case of AWS, *Auto Scaling Groups* to host Mongo, when a node fails, a new one would be created in its place. However, the new node would receive a new IP and would not be able to join the Mongo replica set without modifications to the configuration. The are ways we could accomplish the same in AWS without containers, but none would be so simple and elegant as with Docker Swarm and networking.

What happened to the sample data we created? Remember, we wrote data to the primary Mongo replica `go-demo-db-rs1` and, later on, removed it. We did not use REX-Ray or any other solution to persist data.

Let's enter the new primary Mongo replica:

```
mongo --host go-demo-db-rs2
```

In your cluster, the new primary might be `go-demo-db-rs3`. If that's the case, please change the above command.

Next, we'll specify that we want to use the test database and retrieve all data:

```
use test

db.books.find()
```

The output is as follows:

```
{ "_id" : ObjectId("585d6491660a574f80478cb6"), "title" : \
"The DevOps 2.0 Toolkit" }
{ "_id" : ObjectId("585d6491660a574f80478cb7"), "title" : \
"The DevOps 2.1 Toolkit" }
```

Even though we did not setup up data persistence, all data is there.

The main purpose of Mongo replica sets is to provide fault tolerance. If a DB fails, other members will take over. Any change to data (state) is replicated among all members of a replica set.

Does that mean that we do not need to preserve the state to an external drive? That depends on the use case. If data we are operating with is massive, we might employ some form of disk persistence to speed up the synchronization process. In any other circumstances, using volumes is a waste since most databases are designed to provide data replication and synchronization.

The current solution worked well, and we should seek a way to set it up in a more automated (and simpler) way.

We'll exit the MongoDB and the `go-demo-db-util` service replica, remove all the DB services, and start over:

```
exit # Mongo

exit # go-demo-db-util

docker service rm go-demo-db-rs1 \
    go-demo-db-rs2 go-demo-db-rs3 \
    go-demo-db-util
```

Initializing MongoDB replica set through a swarm service

Let's try to define a better and easier way to set up a MongoDB replica set.

We'll start by creating three `mongo` services. Later on, each will become a member of a Mongo replica set:

```
for i in 1 2 3; do
    docker service create --name go-demo-db-rs$i \
        --reserve-memory 100m \
        --network go-demo \
        mongo:3.2.10 mongod --replSet "rs0"

    MEMBERS="$MEMBERS go-demo-db-rs$i"
done
```

The only difference, when compared with the previous command we used to create `mongo` services, is the addition of the environment variable `MEMBERS`. It holds service names of all MongoDBs. We'll use that as the argument for the next service.

Since the official `mongo` image does not have a mechanism to configure Mongo replica sets, we'll use a custom one. Its purpose will be only to configure Mongo replica sets.

The definition of the image is in the `conf/Dockerfile.mongo` (`https://github.com/vfar cic/cloud-provisioning/blob/master/conf/Dockerfile.mongo`) file. Its content is as follows:

```
FROM mongo:3.2.10

COPY init-mongo-rs.sh /init-mongo-rs.sh
RUN chmod +x /init-mongo-rs.sh
ENTRYPOINT ["/init-mongo-rs.sh"]
```

`Dockerfile.mongo` extends the official `mongo` image, adds a custom `init-mongo-rs.sh` script, gives it execute permissions, and sets it as the entry point.

`ENTRYPOINT` defines the executable that will run whenever a container is run. Any command arguments we specify will be appended to it.

The `conf/init-mongo-rs.sh` (`https://github.com/vfarcic/cloud-provisioning/blo b/master/conf/init-mongo-rs.sh`) script is as follows:

```bash
#!/usr/bin/env bash

for rs in "$@"; do
    mongo --host $rs --eval 'db'
    while [$? -ne 0 ]; do
      echo "Waiting for $rs to become available"
      sleep 3
        mongo --host $rs --eval 'db'
    done
done

i=0
for rs in "$@"; do
    if [ "$rs" != "$1" ]; then
        MEMBERS="$MEMBERS ,"
    fi
    MEMBERS="$MEMBERS {_id: $i, host: \"$rs\" }"
    i=$((i+1))
done

mongo --host $1 --eval "rs.initiate({_id: \"rs0\", version: 1, \
members: [$MEMBERS]})"
sleep 3
mongo --host $1 --eval 'rs.status()'
```

The first section loops over all DB addresses (defined as script arguments) and checks whether they are available. If they're not, it waits for three seconds before repeating the loop.

The second section formats a JSON string that defines the list of all members (id and host). Finally, we initiate the replica set, wait for three seconds, and output its status.

This script is a slightly more elaborate version of the commands we executed previously when we set up the replica set manually. Instead of hard-coding values (for example: `service names`), it is written in a way that it can be reused for multiple Mongo replica sets with varying number of members.

All that's left is to run the container as a Swarm service. I already built the image as `vfarcic/mongo-devops21` and pushed it to Docker Hub:

```
docker service create --name go-demo-db-init \
    --restart-condition none \
    --network go-demo \
    vfarcic/mongo-devops21 $MEMBERS
```

When the script is finished, the container will stop. Typically, Swarm would interpret a stopped container as a failure and re-schedule it. That's not the behavior we need. We want this service to perform some tasks (configure replica set) and stop when finished. We accomplished that with the `--restart-condition none` argument. Otherwise, Swarm would enter into an endless loop of continuously re-scheduling a service replica that keeps failing a few moments later.

The command of the service is `$MEMBERS`. When appended to the `ENTRYPOINT`, the full command was `init-mongo-rs.sh go-demo-db-rs1 go-demo-db-rs2 go-demo-db-rs3`.

Let's confirm that all services (except `go-demo-db-init`) are running:

```
docker service ls
```

The output is as follows:

```
ID             NAME              REPLICAS   IMAGE
11pus9pvxoj6   go-demo-db-rs1    1/1        mongo:3.2.10
59eox5zqfhf8   go-demo-db-rs2    1/1        mongo:3.2.10
5tchuajhi05e   go-demo-db-init   0/1        vfarcic/mongo-devops21
6cmd34ezpun9   go-demo-db-rs3    1/1        mongo:3.2.10
bvfrbwdi5li3   swarm-listener    1/1        vfarcic/docker-flow-swarm-listener
djy5p4re3sbh   proxy             3/3        vfarcic/docker-flow-proxy
--------------------------------------------------------------------
COMMAND
mongod --replSet rs0
mongod --replSet rs0
go-demo-db-rs1 go-demo-db-rs2 go-demo-db-rs3
mongod --replSet rs0
```

The only service that is not running is `go-demo-db-init`. By this time, it finished executing and, since we used the `--restart-condition none` argument, Swarm did not re-schedule it.

We already developed a level of trust, and you probably believe me that the `go-demo-db-init` did its job correctly. Nevertheless, it doesn't hurt to double-check it. Since the last command of the script output the replica set status, we can check its logs to see whether everything is configured correctly. That means we'll need to go one more time into trouble of finding the IP and the ID of the container:

```
DB_INIT_IP=$(docker service ps go-demo-db-init \
    | tail -n 1 \
    | awk '{ print $4 }' \
    | cut -c 4- \
    | tr "-" ".")

DB_INIT_ID=$(docker -H tcp://$DB_INIT_IP:2375 \
    ps -aq \
    --filter label=com.docker.swarm.service.name=go-demo-db-init)

docker -H tcp://$DB_INIT_IP:2375 logs $DB_INIT_ID
```

The relevant parts of the output of the `logs` command are as follows:

```
MongoDB shell version: 3.2.10
connecting to: go-demo-db-rs1:27017/test
{
        "set" : "rs0",
        "date" : ISODate("2016-12-23T18:18:30.723Z"),
        "myState" : 1,
        "term" : NumberLong(1),
        "heartbeatIntervalMillis" : NumberLong(2000),
        "members" : [
                {
                        "_id" : 0,
                        "name" : "go-demo-db-rs1:27017",
                        . . .
                        "stateStr" : "PRIMARY",
                        . . .
                },
                {
                        "_id" : 1,
                        "name" : "go-demo-db-rs2:27017",
                        ". . .
                        "stateStr" : "SECONDARY",
                        . . .
                },
```

```
                    {
                        "_id" : 2,
                        "name" : "go-demo-db-rs3:27017",
                        ...
                        "stateStr" : "SECONDARY",
                        ...
                    }
        ],
        "ok" : 1
    }
```

Mongo replica set is indeed configured with all three members. We have a working group of fault tolerant set of MongoDBs that provide high availability. We can use them with our go-demo (or any other) service:

```
docker service create --name go-demo \
    -e DB="go-demo-db-rs1,go-demo-db-rs2,go-demo-db-rs3" \
        --reserve-memory 10m \
        --network go-demo \
        --network proxy \
        --replicas 3 \
        --label com.df.notify=true \
        --label com.df.distribute=true \
        --label com.df.servicePath=/demo \
        --label com.df.port=8080 \
        vfarcic/go-demo:1.2
```

There is only one difference between this command and those we used in the previous chapters. If we continued using a single address of the primary MongoDB, we would not have high availability. When that DB fails, the service would not be able to serve requests. Even though Swarm would re-schedule it, the address of the primary would become different since the replica set would elect a new one.

This time we specified all three MongoDBs as the value of the environment variable DB. The code of the service will pass that string to the MongoDB driver. In turn, the driver will use those addresses to deduce which DB is primary and use it to send requests. All Mongo drivers have the same mechanism to specify members of a replica set.

Finally, let's confirm that all three replicas of the go-demo service are indeed running. Remember, the service is coded in a way that it would fail if the connection to the database could not be established. If all service replicas are running, it is the proof that we set up everything correctly:

```
docker service ps go-demo
```

The output is as follows (IDs and ERROR columns are removed for brevity):

```
NAME        IMAGE                  NODE               DESIRED STATE
go-demo.1 vfarcic/go-demo:1.2 ip-172-31-23-206 Running
go-demo.2 vfarcic/go-demo:1.2 ip-172-31-25-35  Running
go-demo.3 vfarcic/go-demo:1.2 ip-172-31-25-35  Running
-------------------------------------------------
ERROR
Running 11 seconds ago
Running 9 seconds ago
Running 9 seconds ago
```

What now?

Not all stateful services should be treated in the same way. Some might need an external drive mounted, while others already have some kind of a replication and synchronization incorporated. In some cases, you might want to combine both mounting and replication, while in others replication itself is enough.

Please keep in mind that there are many other combinations we did not explore.

The important thing is to understand how a service works and how it was designed to persist its state. In many cases, the logic of the solution is the same no matter whether we use containers or not. Containers often do not make things different, only easier.

With the right approach, there is no reason why stateful services would not be cloud-friendly, fault tolerant, with high availability, scalable, and so on. The major question is whether you want to manage them yourself or you'd prefer leaving it to your cloud computing provider (if you use one). The important thing is that you got a glimpse how to manage stateful services yourself.

Let's destroy the cluster before we move on:

```
exit

terraform destroy -force
```

15

Managing Secrets in Docker Swarm Clusters

Docker 1.13 introduced a set of features that allow us to centrally manage secrets and pass them only to services that need them. They provide a much-needed mechanism to provide information that should be hidden from anyone except designated services.

A secret (at least from Docker's point of view) is a blob of data. A typical use case would be a certificate, SSH private keys, passwords, and so on. Secrets should stay secret meaning that they should not be stored unencrypted or transmitted over a network.

With all that being said, let's see them in action and continue our discussion through practical examples.

All the commands from this chapter are available in the `14-secrets.sh` (https://gist.gi thub.com/vfarcic/906d37d1964255b40af430bb03d2a72e) Gist.

Creating secrets

Since a single node is more than enough to demonstrate Docker secrets, we'll start by creating a one node Swarm cluster based on Docker Machines:

```
docker-machine create \
    -d virtualbox \
    swarm
eval $(docker-machine env swarm)

docker swarm init \
    --advertise-addr $(docker-machine ip swarm)
```

A note to Windows users

The recommendation is to run all the examples from *Git Bash* (installed through *Docker Toolbox* as well as *Git*). That way the commands you'll see throughout the book will be same as those that should be executed on *OS X* or any *Linux* distribution.

We created a Docker Machine node called swarm and used it to initialize the cluster.

Now we can create a secret.

A note to Windows users

For mounts (a secret is a mount as well) used in the next command to work, you have to stop Git Bash from altering file system paths. Set this environment variable.
```
export MSYS_NO_PATHCONV=1
```

The format of the command that creates a secret is as follows (please do not run it):

```
docker secret create [OPTIONS] SECRET file|-
```

The secret create command expects a file that contains a secret. However, creating a file with unencrypted secret defies the purpose of having secrets in the first place. Everyone can read that file. We could, delete the file after pushing it to Docker but that would only create unnecessary steps. Instead, we'll use – that will allow us to pipe standard output:

```
echo "I like candy" \
    | docker secret create my_secret -
```

The command we just executed created a secret called my_secret. That information was sent to the remote Docker Engine using TLS connection. If we had a bigger cluster with multiple managers, the secret would be replicated among all.

We can inspect the newly created secret:

```
docker secret inspect my_secret
```

The output is as follows:

```
[
    {
        "ID": "9iqwc8zb7xum7krgm183t4mym",
        "Version": {
            "Index": 11
    },
        "CreatedAt": "2017-02-20T23:00:48.983267019Z",
        "UpdatedAt": "2017-02-20T23:00:48.983267019Z",
```

```
        "Spec": {
            "Name": "my_secret"
    }
    }
]
```

The value of the secret is hidden. Even if a malicious person gains access to Docker Engine, the secret would still be unavailable. Truth be told, in such a case, our worries would be much greater that protection of a Docker secret but I'll leave that discussion for some other time.

Now that we have encrypted the secret and stored in Swarm managers, we should explore ways to utilize it within our services.

Consuming secrets

A new argument --secret was added to the docker service create command. If a secret is attached, it will be available as a file in the /run/secrets directory inside all the containers that form a service.

Let's see it in action:

```
docker service create --name test \
    --secret my_secret \
    --restart-condition none \
    alpine cat /run/secrets/my_secret
```

We created a service called test and attached the secret called my_secret. The service is based on alpine and will output the content of the secret. Since it is a one-shot command that will terminate quickly, we set --restart-condition to none. Otherwise, the service would terminate a moment after it's created, Swarm would reschedule it, only to see it terminate again, and so on. We would enter a never-ending loop.

Let's take a look at the logs:

```
docker logs $(docker container ps -qa)
```

The output is as follows:

```
I like candy
```

The secret is available as the /run/secrets/my_secret file inside the container.

Before we start discussing a more real-world example, let us remove the service and the secret we created:

```
docker service rm test

docker secret rm my_secret
```

A real-world example of using secrets

The *Docker Flow Proxy* (`http://proxy.dockerflow.com/`) project exposes statistics that should be reserved for internal use only. Therefore, it needs to be protected with a `username` and `password`. Before *Docker v1.13*, situations like that one would be handled by allowing users to specify username and password through environment variables. *Docker Flow Proxy* is no exception and, indeed, has the *environment variables* (`http://proxy.docker flow.com/config/#environment-variables`) STATS_USER and STATS_PASS.

The command that would create the service with custom `username` and `password` would be as follows:

```
docker network create --driver overlay proxy

docker service create --name proxy \
    -p 80:80 \
    -p 443:443 \
    -p 8080:8080 \
-e STATS_USER=my-user \
-e STATS_PASS=my-pass \
    --network proxy \
-e MODE=swarm \
    vfarcic/docker-flow-proxy
```

While that would protect the statistics page from ordinary users, it would still leave it exposed to anyone capable of inspecting the service. A simple example is as follows:

```
docker service inspect proxy --pretty
```

The relevant part of the output is as follows:

```
...
ContainerSpec:
  Image:      vfarcic/docker-flow-
proxy:latest@sha256:b1014afa9706413818903671086e484d98db669576b83727801637d
1a3323910
  Env:        STATS_USER=my-user STATS_PASS=my-pass MODE=swarm
...
```

The same result that does not reveal confidential information could be accomplished with the commands that follow:

```
echo "secret-user" \
    | docker secret create dfp_stats_user -

echo "secret-pass" \
    | docker secret create dfp_stats_pass -

docker service update \
    --secret-add dfp_stats_user \
    --secret-add dfp_stats_pass \
    proxy
```

We created two secrets `dfp_stats_user and dfp_stats_pass` and updated our service. From now on, those secrets would be available inside service containers as files `/run/secrets/dfp_stats_user` and `/run/secrets/dfp_stats_pass`. If a secret is named the same as the environment variable, is in lower case, and has the `dpf_ prefix`, it will be used instead.

If you inspect the container one more time, you'll notice that there is no trace of the secrets.

We could stop here. After all, there's not much more to be said for Docker secrets. However, we got used to Docker stacks and it would be great if secrets would work in the new YAML Compose format.

Before we move on, let's remove the `proxy` service:

```
docker service rm proxy
```

Using secrets with Docker Compose

True to the mission to have the same features available in all supported flavours, Docker introduced secrets in Compose YAML format *version 3.1.*

We'll continue using *Docker Flow Proxy* to demonstrate how secrets work inside Compose files:

```
curl -o dfp.yml \
    https://raw.githubusercontent.com/vfarcic/\
docker-flow-stacks/master/proxy/docker-flow-proxy-secrets.yml
```

We downloaded the `docker-flow-proxy-secrets.yml` (https://github.com/vfarcic/docker-flow-stacks/blob/master/proxy/docker-flow-proxy-secrets.yml) stack from the `vfarcic/docker-flow-stacks` (https://github.com/vfarcic/docker-flow-stacks) repository.

The relevant parts of the definition of the stack are as follows:

```
version: "3.1"

...

services:

  proxy:
    image: vfarcic/docker-flow-proxy:${TAG:-latest}
    ports:
      - 80:80
      - 443:443
    networks:
      - proxy
    environment:
      - LISTENER_ADDRESS=swarm-listener
      - MODE=swarm
    secrets:
      - dfp_stats_user
      - dfp_stats_pass
    deploy:
      replicas: 3

...

secrets:
  dfp_stats_user:
    external: true
  dfp_stats_pass:
    external: true
```

The version of the format is 3.1. The `proxy` service has the two secrets attached. Finally, there is a separate `secrets` section that defines the `secrets` as `external` entities. The alternative would be to specify secrets internally.

An example would be as follows:

```
secrets:
    dfp_stats_user:
        external: true
    dfp_stats_pass:
        external: true
secrets:
  dfp_stats_user:
    file: ./dfp_stats_user.txt
  dfp_stats_pass:
    file: ./dfp_stats_pass.txt
```

I prefer the first option that specifies secrets externally since that does not leave any trail. In some other cases, secrets might be used for non-secretive information (we'll discuss it soon) and using internal secrets specified as files would probably be a better option.

Let's run the `stack` and check whether it works:

```
docker stack deploy -c dfp.yml proxy
```

Statistics themselves are useless if there is no data so we'll deploy another service that will be reconfigured in the `proxy` and `start` generating some stats:

```
curl -o go-demo.yml \
    https://raw.githubusercontent.com/vfarcic/\
go-demo/master/docker-compose-stack.yml

docker stack deploy -c go-demo.yml go-demo
```

Please wait a few moments until the services from the `go-demo` stack are running. You can check their status by executing `docker stack ps go-demo`. You might see `go-demo_main` replicas in the failed status. Do not panic. They will continue failing only until the `go-demo_db` is starts running.

Now we can, finally, confirm that the `proxy` is configured to use secrets for authentication:

```
curl -u secret-user:secret-pass \
"http://$(docker-machine ip swarm)/admin?stats;csv;norefresh"
```

It works! With only a single additional step `docker service create`, we made our system more secured

Common ways to use secrets

Until secrets were introduced, a common way to pass information to containers was through environment variables. While that will continue being the preferable way for non-confidential information, part of the setup should involve secrets as well. Both should be combined. The question is which method to choose and when.

The obvious use case for Docker secrets are secrets. That was obvious, wasn't it. If there is a piece of information that should remain invisible to anyone but specific containers, it should be provided through Docker secrets. A commonly used pattern is to allow the same information to be specified as either environment variable and a secret. In case that both a set, secrets should take precedence. You already saw this pattern through *Docker Flow Proxy*. Every piece of information that can be specified through environment variables can be specified as a secret as well.

In some cases, you might not be able to modify code of your service and adapt it to use secrets. Maybe it's not a question of ability but lack of desire to modify your code. If you fall into the latter case, I will, for now, restrain myself from explaining why code should be continuously refactored and imagine that you have a very good reason for it. In either case, the solution is usually to create a wrapper script that transforms secrets into whatever your service needs and then invoke the service. Put that script as CMD instruction in *Dockerfile* and you're done. Secrets stay secrets and you don't get fired from refactoring your code. To some this last sentence sounds silly but it's not uncommon for companies to consider refactoring a waste of time.

What should be a secret? No one can truly answer that question for you since it differs from one organization to another. Some of the examples would be usernames and passwords, SSH keys, SSL certificates, and so on. If you don't want others to know about it, make it a secret.

We should strive for immutability and do our best to run containers that are exactly the same no matter where they run. True immutability means that even the configuration is always the same across all environments. However, that is not always easy and is sometimes even impossible to accomplish. Such a situation could be a good candidate for Docker secrets. They do not necessarily have to be used only as means of specifying confidential information. We can use secrets as a way to provide information that differs from one cluster to another. In such a case, pieces of configuration that should differ from one environment to another (example: staging and production clusters) can be stored as secrets.

I am certain that there are quite a few other use cases I didn't even think about. After all, secrets are a new feature (a few weeks old from the day of this writing).

What now?

Remove your Docker Machine VM and start applying secrets to your own Swarm cluster. There's not much more to be said (for now):

```
docker-machine rm -f swarm
```

Appendix

Monitor Your GitHub Repos
with Docker and Prometheus

By **Brian Christner**

GitHub is full of great code, information, and interesting statistics. GitHub repositories are full of statistics that make perfect candidates to graph with Grafana. The best way to graph this data is, of course, with Docker and Prometheus.

Prometheus contains an impressive list of *Exporters* (`https://prometheus.io/docs/instrumenting/exporters/`). These Exporters range from APIs to IoT. They can also integrate with Prometheus and Grafana which produce some beautiful graphs.

Docker, Prometheus, and Grafana

My base setup for anything monitoring related is the Docker, Prometheus, and Grafana stack. That is the baseline I work from and add components like Exporters. I have created the *GitHub-Monitoring Repo* (`https://github.com/vegasbrianc/github-monitoring`). It contains a Docker compose file which makes this stack simplified and easy to start.

Getting started

Prerequisite Ensure you have a Docker host running the latest versions of Docker engine and compose. Next, clone the *GitHub-Monitoring* (`https://github.com/vegasbrianc/gith ub-monitoring`) project to your Docker machine.

We can start configuring the project based on your requirements. Please edit the *Prometheus Targets* (`https://github.com/vegasbrianc/github-monitoring/blob/master/prometheu s/prometheus.yml`) if you need to track additional Exporters or targets. They are located in the static configs section at the end of the file. The Exporter uses the name metrics with port `9171`:

```
static_configs:
- targets: ['node exporter:9100','localhost:9090', 'metrics:9171']
```

Configuration

Create a GitHub token to use for this project. That prevents us from hitting API limits imposed by GitHub for non-authenticated traffic.

Navigate to *Create GitHub Token* (`https://github.com/settings/tokens`) where we will create a token for this project.

Please do the steps that follow:

- Provide a description of the token.
- Select scopes (our project only requires the `repo` permissions).
- Click the generate token button.
- Copy the token ID and store it in a safe place. That is the equivalent of a password so don't keep it in a public place.

Edit the `docker-compose.yml` (`https://github.com/vegasbrianc/github-monitoring /blob/master/docker-compose.yml`) file with your favorite editor. Scroll to the end of the file where you will find the metrics service section.

First, replace the `GITHUB_TOKEN=<GitHub API Token see README>` with the token you generated earlier. Next, replace the `REPOS` with your desired repositories you want to track. In my example, I have selected the Docker and `freeCodeCamp` repositories as they offer lots of movement and stats.

The configuration is as follows:

```
metrics:
   tty: true
   stdin_open: true
expose:
   - 9171
image: infinityworks/github-exporter:latest
environment:
   - REPOS=freeCodeCamp/freeCodeCamp,docker/docker
   - GITHUB_TOKEN=<GitHub API Token see README>
networks:
   - back-tier
```

Once configurations are complete, we can start it up. Run the command that follows from the `github-monitoring project` directory:

```
docker-compose up
```

That's it. Docker Compose builds the entire Grafana and Prometheus stacks auto-magically. The compose file also connects the new GitHub Exporter to our baseline stack. I choose to run docker-compose without the –d flag initially. That makes it easier for troubleshooting since log entries are printed directly to the terminal.

The Grafana Dashboard is now accessible via: `http://<Host IP Address>:3000` (example: `http://localhost:3000`).

Please use `admin` as username and `foobar` as password (it is defined in the `config.monitoring` file that sets out a few environment variables).

Post configuration

Now we need to create the Prometheus Datasource to connect Grafana to Prometheus:

- Click the Grafana menu from the top-left corner (looks like a fireball)
- Click **Data Sources**
- Click the green button **Add Data Source**

Refer to the following image to add a Grafana Data source:

Figure A-1: Add Grafana Data Source

Install dashboard

I created a Dashboard template which is available on *GitHub Stats Dashboard*(https://graf
ana.net/dashboards/1559). Download the dashboard and select from the Grafana menu ->
Dashboards -> **Import**

This dashboard is a starting point to help you get started with graphing your GitHub
Repos. Please let me know if you have any changes you would like to see in the dashboard,
so I can update Grafana site as well.

Figure A-2: GitHub Grafana Dashboard

Conclusion

Prometheus in combination with Docker is a powerful yet simple way to monitor different data sources. The GitHub Exporter is one of the many amazing Exporters available to Prometheus.

About the author

Brian Christner hails from Arizona but now resides in the Alps of Switzerland. Brian spent a large portion of his career in the casino industry where he made sure the house always won. Brian is a nominated member of the Docker Captain's program and a seasoned cloud architect. He is also a cloud subject matter expert in the topics of Docker, Cloud Foundry, IaaS, PaaS, DevOps, CI/CD and, of course, container monitoring. Brian is passionate about advocating for cloud and containers. When Brian is not busy trying to containerize everything he can be found riding his mountain bike or skiing in the Swiss Alps.

Twitter - @idomyowntricks

Website - www.brianchristner.io

Index

CPSIA information can be obtained
at www.ICGtesting.com
Printed in the USA
LVOW09s0103290917
550484LV00003B/59/P